FREEDOM AND THE CAPTIVE MIND

A VOLUME IN THE NIU SERIES IN
Orthodox Christian Studies
Edited by Roy R. Robson

For a list of books in the series, visit our website at cornellpress.cornell.edu.

FREEDOM AND THE CAPTIVE MIND

FR. GLEB YAKUNIN AND ORTHODOX CHRISTIANITY IN SOVIET RUSSIA

WALLACE L. DANIEL

NORTHERN ILLINOIS UNIVERSITY PRESS
AN IMPRINT OF
CORNELL UNIVERSITY PRESS
ITHACA AND LONDON

Copyright © 2024 by Cornell University

All rights reserved. Except for brief quotations in a review, this book, or parts thereof, must not be reproduced in any form without permission in writing from the publisher. For information, address Cornell University Press, Sage House, 512 East State Street, Ithaca, New York 14850. Visit our website at cornellpress.cornell.edu.

First published 2024 by Cornell University Press

Library of Congress Cataloging-in-Publication Data

Names: Daniel, Wallace L., author.
Title: Freedom and the captive mind : Fr. Gleb Yakunin and Orthodox Christianity in Soviet Russia / Wallace L. Daniel.
Description: Ithaca [New York] : Northern Illinois University Press, an imprint of Cornell University Press, 2024. | Series: NIU series in Orthodox Christian studies | Includes bibliographical references and index.
Identifiers: LCCN 2023059465 (print) | LCCN 2023059466 (ebook) | ISBN 9781501777332 (hardcover) | ISBN 9781501777349 (paperback) | ISBN 9781501777356 (epub) | ISBN 9781501777363 (pdf)
Subjects: LCSH: I︠A︡kunin, Gleb, 1935–2014. | I︠A︡kunin, Gleb, 1935-2014—Influence. | Russkai︠a︡ pravoslavnai︠a︡ t︠s︡erkov'—History—20th century. | Russkai︠a︡ pravoslavnai︠a︡ t︠s︡erkov'—History—21st century. | Church and state—Russia (Federation) | Freedom of religion—Russia (Federation)
Classification: LCC BX597.I18 D36 2024 (print) | LCC BX597.I18 (ebook) | DDC 261.70947/09045—dc23/eng/20240220
LC record available at https://lccn.loc.gov/2023059465
LC ebook record available at https://lccn.loc.gov/2023059466

To my granddaughter Isobel Lee (Zazie), who brings joy into my life

Contents

List of Illustrations ix
Preface xi
Chronology xii
Note on Transliteration xvii

	Introduction	1
1.	Beginnings	11
2.	The Letters	31
3.	The Awakening	53
4.	Western Perceptions and Soviet Realities	73
5.	Gleb Yakunin, Henry Dakin, and the Defense of Religious Liberty	95
6.	"I Thank God for the Fate He Has Given Me"	119
7.	The Outcast	138
8.	Return	155
9.	Lifting the Cover	175
10.	Priest and Politician	198
11.	Hope and the Twisted Road	221

Acknowledgments 243
Notes 247
Bibliography 299
Index 321

Illustrations

2.1. Fr. Gleb Yakunin, Fr. Nikolai Eshliman, and Feliks Karelin, 1965 — 42
4.1. Fr. Gleb Yakunin, summer of 1976 — 83
5.1. Yakunin and family, mid-1970s, daughter Mariia, son Aleksandr, Yakunin, and wife Iraida Yakunina — 97
5.2. Lev Regel'son, Fr. Gleb Yakunin, and Viktor Kapitanchuk, mid-1970s — 99
5.3. Varsonofi Khaibulin, Viktor Kapitanchuk, and Fr. Gleb Yakunin, founders of the Christian Committee for the Defense of Believers' Rights in the USSR — 111
6.1. Yakunin's family, taken soon after his arrest in 1979, daughter Mariia, son Aleksandr, daughter Anna, and wife Iraida Georgievna — 126
6.2. Tat'iana Velikanova in exile, 1984 — 127
7.1. House in Siberian village in which Yakunin lived in exile, 1985–87 — 149
8.1. Yakunin campaigning for office, early 1990s — 161
9.1. Fr. Georgii Edel'stein and Zoia Krakhmal'nikova, 1990s — 177
10.1. Fr. Georgii Edel'stein, Fr. Gleb Yakunin, and Viktor Aksiuchits, early 1990s — 201
11.1. Icon of Fr. Aleksandr Men, Apostolic Orthodox Church, early 2000s — 231
11.2. Mariia Yakunina and her husband Aleksei Belov in their studio, 2018 — 238
11.3. Viktor Popkov and Tat'iana Lebedeva, former members of the Christian Seminar in Moscow, 2018 — 240
11.4. Fr. Gleb Yakunin in the last years of his life — 241

Preface

My interest in Gleb Yakunin emanated from two sources. First, this interest began during the writing of my biography of Father Aleksandr Men. The two became friends in their student years and continued when both were young priests in the early 1960s. A few short passages about Yakunin could be found in books about religious dissidents in the Khrushchev and Brezhnev periods, but with few exceptions, little substantial information about Yakunin appeared in print beyond his protests over the Soviet state's persecution of religious believers. His association with Aleksandr Men and the letters Yakunin wrote to Western leaders raise many questions. What motivations lay behind the actions and positions he took? What political and religious context underlay them and produced the consequences that followed? Why did the Soviet government and powerful members of the Orthodox hierarchy go to such lengths to disparage Yakunin and erase his memory from the history of his time?

The second reason relates to an initial encounter with Gleb Yakunin. In May 2007, thanks to the assistance of his friend and colleague, the Russian scholar Elena Volkova, I interviewed Yakunin in an apartment in the Moscow suburbs. The interview took place over most of an afternoon. Although the purpose of our conversation primarily focused on his relationship with Aleksandr Men, it could not have avoided touching on various aspects of Yakunin's own life and perspectives. The person I interviewed did not match the stereotypes of him portrayed earlier in Soviet and post-Soviet accounts as a quarrelsome, ambitious, self-serving, and judgmental individual, but a mild-mannered, open spirited, and humble person, who had a lively sense of humor and a curiosity about all manner of subjects. He made no effort at self-aggrandizement. When asked whether he intended to write an autobiographical account of his many exploits, he rejected that possibility. He had no desire to relive the past, but in the little time he had left, he hoped to contribute in some small way to Russia's future. He expressed neither the wish nor the will to write his story, but hoped that someone else might have an interest in his saga and his efforts to defend the constitutional rights of those who were persecuted in an extremely harsh political environment.

Chronology

1934   Gleb Pavlovich Yakunin is born in Moscow to Pavel Ivanovich and Klavdiia Iosifovna, who had recently moved to Moscow from Anan'ev in Ukraine. Pavel Ivanovich, a professional violinist, finds employment in a Moscow symphony orchestra.

1941   After the German invasion, the family moves for protection to the deep interior of the country.

1944   Near the end of the war, the Yakunin family returns to Moscow. Shortly afterward, Pavel Ivanovich dies of heart attack, leaving Klavdiia Iosifovna alone to raise her son.

1945   Gleb Yakunin continues his education in the Moscow school system, specializing in the sciences, especially biology.

1952   Yakunin enters the Institute of Zoology in the southern suburbs of Moscow.

1953   Yakunin meets Aleksandr Men, a student at the same institute, and the two become fast friends. As their friendship develops and under Men's influence, Yakunin, an atheist, begins to forsake his atheistic beliefs.

1955   The Institute of Zoology moves to a new home in Irkutsk, Siberia, and a large part of its faculty and students, including Yakunin and Men, move also. Yakunin and Men room together.

1956   Yakunin and Men explore Irkutsk, visit churches of diverse confessions, study biology, and discuss theology. Yakunin develops an interest in the history of the Catacomb Church in Russia.

1957   Influenced by Men but also by other people and experiences in Irkutsk, Yakunin converts to Christianity. He reads Nikolai Berdiaev's *Philosophy of Freedom* and *The Meaning of Creativity*, both of which make a large impact on his worldview.

1958   Despite Men's expulsion from the institute, Yakunin remains determined to complete his course of study and the required service after graduation. He makes a decision about his long-term goal: to study for the priesthood.

1959   He meets a young woman in Irkutsk, Iraida Georgievna Semenova, falls in love with her, and proposes marriage. Determined to complete her education first, Iraida Semenova asks him to wait for her. After graduation, Yakunin returns to Moscow.

1960   Yakunin enrolls in the Moscow Theological Seminary.

1961   He marries Iraida Georgievna, who by then has completed her course of study and moved to Moscow. Accused of stealing a book from the library, Yakunin is expelled from the seminary.

1962   May: Iraida gives birth to the first child, Mariia.
August: Yakunin is ordained as a deacon in the Orthodox Church and less than two weeks later is consecrated as a priest and appointed to serve in the city of Zaraisk. The church soon transfers him to the city of Dmitrov, where he would serve for the next three years.

1963   Yakunin encounters Archbishop Yermogen at Fr. Aleksandr's parish at Alabino.

1965   Yakunin and Fr. Nikolai Eshliman send two letters, the first to Patriarch Aleksii I and the second to the chairman of the Supreme Soviet, Nikolai Podgorny.

1966   Patriarch Aleksii I suspends Yakunin and Eshliman from the priesthood.

1968   Boris Talantov writes "The Moscow Patriarchate and Sergianism" and "Sovetskoe obshchestvo, 1965–68," both of which support the views of Yakunin and Eshliman.

1969   Fr. Sergii Zheludkov's letter to Andrei Sakharov calls for freedom of thought and speech.

1974   The Christian Seminar, a religious-philosophical seminar, is formed in Moscow. The gathering attracts young people who are searching for an approach to life and truth different from the Soviet perspective.

1975   April: Yakunin and Lev Regel'son write an "Appeal" to Christians in Portugal. In the same month, they communicate with Soviet authorities on topics concerning the date of the upcoming "subbotnik."
May: Yakunin and Regel'son write an "Appeal for the Glorification of Russian Martyrs in the USSR."
October: Yakunin and Regel'son send a letter to the World Council of Churches, meeting in Nairobi. The letter deals with violence and persecution of religious believers of numerous confessions and it results in heated discussion.

1976   Yakunin serves as one of the founders of the Christian Committee for the Defense of Believers' Rights in the USSR.

June: US House Subcommittees on International Political and Military Affairs and on International Relations discuss the issues raised by Yakunin and Regel'son in their letters to the World Council of Churches and elsewhere.

1977 The Christian Committee develops a relationship with a San Francisco entrepreneur and publisher Henry S. Dakin, who agrees to publish many of the committee's documents.
April: Yakunin is the subject of a scathing two-part article written by Boris Roshchin and published in *Literaturnaia gazeta*. Yakunin responds to the attack.

1978 Yakunin joins the Christian Seminar.

1979 August: Yakunin publishes "The Russian Orthodox Church Today and Perspectives on a Religious Revival in the USSR."
September: the KGB searches Fr. Gleb's home.
November: Yakunin is arrested.

1980 Yakunin is tried in Moscow and charged with violating Article 70 of the Criminal Code of the RSFSR. He is sentenced to five years in strict-regime camps and five years in exile.

1981 Yakunin is transported to a forced labor camp, the notorious Perm-37.
September: Yakunin writes an "Appeal" to President Leonid Brezhnev protesting the seizure of the Bible and other religious literature by camp authorities.
October: Yakunin writes "An Appeal to Western Christians" asking for their prayerful support of political prisoners in the camps. He begins a hunger strike. He starts writing his narrative poem "Eulogy of a Simple-minded Fool of God: In Honor of God, the Universe, and the Homeland."

1984 Yakunin arrives in a Siberian village, located in Ust-Maiskii ulus, in a remote corner of Yakutia, to begin his five-year term of forced exile. He continues to work on his narrative poem.

1987 After Mikhail Gorbachev grants amnesty to political prisoners, Yakunin is freed and returns to Moscow.

1988 Yakunin is reinstated as an Orthodox priest and assigned to a church on the outskirts of the city of Shchyolkovo.

1989 Yakunin serves as leader of a movement called "The Church and Perestroika," which aims at following a key goal of Gorbachev's perestroika.

1990 While serving as a priest, Yakunin decides simultaneously to run for election to the Congress of People's Deputies. He participates in a new group that calls itself the Russian Christian Democratic Movement. He plays a large part in the parliamentary commission to revise the Russian law on freedom of conscience. He is convinced that Russia's future depends on overcoming the cult of the leader and also its messianic vision.

1991 Yakunin plays an active part in defusing the opposition movement aimed at overthrowing the newly elected government of Boris Yeltsin. He is selected as a member of a small parliamentary commission to investigate a special section of KGB archives that monitors the Orthodox Church and other religious organizations.

1992 Yakunin faces a crucial decision about continuing to be involved in Russian politics. He resolves to remain a part of the political process.

1993 Patriarch Aleksii II orders Orthodox priests to refrain from engaging in Russian politics. Nevertheless, Yakunin wins a seat in the Federal Assembly of the State Duma. In October, the Holy Synod orders Yakunin again defrocked for disobeying the patriarch's command. Yakunin decides to fight back.

1994 In two open letters to Patriarch Aleksii II, Yakunin accuses the Holy Synod of acting illegally in defrocking him.

1995 March: Yakunin writes two letters to President Yeltsin in which he expresses strong criticism of the Moscow Patriarchate and its failure to meet the needs of the Russian people. He supports the Protestants' activities in Russia.
September: ultranationalists physically attack Yakunin on the floor of the Federal Assembly.

1996 Yakunin pledges allegiance to the Ukrainian Orthodox Church-Kyivan Patriarchate.

1997 February: The Assembly of Archbishops of the Russian Orthodox Church excommunicates and anathematizes Yakunin for disobedience.
April: Yakunin files suit against Alexander Dvorkin.
September–October: Yakunin strongly protests the 1997 newly revised Law on Freedom of Conscience and Religious Associations, approved by President Yeltsin.

1999 Yakunin expresses opposition to the appointment of Vladimir Putin as President Yeltsin's successor.

2000 Yakunin helps with the creation of the Apostolic Orthodox Church. He establishes a parish in Moscow, and it canonizes Fr. Aleksandr Men.

2006 April: Yakunin writes critique of Metropolitan Kirill's Russian alternative to the Universal Declaration of Human Rights and Dignity and takes strong exception to Kirill's views.
2008 Yakunin begins to experience health problems and receives a diagnosis of a neurological disease.
2012 Yakunin supports the three young women of "Pussy Riot."
2014 Yakunin dies on December 25, 2014.

Note on Transliteration

I have used the standard Library of Congress method of transliteration throughout this book but have altered some Russian spellings of proper names. Russian surnames that are well known to an English-speaking public are given in their common spelling (for example, Dostoevskii becomes Dostoevsky, Iakunin is transliterated as Yakunin). In the case of published works in English, I have used the writers' spelling of Yakunin's name when they have written in English. The names Gleb Yakunin, as well as Aleksandr Men, have been used throughout the book, in the text, notes, and bibliography. The only exceptions are Russian-language titles of books and articles.

Introduction

Gleb Yakunin's arrest on November 1, 1979, represented a turning point in his efforts to secure freedom of thought and belief for religious groups in the Soviet Union. Serving as a priest until he was suspended by Patriarch Aleksii I, Yakunin's activism for freedom of conscience included sending letters and appeals to Soviet political and religious authorities within the Soviet Union and abroad. His arrest and the story underlying it offer insights into the challenges he posed to the Orthodox Church and the Soviet state.

On September 27, a month before his arrest, KGB offices in Leningrad had issued an order for a search of his home in Moscow.[1] The next morning, at a quarter to nine, KGB officers knocked at the door of his house at 30 Dubenko Street in a quiet neighborhood of the city. When he opened the door, the officers showed him their search warrant, entered, and began searching for potentially seditious materials.

They started with Yakunin's brown corduroy jacket on a hanger in the vestibule, and in it they discovered a small telephone book containing a list of foreign names, business cards, and several handwritten notes, all of which they confiscated.[2] These items, Elena Volkova writes, "represented a veritable portable office."[3] The officers then moved through the living rooms, searching the bookshelves, a secretary desk, and a bedside table. They looked under the television, under the bed, in a sideboard, and in the kitchen, where they found Yakunin's dark brown leather briefcase and its trove of provocative materials.[4]

By the end of their search, the KGB officers had confiscated more than eighty items. Their official report listed envelopes crammed with letters, folders of diverse documents, a bag and a suitcase stuffed with writings and émigré journals, and the archive of the Christian Committee for the Defense of Believers' Rights. They had pulled numerous volumes from the bookcase, many of which were published abroad and brought into the country by foreign guests—Russian copies of John Stuart Mill's *On Liberty*, *Conversations with the Priest Dmitrii Dudko*, Alexander Zinov'ev's *Notes of a Night Watchman*, E. Svetlov's (Aleksandr Men's) *Messengers of the Kingdom of God*, and a 704-page volume of hymns.[5] Before leaving Yakunin's home at eight-thirty that evening, the officers stamped the KGB's seal on the bundle of confiscated items and presented a list of the materials for Yakunin and his wife Iraida to sign. Both refused.[6] KGB officials had searched his home twice before—in the spring and earlier that same month.[7] The third search on September 27 served as the basis for a criminal charge against him for allegedly seeking to undermine the Soviet state.

Fr. Gleb might have anticipated the events of that late September evening. A year earlier, state officials, who were well acquainted with his activities on behalf of religious believers of different faiths, had offered him and his family the opportunity to emigrate. Unlike many others given the choice, he elected to remain in his country, believing that he had the responsibility to stay.[8] The police issued a stern warning to Yakunin to desist in his activities or face severe consequences. He persisted, maintaining that he only intended to redress the illegal transgressions committed by local officials against the Soviet Constitution and its guarantee of freedom of conscience.

For some time, state officials had been monitoring the meetings of Moscow's Christian Seminar.[9] Yakunin was a friend of several members and had attended some of their gatherings.[10] KGB arrests of seminar members in the summer of 1979 held ominous foreboding for Yakunin, as did two earlier events suggesting that the KGB's relative tolerance of Yakunin's activities was coming to a head. The Soviet government aimed to undermine such activism before what a Soviet journalist called an "infection of the body politic" spread into the country's "life blood."

In 1976, the head of the KGB, Yuri Andropov, labeled the prominent Soviet physicist and leading human rights advocate Andrei Sakharov "Domestic Enemy Number One" of the Soviet Union.[11] Although the Nobel Prize winner remained free (temporarily), other people associated with the human rights movement suffered a different fate. In 1977 and 1978, the police arrested Yuri Orlov, Aleksandr Ginzburg, and Anatolii Shcharansky, well-known human rights activists.[12] Up to that point, the arrests had focused primarily on the leading participants in the Helsinki Monitoring Group organized by Sakharov in his apartment on May 12, 1976. The circle soon widened. From people who publicized violations of human rights, it moved on to principal spokespersons for the resurgence of religion in the Soviet Union. On November 20, 1978, the KGB jailed Aleksandr Ogorodnikov and, shortly thereafter, sought to suppress the discussion circles he had created. Given this tightening band of arrests, Fr. Gleb had to understand that the secret police would soon come for him.

The late 1970s and the spring of 1980 were times of high political tensions. The Soviet invasion of Afghanistan in December 1979 received world condemnation six months before the Olympic Games, scheduled for the summer in Moscow. Roughly three hundred thousand visitors were expected and what the Soviet leadership under President Leonid Brezhnev emphatically did not want to see were local citizens protesting Soviet violations of human rights and religious liberty. Perhaps even more important, the leadership wished to prevent the further spread of religious belief among its citizenry, an "infection" that the massive incursion of foreigners could exacerbate.

As part of the leadership's efforts, two people whose names had become synonymous with human rights and religious liberty were arrested on the same day in November 1979: Tat'iana Mikhailovna Velikanova (1932–2002) and Fr. Gleb. Velikanova was the coeditor of the widely distributed samizdat publication *A Chronicle of Current Events*, a bimonthly publication that exposed violations of civil liberties by the political authorities.[13]

Like Velikanova, Yakunin's writings transcended national boundaries, reaching out to organizations in the defense of freedom of conscience. His was a searing voice that came not from secular society, but from within the Orthodox Church. Yakunin criticized the church for its complicity with the Soviet government, for its refusal to stand up for the persecuted, and, above all, for its silence. The church, he maintained, had betrayed its sacred mission.

When the police arrested Fr. Gleb, he left behind his wife and three children. Incarcerated in the infamous Lefortovo Prison in Moscow to await trial, he had little doubt that he faced a long and torturous road. With Fr. Gleb imprisoned and vilified in the press, his young family was left without visible means of support as winter approached. They relied on their faith, along with their closest friends and supporters, to provide material aid and psychological sustenance.

Yakunin's arrest and subsequent trial, and his activities leading up to them afforded an opportunity for various people to speak about him, and they offered different perspectives on the man and his significance. Three of them bear mention because they exemplify the diversity of views. Collectively, they raise issues that provide the touchstones for this book.

The first, Anatolii Levitin-Krasnov, was a well-known Orthodox layperson and public intellectual, who had written many incisive articles on church and state in the Soviet Union. Although he emigrated from the Soviet Union in September 1974 and settled in Switzerland, he remained in touch with prominent members of the intelligentsia and continued to write on religion and politics. In February 1977, he published a widely read article analyzing religious life in the Soviet Union in which he noted that he had read "with great sadness" the speeches of Orthodox Church leaders and the vapid articles in the *Journal of the Moscow Patriarchate*. They repeatedly distorted the nature of religious life in the Soviet Union, he wrote, and offered an idealized fantasy about the peaceful conditions that existed throughout the country. He referred to what he called the "semi-comical pronouncements of the Patriarch," which presented a false picture of reality.[14] "It appears," Levitin-Krasnov wrote, "that religious life in Russia is dead, silent, covered by a thick layer of ice. And then suddenly an ice hole, a source of living waters."[15]

Levitin-Krasnov attributed the breakthrough to three people whose activities provided a picture of living realities, as opposed to the fictitious images presented by church and government authorities: he named the physicist Lev Regel'son, the popular priest Fr. Dmitrii Dudko, and Fr. Gleb Yakunin. Levitin-Krasnov praised all three for their courage, breadth of vision, insistence on facts, and challenges to the state-imposed ideology. He objected to the portrait of Yakunin represented in the press, maintaining that this depiction bore little resemblance to reality. By describing Yakunin as an enemy of the Soviet system and a degenerate member of the Orthodox priesthood, the press was creating a fantasy.

Levitin-Krasnov portrayed Fr. Gleb as a dedicated Orthodox priest whose actions in defense of religious believers came from a deep-seated adherence to his Orthodox faith. Married to Fr. Gleb's aunt, Levitin-Krasnov related how he had known Yakunin since childhood and characterized the priest as a seeker of truth, a person of integrity, and a man committed to public service, with a particular interest in serving the dispossessed. Levitin-Krasnov cited Fr. Gleb's many appeals to state authorities and the patriarch on behalf of religious believers of diverse faiths. These numerous appeals had both angered the government and incurred the Moscow Patriarchate's "violent hatred. Persecuted by civil and religious authorities, this Fr. Gleb Yakunin—a noble man and a true Christian—continued his work," Levitin-Krasnov wrote. "He has earned his name in the annals of his church and his country forever."[16]

A second assessment of Gleb Yakunin came from the writers Feliks Svetlov and Zoia Krakhmal'nikova, husband and wife, who were Orthodox Christians. Their article about Yakunin, written immediately after his arrest and that of Tat′iana Velikanova, was published in samizdat.[17]

Both, Svetlov and Krakhmal′nikova maintained, had endeavored to create a more compassionate and humane Russia. Both had done so in the name of a higher form of Christianity than the church itself practiced. "The lives and activities of these remarkable individuals," they wrote, "had served to revive what seemed to be forgotten in Russia, the living tradition of Christian compassion, which from time immemorial Orthodox Christians had conferred on the Russian people, regardless of their social rank."[18] Svetlov and Krakhmal′nikova attributed the roots of this ancient wisdom to the Holy Scriptures, which were deeply embedded in Velikanova and Yakunin:

> For I was hungry and you gave Me food; I was thirsty and you gave Me drink; . . . I was sick and you visited Me; I was in prison and you came to Me. . . . And the King will say to them, "Assuredly, I say to you, inasmuch as you did it to one of the least of these My brethren, you did it to Me." There is not one person—whatever religion one confessed—not one person—whatever the nationality to which one belonged—who has not found in them help, support, and defense. Not tens, not hundreds, but thousands of people know this.[19]

Their article made a strong plea that the sacrifices of Velikanova and Yakunin must not be forgotten. They concluded by emphasizing that the arrests of these two people were not personal matters but had broader significance: "They were a blow that struck at the living, suffering heart of Russia."[20]

A third perspective comes from a much different source. In the late 1970s and early 1980s, Vladimir Alekseevich Kuroedov was a prominent Soviet historian and chair of the Council for Religious Affairs.[21] Kuroedov's published works mainly dealt with church and state relations. His *Religion and the Church in Soviet Society* (*Religiia i tserkov′ v Sovetskom gosudarstve*), issued in a large number of copies, devoted several pages to Fr. Gleb Yakunin.[22]

In this book, as in many of his other writings, Kuroedov invariably placed his main arguments within the context of Soviet principles on religious liberty. Soviet legislation, he claimed, fully protected and guaranteed freedom of conscience, a fundamental right enshrined in Article 52 of the Soviet Constitution. The founders of Marxism-Leninism, Kuroedov pointed out, repeatedly warned against using any form of violence or taking discriminatory actions against religious believers, and while they had emphatically viewed religion as anachronistic, the founders respected the rights of individuals to their own religious beliefs. Yet bourgeois propagandists, Kuroedov maintained, had spread every "cock and bull" story about the policies of the Soviet Union and the suppression of freedom of conscience.[23] Religion, supported and generously financed by capitalist interests, served as a major tool in the ideological assault of Western powers against the Soviet Union.

In Kuroedov's view Yakunin was not a positive character, either in his upbringing, his role as a priest, or in his conflict with the church. He questioned the purity of Yakunin's motives in his desire to become a priest. Citing a letter from several parishioners of Yakunin's former church, Kuroedov claimed that as a young cleric Fr. Gleb always had an eye for "calculating the value of an icon and the money in the church's collection plate."[24] Yakunin had become known as a "great martyr" to the cause of truth in the Western world, but, the parishioners charged, "we see Yakunin not as a shepherd of God, but as a felon." Kuroedov targeted Yakunin's connection to the American entrepreneur Henry Dakin's Washington Research Center in San Francisco, his letters to Western political leaders, his outreach to world religious organizations, and the relationships he forged with Russian émigré journals such as *Posev*, *Russkaia mysl'*, and others. He asserted that these efforts had one ultimate goal: the subversion of the Soviet Union.[25]

The perspectives on Yakunin summarized above raise several questions about his motivations, activities, and place in the political and religious history of Russia in the second half of the twentieth century and the first decades of the twenty-first. Did Kuroedov's portrayal of Fr. Gleb as an extremist, an enemy of the church and the Soviet state, represent an accurate assessment, or did it conceal another purpose—an effort to stigmatize a growing religious awakening that threatened the state's ideological foundation? Also, why did Gleb Yakunin, originally educated as a wild-game biologist, become an Orthodox priest during a time when his society strongly discouraged that vocation? What persons and writers shaped Yakunin's commitments and made him a primary spokesperson for religious freedom? How did the social, political, and religious setting in which he lived influence his decisions and lead him to rebel against the church and the state? How and why did Fr. Gleb Yakunin seek to cultivate relationships with the West and particularly with a certain person in the United States? What did Yakunin mean by "freedom of conscience" in the context of the Soviet Union, and later, in post-Soviet Russia, and what obstacles did he face in defending it?

Gleb Yakunin's life spans many of the most important events in the Soviet Union and post-Soviet Russia in the past century. Born in 1934 in Moscow, at the beginning of Stalin's Great Purges, he lost his father during World War II. He was raised by his mother, a staunch Orthodox believer, and two aunts, who held fast to the ritualistic practices of the Russian Church. Fatherless and like other Russian youths in the late 1940s, he spent his early teenage years roaming the streets of Moscow. Taught in the dull, conventional Soviet educational system, he had an inquisitive mind and a love of books, particularly those that fell outside the approval of the authorities. His postsecondary schooling took place in the Institute of Zoology, which moved to Irkutsk, Siberia, in 1955. Similar to his friend and classmate, Aleksandr Men, his experiences in Irkutsk shaped his life and perspectives. There, he became acquainted with a multicultural world and diverse religious beliefs. There, too, he made the decision to study for the Orthodox priesthood. He was ordained in 1960, during the worst period of Khrushchev's attack against religious belief and his massive closure of churches.

As a young priest, Fr. Gleb strongly believed that the survival of the church depended on its willingness to reform and its ability to reach out to the world. The letters he and his fellow priest Nikolai Eshliman sent to the Russian patriarch and the head of the state expressing this view resulted in the suspension of both young priests. Undaunted, Yakunin continued to fight against the system, writing letters to the World Council of Churches in 1975 and to various other world leaders, exposing the persecution of religious believers in the Soviet Union. Additionally, he participated in what he believed was a coming religious Renaissance among young members of the intelligentsia in the 1970s, served as a founding member of the Christian Committee for the Defense of Religious Believers' Rights in the USSR and, in an act of utter defiance of the political authorities, transported the committee's materials to the US entrepreneur and publisher Henry S. Dakin, an act that ultimately resulted in his arrest, imprisonment, and exile to Siberia.

Supported by his wife, Iraida, and his family, Yakunin refused to confess to his alleged anti-Soviet activities. Like other political prisoners, he was released from exile by President Gorbachev's general amnesty in 1987. On his return to Moscow, he was appointed head priest of a small parish in the Moscow region. There, he engaged in a whole flurry of activities. While serving as a priest, he ran for political office, served in the Congress of People's Deputies, and, after the fall of the Soviet Union in 1991, worked on the small parliamentary commission to investigate the heretofore closed archives of the KGB, which resulted in a series of explosive revelations. Pressured by church authorities to give up his political activities and focus solely on his responsibilities to his parish, he refused, an act of defiance that again led to his suspension from the priesthood and, eventually, in 1997, to his excommunication from the Russian Orthodox Church. The principles to which he held firmly—freedom of conscience, church reform, *sobornost'* (conciliarity), reconciliation, and repentance—were activated in the Apostolic Orthodox Church, which he helped found in 2000 and in which he served until the end of his life. He remained a sharp critic of the Moscow Patriarchate, authoritarian government, political violence, and a closed society until his death on December 25, 2014. His legacy is a testimony to defiance against the established power, a strong yet understudied theme in Russian history.

The Russian Orthodox Church does not list the name of Gleb Yakunin in its official encyclopedia; nor is there any mention of his myriad activities in defense of religious believers against persecution by the Soviet state. These omissions negate neither his historical significance nor his role in calling both the church and the state into account. The story of the Russian Orthodox Church in the twentieth century cannot be fully understood without coming to terms with Yakunin and the many voices he represented—in all their aspirations, circumstances, and struggles.

In the first two decades of the twenty-first century, no serious study of Yakunin's life and activities appeared in print, and he seemed nearly forgotten in public memory. In 2021, however, in rapid succession, three significant books on Yakunin were published, all of them written by knowledgeable Russian scholars. The first, authored by Volkova, titled *The Colossal Gleb: The Most Forbidden Priest* (in Russian, my translation), is an intimate portrayal of Yakunin's heroic efforts to defend religious believers of all confessions against state persecution and the church's seeming indifference to their plight.[26] The volume is particularly strong in its inclusion of lengthy excerpts from materials held in KGB archives, which Yakunin originally unearthed, the testimonies of family and friends, memoirs, and Yakunin's poetry, all of which in combination offer an informative and moving portrayal of his aspirations and activities.

The second book, *Gleb Yakunin (1934–2014): Orthodox Human Rights Defender, Priest, Deputy, and Poet* (in Russian, my translation), adds a unique perspective. Written by Georgii Vasil′evich Rovenskii, a local historian and the author of more than three hundred books on the city of Shchyolkovo, nineteen miles northeast of Moscow, and its surrounding region, this short work focuses on Yakunin's significance within that region.[27] The author aspires to revive and preserve Yakunin's memory in the face of efforts to forget the past and the men and women who kept humanistic values alive in the Soviet era.

The last of the three, *Fr. Gleb Yakunin: The Difficult Way of the Truth-Seeker* (in Russian, my translation), by the historian Sergei Sergeevich Bychkov, is a fact-based, well-researched, nonideological account of Yakunin's lifelong efforts to secure religious freedom in the former Soviet Union.[28] An acquaintance of Yakunin's for over forty years and the author of four books on the Russian Orthodox Church, Bychkov centers his biography on the major questions of ecclesiological debate in the past century: "What is the Church?" "How should it relate to the state and to the community?"

My book owes a debt of gratitude to all three of the abovementioned works. It relies on them, particularly Volkova and Bychkov, for factual details on several aspects of Yakunin's life and his break from the Moscow Patriarchate. In two ways, however, the account in my book takes a different approach to the subject.

First, more emphasis is placed on the significance of the international relationships that Yakunin cultivated. His activities sparked interest that went beyond the Soviet state and included the responses to the well-known letter he and his colleague Lev Regel'son wrote to the World Council of Churches in 1975, the perceptions he and others created about the grassroots realities of life in the former Soviet Union, as opposed to the picture Soviet leaders and the media attempted to draw, the support he received from abroad during his time in a Siberian labor camp and in exile, the outreach he and the members of his committee for the defense of believers' rights cultivated with the US entrepreneur Henry S. Dakin, and his efforts on behalf of religious believers that reached across confessional boundaries. Although he remained a citizen of Soviet Russia, Yakunin thought more broadly about citizenship and humanity than about national allegiances.

The materials in the Keston Archive at Baylor University, particularly those that document the persecution of religious believers, fit the narrative of the Soviet Union as an oppressive state. Some documents in the archival collection were used by political interests during the Cold War. Keston College in Great Britain, the original creator of the archive, however, never received funding from state agencies, and its employees did not view themselves as agents of the state. They had little control over how the documents were used outside the archive's domain, and such uses belong to another study. In this book the focus is on Fr. Gleb Yakunin, his activities and his struggles to support human rights and religious freedom. These themes spoke to global concerns that transcended the Cold War. In the 1970s, especially, they became an important part of the "quest for personal meaning and authenticity."[29]

Second, the theoretical framework for this book is derived from the Polish poet Czesław Miłosz's classic book-length essay *The Captive Mind*, written shortly after he left Poland for the West in the early 1950s. Miłosz had recently witnessed Stalin's tanks in the streets of Wilno (now Vilnius), the destruction of the Warsaw ghetto, and the Soviet suffocation of Poland. *The Captive Mind* seeks to explain why so many thinking people choose to sacrifice their independent lives and pay homage to an authoritarian political order. Miłosz explores the inner fears of people who surrender their personhood and their own freedom of thought for the promise of a bright, fantastic future in which neither shadows nor darkness exist. He calls this the "New Faith," whose magical influences have proved attractive to large numbers of intellectuals in the past century and, by inference, in the present.

In such a society, a few people resist and struggle to maintain their mental independence, but the vast majority submerge their identity in the New Faith. They acquire a different understanding of truth than that of the past. Truth is malleable, always in motion, and interdependent on a whole host of circumstances beyond their control. A magical power replaces the "objective search for truth and beauty," and metaphysical thought, in all its forms, is denigrated as being too intellectual, as well as too close to religion. Poets, therefore, are deemed especially dangerous and their work harmful to the compliant spirit of an authoritarian state. Thus, the government targets them first as enemies of the New Faith.

A major theme of Gleb Yakunin's story concerns his opposition to this notion of the captive mind. He challenged the political and religious structure that sought to crush freedom of thought. Russian history contained a strong tradition of dissent that existed alongside an authoritarian system that sought to compel compliance. Yakunin was part of that tradition, a rebel who never felt at home in a society that required submission and servitude. He was not without flaws and miscalculations. He put his wife and three children through periods of hardship and deprivation. Nevertheless, he had an indomitable spirit, a willingness to take great personal risks in pursuit of causes he considered just.

The roots of Yakunin's rebellion against the church and the state lay deeply embedded in his upbringing and personality as well as the specific impediments he encountered throughout his life. Although an Orthodox priest, he did not recognize Orthodoxy as the only authentic religious body in Russia, but endeavored to reach out to other confessions in defense of their legal rights and appreciation of their aspirations and beliefs. This book seeks to tell his story, his triumphs and disappointments, and above all his perseverance in the face of formidable challenges.

CHAPTER 1

Beginnings

The town of Anan'ev is located in the Odesa region in southwestern Ukraine on the northern coast of the Black Sea. In the late eighteenth century, as a result of the Partitions of Poland and Empress Catherine II's imperial projects, the Russian Empire acquired a large number of Jewish settlers, who lived in what later became known as the Pale of Settlement. A thriving commercial center within the Pale and known as the "pearl of the Black Sea," Odesa enjoyed a large multiconfessional and multicultural population. It was the birthplace of both the great poet Anna Akhmatova and the founder of jazz music in the Soviet Union, Leonid Utyosov. In the late nineteenth and early twentieth centuries, the area around Odesa was a rich agricultural center where local inhabitants cultivated grains, oilseeds, fruits, and vegetables. Located a short distance inland, Anan'ev also had a thriving textile industry. Founded in 1753, the town attracted Jewish settlers. In 1926, they numbered 3,516 out of a total town population of 18,230, and many of them worked in the town's textile enterprises.[1] Life in Anan'ev, however, did not consist of peace and security. Some of the country's most violent pogroms took place there: on April 27, 1881, antisemitic mobs demolished 175 Jewish homes and 14 small businesses, most of them in the poorer parts of the town; on October 17, 1905, gangs murdered 44 Jews and plundered a large number of shops; and in early 1920, a marauding band killed 220 of the 300 members of a Jewish defense organization.[2]

In the 1920s, in Anan'ev, lived two families who would play a large part in the Yakunins' story. The Zdanovs were the first of these. A family of small crafts-making people, they had moved to the area from Poland. Orthodox believers who had converted many years earlier from Catholicism, the Zdanovs practiced their Orthodox faith assiduously and raised their children to do the same. Living next door to them were the Yakunins. Descendants from the Russian nobility, they enjoyed a prestigious status before the Russian Revolution. The grandfather was once the vice-governor of Samara province in southwestern Russia, then governor of the prominent Novgorod district in the north. After the revolution, he and his wife moved to the south, bought a house in Anan'ev, and settled there to raise their children, of which they had many.[3] Their talented oldest son, Pavel Ivanovich Yakunin, completed the university and afterward matriculated at the conservatory, where he specialized in playing the violin.[4] He then made a decision that proved extremely unsatisfactory to his parents, particularly his father: he asked his neighbor's daughter, Klavdiia Iosifovna Zdanovskaia, whom he had known since his childhood, to marry him. His father considered her much below the status of his son. Poorly educated but lively, warm-spirited, and extroverted, this black-haired young woman expressed strong devotion to Pavel Ivanovich and the family life they both desired.

Wishing to establish themselves on their own, in the early 1930s, Pavel Ivanovich and Klavdiia Iosifovna moved to Moscow. They settled in the capital when Moscow was undergoing a large population expansion, a time of rapid economic growth, and a period when optimism about the Soviet Union's prospects seemed nearly unlimited. Pavel Ivanovich found employment as a professional violinist fulfilling a lifetime ambition, and he and his young wife enjoyed what appeared to be a promising future in a country on an upward trajectory, when most Western economies were mired in the Great Depression.

In 1934, shortly after the Yakunins settled in Moscow, Klavdiia Iosifovna gave birth to their son, Gleb Pavlovich. This event added to their sense of well-being, and the two parents were overjoyed by the bright, energetic child in their midst to whom they devoted a great deal of attention. As the child grew, they were delighted by his kindheartedness and his curiosity about nearly everything, but also by his interest in learning, which was sometimes tempered by a mischievous personality. Music, tenderness, and care for each other pervaded the entire household, which created for the child a warm, nurturing environment fostering his confidence in his capacity to make his own way in the world. The feeling of well-being, however, did not endure for long. As the German army rolled across the Soviet frontier on June 22, 1941, life in Moscow descended into chaos, and many families, including the Yakunins, left the city for the deep interior. In 1943, as the Soviet army succeeded in pushing back the German forces from Moscow, Pavel Ivanovich, unable to find employment suited to his musical skills, decided to return to the capital city, temporarily leaving his wife and son in the Russian interior. In Moscow, however, during those wartime conditions, he had no success in landing a position as a violinist and found work only as a boiler man. Pavel Ivanovich was unaccustomed to the physical demands of his job. His body steadily weakened from stress and the scarcity of food in a city whose main lines of supply were in near total disarray. In 1944, he suffered a heart attack and died. His unexpected death left Klavdiia Iosifovna, unemployed and a single mother, the parent of a ten-year-old child, without a regular means of financial support.[5]

The family's situation soon underwent another major change. In 1945, at the end of World War II, Gleb "acquired two additional mothers" who, according to his later friend Anatolii Levitin-Krasnov, strongly shaped the world in which Yakunin grew up: two of Gleb's aunts, having fought at the front in the war, resettled in Moscow, where they and his mother doted on the fatherless child. The whole family spent a lot of their time in church; they were not only religious, but deeply churched: "Icons and lighted lamps in all the rooms of their apartment," Levitin-Krasnov wrote, "the constant attendance in churches, the acquaintances with priests, and also the meticulous observance of Orthodox rituals—this was the style of the family."[6]

In reality, however, Gleb Yakunin grew up in two different and conflicting spheres: the world of the church, so passionately embraced by his mother and aunts, who fervently sought to pull him into its orbit, and the world of the school and Soviet culture, which moved in an opposite direction. In the late 1940s and early 1950s, the Soviet government and its educational institutions pursued a rigorous atheistic agenda. Although the government had relaxed its policy of closing Orthodox Churches and permitted the reopening of some religious institutions, beginning in 1943, official policy continued to use atheistic propaganda as a means to reeducate the population. The entire school system required atheistic teaching.[7] Caught between these two competing worldviews, the young Gleb Yakunin could not have avoided making some difficult choices. At the age of fourteen, he declared himself an avowed atheist.[8]

Yet this declaration did not prevent Yakunin from exploring fields that offered a different view from the one his teachers attempted to drum into their students. At the time, in the secondhand bookstores in Moscow, one could still find older works in philosophy, theology, and history, and Yakunin often haphazardly scoured these bookshops. As a bright and intellectually rebellious teenager, he developed a special interest in ancient religions and their various responses to the gods and the mysteries of creation. He had a curious mind, one that, even at an early age, desired to investigate more fully subjects his classes in school only touched upon, and this inquisitiveness, combined with skepticism toward official pronouncements, already characterized his personality. He took little at face value—neither the ritualistic religion of his mother nor the ideological certainties articulated by the political establishment.

A New Friend

Like most other Soviet youths of his generation, Yakunin had a strong disposition toward the sciences. In making the decision about his future, according to Levitin-Krasnov, "he chose for himself an unusual profession—that of hunter and biologist. The romantic attracted him, the romance of nature, the forest, and wild animals. Before him stood the image of Lieutenant Glahn and other heroes of [the novels of Knut] Hamsun."[9] The young Yakunin, Elena Volkova writes, dreamed of becoming "a man with a weapon, a person of strength, who had the ability to defend himself and others, to spend his days in the forest, hunting his own food, enjoying nature, and singing songs by the campfire. After the small rooms in Moscow's communal apartments, school drills, yard punks, wars, repressions, and sweaty fear, to suddenly turn into a free person, who awakened in a haystack, shared wine with others at a hunting stand, and filled his breast with freedom . . . this was his dream."[10]

After finishing his secondary education, therefore, Yakunin enrolled in the Institute of Zoology, which focused on fur-bearing mammals and was located in the southern suburbs of Moscow. This decision would change his life in major ways, particularly because of a noteworthy relationship he developed and the experiences he encountered at the institute. It was here that he met another student, Aleksandr Men, who had a similar interest in biology and who would have a formative influence on the young Yakunin's worldview.

On a Sunday afternoon in 1953, Gleb Yakunin was aboard the suburban train that took him from his home in Moscow to the institute. He noticed a young student sitting alone in a corner of the car and reading. Yakunin had never seen him before, and out of curiosity, approached the unknown student, who, he quickly learned, was Aleksandr Men. Yakunin—redheaded, short in stature, and with a pleasant look on his face—politely inquired about the book his new acquaintance was reading. Then, in a low voice, Yakunin asked him whether he had any books on Eastern religions and mysticism. The subjects lay outside the Soviet mainstream; in the late Stalin period, a person with an abiding interest in these topics would have instantly aroused suspicion. Immediately, Men became wary, not knowing whether the stranger intended his question to be a provocation. Uncertain about how to respond, Men gave a generic answer, mentioning only a standard Soviet textbook. "That is not what I asked you," retorted Yakunin.[11] The two students struck up a conversation about different subjects, which revealed that they had much in common, including a love of books. Both were voracious readers and both had an interest in world religions, the sciences, and the relationship between religion and science. This began a long-lasting friendship that, in Yakunin's case, changed his view about many topics. Yakunin had not abandoned his atheistic beliefs, but, as he later told me, he was in the process of seeking his own way.[12] His encounter with Aleksandr Men took place at an opportune time in his life:

> I was not a Christian at that time but, as the saying goes, "I was on the way." When I was a child, my mother often took me with her to church. She was a devout believer, but, as is often the case, also somewhat simpleminded. Naturally, she could not answer the many questions that had steadily emerged in my mind. She was a traditionalist, who abided by all the church traditions without questioning them, as she had been taught to do. But growing up in the general environment of the 1930s and '40s, in effect, I lost my childhood faith in God, and by the age of ten or eleven, I had become a diehard atheist. Later, however, primarily through my reading in philosophy, and the humanities, I gradually became an idealist of sorts. I recognized the existence of God, but not as something concrete and real. . . . It was at that point that I met Aleksandr Men and we became friends. . . . Under his influence and through my connections with several other Moscow friends, some very intelligent people, I had started to take an interest in Christianity.[13]

In 1955, the Soviet government decided to relocate the Institute of Zoology to the central Siberian town of Irkutsk, a main juncture on the Trans-Siberian Railroad and in the heartland of the institute's teaching and research. The location would give students firsthand exposure to the main resources of their study as well as to the furs that had become such valuable commodities on the international market and major sources of revenue for the Soviet state. The city was a crossroads of diverse nationalities and languages, which exposed a person directly to different social and religious ways of thought and belief. In this frontier city, state control over various institutions was not nearly as restrictive as in Moscow and the central regions of the country. Moreover, the city's historical and cultural significance predominated over an enormous part of the Soviet Union. Since the time of Peter the Great, Irkutsk had served as the administrative center of eastern Siberia, extending from the Yenisei River to the Pacific Ocean. For the past two hundred years, the city had been a central location to which the government had sent political exiles as well as the Polish citizens whose lands the Russian state had incorporated; Irkutsk, therefore, had one of the largest concentrations of Catholics in the Soviet Union. It also contained large settlements of Old Believers, the Orthodox sect that had left the church in 1666 in protest against the state's required church reforms.[14]

"At first, he [Men] did not like Irkutsk," Zoia Maslenikova writes. "The atmosphere was heavy and gloomy, and the same endless taiga oppressed him. He disliked the wooden pavement, the thick, broad faces, the squat wooden houses, the soot from the factory chimneys, the objects hanging over the streets."[15] The move placed Yakunin and Men in an unfamiliar city whose diverse population and flat layout required a significant adjustment in their perspectives. Gone were the cultural attractions of Moscow, and in their place were the rough-hewn, simplistic ways of a frontier city. The city and its environs had to grow on them, and, in time, both of them developed a liking for the multiethnic population and its diverse customs. Irkutsk had much to offer to a young person in the process of questioning everything, seeking new perspectives on life and belief. Its relative openness, the friendliness of its people, and its hospitality to outsiders made the city an attractive place to study and to broaden one's outlook on society as well as the multiethnic and religious composition of the Soviet Union.

Yakunin and Men chose to room together in Irkutsk. They elected, however, not to live with other students in the institute's dormitory, but to settle elsewhere, so they could pursue their interests without the distractions of other students. They found a place in a rooming house on the outskirts of the city. The institute's curriculum was not intensely rigorous, so they had plenty of time to explore the city and its surrounding area; they also had the opportunity for conversations with each other about mutual interests. The living arrangements they secured in Irkutsk brought the two students close together, although in theological matters, at this time in their lives, Men was far more advanced than Yakunin. Baptized in the Orthodox Catacomb Church as a baby, Men had been raised in the Catacomb Church in Zagorsk (Sergiev Posad), and the spiritual life he led was anything but the ritualistic forms of practice that Yakunin, at an early age, had learned to dislike. Tutored by several outstanding priests and a remarkable nun who encouraged him to discover the deepest wellsprings of Orthodox tradition, the young Men had known some of the best and most creative teaching the church had to offer.[16] In addition, Men's mother and "aunt" had recognized his unusual intellectual gifts, and they exposed him at any early age to philosophical and theological texts much more advanced than anything the school system had to offer. As a result, by the time he and Yakunin teamed up, Men had already acquired a vast reservoir of knowledge about a wide variety of topics, both Russian and Western, and he imparted some of it to Yakunin. "We talked a great deal," Yakunin said, "about the role of the Orthodox Church in society and what it ought to look like in the future of Russia."[17] Men gave Yakunin a firsthand tutorial about the history of many related subjects.

When he arrived in Irkutsk in the fall of 1955, Aleksandr Men brought with him a large trunk filled with books and papers that he intended to use in writing a history of religion from its origins to the birth of Jesus Christ. He had already written a draft of the first volume and intended to continue his work on this ambitious project while a student at the institute. Already in the middle of writing the second volume of the history, he had tentatively titled it *Magic and Monotheism: The Religious Path of Humanity up to the Epoch of the Great Teachers*. In Gleb Yakunin, he had a trusted friend with whom he could discuss his work and share ideas, someone who also had a keen interest in learning. Their friendship developed at a fortuitous time for both young men.

Yakunin's relationship with Men contributed to his future development in one additional way: Men had a long-lasting effect on his friend's theological outlook. Yakunin's view of Christianity closely paralleled the views Men expressed in his *History of Religion*.[18] In the early drafts of that multivolume work, Men understood Christianity as only in the first stages of its development. It was not yet completed, and people who claimed to have absolute knowledge of truth were misguided. His was not a static model of world history, but a dynamic one "[in] which the whole cosmos is in movement," constantly evolving towards something different from what existed earlier.[19] History was evolutionary, and Christianity followed a similar pattern. This understanding of Christianity strongly imprinted itself on Yakunin. He would later take a firm stand against conservative apologists for Christianity who aspired to preserve the past and "close the doors" against attempts to breathe fresh air into Christianity.[20] He would also acknowledge his debt to Aleksandr Men for opening his eyes to a deeper and clearer conception of Christianity than he had previously known. Yakunin emphasized his debt to his friend in a long narrative poem he wrote later in his life:

> This very menu
> For the poor in spirit,
> Came into being from the penetrating thought
> Of Aleksandr Men.[21]

When Yakunin and Men lived together in Irkutsk, the ideas in *Magic and Monotheism* were on Men's mind, and he had little reticence about sharing them. He had begun to develop his ideas on sin, suffering, and evil, themes to which he returned in all the volumes of his *History*.²² As Men used the term, "magic" represented the desire "to be like God"; it denoted the aspiration to "acquire the power of God" and to remake the world to fit one's own image. He connected it to the biblical view of original sin and the separation from God. This estrangement marked a spiritual sickness, the revolt against God, and the near total focus on the self. *Magic* placed the self, not others, at the center of existence and worship; it promoted a blind religion and "an almost maniacal faith in all-powerful rituals, incantations, and pledges."²³ In his later critique of Stalinism, Yakunin expressed similar views of the incantations and rituals as well as the cult of power that the Stalinist system promoted. The church, he would argue, had fallen under the sway of this all-embracing power.

Most important, in *Magic and Monotheism*, by drawing on anthropological studies of primitive societies, Men showed how magic could exercise a dominant influence over an entire group, encouraging people to meld with their native tribe. In this tribal setting, a person "did not have his own life, his own judgment, his opinion, and his own doubts, but fell under the hypnosis of 'collective ideas.'"²⁴ Men cited the French philosopher and anthropologist Lucien Lévy Bruhl's study of the primitive mentality to show how these ideas were passed from generation to generation.²⁵ In a primitive society, according to Lévy Bruhl, ideas were "imposed on individuals in the group, awakening in them, according to their circumstances, feelings of respect, fear, worship, etc. and how they should relate to different objects in the world."²⁶ In such a collective society, individuals relinquished their capacity to exercise their own free will. Subjugation made the society easier to govern, manipulate, and control. What Men called the tsar-magician endeavored to gain total domination over the creative impulses of the state's citizens and to suppress the freedom that lay at the core of Christianity.²⁷

It is difficult to discern precisely when, during his student years, Gleb Yakunin embraced these ideas. But a close look at Men's central beliefs, those already present in his early writings, suggest that Yakunin, in coming to Christianity, found them compatible with his own understanding. Like Men, Yakunin viewed Christ as unique, as more than a teacher, and as different from other prophetic voices of the ancient world. Christ offered a new way of looking at human beings as containing a divine and creative presence.²⁸ Threaded through all of history, two opposing forces had emerged, and they continued to play out, even within the Christian Church: "On one side, a creative, always searching movement," illustrated by a "dynamic spirituality" and "reverence for the Almighty." On the other side, a turning inward, accepting repression of the mind, and prizing comfort above all else, attitudes that are fully compatible with the worship of pagan secular rituals and static symbols of faith.²⁹ The conflict between these two opposing forces ran throughout Men's *History of Religion*. They provided a religious and intellectual framework from which Yakunin drew as he began to develop his own ideas about the role of the church in the world.

In addition, Yakunin's experiences in the multiethnic region of Irkutsk led him to appreciate, firsthand, the desires and human sensibilities of these diverse nationalities. These experiences made Yakunin a strong advocate for an open form of Christianity that reached outward, broke through the self-imposed barriers, and exhibited compassion for all of humanity.[30] A Christianity based on fear and exclusion was not a correct understanding of Christ's teachings or of the Apostle Paul's view that in Christianity "there is neither Jew nor Greek, there is neither slave nor free, there is neither male nor female; for you are all one in Christ Jesus" (Galatians 3:28). Reconciliation between different religious faiths would become major goals of both Men and Yakunin, although their approaches eventually took very different forms. As students in a frontier city, in order to broaden their theological understandings, they began to take a closer look at the Orthodox Church for comparison with the practices of other religious traditions.

Religious Communities in Irkutsk

The visits of Yakunin and Men to various churches in Irkutsk and the surrounding area began out of curiosity. Because the earlier experiences of both students had chiefly taken place in Moscow (in Men's case, also in Zagorsk), they wanted to compare the two settings, primarily to get a better view of religious life in this distant provincial city. As a longtime member of the Orthodox Church, Men quickly became a regular participant in the main Orthodox Church in Irkutsk, where he developed a relationship with the head priest and several diocesan officials.[31] Yakunin occasionally went with him, although the services left him uninspired. Both men were disappointed by the church's passivity and the priest's failure to explore important matters of faith more deeply and speak to social concerns. The differences with other religious communities they visited were "striking," Men wrote. "A half-empty church, the disorganized order of the service, depressed, melancholy elderly women, [and] a very short sermon heavily laden with political information (something about China)" distressed him, and these weaknesses similarly made a strong impression on Yakunin.[32] Neither young man found there the kind of open, creative approach that both of them desired.

Visits to a local Catholic community produced a different response. Yakunin and Men went there several times and soon developed a friendship with a young Catholic priest with whom they had many lively, wide-ranging conversations. Well-read, highly intelligent, and open-minded, the priest had traveled abroad, studied in the Vatican, and only recently returned to Russia. He was conversant with the writings of contemporary Catholic theologians who advocated dialogue with other religious confessions, a proposal he impressed upon Yakunin and Men. The priest did not at all fit the stereotypes of Catholic priests described in the Soviet press as poorly informed, doctrinaire, and slavish followers of the Roman pope. He invited them to attend Catholic services. Again, however, they were disappointed. They found the services to be mechanical, unimaginative, and not particularly welcoming, although the priest privately exhibited none of the qualities they witnessed in the services.[33]

Irkutsk had many different Protestant denominations, and they attracted the attention of the two students. They visited a Baptist church, whose membership, Men wrote, consisted mainly of local factory workers who warmly welcomed them into the service. Yakunin and Men observed there the kind of close-knit, welcoming church community that they admired and rarely saw elsewhere. But they did not find the services themselves appealing and they expressed disappointment at the theological shallowness of the pastor and the congregants. The pastor spoke extremely well to the members of the church community, but neither student appreciated his theological approach. They did not return.[34]

Men and Yakunin had conversations with other religious leaders in the city, including a Muslim imam, whom they found extremely well-read and personable. An Orthodox priest, a Fr. Vladimir, who served in a small church near Lake Baikal, however, unexpectedly made the greatest impression on Yakunin. "He was a very unique priest who had once served as a history teacher in Ukraine before his arrest by the state security police. We visited him shortly after his release from prison. With him, we developed a feeling of mutual trust. It was from him that I learned about the true history of the church, including the Catacomb Church."[35]

In addition to providing the chance to explore the environs of Irkutsk, the atmosphere of the institute had one other advantage: it connected study in the classroom to life in the world outside. Although it had a firmly set academic curriculum, the institute allowed plenty of time for leisure pursuits, personal exploration, and fraternization. The teaching faculty encouraged students to get acquainted as much as possible with the natural world, an opportunity that the Institute of Zoology readily accommodated, particularly during the summer months. Valentina Bibikova, a fellow classmate, remembers that "life was gay and happy":

At the end of the first year, we decided to camp in the Prioksko Nature Reserve. We needed money for a gun for someone, a camera for someone, and shoes for still another. Our everyday dress consisted of a ski suit, sneakers, and a backpack, and Alik (Aleksandr) also wore a summer hat. We were told to check the nature reserve's hollows for tits, flycatchers, bats, and small animals. We lived on the cordon; in the evenings, we boiled potatoes over a fire, caught from the Oka the unique fish of those years, and brought back what we could find in nearby village shops: crabs, cod liver in butter, and bread. Aleksandr Men played a guitar, and we listened to the sounds of the forest at night and the fish splashing in the river.[36]

In the late summer months, students were sent to a summer camp where they helped to harvest the crops. By day, they gathered potatoes, and in the evening, they typically swam and sat around a campfire, where they told stories and sang folksongs, accompanied by a guitar that one of them had brought.[37] Men and Yakunin were assigned different camps that were some distance apart. Near the end of the season, anxious to be reunited with his friend, Men journeyed to the camp where Yakunin was quartered, and the two of them went several times to speak with the above-mentioned Fr. Vladimir. Yakunin and Men learned that he had taught in a secondary school before becoming a priest. After being imprisoned for several years in the Gulag, he had recently been released as part of the large number of church officials freed after Nikita Khrushchev's anti-Stalin speech in February 1956. To Yakunin, the meetings with Fr. Vladimir proved a revelation. As he recounted: "It was there, during our conversations, with Aleksandr present, that I learned for the first time that Aleksandr's mother and aunt were not connected with the churches of the Moscow Patriarchate, but with the underground church. Aleksandr and I had long conversations with Fr. Vladimir, and he educated us about the true history of the church. He said that the official Orthodox Church was not the real church; the true church was the one that operated underground. . . . Aleksandr knew much of this history already, but, to me, it was shocking."[38]

In the conversations with Fr. Vladimir, Yakunin learned about the Catacomb Church and the conditions that had spawned its emergence after the revolution. In 1927, under enormous political pressure from the government, Metropolitan Sergei, the locum tenens of the Orthodox Church, pledged the church's loyalty to the new Bolshevik power, and Orthodox priests were required to do likewise. In order to preserve their status and to prevent what they feared would be the church's destruction, most priests complied with the requirement, but not all were willing to compromise either their own or the church's integrity. At great risk to their lives, these priests went underground and continued to hold services in secret, often in the most dangerous circumstances for them and their parishioners. These underground communities emerged in many places in the Soviet Union, sustained by the belief that they were upholding the purity of the Orthodox faith without giving in to the atheistic state and compromising time-honored traditions.[39] By the late 1950s, most Soviet citizens had no knowledge of this history.[40]

In Aleksandr Men, Yakunin had with him a fellow student who had spent his early years in the Catacomb Church in Zagorsk. Men's experiences with the elders in that unofficial church community had deeply shaped his theological perspectives and vision of what the church should be.[41] The priests who served in the Catacomb Church in Zagorsk had the same approach as the famous Optina pustyn' elders in their relationships with the people they came in contact with. In the Optina pustyn' monastery, the elders engaged in open conversation with people, counseled them, and gave them guidance in their lives. After the Bolshevik government closed the Optina monastery in 1923, its traditions lived on in the Catacomb Church in Zagorsk, where Fr. Serafim (Batiukov), who served there after having spent part of his early training at Optina pustyn', formed a warm, caring community. When he first heard of the Catacomb Church, Gleb Yakunin learned of a church community that operated outside the heavy-handed influence of the government, a memory that remained with him for a long time.[42]

In addition to his conversations with Fr. Vladimir, Yakunin's views of his society were sharpened by yet another experience he had during his student years. The rooming house where he and Men lived was located near a railroad track, on the other side of which stretched a large, open field. On a clear day, in the early morning, they could see a line of prisoners shuffling along, slumped over, heads bent down being marched to their daily work in the fields nearby. Even on bitterly cold mornings, Yakunin and Men witnessed the procession, and the image of prisoners' plight made a deep impression on both students.[43] Growing up in Moscow, Yakunin obviously knew about the labor camps, but in Irkutsk, he witnessed them firsthand, and this experience burned in his consciousness. His compassion for the voiceless in the camps and his understanding of the reasons for their incarceration made him acutely aware of the dichotomy between the state's rhetoric about a free society and the social realities he encountered.

In Irkutsk, following his conversion to Christianity, Yakunin began to think a great deal about the fate of the church, particularly with regard to its responsibility to the outcast members of Soviet society. In the weeks following their conversations with Fr. Vladimir, he and Men spent a great deal of time talking about what the Orthodox Church would look like "free of intimidation by the KGB and free of state control." They discussed "what it would take to reform the church, and how, in present circumstances, to make this reform a reality."[44] Yakunin well understood that their aspirations represented youthful ideals. In hindsight, however, in looking back over the course of his career, key aspects of Yakunin's character as well as one of his perceived flaws, were already apparent at this time. All his life he continued to imagine that change was forthcoming and that with courage and the right approach, a new beginning could be achieved. Despite the most difficult of circumstances, he held firmly to a positive view of the world and the human beings he encountered. He had little use for pessimists, those who were indifferent to social injustices, or those who remained compliant with the institutions that fostered those injustices. Regrettably, though, he often underestimated the challenges he faced and the support he had for what seemed to him to be reasonable changes. The miscalculations, even with the best of intentions, would subject him to much suffering.

Yakunin's long-term goal was to liberate the church from the domination of the political powers. During his student years in Irkutsk, he had not fully defined this ambition, but it had begun to form in his mind. Like Men, and perhaps under his influence, Yakunin already understood that for the Orthodox Church to be effective and to develop an authentic voice, it had to be open to the world. Based on the Gospels, this openness would serve as one of the distinctive features of Aleksandr Men's later vocation as an Orthodox priest. It also played a significant role in Yakunin's future endeavors and gave him a powerful, if controversial, voice.

Although the two friends would take vastly different roads, they shared the belief that the church ought not to turn its vision of the world inward, as it had done since the late 1920s. It had to serve the society actively, speak to its needs, develop a compelling voice for those individuals searching for a holistic view of life, and reach out to a suffering humankind. It had to find the means to educate the members of Russian society in the fundamental teachings of the Orthodox tradition and the Holy Scriptures during a time when the state's assault on religion had nearly obliterated those teachings from the minds of the Russian people.[45]

The questions that arose during his experiences in Irkutsk concerned Yakunin (as they had Men) long after he graduated from the institute. These questions were not determinative, and he considerably refined them later, but Irkutsk and his relationship with Men essentially focused the main issues in his mind. He wondered how the church might uncover the sources of its tradition and, most important, convey these sources effectively to the Russian people. During a time when state policies narrowly restricted its ability to reach people beyond the physical boundaries of its property, he recognized the importance for the church to express its compassion for people in need, including those who aspired to practice their faith freely. In Irkutsk, after his conversion to Orthodox Christianity, Yakunin most likely began to question the capacity of the Moscow Patriarchate to satisfy the spiritual needs of the Russian people. He connected the official church with state violence, the suppression of believers, and a reluctance to address the problems that concerned him.[46]

It is unknown precisely when Gleb Yakunin made the decision to become a priest. His association with Men and their conversations about the role of the church in Russian society played a part. Most likely, this idea formed only gradually in his consciousness. He would have seen the vocation of priest, if practiced responsibly, as an enormous challenge, particularly given the severe obstacles the priesthood faced. Given the patriarchate's passivity toward the defense of the priests who failed to strictly adhere to the state's dictates, he could have expected little support from the church hierarchy. During his stay in Irkutsk, however, he had come to see the importance of the church and the need for its dynamic presence in Soviet life, despite the challenges. "By my nature, I am a fighter," Yakunin later claimed.[47] In his early twenties, this quality of his personality had already begun to manifest itself in his choice of vocation.

Discovering Berdiaev

Like Men, Yakunin had a love of reading, and the two of them often scoured the antiquarian bookstores in Irkutsk in search of books not easily found in Moscow. After Men discovered a stack of old volumes in the church where he worked as a part-time boiler man, their reading intensified. Someone had discarded the books, leaving them in a closet in the church where they were gathering dust, and a cleaning lady told Men to take any of them he wished.[48] Several volumes in this treasure trove of books were written by the talented leaders of Russia's religious and philosophical circles at the end of the nineteenth and beginning of the twentieth century. Men devoted a great deal of time to reading their works and introduced Yakunin to several of them, including the work of Nikolai Berdiaev, who would have a large influence on his fellow student.[49]

Born in 1874 (d. 1948) to a noble family in Kyiv Berdiaev had an aristocratic upbringing. As a student at the University of Kyiv, he converted to Marxism and joined a radical Social Democratic group. But he never fully embraced Marxism and was never comfortable with its narrowly focused, restrictive views on human freedom. After his expulsion from the university for his political activities and his exile in Vologda, in 1924, Berdiaev moved to Paris. His encounters with leading intellectuals such as Sergei Bulgakov, Zinaida Gippius, and Dmitry Merezhkovsky led him to renounce his Marxist affiliations. Several reasons accounted for his change of mind. The Marxist perspective claimed to be a totalistic view of human existence, but it did not explain everything, including such irrational feelings as love, compassion, and self-sacrifice. Since childhood, Berdiaev wrote, he had always had a predisposition to religious questions. Most important, while in Paris, he read the great Slavophile philosopher and poet Aleksei Khomiakov, whose writings opened up a completely new world for the young Berdiaev. "His [Khomiakov's] idea of freedom as the ground of Christianity and the Church had a special significance for me," he noted.[50] He developed a strong belief in the importance of the free, unfettered personality and one's right to choose one's own course in the world.

After his return to Russia in 1908, Berdiaev worked as a journalist and a teacher of philosophy, all the while moving closer to Orthodoxy, although he had difficulty with the church's administrative structure and its leadership's narrow-minded views of society. But the beauty of Orthodoxy, the creativity of its teachings, and its emphasis on spiritual freedom spoke profoundly to him. After the revolution, he stayed in Russia, for a brief time serving as a professor of philosophy at Moscow University and teaching at a private institution, the "Free Academy of Spiritual Culture."[51] During this period, Berdiaev wrote his first significant works: *The Philosophy of Freedom* (1911) and *The Meaning of Creativity* (1916), books containing central themes on which he elaborated in his later publications.[52]

It was the first of these books that Aleksandr Men recommended to his friend when they were students in Irkutsk, and Gleb Yakunin read it for the first time then.[53] He would repeatedly return to it for guidance and ideas, several of which, given his evolution as a student, would have had an immediate appeal.

In his *Philosophy of Freedom* (as well as *The Meaning of Creativity*), Berdiaev emphasized the importance of the free human personality, which he contrasted with the mentality of the crowd. This personal gift, which the Creator gives to every individual, must be allowed to develop freely and permitted to act and to think unrestricted by outside pressures to conform. The free personality, he maintained, was "one of the highest features of spirituality"; it was, he asserted, the very "image of God" that lived in each person; it represented a person's "I."[54] Mass society tended to reduce the human being to a cog in a vast machine, a number, an address, a particle in a whole society. Christianity, in contrast, underscored the supreme importance of the person as a child of

God. *The Philosophy of Freedom* defended "personalism" as the sacredness of the individual against the impersonal forces brought about by recent scientific discoveries, technology, and attempts to reduce human beings to automatons.

Freedom, Berdiaev maintained, allowed the individual to make a choice, a choice that was mystical and formed the very essence of creativity.[55] Freedom meant spiritual freedom, the capacity and openness to hear one's own calling and the willingness to respond to that calling, despite the powerful societal pressures that pulled one in a different direction. Religion, he claimed, did not lead to a sense of dependence, but to a "sense of independence." "If God does not exist," Berdiaev wrote elsewhere, "a person is a being wholly dependent on nature or society, on the world or the state. If God exists, the person is a spiritually independent being; and the individual's relation to God is to be defined as freedom."[56]

As a student in the process of rejecting the atheism he had formerly and unthinkingly adopted, Gleb Yakunin found these ideas liberating. They encouraged him to seek his own course and affirmed the legitimacy of his ultimate decision. In concert with Men, Yakunin began to conceive of the spiritual as an essential part of human creativity. Spirituality flourished when it had the chance to develop freely, whether in the world or within the individual. Like Berdiaev, Yakunin would come to abhor the objectification of nature and human beings that turned them into passive objects for profit or human pleasure. Berdiaev despised and characterized as sins against God all forms of slavery and all attempts to delimit the "freedom of the creative soul." Yakunin held a similar belief for the rest of his life. It strengthened his commitment to "freedom of conscience," which soon became one of the core elements in his theology.

All too often, Berdiaev noted, people willingly sacrificed their freedom, the most important possession a person had, in exchange for security, certainty, and material gain. He cited a passage from Dostoevsky's "Legend of the Grand Inquisitor" from the novel *The Brothers Karamazov*, in which the Grand Inquisitor reproaches Christ: "You desired the freedom of man, that he should follow you freely, seduced and captivated by you."[57] In this statement, Berdiaev wrote, Dostoevsky clearly showed the meaning of Christian freedom: "Man must carry the burden of freedom in order to be saved. Christianity offers freedom in Christ. Salvation through the use of compulsion is impossible and useless."[58] The church, Yakunin maintained, must never become part of the government, because when it did, it sacrificed its most precious gift, its internal freedom. When the church allied itself with the government in pursuit of power and gain, rather than in the defense of its own internal freedom, the church's mission was corrupted.[59] The church had to retain its capacity to criticize state actions, and it had to strengthen its compassionate voice in order to have a creative presence in the world. Observing the subservience of many Orthodox priests and their failure to remain true to what Berdiaev had referred to as the "divine principle in life," Yakunin saw the vital need for church reform. As he began to define his own future calling, he also understood the direction he had to follow.

Road to the Church

Looking backward at Gleb Yakunin's life, one might have the impression that his pathway to the priesthood had a consistent trajectory. But this would be a mistaken impression. He faced many practical obstacles, including the temporary loss of his friend and confidant Aleksandr Men, whom the institute expelled in May 1958, several weeks before Men's scheduled graduation.[60] Yakunin remained determined to complete his course of study and to graduate from the institute. Lacking any formal education in theology and church history or the qualifications that would ease his admittance into the priesthood, he had to decide on the best course to follow.

Before his graduation from the institute and his departure from Irkutsk, one other event took place in Yakunin's life that had a significant influence on his future. He and Men often worshipped at Znameniia Presviatoi Bogoroditsy (Church of the Miracle, Sign of the Most Holy Theotokos), the Orthodox Church in the city center. Singing in the church choir was a young woman, Iraida Georgievna Semenova, to whom Yakunin immediately felt an attraction. They became friends, and after meeting with her several times, he felt this attraction even more profoundly. Subsequently, she invited him to her home to meet her parents. For Yakunin, the meeting did not turn out to be a pleasant experience. Iraida's father, a former soldier who had fought at the front in World War II, worked as a carpenter in the military hospital in Irkutsk, and the family lived in an apartment on hospital grounds. Iraida's father took an instant dislike to Yakunin. Strongly antisemitic, he took the redheaded Yakunin to be Jewish and was overtly rude to him. Iraida's mother, however, treated him kindly, and the two got along from the outset. Iraida invited Yakunin a second time, for tea, thinking her father would be away. Soon after Yakunin arrived, however, Iraida learned that her father had left work early and soon planned to return home. To avoid a confrontation, the two of them quickly left the apartment and conducted their courtship as they walked on the street.[61]

Iraida's acquaintance with Gleb Yakunin, which began in 1957, soon developed into a romance. Sometime later that same year, he proposed marriage to her. He was twenty-three years old and she was eighteen and only at the beginning of her advanced schooling. She went to seek her mother's counsel: "I like him," Iraida said, "but I am not ready to get married. I want to study to find my own pathway in life, which I have not yet discovered." "Well, then, tell him 'No!' Mama advised. And I did so."[62]

Iraida had wanted to be a doctor, but, following an unsuccessful foray into medical school, she enrolled in a technical institute where she studied economics to become an accountant. Meanwhile, Gleb Yakunin graduated from the institute in Irkutsk, served the compulsory term as a forest ranger, and returned to Moscow. At the same time, he kept up his relationship with Iraida, often sending her letters and packages filled with "journals and books about art and various other subjects in an attempt to enlighten me," she later recalled. Before he left Irkutsk, he had told her that he would wait for her until she was ready to marry and asked her how long it would be.[63] Although she did not give him a definite answer, Yakunin was patient, convinced he had found his future wife.

In retrospect, the two made a good match. Iraida had been raised in an Orthodox family in which the mother, a committed believer, had attempted to instill the Orthodox faith in her three children. She had them in church each Sunday, although, at the time, believers in God were ridiculed and often provoked by other children. "Not just a few times did others challenge us in school and demand that we remove the cross from our neck and try to forbid us to go to church."[64] Neither she nor her siblings ever relented; her two brothers served at the altar in the church, and she sang in the church choir.[65] In remaining committed to her, Gleb Yakunin knew that he had found a steadfast person whose life experiences fit well with the life of an aspiring young priest. While he may not have been fully conscious of it, his selection of Iraida replicated his own father's choice, since he, too, had chosen a young woman from a simple, uneducated, working-class family with whom he would have an enduring relationship.

When he returned to Moscow in 1959, Yakunin did so alone. A year later, he matriculated in the Moscow Theological Seminary and began his studies for the priesthood. He could hardly have chosen a less opportune time to become a priest. The previous year, beginning in February 1959, the Soviet premier Nikita Khrushchev had called for a transition in the state's approach to religion, moving from active propaganda to a more aggressive approach in which church hierarchs were targeted for removal and churches were closed down. In December, an antireligion storm was underway, and one month later, in January 1960, the assault intensified with the mass closure of churches, the prohibition of pilgrimages and church charitable work, and the publication of hundreds of thousands of atheistic tracts.⁶⁶ The authorities also decreed that a specified distance separate churches in towns and villages and made it illegal for a priest to represent more than one church.⁶⁷ The effects of this policy resulted in the closing down of rural churches throughout the country.⁶⁸

Gleb Yakunin had hoped the Moscow Theological Seminary would be a place of learning and excitement. Instead, he found neither the curriculum nor the professors to be inspiring. He quickly became aware that he would have to accomplish any learning on his own. He lasted less than a year in the seminary. Late in his first year, he borrowed a book from the library: Nikolai Berdiaev's *Filosofiia svobody* (The Philosophy of Freedom). Shortly after he checked out Berdiaev's book, the Party's Literature Control Office instituted a purge at the Ecclesiastical Academy's library of certain volumes deemed unsatisfactory. These writings included the collected papers of the Kyivan theology professor Archpriest Pavel Iakovlevich Svetlov and Nikolai Berdiaev's *Filosofiia svobody*. Yakunin loved Berdiaev's book, considered it a rare and penetrating work on the meaning of freedom, and he knew that when he returned the book, it would disappear. He told the authorities he had lost it. Archimandrite Leonid (Poliakov), a professor who sympathized with Yakunin, said to him, "Gleb, try to return the book at any cost; otherwise, they will expel you, and I will not be able to defend you." As soon as he heard this, Yakunin recounted, "I went on the black market and bought a copy of Berdiaev's book, but without the library stamp, of course. I told the authorities that I was returning an exact copy in the place of the lost one." That did not satisfy them, although they immediately confiscated the copy and then told the seminary's rector to "expel Gleb Yakunin, because he checked out a library book; however, after an urgent demand for its return, he submitted a totally different copy." "I was 'guilty' of an immoral act—I had tried to steal a book, and on this basis, they dismissed me from the seminary."⁶⁹

Despite this setback, Yakunin soon experienced several developments that placed his life on a more positive trajectory. While in Moscow, he had continued writing letters to Iraida Georgievna in Irkutsk, affirming his desire to marry her, and in 1961, after completing her course of study, which qualified her as a bookkeeper, she moved to Moscow to be near him. Unable to secure a prominent position in the church, Yakunin took a low-ranking post as a psalm reader in the northwestern suburbs of Moscow. Several days after Iraida's arrival, they married. The wedding was simple, Iraida recalled ("We had little money"), and Fr. Aleksandr Men organized everything at the dacha of Fr. Vladimir Rozhkov, where all their friends gathered.⁷⁰ The wedding was the joyous culmination of an extended courtship during which Yakunin never wavered in his devotion to her.

In May 1962, Iraida gave birth to their first child, a daughter whom they named Mariia, who immediately became one of the most beloved people in Yakunin's life. Another fortunate development soon followed. On August 9, 1962, Yakunin was ordained as a deacon, and the next day Archbishop Leonid (Poliakov), in a ceremony held in the Novodevichy Monastery in Moscow, consecrated him as a priest.[71] The church appointed him to serve as second priest in Zaraisk, a small medieval fortress town in western Russia, some 101 miles from Moscow. Iraida worked as a bookkeeper in Moscow, where, despite the distance Yakunin had to travel, they lived with Yakunin's mother in a small room on Zhukovskaia Street in central Moscow. A curtain divided the fourteen-meter room in which all four of them lived. Yakunin's mother slept on one side of the curtain, and Yakunin, Iraida, and their daughter on the other.[72]

A short time later, the church transferred Yakunin from Zaraisk to the medieval city of Dmitrov, forty miles from Moscow and much closer to his home. Located north of Moscow, the city lay on a once major trading route to the north through which grain from the south had once moved, and fur pelts had been transported southward to Moscow. Dmitrov was also the site of magnificent churches whose golden cupolas loomed over the city's landscape. These churches and nearby monasteries suffered greatly during the antireligion campaigns, and most of them were closed or converted into museums. A small church lying on the outskirts of the city remained the only open establishment, and it attracted people from all the surrounding towns and villages.[73] Fr. Gleb would serve this church for the next three years, marking an extremely joyous time in his life. Happily married, the father of an infant daughter, and the head priest of an Orthodox parish, he thrived, even in these challenging times. By all these measures, he was successful. Of Yakunin's three years in Dmitrov, Levitin-Krasnov wrote, "[Fr. Gleb] was respected and loved by his parish and the people; a person of rare kindness and utmost humility, he won the respect of all people who met him."[74] Yakunin could not have known that an explosive event lay immediately ahead and change his entire relationship to the church and the trajectory of his life.

CHAPTER 2

The Letters

In the last two months of 1965, letters sent by two young Russian parish priests, Fathers Gleb Yakunin and Nikolai Eshliman, shattered the widespread view of the Russian Orthodox Church as submissive and malleable. Although the letters were group composed, the two young priests signed them, thus taking on the responsibility of being the public face of the messages. The names of the two priests were then little recognized in the Soviet Union and the Western world. The first letter, dated November 21, they delivered to the head of the Russian Orthodox Church, Aleksii I, patriarch of Moscow and All-Russia; the second, written on December 15, addressed the chair of the Presidium of the Supreme Soviet of the Soviet Union, Nikolai I. Podgorny.[1] In the context of the letters sent to Aleksii I and Podgorny, statements attributed herein to Yakunin and Eshliman, the only signatures on the documents, represent the thoughts and conclusions of the larger group with whom they collaborated.

The two letters, which challenged the Russian state and the Orthodox Church, soon received near universal attention. Excerpts were widely published and distributed, and these published accounts focused on the writers' accusations of widespread persecution of religious believers, and included a demand that the patriarch stand up to the government's violations of the Soviet Constitution. Historians and journalists have examined these letters, particularly the lengthy first one addressed to Patriarch Aleksii I, for their political content, which, during the Cold War, neatly fell into the narrative of the Soviet Union as an oppressor nation. But the time has come for a closer look at the documents and at the Orthodox Church and its practices at a crucial moment in the history of the Soviet Union.

The two letters reached Western Europe and the United States in the late spring and early summer of 1966 and immediately created a sensation. The National Council of Churches, which made the letters public in the United States, called them new evidence of a "not so quiet revolution inside the Russian Orthodox Church in Moscow." In London, Victor Frank, the son of the early twentieth-century Russian philosopher-theologian Semen Frank, described the letters as rare and incisive portraits of life inside the church. "Hitherto," he wrote in the progressive Catholic weekly the *Tablet*, "most scholars had to rely either on Soviet press accounts or the isolated testimonies of individual believers, many of them devout but inarticulate humble folk. What we have now in the shape of this letter [to the patriarch] is a highly articulate analysis of the church-state relationship in the Soviet Union, an analysis made by two young Orthodox priests of Soviet nationality." Expressing its surprise at the appearance of the letter to the Soviet president, the *Christian Century* called the first letter a document of "extraordinary historical importance." But in the Soviet Union, perhaps taken aback by the letters' reception and interpretation in the Western world, the view was much different: Western writers were simply misinformed; they misread the actual realities of religious life in the Soviet Union. The prominent Soviet journal *Science and Religion* called the two young priests "ecclesiastical extremists" who were attempting to "push the church into a position of political opposition to the regime." Given the political passions Eshliman and Yakunin stirred and the uproar over their letters, it bears another look at the context for their actions and the immediate consequences, both for them and for the church. The story of these letters began long before 1965.[2]

A Gathering of Young Priests

In 1962, a group of young priests came together in the village of Alabino in the environs of Moscow, southwest of the city. As newly minted priests fresh out of the seminary or other educational institutions, none of them held positions of prominence within the Orthodox Church. Nearly all of them had recently received appointments to village parishes where they came face-to-face with the difficult realities of their calling. They gathered in Alabino to discuss the problems they encountered, to support each other in their separate endeavors, and to share the results of their individual efforts to reach people both within and outside the church. The priests prayed together, asking for divine guidance, and read the Gospels, seeking inspiration for the mission they collectively shared.

The priests were also reform-minded. They well understood the harsh conditions in which they served and recognized that the church itself was the source of many of their problems, thanks, in part, to the low levels of education held by many of their superiors and the fear these superiors had of taking any kind of bold action. But mostly, the difficulties came from outside the church. Beginning in 1959, the Orthodox Church experienced the second great wave of religious repression in Soviet times. Large numbers of churches and monasteries were closed, a virulent antireligion campaign began in the press and other media, and educational and cultural institutions portrayed religious beliefs as superstitious holdovers from the past that would soon be left behind.[3] The new journal *Science and Religion*, which began publication in 1959, publicly spearheaded this effort, describing many of the giants of Russian cultural history as atheists. The Soviet premier Nikita Khrushchev vowed to extirpate religion from Soviet life, and the years 1962 and 1963 represented the high-water mark of this effort.[4]

To the young priests who met at Alabino, as to all other Orthodox servitors, the Soviet government's passage of parish reform in 1961 represented an especially onerous restriction on their activities. The parish reform was passed by a hastily convened Council of Bishops whose members were summoned to the Holy Trinity Monastery at Zagorsk on July 18, 1961, given the decree that had already been prepared, and forced to sign it on the same day. The decree crippled the priests' authority in their parish and took away all their rights there, with the exception of allowing them to conduct church services. Authority was placed in the hands of a government-appointed council of twenty people, the *desiatniki*, which were often composed of older citizens and people with mental illnesses or avowed atheists—all of which made effective management of the parish extremely difficult. Most often, rights within the parish fell under the jurisdiction of the local police. This decree represented a breach of canon law as well as a serious infringement on the Soviet Constitution of 1918. In the early 1960s, Russian Orthodox parishes became subject to all kinds of arbitrary actions carried out by state representatives.[5]

Normally, the priests who met regularly at Alabino complained about the 1961 decree and its hindrance to their activities. Nevertheless, it is important to keep in mind that their meetings aimed at an objective larger than this one piece of legislation. They were concerned, more broadly, with the Orthodox Church's traditional mission and how best to fulfill that mission. These clerics were not radicals who aspired to overturn Orthodoxy's theological message; but they were rebels against the status quo, against the static mindset that they witnessed around them, and against the policies that prevented them from reaching out to people. In the early 1960s, unpublished decrees issued by Khrushchev's government required clergy to provide a written application each time they conducted christenings, funerals, and weddings. They could not conduct any special religious service in a believer's private residence without special permission of the local officials.[6] They wanted these restrictions removed. Moreover, they wanted the church reformed and returned to its proper roots.

Leading Voices

The group of priests that met regularly numbered about ten members. Some of them did not want their names known, and they have remained anonymous. Others, however, soon became well known; for diverse reasons, they would play prominent roles in Russia's religious history in the second half of the twentieth century, and they included Aleksandr Men, Gleb Yakunin, Nikolai Eshliman, and Dmitrii Dudko.

Fr. Aleksandr Men was the leader of the group. It was likely his initiative that first brought the members together; originally, he served as second priest in the Alabino parish, the place of the gatherings. Only two years had passed since his ordination into the Orthodox priesthood, and Alabino was his first posting. The head priest was older and in poor health, and left most of the active duties in the parish to his young associate. In 1961, a year after Men's posting, the elderly priest died, which left the twenty-six-year-old Fr. Aleksandr in charge of the parish. Until the late 1980s, near the end of his life, this would be the only time he had the opportunity to serve as head priest. Broadly educated and an inveterate reader of the sciences and theology, he had already begun to write the impressive, deeply researched books on the Gospels and the history of religion that could only be published in Russia many years later. Men had a lively curiosity and searching mind, an attribute that would make him very attractive to the Russian intelligentsia, who had already heard of this unusually gifted young priest and came out to Alabino in increasing numbers to meet him. Fr. Aleksandr also had an uncommon ability to speak across educational boundaries and relate to simple people. His magnetic personality drew many different kinds of people to him, occasionally including some with unsavory motives. He never wavered in his resolve to serve people. In 1962, the church transferred him to the provincial parish of Tarasovka, a settlement on the railway line between Moscow and the famous Orthodox Church center of Zagorsk. The circle of young priests who began at Alabino moved with him.[7]

Fr. Gleb Yakunin was in the first months of his priesthood. Men had played a major role in converting Yakunin, previously an atheist, to Christianity (discussed in chapter 1). Yakunin freely admitted his personal and intellectual debts to Men both in his later poetry and in his theological commitments. Psychologically, however, the two young priests were very different. Although well-read, broadly educated, and possessed of a curious mind, Yakunin had a fiery temperament and sometimes acted impulsively, with scant regard for the consequences. He did not hesitate to speak out boldly, and often loudly, against acts that he considered unjust. Men was the deeper thinker, the more scholarly student of history and philosophy, Yakunin the more politically active person, who had little hesitation in challenging authority. Like Men, he made friends easily, although Men proved much more circumspect in his closest affiliations than Yakunin. Both, however, had a deep commitment to the Orthodox Church and to the belief that it needed to reach far beyond the narrow physical boundaries that the Russian government prescribed.

Fr. Nikolai Eshliman was one of the older members of the group. Thirty-four years old when he joined the gathering in 1964, he had a lively personality, was a gifted storyteller, and had a large number of friends. A member of the Moscow intelligentsia, Eshliman and his wife, Irina, in their younger years held open court in their one-room apartment in the city of Dmitrov, where their intelligentsia friends gathered to drink and hold long conversations about literature and the arts. Aleksandr Men met Eshliman in 1956, and the two immediately became friends, although they had dissimilar backgrounds and personalities. Many people took Eshliman to be Jewish because of his last name, but, in reality, he was a descendent of Scottish forebears whose name was Ashley and who, as skilled craftspeople, had immigrated to Russia during the period of Catherine the Great. Eshliman's mother was a member of the Russian nobility who had passed on to her son the social mannerisms and speech of her class. "He was an aristocrat—and I was never one of them," Fr. Aleksandr explained. "Nikolai was an aristocrat at heart, a person with majestic aristocratic manners, mixed in with artistic qualities. He played the piano well, sculpted something, drew—there was something bohemian in him."[8] Eshliman worked first as an artist, a reconstructionist of church art. But in his early thirties, he changed course; he enrolled in the Moscow Theological Academy to study for the priesthood. He was ordained in 1961. Once he entered this vocation, he threw his whole being into it. He served with a passion and grace one rarely saw, Men said. "He preached excellently. His people loved him. . . . I myself attended his services and saw how his people loved him—because he was a gentleman, in the best sense of this word. His parishioners somehow felt in him a 'gentleman'—they sensed this immediately."[9] Eshliman served in a large church a short distance from Moscow before his transfer to a church in the center of the city.

Father Dmitrii Dudko was the senior member of the group. He had also traveled the most difficult personal road to reach this point in his life. Forty years old, he came from a peasant village in the deep interior of Russia, the son of hardworking parents who struggled night and day to provide sustenance for their nine children. Dudko vividly remembered the Stalinist collectivization campaign, when state officials entered their hut and asked the family for all the grain they possessed. He recalled his father's protest, his cry to the grain collectors that he would not be able to feed his children, and the indifference of a state official as he removed the family's one remaining sack of grain. A bright and curious child, Dudko stood out from all the other children in the village; he was an avid reader, absorbing every book he could get his hands on, including the Gospels, which he read at an early age. After the war, he heard of an open seminary in Moscow and, in 1946, he left his village to enroll.

The seminary, housed in Novodevichy Monastery in the same quarters that Tsarevna Sofiia had once lived, served as the first step to a vocation filled with numerous twists and turns. Achieving high marks on the entrance exams, he enrolled in Moscow's premier religious institution, its Theological Academy, where he prepared for the priesthood. His studies, however, were interrupted. He was arrested, ostensibly for his poetry, but in reality for being what the police considered an "unreliable person," and from there he followed the usual path for those arrested: the Lubyanka and Butyrka prisons, followed by a labor camp in the Ural Mountains where he spent eight and one-half years.[10] The labor camp, despite its harsh conditions, exposed him to a wide assortment of people, from the coarsest, most foul-talking individuals to the most highly educated intellectuals of the "old school." The camp became, for Dudko, his "university"; but most of all, according to a close friend, Anatolii Levitin-Krasnov, in the time he spent there, he prayed.[11] In 1956, he was rehabilitated and he returned to Moscow and the Theological Academy to write his dissertation. He completed it two years later, and titled it "Sobornost' and the Church" (*Sobornost' i Tserkov'*), which expounded on the view of the Russian philosopher/theologian Nikolai Berdiaev that freedom was the foundation of the Church community. Otherwise, Dudko argued, the Church would become heavily contaminated with papism, an illness that had become embedded in Russian Orthodoxy.[12] Dudko was ordained as a deacon in November 1960 and shortly afterward as a priest. In 1962, when he became an active member of the gathering of young priests, he served in the Church of the Kazan' Virgin in Moscow.[13] Short in stature, balding, with wire-rimmed glasses, he was fearless in his approach to Christianity and his critique of the church.[14]

The group of priests who gathered around Fr. Aleksandr Men represented some of the best and brightest of the Russian Orthodox clergy. All of them were well-educated and deeply steeped in the Gospels and Orthodox theology. All had their family roots in the Russian people; not one of the four came from a clerical family, and they maintained their ability to address the common people. All four believed the church had to become more accessible to people, young and old, and they were not to be hindered by obstacles, whether from within the church or from without, that prevented them from fulfilling what they believed to be their appointed mission. All four were married: Men to Natal'ia Fedorovna, a bookkeeper who worked in Zagorsk; Yakunin to Iraida Georgievna, who was employed part time in a Moscow office; Eshliman to Irina, a fellow artist and the granddaughter of the former Russian prime minister Sergei Witte; and Dudko to Nina Ivanovna, who worked in an office on the other side of Moscow from their house. All four priests—and one might well assume the other members of their group—held out hopes that the church could be reformed and made again into a powerful presence in people's lives. In the early 1960s, they were virtually unknown. In a short time, their activities would no longer be shrouded in obscurity.

A Frequent Visitor

By 1963, Archbishop Yermogen (Aleksii Stepanovich Golubev) already had a reputation as one of Russia's most accomplished religious leaders and a staunch defender of the Orthodox Church. In this same year, shortly after he moved to a diocese near the town of Kaluga, he began to visit the gathering of priests meeting in Alabino. The presence of such a distinguished clergyman had a large influence on the group that formed around Fr. Aleksandr Men.[15] Erudite, accomplished, and knowledgeable about the inner workings of the church and its conditions in the countryside, Yermogen had experienced the best and the worst of dealing with both the church hierarchy and state authorities. In the past, he had been extremely skilled at navigating through the treacherous political waters in which the Orthodox Church operated.[16]

After World War II Yermogen sought to keep churches open in each of the dioceses he served. Despite heavy pressure from the local authorities to close them, he managed to persuade local officials to leave churches under his jurisdiction alone, fearlessly resisting arbitrary attempts to eliminate their operations. In the late 1940s, Patriarch Aleksii I sent him to Samarkand to serve as a pastor; following Yermogen's outstanding service in the large Uzbekistan city, in 1956, the patriarch appointed him bishop of Tashkent and Central Asia. There again he was remarkably active, expanding the local church council three times and building the "largest church complex successfully completed by the Russian Orthodox Church since the Revolution."[17] This accomplishment earned him accolades from Patriarch Aleksii I, who elevated him to the rank of archbishop and "congratulated him in the warmest terms."[18]

Yermogen's energetic efforts on behalf of the church, however, did not escape criticism. In 1959, simultaneous with the beginning of Khrushchev's antireligion campaign, the Tashkent press launched a vicious attack on him and other priests in his diocese.[19] As the attack intensified, the patriarch transferred Yermogen to Kaluga, in central Russia. After a successful beginning, however, he soon ran into difficulties with a Soviet official, Fr. P. Riakov, who wanted to make all appointments within the diocese himself, presuming that the archbishop would simply "rubber-stamp" his selections.[20] Yermogen viewed these actions as an unacceptable infringement on the church's prerogatives.

These limitations on the church's authority and the interference of secular officials in religious activities were not limited to the Kaluga diocese but widespread. They had become increasingly problematic since the 1961 parish reform, so in the summer of 1965, Archbishop Yermogen and eight bishops delivered a petition to the patriarch asking him to redress the abuses. Led by Yermogen, the delegation lamented what they called detrimental interference in their operations and requested that the patriarch rescind the parish reform.

It was a bold act, but one conceived in the hope that members of the delegation would receive a sympathetic hearing. The response they received, however, was the opposite of what they had wished. The bishops had demanded that the patriarch, for the sake of the church, no longer act as a submissive agent of the Soviet government. In his response to the bishops, however, Patriarch Aleksii I bowed to the pressure of the head of the Council for Religious Affairs, V. A. Kuroedov, and rejected their appeal. The patriarch summoned Archbishop Yermogen to appear before the Holy Synod, where he accepted full responsibility for the bishops' conduct.[21] Ordered to express remorse for his actions and delete his name from the declaration, the archbishop refused. The patriarch's response came almost immediately. Again, under pressure from the head of the Council for Religious Affairs, Yermogen was removed from his Kaluga diocese and forced into retirement at the Zhirovitskii Monastery in Belorussia. Yermogen never left the Zhirovitskii Monastery: he died there on April 7, 1978.[22]

Blueprint for Regeneration

Historians and others have generally attributed Archbishop Yermogen's dismissal with being the catalyst behind the larger group's decision to send the letters they wrote to Patriarch Aleksii I and Chairman Podgorny.[23] The timing of the two letters came almost immediately after the negative response Yermogen received. The group's outrage at this turn of events must have precipitated their actions, their efforts to add their own voices to attempts to redress their grievances about the church's plight. Yermogen had opened the door to a frank discussion of these injustices and for a return of the Orthodox Church to its proper role in Russian life. Yakunin and Eshliman wanted to show that the ideas articulated by Archbishop Yermogen and the eight bishops had wider support inside the church than the patriarch imagined. "The indications are that unless the patriarch and his advisors in Moscow give more weight to the demand for reform than they have yet done," a leading scholar wrote, "they will find themselves increasingly isolated from their church—particularly from its younger members who did not endure the terrors of Stalin's purges."[24]

But other reasons also underlay the writing of the two letters. Many of the ideas put forward in the letters had long been discussed in the gathering of young priests around Fr. Aleksandr Men. The members of the group strongly believed in the need for Russian Orthodox Church reform. They wanted the church to be more responsive to people, and they hoped to enhance its voice in Russian life. The members were Russian patriots; they had seen the Orthodox Church spring back to life during World War II, when Stalin had permitted its resuscitation, and they had witnessed its contributions to the victory over the Nazi invaders. They knew the church's potential to enliven the countryside, but only if the shackles hindering its activities were removed, allowing it to play the role endowed on it by history and tradition. Archbishop Yermogen's visits to the gathering and encouragement of their ideas had furthered their thinking.[25] The presence of the prestigious senior leader of the church had given them hope that their desires for reform had widespread support among the Russian clergy.

Despite the outcome of Yermogen's declaration to the patriarch, the timing was right for reform. A year earlier, in October 1964, Nikita Khrushchev had been dismissed and a new administration had come into power. Participants in the gatherings at Alabino and Tarasovka could well remember what had taken place shortly after Stalin's death in 1953 and how that period had opened up a Pandora's box, bringing with it a "thaw" and fundamental changes in the state's relationship with its citizens. Many of the most egregious abuses of the previous epoch had been rescinded. A similar expectation now presented itself. The country's new leaders severely criticized Khrushchev, accusing him of "subjectivism," "harebrained scheming," ignorance, and reaching "half-baked conclusions."[26] The opportunity to make known to both the upper echelons of the government and the church the abuses and legislative inconsistencies of the recent past would surely provoke fundamental reform.

The letters that the group composed did not emerge as spontaneous compositions. The writing took place over a two-year period, during which their content went through many drafts, beginning with a short piece written by Anatolii Levitin-Krasnov.[27] During the next two years, some fifteen to twenty priests proposed ideas for inclusion in the letters, including Archbishop Yermogen, Fr. Aleksandr Men, and newcomers to the group such as Lev Regel′son, Feliks Karelin, and Viktor Kapitanchuk.[28] Fr. Aleksandr wrote a three-page draft of the letter to the patriarch, protesting the harmful effects of the parish reform, and asked Yakunin to read it. "No, this is entirely inadequate," Fr. Gleb responded. "It is necessary to hammer them! Hammer! So that it hits them hard."[29]

The letters, therefore, represented a corporate endeavor, an ambitious plan to remove the heavy shackles on the church and provide a blueprint for the future role of the Orthodox Church in Russia.

In drawing up the plan, the priests knew they would have little chance of success without additional support. "We knew very well that we could not accomplish anything tangible without the backing of our bishops," Yakunin said. "We sought out bishops sympathetic to our cause; one of them was Archbishop Yermogen, and all of us spent a lot of time meeting with him personally."[30] Yakunin believed they had the backing of many other bishops who longed for the Orthodox Church to recover its past traditions. Yakunin also believed, perhaps naively, that Patriarch Aleksii I "secretly supported the reformist movement" and that "letters like ours were needed" to encourage the government to make certain changes in its policies toward the Orthodox Church.[31] Whereas others might have failed in the past, Yakunin thought the patriarch was simply waiting for a significant moment to reassert the church's rightful place in the state.

Frs. Gleb Yakunin and Nikolai Eshliman knew that they were taking enormous risks. In putting their names on the two letters, the priests realized the dangers they faced and what it would mean not only to the futures of their priesthoods but also to their families. Both men had studied Russian history and were fully conscious of reformers inside and outside the church who had failed and suffered the consequences. "We well understood that we were like kamikazes and that sooner or later the state might come crashing down on us. . . . But the church needs not only prophets but a prophetic role in society," Yakunin said.[32] The two men signed the letters thinking they were contributing to that prophetic role. Yakunin and Eshliman assumed that many others would affix their names to the letters, but they turned out to be mistaken. Whether out of fear, reconsideration, or personal reasons, others did not follow through, leaving the signatures of Yakunin and Eshliman as the only names on the letters, the only two to go forward.

The ultimate goals of the letters were not only religious but also social. "In those times, many of us who had come to know the church," Yakunin said, "believed the church had to be not only a way of performing the liturgy, but had to be something more, and we were looking for ways to bring about a renaissance in the church, a revival of sorts so that the church could compete and be viable in our society."[33] Making the church more energetic and giving it greater relevance to the needs of the people were the primary reasons underlying the two letters. How were these purposes to become realities? How did the letters portray a coming religious renaissance in Russian society?

Although they included plenty of harsh accusations, the letters represented much more than a criticism of the governing apparatus. They offered a blueprint for the church's regeneration and a prospectus of the Orthodox priesthood's role in that revival. Viewed in its full context, the letter addressed to Patriarch Aleksii I had a central theme: to become effective, the Orthodox Church had to recover its authentic voice. The authors of the letter emphasized the church's silence during some of the most cataclysmic events of the twentieth century. This silence betrayed the church's mission of advising the ruler and providing succor to the people when moral issues confronted both of them. Yet, for many years, the church had failed to fulfill its obligations. Its silence bespoke a "spiritual weakness," a sinful lack of responsibility, and the letter writers called upon the patriarch, as the conscience of the Russian Orthodox Church, to redress this grievance. The patriarch's smothering quietude was no longer tolerable. As parish priests, the authors said, we "consider it impossible to remain silent about those who transgress the rights of the church. These transgressions have produced a dangerous situation and, for all of your pastors, they are the reasons for ever growing anxiety, constant worry, and many embarrassing situations."[34]

As Yakunin had desired, the letters placed the church's present problems in the larger context of Russian history. They sought to remind the patriarch of the historical ideal of the relationship between the Orthodox Church, as the bearer of Russia's moral traditions, and the government as the protector of the Russian land. Although the letters offered only a general outline, they referenced the period before the time of Tsar Peter I and his Ecclesiastical Regulation of 1721. Before Peter I, the church and the state had operated cooperatively, with the state seeking the church's spiritual support and blessing

FIGURE 2.1. From left to right, Fr. Gleb Yakunin, Fr. Nikolai Eshliman, and Feliks Karelin, 1965. Courtesy of the Keston Center for Religion, Politics, and Society, Baylor University, Waco, Texas.

(*simfoniia*) in matters concerning the citizens' welfare. In turn, the church sought the state's material support in order to care for the lives of its citizens. In early Russian history, according to the letters that Yakunin and Eshliman sent forward (see figure 2.1), the church had fulfilled this mission, and it had made a singular contribution to the national development of the Russian state and was "inseparably connected with the fate of the Russian people."[35] During some of the darkest periods of the past, the thirteenth and fourteenth centuries, when the country lay under the Mongol yoke, the Orthodox Church had preserved the sense of national unity among the people. During a time when brutality had flourished everywhere, the Orthodox Church had offered moral guidance. Additionally, it had provided the ideological underpinnings to the unification of Russian lands under the leadership of Moscow.

The historical excursion provided in the letters represented a simplistic, overgeneralized portrait of the church's relationship with the state. The main purpose of this depiction, however, lay in reminding the authorities of the church's significant role in defining the identity of the Russian people. The letters also attempted to bring attention to the importance of the All-Russian Church Council of 1917–1918, convened after the fall of the tsarist government, which endeavored to restore the symphonic ideal that had prevailed before the secular reforms of Peter I. The Church Council rejected the drawing of a hard line between spiritual and secular authorities and likened the act to the desire that "sun should not shine, fire should not warm up. By the internal law of her existence, the church cannot renounce her calling to enlighten, to transform the whole of human life, to imbue it with her rays."[36]

The contributions of the church, therefore, extended beyond Russia's spiritual consciousness to the evolution of Russian culture. On this topic, the letter to the patriarch presented an argument that countered the prevailing communist ideology, to what they called compliance with this "primitive ideology" and the patriarch's failure to articulate publicly a dissenting point of view. They maintained that it was incorrect to depict science and religion as entirely separate disciplines; historically, "science and faith independently contributed to and strengthened each other."[37] As support, the letter to the patriarch referenced the Russian pioneering giant of the sciences Mikhail Lomonosov, the founder of Moscow University. Bolshevik historians had made him out to be a staunch atheist, but, in reality, he represented the opposite. In his famous ode "To God," his poetry, and his other writings, Lomonosov gave thanks for the inexplicable benevolence of God and the gift of creativity that Lomonosov viewed as endemic in human beings.[38]

A primary theme of the letter to the patriarch consisted of the creative power of human beings and its divine source. This divine source marked the highest forms of Russian culture: the masterpieces of early icon painting, the writings of the Church Fathers, the poetry of Alexander Pushkin, the classical nineteenth-century writing and art of Nikolai Gogol, Fyodor Dostoevsky, Fyodor Tyutchev, Leo Tolstoy, Vladimir Solov'ev, and Viascheslav Ivanov.[39] The letter made a polemical argument, but its purpose went beyond polemics to reminding the patriarch of his responsibility to uphold his sacred obligations to the church and overcome his silence. Additionally, the letter emphasized the large treasure house of spiritual riches that the official establishment generally ignored. That valuable collection held a substantial contingent of Russian thinkers who needed to be rediscovered, ranging from the nineteenth-century writers Aleksei Khomiakov and Konstantin Leontiev to the twentieth-century theologian-philosophers Frs. Nikolai Berdiaev, Sergei Bulgakov, and Pavel Florenskii.[40] Most important, all these giants of Russian culture had been nourished within the bosom of the church; they represented an "open spirit," a constant desire to see the world afresh. They were the opposite of the "closed mentality" that turned inward, disconnected from worldly realities and exigencies.

In expressing the relationship between religion and Russian culture, the letter to the patriarch is remarkably like those ideas expressed nearly twenty-five years later by Fr. Aleksandr Men. In the late 1980s, Men similarly sought to stake a claim to earlier cultural traditions. He interpreted the Incarnation as a call to creativity, a concrete summons to reach out to the world, not to reject or turn away from it.[41] Creativity, Men said, expressed a "spontaneous movement within the person . . . some kind of ringing in the soul, a desire for transformation coming from the depths of one's being," diametrically opposed to submission to some external authority.[42] In his lectures in the late 1980s, presented shortly before his death in 1990, Fr. Aleksandr discussed many of the same creative people mentioned in Yakunin's and Eshliman's letter to the patriarch.[43] He sought an accessible bridge to earlier cultural traditions, reaching back beyond the Soviet state in an attempt to recapture certain ways of thinking. It may be that the similarities between Fr. Aleksandr's lectures and the earlier letter were incidental. But, given the parallel thoughts, it is more likely that Fr. Aleksandr, as a member of the group of young priests who met in the 1960s, wrote that part of the letter dealing with history and creativity.

According to the letter writers, the church had labored for a long time under a "heavy burden." They attributed this to two reasons: first, church leaders had too willingly submitted to the demands of lay authorities who ought not, by canon law, to exercise command over them. This acquiescence began more than two hundred years ago, with the Ecclesiastical Regulation of Peter I. It had continued under the Bolsheviks, but with one major difference: after the Russian Revolution, lay officials were replaced by atheistic authorities, with devastating effects on the self-government of the church. The second reason, related to the first, was that parish life, the lifeblood of the church, had suffered a heavy blow. Under the Bolshevik government, the scope of the parish's activities had diminished and was eventually stifled. Consequently, the capability of the church to fulfill its proper functions had greatly suffered.[44]

In making these extremely negative assertions about the Synodal Church, however, the letter writers' views overgeneralized the state's power over the church. Recent research, particularly the work of the historian Gregory Freeze, has disproved the portrayal of a submissive church in tsarist Russia. In reality, the church had a much larger degree of autonomy than earlier historians often asserted.[45] Moreover, the claim that the new Bolshevik government devastated parish life after the 1917 Revolution is inaccurate. Although the upper echelon of the church suffered a crippling blow, beneath that level, in the 1920s and 1930s, parish life witnessed a reinvigoration and restoration of rights lost under the tsarist regime. Parishioners, including laypersons, took on numerous responsibilities, more than they had previously been allowed to assume.[46]

Presently, with the downfall of Khrushchev's rule, the time was propitious for fundamental reform, in which the patriarch, Yakunin and Eshliman believed, had to take the lead. In hopes that the patriarch would follow suit, the letter offered historical examples of Orthodox leaders and other prominent figures who had courageously stood up to the authorities. The letter referenced the archbishop of Rostov, Georgii Dashkov, who, during the time of Peter I, advocated the resurrection of the patriarchate. In the 1740s, two members of the synod proposed the abolition of Peter I's Ecclesiastical Regulation. In the early nineteenth century, the Russian historian Nikolai Karamzin had emphasized the dangers of autocracy that was unrestricted by any sacred power. The letter to the patriarch quoted other critics of the government's authority over the church, including the bishop of Eniseisk, Nikodim Kazantsev, who, in 1874, decried the illegitimacy of a secular power holding supreme legal authority over a sacred institution. The letter mentioned the Slavophile writer Ivan Sergeevich Aksakov, who likewise pointed out the negative consequences of the Holy Synod; the synod's power, he wrote, "diminished the soul" by replacing "a church ideal with a government ideal." As the late nineteenth-century Russian philosopher Vladimir Solov'ev maintained, this led to an "official church, governed by civil servants, in which the church became only a government institution, a 'secondary branch of a bureaucratic administration.'"[47] The long-term effects on the church's true mission were devastating.

Nearly forty years earlier, the letter to the patriarch observed, the All-Russian Church Council of 1917–1918 had redressed these grievances in its restoration of the patriarchate. But the antireligion campaigns of the Bolshevik regime had again crippled the church, and the stifling controls of church life had turned this sacred institution into a ghost of its true self. The two priests wanted reform, but the letter Yakunin and Eshliman sent expanded their desire for reform into a larger question about the church's identity and purpose in the present-day Soviet Union. By focusing primarily on criticisms of the Soviet government's actions, analysts have generally overlooked this issue. The two priests' condemnation of government policies is an important part but not the only significant aspect of the letter Yakunin and Eshliman sent to the patriarch.

In the text, the word "conscience" appeared four times. The church was viewed as the "conscience" of the nation. Thus, the church embodied a sacred trust: it held the key to the judgment of right and wrong, good and evil, and this capacity could not be obliterated without doing serious injury to the nation's well-being. Yet what the letter called the "asphyxiation of church life" had produced an extremely harmful situation: the church no longer fulfilled its divine task as the arbiter of good and evil.[48] The silence had come about not only because of external acts of violence but also because of an internal view that such silence protected the church, shielding it from total destruction. In reality, the opposite was true. This failure to speak out and to fulfill its role had infected the body of the church with a deadly bacillus, "implanting in it a submissive and pliable conscience."[49]

"The Orthodox Church is indeed the house of God, the focal point of church life, the spiritual table which feeds the incorruptible gifts of divine grace."[50] The letter sent by Yakunin and Eshliman proclaimed the church to be much more than a spiritual space, more than an edifice of stone. It encapsulated the entire sense of religious expression, the encounter with the holy, which, the text claimed, "Orthodox people have loved from earliest times."[51] As Fr. Sergei Bulgakov had written, the beauty of the church had a powerful attraction: it unified spiritual beauty with the beauty of this world.[52] The divine and the human merged in it. It also brought together members of the community, forging bonds between each person and the divine. The callous, widespread closure of churches carried out by the government in recent years, the letter maintained, destroyed those bonds, and it would eventually have catastrophic moral consequences.

When the leaders of the church kept silent and failed to protect their commitment, they betrayed their sacred calling. The bureaucratic structure under which the state had placed the church produced a wholesale corruption of its purpose and foundation. By passively submitting to this bureaucratic structure, the leadership of the church violated the "sacred treasury," the beauty entrusted to it by its predecessors. In passionate—and patriotic—language, the letters called upon the church leadership not to deny this heritage:

> Because not for this did our most Holy Lady take the Russian church under her merciful protection; not for this did the first apostles of the Slavs preach the Word of God; not for this did the glorious army of Russian saints stand in the church, "invisibly praying to God for us"; not for this did St. Sergius—the great servant of God—shine forth in the heart of Russia; not for this did the holy blood of Russian martyrs flow abundantly; not for this have the Easter bells rang out over Russia for a thousand years with such triumph as has never been heard elsewhere in the world.[53]

As an instrument of God, the church assigned a vital role to the ministry. Given the chaos in which the parish priest functioned during the past two decades, and especially recently, the letter to the patriarch attempted to redefine that important position. Pastoral obligations served as the "foundation of the church," and the priest always had to reach out to his people. If state authorities severely hampered the priest's activities, he could not fulfill this time-honored responsibility. He had an obligation to pray for his people, to be present in their homes during times of suffering, to conduct wedding ceremonies, to perform requiems for the deceased, and to baptize children, both in private homes and in cemeteries, all of which he should be able to do without special state authorization.[54] He had to manage effectively the economic and administrative affairs of the parish.[55] During times of profound suffering, "who else, if not the pastor, must lay down his life for the sheep and protect his flock from destruction."[56] Yet in all these instances, recent government regulations put obstacles in the path of each priest's capacity to carry out his responsibilities.[57]

The letter Yakunin and Eshliman sent mentioned "freedom of religion" and "freedom of conscience" only twice, but both terms were placed at strategic points. The first the letter called a "sacred right," while the second it emphasized when discussing the teaching of children.[58] Both terms were cited in relation to the government's illegitimate interference into the realm of the sacred. The Soviet Constitution of 1918 guaranteed "freedom of religion."[59] When the church allied itself with the government and submitted to that authority, it lost its quest for social justice and corrupted its divine mission.[60] The church ought never to give up the sacred meaning of religious freedom and freedom of conscience, yet it had surrendered both in the false hope that its survival depended on such a sacrifice. These freedoms had to be reclaimed for the Russian Church to experience a renaissance.

The Language of Protest

In addition to their letter to the patriarch, Yakunin and Eshliman sent a second letter, which was addressed to the chair of the Supreme Soviet of the USSR. Written on December 15, 1965, it contained numerous accusations and charges directed against the state authorities. The letter underscored the constitutional right to protest against what it called the flagrant abuse of the laws. In violation of both socialist and state laws, such transgressions, the letter claimed, were carried out repeatedly by the state authorities.[61]

As distinct from the first letter, the second one couched its argument in clever language in the context of Soviet politics. A main charge justifying the recent dismissal of Nikita Khrushchev as political leader of the Soviet Union, it said, related to "subjectivism and bureaucracy in the leadership."[62] Instead of serving as an office to resolve conflicts and solve problems, Eshliman and Yakunin charged, the Council for Russian Orthodox Church Affairs had exerted control over decisions that rightfully should have been made by the Moscow Patriarchate. This practice had allowed a bureaucratic office to interfere in the internal life of church bodies. This madness, according to the second letter, had not ended with Khrushchev's ouster.⁶³ The atmosphere of "antireligious fanaticism," so rampant in the recent past, had erupted in many locales, to the detriment of state stability.⁶⁴

The letter to Nikolai Podgorny made several specific charges about bureaucratic interference in the internal affairs of the church. Representatives of the Council for Russian Orthodox Church Affairs had repeatedly issued unofficial, arbitrary oral decrees; removed and transferred clergymen from one diocese to another; displaced and ruined sacred objects; closed a massive number of churches; destroyed religious art; and violated the separation of church and state. "A persistent legacy of the period of arbitrariness" remained and had to be rooted out.⁶⁵ The above-mentioned violations of the separation of church and state, which the Soviet Constitution, the fundamental law of the land, had guaranteed, the letter boldly said, represented criminal offenses.⁶⁶ State officials often concealed their illegal actions. Using language straight out of the past, when Soviet leaders had asked the people to report violations of socialist legality and incidents of property destruction to the security police, Yakunin and Eshliman, as senders of the letter, claimed it their responsibility to bring those acts of subterfuge to the attention of the authorities.⁶⁷

If the letter addressed to the patriarch had pleaded with him, as head of the Russian Orthodox Church, to fulfill his historic responsibilities, the letter addressed to the chair of the Presidium demanded that he redress "flagrant violations" of the laws. The second letter was an aggressive document. It was not a petition, did not make requests, and was not a supplication from citizens of the state. Rather, the language was harsh, accusatory, and fearless. It charged state officials with carrying out "scandalous policies," radically distorting the laws, and willfully violating the core principles of socialist justice. Earlier, Archbishop Yermogen had counseled Yakunin, Eshliman, and their fellow priests not to go too far and not to act too precipitously. "He told us that we had to be careful and try not to make matters worse than they were," Yakunin said.⁶⁸ Whether they acted too rashly or idealistically may be subject to dispute. They had assumed, mistakenly, as it turned out, that their protests to the leadership would receive broad support. In the end, however, they acted alone. Why, then, did Yakunin and Eshliman take such an aggressive, uncompromising stand that was almost certain to provoke a strong response?

Who Wrote the Letters?

The authorship of the letters to the patriarch of Moscow and All-Russia and to the chairperson of the Presidium of the USSR remains a debatable question. As this chapter has argued, many members of the group of young priests who gathered around Fr. Aleksandr Men contributed to the letter, both directly and indirectly. The precise origins of the letters might be inferred during a conversation between Men and Yakunin about letters written by numerous small-town priests concerning the onerous burdens placed on them by the 1961 parish reform. Fr. Aleksandr put forth the idea about writing a group letter that would make an authoritative statement about these obstacles and questioning the legitimacy of the 1961 Church Council that had endorsed the parish reform. According to Men, Yakunin "was ecstatic at the idea and kissed me in his enthusiasm."[69] He immediately began to put the plan into action. He spread the idea among others in their group, including Nikolai Eshliman, Fr. Dmitrii Dudko, and Anatolii Levitin-Krasnov. Fr. Aleksandr and Levitin-Krasnov had formed a close friendship. Not surprisingly, he was drawn into the discussion of writing a letter to Patriarch Aleksii I on the revitalization of the Russian Orthodox Church.

The group met in Fr. Aleksandr's home in Semkhoz to discuss what needed to be done.[70] Their meeting must have been a lively occasion, filled with spirited conversation about both the possibilities and the risks. All the participants shared the view that something had to be done to protest the oppressive conditions under which the church operated. They also believed they had to expand the number of participants in their plan. They soon did so, holding a subsequent gathering at Eshliman's country dacha and attended by ten guests who generated concrete ideas about how to move forward. That meeting led to Fr. Aleksandr Men's composition of the three-page document setting forth their objectives and raising a whole series of questions about church policy. Levitin-Krasnov also developed a ten-page essay that went much farther, in which he elaborated on the church's role in Russian national life and criticized the church leadership for its failures to defend that role.[71]

Yakunin was eager to act.[72] He believed the issues were too important to wait, and in this he was joined by Nikolai Eshliman. But the actual composition of the letters still needed to be worked out, the ideas coming from various people had to be integrated, and the precise wording of what would be an explosive document remained to be done. Fr. Aleksandr, who had the requisite writing and editorial skills to carry out these tasks, did not wish to participate. Following the response to Archbishop Yermogen's petition, he was uncertain about whether the present was the most propitious time to send the letters his fellow priests had in mind. He wanted a lot more deliberation before taking such a large risk. Moreover, despite his regard for Yakunin as a person, he did not take too seriously the chance that the letter would actually come to fruition. "I knew that Gleb would never write one line," Fr. Aleksandr said, "and Nikolai would actually produce something, but very slowly—terribly slowly—super slowly, and he would not finish it. Therefore, I was not especially concerned."[73] Both Yakunin and Eshliman, Fr. Aleksandr believed, were too busy carrying out their day-to-day priestly duties to devote themselves to the time-consuming task of writing these letters.[74]

At this point, a fateful turn of events took place. Sometime earlier, a new arrival in Men's parish impressed nearly everyone who had gathered there. Eventually, this newcomer was to become extremely controversial, but at first, he had a very positive impact. This person, Feliks Karelin, was a brilliant talker who could, Men said, "speak for hours 'as though out of a book.'"[75] An expert in Byzantine art and theology, an erudite spokesperson, and charismatic character, he quickly acquired a following among some of the young people in the parish.

Karelin had once been a member of a group of young intellectuals who had come together in Moscow to study religion and philosophy. When the police had arrested members of the group years earlier, Karelin was among them. He spent ten years in a prison camp, which had been his "university education." In the camps, among professors, scholars, and intellectuals who were also serving prison sentences, he acquired firsthand, specialized knowledge of the history and theology of Byzantine culture. Liberated from prison during Khrushchev's "thaw," he married a Russian actress and lived in several places, including Tashkent and Irkutsk. In Irkutsk, at the same time that Men and Yakunin were students, he had heard of Men and tried, unsuccessfully, to meet him. But in the early 1960s, in Moscow, he encountered Gleb Yakunin; the two became friends, and Yakunin, charmed by Karelin, brought him to Men's parish.

In the parish, shortly after Karelin's arrival, two circles formed: the first, around Karelin, focused on reading and discussing Russian theology and philosophy, particularly writers such as Vladimir Solov'ev, Nikolai Berdiaev, Sergei Bulgakov, Pavel Florenskii, Nikolai and Evgenii Trubetskoi, Vasilii Bolotov, and others. This circle included Gleb Yakunin, Lev Regel'son, a former physicist; Viktor Kapitanchuk, a church art restorer; and several others. A second circle, centered around Fr. Aleksandr Men, read more broadly than the first, both in the Russian religious and philosophical tradition and outside it. Members wanted to become better acquainted with the exciting new developments in worldwide theology by reading and discussing writers from diverse religious perspectives such as Constantin von Tischendorf, Karl Barth, Emil Brunner, Paul Tillich, Karl Rahner, and Hans Küng, whose books they could find in Russian translation.[76]

Given their members' strong personalities and different approaches, the two groups were perhaps destined to break apart. "As long as we were together, the very atmosphere of brotherhood and community prevailed," wrote Lev

Regel'son.⁷⁷ But when they met separately, which increasingly became the case, tension between their theological approaches came into full view, and Fr. Aleksandr grew worried about the deleterious effects on the parish as a whole. But in the meantime, in 1965, it was Feliks Karelin and two of his associates, Viktor Kapitanchuk and Lev Regel'son, who played the leading parts in taking the various proposals and unfinished papers, synthesizing all the ideas, and refining them into completed documents.⁷⁸ Yakunin's contribution consisted only of a set of general ideas.⁷⁹ In their final iteration, both letters to the patriarch and the government bore Karelin's strong editorial imprint. The passionate tone of the letters, so pronounced in many of the parts, corresponded to similar aspects of his own personality.

Tempestuous, uncompromising, and extraordinarily intelligent, Felix Karelin was an extremely complex and controversial person. Rumors circulated widely in the parish. During his early years as a member of the religious study group in Leningrad, there is good evidence that he served as an informer for the secret police. He was named after Felix Dzerzhinsky, the infamous head of the original state security police, the Cheka, to whom he was related. It was said that in the prison camp, in order to prove his innocence after he was accused of being a provocateur and was threatened with death, he knifed to death a man who was believed to be a police informant.⁸⁰ In his memoirs, Fr. Aleksandr provided the following portrait of Karelin:

> He was a man with a systematic type of intelligence, which could have been advantageous to both church and business, if it had not been for his unrestrained nature. . . . As soon as we became acquainted, Karelin took me into a separate room and began straight away to tell me about how he had been in solitary confinement and how in that unpleasant place, he, for some reason, had drawn a six-pointed star on the wall and started to meditate on it. Whole systems of creation had constructed themselves within him, systems of redemption—a whole lot of things. I looked upon him with such sadness, as if he were a madman, that he soon stopped telling me about those convoluted beliefs.⁸¹

While Fr. Aleksandr always had suspicions about Karelin and questioned his motives, ultimately, he found him to be an honest, if misguided, person. Men described him as Stavrogin-like, referring to the character in Dostoevsky's novel *The Possessed*—a generous person with a charismatic personality "who led those young men astray and destroyed all of them."⁸²

Although he played only a marginal role in the actual writing of the 1965 letters, Gleb Yakunin sincerely believed everything they said. In ultimate acts of courage, he and Nikolai Eshliman signed both letters, the only two priests whose names appeared on them. Convinced that the letters told the truth to all who might read them, Yakunin and Eshliman firmly believed that the Orthodox Church could not fulfill its historic responsibilities to the Russian people until it stood up for this truth.

In an action that eventually cost them dearly, they distributed copies of the letter to the patriarch to all the bishops in the Russian Orthodox Church. Yakunin and Eshliman assumed that it was within their judicial and canonical rights to do so as members of the wider church body.[83] Furthermore, perhaps naively, but in good faith, they believed that their fellow clergy held the same views, awaited such a statement of principles, and would stand behind them. The time had come, Yakunin and Eshliman maintained, for the Russian Orthodox Church to break its prolonged silence.

They expected that the patriarch would quickly respond and awaited his reply. For months, Yakunin and Eshliman heard nothing. But then the response did come, and it was not what they had either hoped or expected.

CHAPTER 3

The Awakening

Gleb Yakunin and Nikolai Eshliman had sent letters to Patriarch Aleksii I and Nikolai Podgorny hoping that their communications would be well received. They reasoned that their letter would give the patriarch the political leverage to redress the grievances of the church and give him courage to stand up to the governing authorities, the new leaders of the government who had berated Khrushchev for his irrational schemes. Although these leaders had not mentioned the church in their criticism of Khrushchev's "harebrained" policies, it would only be a matter of time, Yakunin and Eshliman reasoned, before the new authorities rescinded his antireligion campaign. A new direction was in the offing. In nervous anticipation, they waited for a response.[1]

Born in 1877, Patriarch Aleksii I (Sergei Vladimirovich Simanskii) had lived through some of the most tumultuous years in Russian history. During World War II, he served as metropolitan of Leningrad and Novgorod. For two years he remained in Leningrad during the worst time of the German blockade, as the city and its citizens endured prolonged suffering from severe shortages of food and fuel. For his efforts in helping to organize the city's defense, the Soviet state awarded him the Order of the Red Banner of Labor four times. In September 1943, he was one of three church leaders who met with Stalin in the Moscow Kremlin, a meeting that resulted in the historic restoration of the Moscow Patriarchate. A year later he was elevated to the patriarchy.

Like his predecessors, Aleksii I was characterized by docility and compliance with the orders of the state during his tenure. He had signed off on the Parish Reform of 1961, backed by the Soviet authorities, which aimed to cripple the church. In December 1964, a month after Khrushchev's fall from power, the patriarch warned priests in the Moscow diocese against lax compliance. He reminded them that the baptism of young children required state registration.[2] In 1965, now in poor health, the eighty-seven-year-old patriarch relied heavily on his closest confidants for advice. After a lifetime of state service, he was not inclined to go against the wishes of the governing authorities. Yakunin and Eshliman's letter encouraging him to stand up to the government's flagrant abuses of power called for action that exceeded his personal capacities.

It would be an inordinately long time before Yakunin and Eshliman received the patriarch's reply. These were months of agonized waiting, and both young priests were consumed with uncertainty about their futures. They had taken a courageous stand that few had attempted in the past forty years, knowing that their careers lay in the balance. Finally, on May 23, 1966, nearly six months after sending their first letter, the patriarch's written response arrived. Aleksii I's answer was even much harsher than they had expected. The patriarch expressed little sympathy for their recommendations. He accused Eshliman and Yakunin of behavior "prejudicial to the church" and of an act that sought to sow discord in the body of the church, thus disrupting its internal peace. He charged them with engaging in "evil activity" unworthy of their calling as priests.[3] He demanded that they recant their words and express repentance, and until they recanted and pleaded for forgiveness, the patriarch suspended them from their duties as priests.[4]

Neither Eshliman nor Yakunin were willing to recant. They believed they had told the truth, which, they said, "can never sow discord in the church." They claimed that the patriarch had not addressed their concerns, elected to disregard them, and unjustly accused them of violating canon law. "If His Holiness the Patriarch considers that there is falsehood in our letter, then he should have exposed it," they responded. "If in the secret place of his heart His Holiness knows that we have spoken the truth, how can he state that we are sowing discord?"[5]

Psychologically, the reactions of the two young priests could hardly have been more different. The patriarch's dismissal of the letter and his personal criticisms of the authors crushed Eshliman's spirit. When I later asked Yakunin about Eshliman's subsequent life, Fr. Gleb did not wish to speak about it, saying that the subject "was too painful."[6] Suspended from the priesthood and unable to fulfill what he regarded as a sacred calling, he descended into deep depression. The talented, outgoing, and engaging Fr. Nikolai Eshliman resigned from all dissident activities and entirely dissociated himself from the church. During the next few years, he withdrew into himself, lost much of his former drive, later suffered from ill health, and died in 1985 at the age of fifty-seven.[7] Fr. Gleb, in contrast, was determined more than ever to fight what he perceived as the hypocrisy of the patriarchate and the Soviet government.[8]

Death or Rebirth?

In coming to power in Russia, the Bolshevik Party claimed to be riding a deeply rooted historical trend in which religion would soon die out. Religion, the Bolshevik leaders believed, belonged to the past, had served as an instrument of exploitation by the ruling class, and had originated in superstition and mythology. An industrial, scientific, and rational public order promised to kill off naturally what remained of a backward-looking set of beliefs. In 1922, elaborating the new Soviet ideology, Vladimir Lenin called Christianity a naive faith whose extirpation "was essential for our struggle against the governing religious obscurantists."[9]

In the late 1960s and the 1970s, members of the Soviet elite considered the victory over this vestige of the past nearly won. In May 1976, the deputy chair of the Council for Religious Affairs, Vasilii Grigor'evich Furov, gave a lecture on the status of religious belief in which he announced that religion in the Soviet Union had nearly disappeared. In the past five years, he boasted, about 700 religious establishments had passed from existence, and about 1,000 Orthodox Churches once registered as active congregations had closed. The Soviet Union had ten times fewer Orthodox Churches than existed in pre-revolutionary Russia (their number had declined from 77,676 to 7,500). Catholic Churches, which once totaled 4,200 in the Baltic region, had now shrunk to 1,000. In regions where Islam had flourished, only 1,000 mosques remained out of 24,000, and the number of Jewish synagogues had decreased from 5,000 to 2,020, only 92 of which were registered; fifty rabbis were all that remained.[10]

In his lecture, Furov characterized the relationship between church and state as "normalized," a condition evidenced by formerly recalcitrant priests having reformed and allied themselves with the government. Most of them, he said, supported government policies and were staunch advocates of Soviet patriotism. Harmony and goodwill described the bond that existed between the remaining churches and the Soviet government, a condition attributed to the "modernist, reforming tendencies" that "were penetrating ever deeper into parish life, actively supporting the domestic and foreign policy of the USSR."[11]

Furov did not gloss over people, vestiges of the past who expressed "anti-Soviet" views. He named three who articulated "anti-Soviet" ways of thinking: the Orthodox Hierodeacon Varsonofi Khaibulin, the physicist Lev Regel'son, and the mathematician Igor Shafarevich. As will be discussed later, Khaibulin and Regel'son had a close relationship with Gleb Yakunin. Sharfarevich had recently published abroad a short book on religious legislation in the USSR, which, Furov claimed, expressed opposition to Soviet policy on the church.[12] According to Furov, these three were aberrations. In a concluding statement to his lecture, one filled with irony, he spoke of the possibility of state support for the church even as the state continued to wage ideological war against it.

At the end of the 1970s, just a few years after Furov's assessment, Gleb Yakunin expressed a much different view of the church's present condition. Instead of speaking about "modernizing trends," he strongly criticized the government's unlawful interference in religious affairs, which, he believed, had significantly weakened the church's presence in Russian life. At every level, from the patriarch to the parish, government policies had corrupted the Orthodox church's capacity to carry out its responsibilities.

Most important, Yakunin maintained that religion was not dying out in the Soviet Union. He spoke of a "Religious Renaissance" among important segments of the population. The contentions that Yakunin advanced presented several questions. In the late 1960s and 1970s, the emergence of this so-called awakening served as a key element in Gleb Yakunin's evolution as a religious activist. It would become a vital part of how he viewed his role in his country's potential transformation.

Fresh Directions

In the mid- to late 1960s, the ideological beliefs and commitments that had so inflamed earlier generations of Soviet citizens had begun to lose their power. Nikita Khrushchev's speech to a closed session at the Twentieth Party Congress in February 1956, in which he denounced his predecessor, Joseph Stalin, as a cruel, despotic, and irrational leader, opened up Pandora's box of questions about the Stalinist system and the ideology that supported it. Following the long Stalinist winter, a period known as "the Thaw" launched a series of disputes that raged across Russian literature, the arts, and the subject of history. Questions about history led to a growing interest in the church's contributions to the development of the Russian state.

Tat'iana Goricheva was a participant in this revival of interest. "In the sixties," she said, "when the breakdown of the myth of Stalin and the ideals of communism began, we saw that culture served as a point of departure. . . . Cultural values helped us come out of the underground towards the light."¹³ Seeking new ways of interpreting Russian history and culture, the generation of the 1960s lacked an immediate bridge connecting them to the past. The bridge had to be discovered. Because prerevolutionary Russian religious history received little attention in schools, and people had no solid body of facts on which to build; the trial-and-error process of discovery often led to many misconceptions, and sometimes to extreme views. Yet increasing numbers of people aspired to know more about particular subjects, especially religion, which the school system had forbidden them to explore.

The desire for knowledge, authenticity, and freedom of expression emerged from several additional sources. In the late 1960s, Yakunin and Eshliman's letter to Patriarch Aleksii I, and other voices were calling freedom of thought and speech essential to human creativity. These voices came from people closely allied with the church. Their writings, widely circulated in samizdat, found a ready audience, above all among those who sympathized with the ideas of Yakunin and Eshliman.

"It is obvious that the absence of freedom is the death of creativity in all aspects of life," wrote Fr. Sergei Zheludkov in his letter to Pavel Litvinov, the human rights activist, on March 30, 1968.¹⁴ An outcast Orthodox priest and a friend of Fr. Aleksandr Men, Zheludkov (1910–1984) sounded the moral voice of the old Russian religious intelligentsia of the late nineteenth and early twentieth centuries. On December 3, 1969, writing to the academician Andrei Sakharov, Zheludkov criticized the Soviet effort to create an illusory world built on faith in pagan rituals and magical incantations.¹⁵ His letter decried the lasting effects of Stalinism that waged war on the human spirit and crushed the creative gifts embedded in each person. He likened the effects to the Nazi indoctrination of Germany, but such a program had lasted only a short period of time. In the Soviet Union, the consequences of Stalinism had penetrated far more deeply, because Stalinism, he said, has continued to "grow in us." It manifested itself in various forms, most importantly in what Zheludkov referred to as "pretentiousness." As a Soviet person, one "has an inexplicable desire to preserve, at all costs, one's own self-respect"; to do so, one "leaves ajar before oneself, in the depths of one's crippled soul, the willingness to adopt a false, historical and current stream of information in order to justify one's own submissiveness."¹⁶ Thus a person believes that the government does not make mistakes and accepts the view that the Russian people do not have the maturity for intellectual freedom, a fabrication that functions like a "fox in the vineyard." Information, therefore, is censored; the press is tightly controlled; it is forbidden to criticize the government; and when confronted with the truth, one finds it painful to accept it.¹⁷

Zheludkov's critique of Stalinism and his view of religion and intellectual freedom as inseparable came from the depths of his Orthodox faith. The freedom to think and speak did not belong to the government. "It does not belong to God"; it belongs to the person; it is part of one's sacred responsibility. He quoted the apostle Paul: "Where the spirit of the Lord is, there is freedom. To freedom you are called."[18] What made Stalinism so vile, he maintained, was that it deprived humans the most precious part of their existence.

If Fr. Sergei Zheludkov's admonitions focused on Stalinism, another significant critic turned his attention to the church itself. Boris Vladimirovich Talantov (1903–1971) was the son of an Orthodox priest, who had been caught in Stalin's wave of arrests in the 1930s and perished in the Temnikov labor camps in Mordovia in 1940. After graduating from the Kirov Pedagogical Institute in Zaraisk, Talantov taught higher mathematics in the institute until he was fired in 1954, after the KGB traced to him an anonymous letter he published in *Pravda* criticizing the illegal actions of the local government.[19]

Although Talantov admired the True Orthodox Church, the schismatic organization that had broken away from the official church, he remained faithful to his tradition. Nevertheless, he was dismayed by its present course—the "lies," "deceit," and repeated "excuses for injustice" perpetuated by the Orthodox hierarchy. He had read the letter Yakunin and Eshliman sent to the patriarch and sympathized with their critique of the church's leadership, as well as the portrayal of the "lawlessness and arbitrary behavior" of local civil administrators.[20] He knew Yakunin well and frequently stopped by his home when traveling to Moscow.[21] The punishment Yakunin and Eshliman received did not prevent him from expressing his own similar views or hinder him from boldly castigating the intellectual servitude that the church had fostered.

Like Yakunin, Talantov traced the problem to Metropolitan Sergei's 1927 agreement pledging the church's cooperation with the Bolshevik government.[22] Its declaration of loyalty had bound the church, a sacred institution, to an atheistic regime. This action had deleterious consequences: instead of the church defining social justice and the meaning of a flourishing society, the Bolshevik government alone determined them. Church theologians thus adopted the communist organization of society, the "only happy and just one" that they claimed the Gospels had always taught.[23] "*In essence*," Talantov maintained, "*adaptation to atheism represented a maniacal union of Christian dogmas and rites with the socio-political views of the official ideology of the CPSU.*"[24] Most insidious, according to Talantov, were the effects on the mentality of church leaders. "Any criticism of the state," its ideology, or the actions of its authorities was not allowed and was viewed "as a deviation from proper religious activity and as counter-revolutionary behavior. People knew that if they spoke out against the arbitrary and illegal deeds of the authorities they would be branded as criminals and subject to arrest."[25] This atmosphere of fear within the body of the church stifled freedom of thought and undermined the creativity that served as the essence of humanity.

The boldness of Talantov's writings did not shield him from the security police. He was arrested in June 1969 and later sentenced to two years in prison for his "anti-Soviet" activities. He died in prison on January 4, 1971, at the age of sixty-seven.

Beneath their harsh criticisms of the present state of affairs in the Orthodox Church and the Soviet state, the writings of Fr. Sergei Zheludkov and Boris Talantov expressed a yearning for an authentic form of Orthodoxy, a return to the ideals they believed essential to a flourishing society. Both men decried the passivity, servility, and fear that covered up the rich cultural resources that lay buried beneath the frozen surface of Orthodoxy's heritage. Zheludkov and Talantov wanted to remove the obstacles that prevented the intellectual and personal exploration of their faith. At the core of their writings was the craving for freedom of thought, speech, and belief. Like the letters of Yakunin and Eshliman, the writings of Zheludkov and Talantov represented a fresh wind blowing within and around the church and opened a gateway for other, younger voices to explore the questions they raised.

The rejuvenated interest, as the theologian Fr. Michael Aksenov-Meerson has pointed out, did not signify the first time such a movement had occurred in the Soviet Union. During and immediately after World War II, the Orthodox Church enjoyed a brief period in which a large number of churches were reopened and religious life flourished.[26] Despite the wave of violence directed against the church in the prewar decade, it had not dampened the desire of the Russian people to restore places of worship. But, as Aksenov-Meerson noted, the revival in the late 1960s differed significantly from its predecessor. The earlier resurrection originated with people who had grown up in the church and were already religious believers. The young generation who led the late 1960s revival had grown up as atheists; they had been educated to consider religion as superstition and had no experience with church life. In addition, unlike their predecessors, who remained committed to the Soviet government, the young generation had no such allegiance.[27] They questioned everything. They especially revolted against the government's intolerance of dissent, its reluctance to admit multiple points of view, and its restrictions on free expression.[28]

By the late 1960s, disillusionment with the Soviet state and its supportive ideology had made deep inroads into Soviet youth. They had become disenchanted with what life under the present regime had to offer, and the state's promised road to the future held little attraction. In their dissatisfaction with the established order and the revolutionary spirit that had animated their predecessors, they resembled similar groups of young people during the same period in France, Great Britain, and the United States. Like them, Soviet youth searched for a deeper and more authentic meaning of life than their predecessors offered. Unlike their counterparts elsewhere, however, Soviet youth were not in rebellion against the capitalist social and economic system. They rebelled against a political order that pushed them into narrowly defined social categories, limited their freedom of choice, and tried to restrict their imagination. In short, they disdained the state's attempt to control the mind and the spirit. They presented a particular challenge to the Soviet authorities, who viewed the "convictions of the young" as essential to the future development of a secular social order.[29]

This refusal to conform to the established order is what drew the future Orthodox priest Michael Aksenov-Meerson into open rebellion. A brilliant student of history at Moscow State University in the early 1960s, he became a dissident at the end of his first year, which resulted in his expulsion. He had decided that he could no longer accept the ideological straitjacket that forced the interpretation of history into a prescribed framework. After leaving the university, he entered a period of uncertainty and confusion about his future course. "I would have become a terrorist," he said, "if, at that time, on a whim, I had not traveled out to the parish of Fr. Aleksandr Men," whose church outside Moscow attracted similar young members of the Russian intelligentsia.[30]

Fr. Aleksandr's reputation as one of a small number of unusually gifted Orthodox priests had rapidly spread in the late 1960s in the Russian capital and other nearby cities. His parish in the small town of Tarasovka, where he served from 1962 to 1970, lay on the railroad line from Moscow to Zagorsk (Sergiev Posad), the traditional seat of Russian Orthodox theology. An ever-increasing number of Russian youth journeyed to Tarasovka each Sunday morning to attend services and engage in conversation with the well-read, open-minded Fr. Aleksandr.[31] A master conversationalist and a staunch believer in the importance of dialogue, Men was a rare example of a priest who expressed openness to the world.[32] During a time when many young people searched for new directions in their lives and questioned everything, Fr. Aleksandr offered them a fresh look at Orthodox Christianity, which they had been taught to denigrate.[33]

The seeds Fr. Aleksandr planted about freedom, faith, and human purpose germinated still further in the writings of Anatolii Levitin-Krasnov.[34] In his early career, Levitin-Krasnov had taught Russian literature in a Leningrad elementary school. Encouraging his students to read the Symbolist poets, he raised questions about the influence of Orthodox Christianity on the poetry of this group of writers, and he discovered that his students had a keen interest in spiritual topics. "I can see before me now those thirty children, pale, disheveled little boys and urchin-like girls with pigtails, all of them with their eyes fixed on me. And I, only twenty-three years of age, wearing the same cheap jacket as they, leaning on the ink-stained teacher's desk and reading . . . making no secret of my religious beliefs."[35] His faith in the promise of Russian youth never wavered, and by the 1970s, Levitin-Krasnov was convinced that Russian youth had set out on a long journey. Everywhere in society, one felt the silence, but also the expectation, he wrote: "The night is over. The sleepers are waking up. Life is beginning to stir. What will the day be like?"[36]

The dialogue Levitin-Krasnov advanced in his writings received a considerable boost in the early 1970s from an Orthodox priest who changed the entire structure of his church services. A short, broad-shouldered, ebullient man with an omnipresent smile, Fr. Dmitrii Dudko had a dynamic preaching style and welcoming approach to newcomers who entered the several churches he served in Moscow and neighboring towns in the late 1960s and early 1970s.[37]

In 1973, Fr. Dmitrii changed the format of his Saturday evening sermons. Instead of a delivering a preconceived message, he initiated a dialogue with members of his congregation. At first, this dialogue largely focused on theological issues, but it soon evolved into other subjects. Controversial questions often came up concerning the relationship between religion and society, personal morality and responsibility, and church and state. Fr. Dmitrii, in the words of an observer, "did not ask for such provocative questions, but he did not avoid them either. He mainly insisted upon basic religious truths, upon Orthodoxy as the living content of life, upon the hopelessness of atheism."[38] Although he did not set out either to challenge authority or to remake the political establishment, the methods Fr. Dmitrii employed threatened to the core the hierarchy's top-down approach to knowledge and truth.

The open character of the Saturday evening meetings was the antithesis of the services offered in other Orthodox Churches. Word of this courageous, approachable, talented priest rapidly spread. His meetings provided an education to the five hundred or six hundred people in attendance, giving them facts and perspectives that they had not heard during their schooling. The discussions continued for nine sessions. At the tenth, Fr. Dmitrii announced that the meetings were being suspended upon orders from Patriarch Pimen.[39] But they had opened doors to questions about certain topics that could not easily be closed.

In the early 1970s, in Leningrad, a thriving underground literary movement that would soon parallel other such movements interested in philosophical discussion and theological searching. This underground organization raised spiritual questions, which resulted in a large outpouring of religious poetry, written in the guise of "holy foolishness" to emphasize the poets' position as outsiders to official Soviet culture.[40] In the mid-1970s, other informal seminars among the young sprang up in Moscow, Leningrad, and several other cities. Their existence directly challenged the state's efforts to build an atheistic political and social order. The seminars almost immediately attracted the interest of the state's agencies of social control, most notably the KGB.

The Participants

Ideas in history do not always move in a straight line, as the English historian J. H. Hexter wrote many years ago; they take a zigzag course, advancing, retreating, and then often reappearing in different forms.[41] One cannot trace a direct line between Fr. Dmitrii Dudko's evening sessions and the student seminars that sprang up a year later. But the questions raised in the earlier discussions about freedom, community, and culture began to be explored more deeply and expansively than they were before.

In September 1974, a little more than a year after the patriarch suspended Fr. Dudko's Saturday evening sessions, a religious-philosophical seminar was formed in Moscow. The seminar invited young people who were interested in learning more about religious issues. It was the brainchild of twenty-four-year-old Aleksandr Ogorodnikov, a former student of the All-Union State Cinematography Institute in Moscow. Born and raised in the provincial town of Chistopol, in the Republic of Tatarstan in east-central Russia, as a youth Ogorodnikov had served as a leader in the Young Pioneers and Komsomol organizations. His pathway to open rebellion against the established order followed a trajectory similar to those of other young members of the Soviet intelligentsia. A top student at all three educational institutions he attended, Moscow State University, the Urals University (he majored in philosophy at both), and the Cinematography Institute, he began to question the philosophical principles of Soviet ideology even before he arrived at the Cinematography Institute, where he hoped to become a film director. The breakthrough moment, he claimed, came after viewing the Italian director Pier Paolo Pasolini's *The Gospel according to St. Matthew*. Pasolini's film closely followed the story of Christ's life, his teachings, and the parables and contrasted them with the actions of the authorities. Soon after seeing the film, Ogorodnikov converted to Christianity and, among his fellow students, made little secret of his newly found faith. Upon learning of his conversion, the institute expelled him.[42]

In early 1974, the plan to organize a special seminar emerged gradually in Ogorodnikov's mind. In the past year, he had met Fr. Aleksandr Men, traveled to his parish many times, and shared his idea with Fr. Aleksandr, who encouraged him and offered advice.[43] Inspired by Fr. Dmitrii Dudkov's Saturday night gatherings, which he had attended, Ogorodnikov created a seminar for open dialogue on questions that concerned many in the group. He established three principal reasons for its existence: to enhance the participants' theological understanding, "which we could not obtain by any other means," to develop a Christian community based on mutual love, and to engage in missionary work.[44] All these purposes violated the ideological underpinnings of the government's political campaign to extirpate religion.

The seminar attracted some outstanding personalities who remained with Ogorodnikov throughout its existence. They included several prominent leaders: Tat′iana Shchipkova, a teacher from Smolensk; Vladimir Poresh, her former student; and Lev Regel′son, a mathematician and physicist who, before his conversion to Russian Orthodoxy, worked at the Moscow Planetarium. Their personal evolutions reveal their attraction to the Christian Seminar and the quest for a more authentic life.

Tat′iana Shchipkova served as a lecturer in the Pedagogical Institute in Smolensk, where she had taught for more than a decade. At fifty years old, she was a rare exception to the young age of most seminar participants, which included her own son and two other Smolensk residents.[45] Shchipkova specialized in classical languages, cultures, and history. In her Latin class, she often managed to integrate several sessions on the rise of Christianity in the ancient world. "I had a usual class on first-year Latin," she wrote. "For thirteen or fourteen years, it had been my practice to teach the students about the culture and history of ancient Rome, as well as elementary Latin grammar." She would give "the first-year students preparatory lessons on the rise of Christianity, on the personhood of Christ, on His parables, and the significance of Christianity in the subsequent fate of Rome, Europe, and humankind."[46]

After joining the Christian Seminar, Shchipkova decided to go further, resolving to be open and honest in her teaching. "On June 7 [1977], I continued my lectures on Christianity and explained to the students that the Christian religion was still alive (the first time that a teacher had told the students of such a thing). I explained to them that, in our time, it is attracting more and more educated people in the Soviet Union, as well as in other countries and that I am a believer myself." Shchipkova continued, "We were not in the habit of telling the truth about ourselves, and so the students were unaccustomed to hearing it. They were stunned by what I said, listened in total silence, and did not ask a single question. Judging by everything, no one ran off to report me."[47]

Word of Shchipkova's confession, however, did reach the administration. In mid-June, she was summoned before the faculty and accused of disseminating religious propaganda. She maintained that she "was not guilty of propagating anything that would risk my work and position." "My goal," she said, "was to give my students a representation of this huge world and its cultural phenomena."[48] Shchipkova recounted that no one in the faculty meeting at which she was charged rose up to defend her, although she remained convinced that some had sympathetic views. The faculty dismissed her from her teaching position for what they called spreading lies.

Vladimir Poresh, like Shchipkova, had grown up in Smolensk and he studied at the Pedagogical Institute there. She recalled him as an extremely talented and sensitive student with an inquiring mind that questioned everything.[49] Poresh often remained after class to ask her about various points in her lecture, Shchipkova said, and sometimes he offered a carefully constructed counterargument. She recalled her sadness when he moved away to enter Leningrad State University.[50]

By the time she next saw Poresh, in late 1969 and again in 1970, he had changed. After the Soviet invasion of Czechoslovakia in 1968, he had become extremely depressed. The Soviets' violent suppression of free thought had convinced him of "his own spiritual enslavement and that of everyone around him."[51] He told her that he had contemplated suicide. But then, Shchipkova recounted, he had managed to work his way through his depression, because when she later encountered him on the streets of Leningrad, sometime in 1973, he expressed joy and hopefulness.

"I have begun a new phase of my life," he told Shchipkova. "I've got to know someone called Sasha Ogorodnikov. We have decided to create a culture within a culture."[52] Poresh said that he had begun to read Russian religious philosophy, and although he found it difficult, he saw in it the spiritual foundation for which he had searched a long time. He and Ogorodnikov had become fast friends, recognizing each other as "fellow travelers," and Poresh had joined Ogorodnikov in creating a similar student seminar in Leningrad.[53]

A third leading participant in the Christian Seminar, Lev Regel'son, came from a distinguished Moscow family. Born in 1929, he was the son of a prominent professor of physics at Moscow State University. His father and grandparents were committed communists who had lived the Stalinist dream of building a new society. Regel'son lived in the home of his grandparents and barely knew his mother.[54] He matriculated at Moscow State University, where he specialized in physics and mathematics, intending to follow the same career path as his father. He was fascinated by inquiry into the physical universe and the process of discovery. "But narrow scientific endeavors did not satisfy him," wrote Levitin-Krasnov, who knew Regel'son well. "He was constantly searching for higher truth," Levitin-Krasnov continued:

> Even in his student years, he was often carried away by the study of philosophy. First, he was enthused by Nietzsche, but was soon a little disappointed by the German philosopher, and turned to the study of Freud, whose works were suppressed and illegal at that time in the USSR. Once, he made a public report on Freud's work at a meeting of young students, which attracted wide attention. The young, inquisitive student did not stop with the study of Freud. He turned to the works of the Russian philosopher Berdiaev, then he took up religion seriously.[55]

During his years working as a physicist, Regel'son simultaneously considered himself a scientist and a religious person, although he had to keep the latter private. Afterward, following his baptism in the Orthodox Church, he was removed from his position and forced to live in the most meager circumstances. He wrote a large number of articles for samizdat publications and was one of the Christian Seminar's oldest and most experienced participants.[56] In the late 1970s in Paris, he published *The Tragedy of the Russian Orthodox Church, 1917–1945*, a unique, invaluable collection of primary documents detailing the assault on religious belief and the compromises the patriarchate made to preserve the church's existence.[57] He also became a close associate of Fr. Yakunin in the struggle for human rights. The two would write a series of significant appeals about the Soviet attack on religious liberty.

Shchipkova, Poresh, and Regel'son were all raised in atheist households. For each of them, the materialist intellectual underpinnings of the Soviet worldview proved unconvincing and led to resentment of the narrow framework it provided. They went in search of something larger, less confining, open to the world of mystery, wonder, and the imagination. Alexander Ogorodnikov described the quest of many of his cohorts as well as their disappointment in what they found in the official church: "Each of us has undergone a complex, sometimes agonizing path of spiritual questing, from Marxist convictions, via nihilism and the complete rejection of any ideology, via attraction to the 'hippy' lifestyle, we have come to the church. We came to it with our questions and our hopes." But "[we were] soon convinced that our problems were ignored in church sermons, which were the only means for the religious education of believers, nor did they have a place in the pages of the church's publication the *Journal of the Moscow Patriarchate*, which, moreover, is inaccessible to the ordinary Christian."[58]

Like most of the other participants in the Christian Seminar, Shchipkova, Poresh, and Regel'son had a higher education. They did not fit the common stereotype advanced in the Soviet media of religious believers as uneducated, superstitious, and unmindful remnants of the past. In a time when there were many captive minds, they raised questions that had no predetermined answers.

Breaking the Chains of Ideology

In 1978, Fr. Gleb Yakunin began attending sessions of the Christian Seminar. "He came to our meetings," said his friends Viktor Popkov and Tat′iana Lebedeva, "although he listened carefully and rarely said much at all."[59] The conversations he heard deepened his understanding of the readings the participants discussed. The quest of these young people inspired him, and he saw them as evidence of a new wave of human consciousness in the Soviet people. They had discovered deeply submerged in the Orthodox faith and in other religious traditions a wealth of thought that contradicted much of what they had heretofore known. This experience of Yakunin's testified to his conviction that a new day had dawned in the Soviet Union, and if left unimpeded, its course was irreversible.

The awakening had not emerged spontaneously; since at least the early 1960s, young people had begun to despair of the lies they witnessed all around them. The thirst for personal freedom, freedom of the spirit, had developed its own momentum. The Christian Seminar, with its searching spirit and the desire of its participants to learn more about Orthodox Christianity, exemplified that momentum. Yakunin grasped the optimism that Aleksandr Ogorodnikov expressed, perhaps too exuberantly, about Russia's present situation: "Russian culture today, while pushing its way out from under the rubble of terror, lies, and delusions, has given birth to an intellectual ferment which neither we ourselves nor the world in general expected."[60]

The Christian Seminar differed dramatically from the cultural and educational setting that its participants had previously known. Mark Popovskii, a young journalist, described a seminar meeting he attended. "In one of the Moscow apartments, in a condition of strict secrecy, the usual religious-philosophical Seminar of young Orthodox people just concluded. More than forty people, the majority of them from the provinces, for two days have discussed problems of philosophy, theory, and contemporary practice of Orthodoxy."[61]

According to Popovskii, seminars similar to the one in Moscow had emerged in Leningrad, Smolensk, Kazan, Odesa, Ufa, Grodno, and Lviv. This was a sign that "in many cities of the country, there are young men and women, for the most part students, teachers, and very diverse kinds of intelligentsia—workers, who have moved away from the official ideology, from the left-wing radicalism and the pathos of the counter-cultural, to Orthodoxy."⁶² The seminar sessions Popovskii attended discussed the relationship between newly converted Christians and the church as well as the writings of contemporary leftist philosophers such as Herbert Marcuse, Erich Fromm, Theodor Adorno, Jean-Paul Sartre, and Michel Jean-Pierre Debré. The topic that most excited the participants was a presentation devoted to "The Culture of the Catacombs, or the Search for Free Forms of Life in Soviet Totalitarian Society."⁶³ The discussants wanted to know how they could successfully create a dynamic, mutually supportive Christian community in the milieu of a totalitarian society. The participants proposed beginning with a summer-school camp organized during the holidays that would attract like-minded people of similar spiritual dispositions. In an isolated location, attendees could discuss a whole range of topics related to their lives and their society. They wanted to raise their children in such an environment.

During his journey, like many other seminar participants, Ogorodnikov had grown sick of what he referred to as the "spellbound spiritual captivity of ideology" and its penetration into every corner of one's life.⁶⁴ In the depths of our despair, Ogorodnikov said, we learned that underneath the outward layer of Soviet existence, "spiritual life quietly and secretly flows, streams into the deep Soviet underground, weaving the light."⁶⁵ This discovery, he said, was what led them to the "eternal truth" of the church and, from there, to Russia's great spiritual writers and philosophers such as Nikolai Gogol, Pyotr Kireevskii, Aleksei Khomiakov, Vladimir Solov'ev, Nikolai Berdiaev, and Sergei Bulgakov.⁶⁶

Yakunin observed that the rising tide of interest in religion among the young was taking place outside the institutional church. According to Yakunin, the Moscow Patriarchate and its lethargic Patriarch Pimen demonstrated little interest in this religious awakening. While they did not attempt to stifle the movement, neither did they offer any encouragement.

Earlier, in 1975, Yakunin, Lev Regel'son, and an associate, Viktor Kapitanchuk, wrote to Patriarch Pimen hoping that he would be more courageous than his predecessor. "Faith without action is dead," they had written. "Most of all, a truly believing heart cannot remain indifferent to the events taking place in the history of the world around us."⁶⁷ This Christian doctrine, calling the church to respond to events taking place in history and its responsibility "to unmask lies and injustices," would become a central theme in Yakunin's life.⁶⁸

In the meantime, members of the Christian Seminar, in Yakunin's presence, continued their quest for an authentic existence, questioning the kind of society in which they wanted to live, which the authorities deemed threatening to the Soviet order.

Raising Questions

On the morning of May 21, 1978, Tat'iana Shchipkova was sitting in her Smolensk apartment, conversing with several members of the Christian Seminar. Aleksandr Ogorodnikov and Viktor Popkov had come from Moscow to visit her, and they were joined by the sympathetic superintendent of her apartment building. Suddenly, they were interrupted by a loud knock on the door. Surprised by the arrival of additional visitors, Shchipkova asked who they were and was told "the police!" They demanded that she open the door immediately, and when she refused, they threatened to force it open. She stepped out into the hallway, slamming the door behind her. The lead police officer showed her a search warrant. "There were five of them who confronted me," she said, a senior investigator named Kleshcheva, an assistant public prosecutor, and three men in civilian clothes. They demanded again that she open the door. When she told them that she had forgotten her key, the public prosecutor called for an ax and ordered the police to break the lock.[69]

The security police had carefully watched Shchipkova's movements, as well as those of other members of the Christian Seminar. The printed materials that circulated among seminar members, including their journal *Obshchina*, deeply threatened the ideological framework of the Soviet state, and while authorities had tolerated the seminar's existence earlier, they no longer exhibited such patience. The police, joined by two witnesses (a cashier and saleswoman from a local store), entered Shchipkova's apartment. The ensuing scene was chaotic, a combination of threats, demands, and belittling comments. The investigators searched every crevice of the apartment, pulling out papers, documents, and any little fragment of writing they could find. Spreading them out on the floor, they examined each one, looking for evidence of anti-Soviet materials. The assistant public prosecutor ridiculed the Christian Seminar, "Nowadays, when we are sending up spaceships, to believe in such nonsense. . . . They thought themselves up a myth, a fairy tale—a fine thing for people to waste their time on!"[70] At one point, as Shchipkova defended the seminar's purpose, its earnest attempt to investigate Russian Orthodoxy, and its theological relevance to the present, one of the women who served as a witness expressed surprise that such an organization existed and conveyed her interest in it.[71]

The search of Shchipkov'a apartment lasted six hours. In the end, the police and their collaborators tied everything into bundles—books, samizdat materials, carbon paper, and manuscripts—and carted them away along with Shchipkova's typewriter. As they departed, the emissaries of the KGB handed her an inventory of condemned books and manuscripts. They asked her voluntarily to surrender all the materials in her possession that defamed the Soviet Union; she responded she had no items that defamed the Soviet state.[72]

The inventory, as well as Ogorodnikov's list of readings for the seminar, offered a firsthand view of the main issues the participants explored. These materials consisted of 108 in all, and included copies of letters to various government officials, essays circulated among Christian Seminar members, and books by late nineteenth- and early twentieth-century Russian philosopher-theologians as well as Western writers. Three of the writers warrant special attention: Vladimir Solov'ev, Aleksei Khomiakov, and Henri Bergson. All three offered alternative views of religion that contributed to Yakunin's evolving understanding of freedom of conscience, creativity, and open-mindedness.

Vladimir Sergeevich Solov'ev (1853–1900) majored in philosophy at Moscow University with an emphasis on the natural sciences and theology. Educated during a time when positivism reigned supreme among Russian educated youth, early on he began to carve out a path different from the positivists. One of Russia's greatest philosophers, Solov'ev had a big influence on a whole generation of Russia's most creative thinkers.

Solov'ev's belief that God had created the universe as a single, interconnected unity lay at the core of his philosophy. When people removed any part of this unity, abstracted and made it into the whole of their perceptions, they engaged in a delusion. "We know that objects before us in the world did not fall haphazardly from the sky in a ready-made state," Solov'ev maintained, "but were composed over time and on the earth. Knowing that they are in a constant state of becoming, we have no reasonable basis to claim that what we see before us is already completed."[73] Humans were essentially creative beings endowed with a divine spirit, capable of making the world a better place, infusing society with this divine spirit, bringing all of humankind closer together. Solov'ev saw this as a fundamental principle of Christianity.[74]

Members of the Christian Seminar, raised on dialectical materialism, found Solov'ev's ideas immensely attractive. He offered the participants a different, more coherent view of the world than they had been taught. Solov'ev's emphasis on creativity and the individual's role in fulfilling a divine plan gave the seminar members a positive view of their own responsibilities. They did not see a conflict between science and faith, although they understood that each sphere represented a distinctive way of knowing. Together, these spheres represented parts of God's creation, divine sources of a universal unity.[75]

Drawing from Solov'ev, Vladimir Poresh wrote, "Our nation has borne incredible suffering which has formed the moral core, the religious foundation, on which a new rediscovered religious consciousness is being built."[76] This religious consciousness, Poresh asserted, remained incomplete and infirm, but he had little doubt in Russia's spiritual power and its role in Russia's eventual transformation.

Speaking of the mindset of present-day Russia, Poresh was adamant in his condemnation as well as his faith in his country's hidden resources: "We do not want talentless vulgarity, the stillness that destroys. We do not want the cynicism and despair that suppress the Word, the meaning of life. We do not want this lying [falsified] peace: we want a just war. Where are you, Holy Russia, Russia of the saints and holy men? We do not believe you are dead."[77]

In its efforts to foster a communal society, the USSR placed little emphasis on the individual. In the attempt to rediscover Christianity, members of the seminar gave special attention to the question of the person and the person's relationship to the parish community.[78] What did freedom of the individual mean in reality, and how, Poresh asked, might it contribute to the creation of a moral order and "religious consciousness?" What did it mean to have an authentic church community, one that operated in freedom, unrestricted by the state? Frustrated by their inability to locate such a community in the contemporary church, members of the seminar looked for guidance in the writings of one of Russia's most prophetic theological minds.

Aleksei Stepanovich Khomiakov (1804–1860), a founding member of the influential nineteenth-century Slavophiles, belonged to the landed nobility that had deep roots in the Orthodox Church. He was a poet, historian, artist, linguist, and theologian, whose writings spoke with a freshness and power that members of the conservative church hierarchy of his time often criticized. Perceiving these writings as revolutionary, church censorship prohibited most of them from being published. As the Orthodox scholar Nicholas Zernov noted, however, Khomiakov's thoughts drew from the deepest recesses of the Orthodox tradition.[79]

Among the subjects that Aleksandr Ogorodnikov listed for discussion, "The Church and Industrial Society Today" stood at the top. He added "The Individual and the Community of the Church." Khomiakov appeared as the first name recorded on the topic. The two subjects concerned the present condition in which Soviet youth had grown up and both suggested the chief interests of the seminar's participants, particularly the question of freedom and community. The treatment of Christ in the Gospels was central to both questions, and Khomiakov's portrayal of Christ addressed them. As Fr. Aleksandr Men later noted in his public lecture on Khomiakov's understanding of Christ:

> He is the victor in the New Testament, but a victor who does not humiliate, who does not destroy, and who preserves human freedom. Freedom is a great gift, which distinguishes us from animals—this is the freedom

that God has carefully endowed us with. Therefore, the appearance of Christ took place without force over the personality and conscience of the human being. Christ always allowed a person the opportunity to turn one's back on Him.[80]

The freedom of choice stood in stark contrast to force and violence. When it operated properly, the church community fulfilled a similar purpose.

In his seminal work, *Tserkov' Odna* (*The Church Is One*), unpublished during his lifetime, Khomiakov defined the church as a fellowship of love, which allowed a person, in living communion with others, to separate from a lonely, ego-driven existence and become part of a living organism. The term "sobornost'," meaning "conciliarity," expressed this unity in freedom and love.[81]

It is easy to see the appeal of Khomiakov's ideas to members of the Christian Seminar. His discussion of love, freedom, and the church community spoke directly to the founding purposes of the seminar and the main interests of its participants. The more a person lived in cooperation with others, the richer and more fulfilled life would be. The church lived not under force or constraint. It was not an authority, as some were wont to say: "God is not an authority, and Christ is not an authority, because an authority is something exterior to us." Rather, the "church is truth. She lives in a person more real than the heart beating in his breast, or the blood running in his veins."[82] In this community, a person found his true calling in freedom and unity with others. These beliefs offered the participants in the Christian Seminar a much different view of life than the ideology under which they had grown up.

The discussion of the role of the church in the contemporary world, the individual and society, and the relationship between the church and freedom raised other questions concerning the church's effectiveness in speaking to the spiritual needs of the Russian people. Such issues related to the relationship between freedom and creativity, as well as the present qualities and ways of thinking that impeded the development of a spiritual community.

The last question—the idea that certain philosophies could be counterproductive for spiritual growth—was the subject of the great French scientist and philosopher Henri Bergson's *Two Sources of Morality and Religion*. Bergson (1859–1941) won the Nobel Prize in Literature in 1927, and several of his works, like other significant foreign books, were translated into Russian shortly after their publication. Many of them could still be found in Soviet antiquarian bookstores, and they remained fresh sources of discussion among segments of the population. *Two Sources of Morality and Religion* was one of these.

In this influential work, Bergson contrasted the evolution and characteristics of what he called closed and open societies.[83] He likened a closed society to a biological organism that attempted to define the functions of each part of the whole and fit them together for the sake of the common good. In such a society, a clan mentality predominated that aimed at preserving the status quo and safeguarding the community against outside attack. In the closed society, according to Bergson, human beings operated as ants in an ant heap.[84] The religious beliefs of the closed society focused on ritual, stability, reproduction, and keeping everything in their predefined order.[85]

In contrast, the open society was less concerned with rigidly defined obligations and put greater emphasis on creativity and progress. The open society accepted that life involved adapting to changing circumstances; it operated much differently from the "anthill." Remaining open to change, new possibilities, and discovery were paramount, and citizens operated not as cogwheels in a well-organized and disciplined mechanism, but as participants in a dynamic community. Religion in the open society emphasized love and grace rather than rigid doctrines and rituals.[86]

Bergson offered seminar members a critique of the closed society, but he did not offer them a prescription for how to construct an open community. His conclusions were a good fit for the seminar participants' quest for a new social order. His *Two Sources* spoke directly to the Soviet Union's political condition, particularly the high value placed by its governing elite on stability, self-preservation, and clan mentality. In a closed society, the questions people raised had answers within a preestablished framework. In a time when there are many captive minds, according to Czesław Miłosz, one must not ask embarrassing questions, but rather accept what one is told, submerging one's identity in the political order.[87]

Seminar participants were fully aware that the security police were present all around them. The arrests of their leaders and the most energetic members would follow in 1978–1979. Yet the conversations their questions stimulated and the critiques they generated about power and violence would continue to germinate and take form in the struggle for human rights and religious liberty. In that quest, Fr. Gleb Yakunin, Lev Regel'son, and other members would play major parts.[88]

The readings and conversations in which Yakunin participated in the Christian Seminar gave him hope for Russia's future. The seminar raised questions and pointed to issues that he saw as essential to the future health of the Orthodox Church and Russian society. He believed that his country held valuable intellectual and spiritual resources that only needed to be released to foster regeneration. The Christian Seminar gave him the confidence to reach out beyond Russia's borders to build sympathetic relationships and seek new sources of support for religious freedom.

CHAPTER 4

Western Perceptions and Soviet Realities

In the 1960s and early 1970s, Russian religious believers sent letters to various émigré publications in the West describing the state's assault on Russian Churches. Their letters detailed the mass closure of churches as well as the harassment of men and women who aspired to continue their religious practices, despite the Communist Party's aggressive campaign to obliterate religious belief in the Soviet Union. Émigré publications in Paris, Prague, and New York willingly published these letters, which provided a clear, if anecdotal, portrait of the pain their writers and families suffered at the hands of the agents of a powerful state. Taken individually, however, the accounts made little dent on Western policy makers. They neither stirred up a debate nor incited a closer look at religious persecution in the Soviet Union. In October 1975, the World Council of Churches received a letter written by Fr. Gleb Yakunin and an Orthodox layperson, Lev Regel'son, that changed the Western response.

Founded in August 1948, in Amsterdam, the World Council of Churches (WCC) represented an international Christian Church organization whose membership extended from East Asia to Western Europe and the United States. Created as an ecumenical movement, the WCC aimed at promoting religious tolerance and mutual understanding between different religious denominations whose beliefs and practices widely diverged. The members pledged to work together to share common experiences and promote Christian unity. As the secretary-general announced the organization's preeminent mission in the opening session in 1948, he stated that the WCC resolved to "speak boldly in Christ's name, to both those in power and to the people, to oppose terror, cruelty, and race discrimination, to stand by the outcast, the prisoner, and the refugee. We have to make of the church in every place a voice for the voiceless."[1]

The WCC was not a church, but a loose conglomeration of widely diverse churches and organizations. The members had a lofty, all-embracing goal: through Jesus Christ, to work toward a peaceful and nonviolent world for all children. The Russian Orthodox Church joined the WCC in 1961 and, from the outset, influenced its agenda. In the first twenty-five years of its existence, the WCC's principal concerns included topics such as national liberation movements, race relations, international reconciliation, and colonialism. In 1975, the WCC's membership totaled more than 260 congregations, representing over a half billion Christians. For more than a decade, some Western denominations had expressed unhappiness about what they considered the leftward focus of the WCC; in the 1970s, these discontented groups threatened to pull out of the organization.[2]

More specifically, the topics raised within the WCC over issues such as humanitarian aid to groups struggling against racism and the stand it had taken against racism in all its forms provoked controversy within and beyond the organization. In response, in 1971, the WCC's Central Committee charged its Church and Society subcommittee to conduct a two-year study on the struggle for social justice and its implications for the actions of the WCC. The subcommittee focused its attention on the potential of violence and nonviolence in the struggle. In its August 1973 report to the WCC's Central Committee, the subcommittee pointed out that its task "was not to initiate a discussion," since that conversation had already taken place in numerous venues, but rather to place the quest for social justice "in a worldwide ecumenical context."[3] Stepping delicately around the controversial and sensitive subject of their assignment, the writers of the report emphasized their desire to help affluent Christians, primarily the white world, better understand the views of other Christians. The final document, drawn up by the WCC's Central Committee in 1973, emphasized that Christians everywhere had a responsibility "as old as Christianity" to speak to a world in which force and violence were always present. Violence took ever-changing forms, which Christianity had to resist, and it particularly had the responsibility to address political authority that promoted social injustice.[4] The document referenced the predominance of violence in South Africa, Latin America, Northern Ireland, the Middle East, and the United States. But it contained no mention either of human rights or religious persecution in countries living under communism. To some members of the WCC, these represented glaring omissions.[5]

Nairobi

Convened in Nairobi in August 1975, the WCC's Fifth Assembly faced all these contentious issues. Before the meeting, however, the leadership could not have anticipated that the organization would soon have to deal with a serious question it had largely avoided in earlier sessions. On October 16, 1975, WCC delegates read an "Appeal" transmitted from Moscow by Yakunin and Regel'son, which dealt directly with violence in the Soviet Union. Although earlier letters from individual religious believers had largely been set aside, the delegates did not ignore this appeal, and it would find its way onto the main agenda of the international meeting. The letter's prominence derived from two fundamental reasons: its timing and the actions of the African organizers of the sessions.[6]

In 1975, human rights had emerged as a major issue of international concern, which generated passionate interest, especially in the United States and Western Europe. Not surprisingly, in some groups within the WCC, it likewise ascended to the top of their agenda, and the communication from Yakunin and Regel'son immediately attracted their attention. Except for a chance decision, however, it is unlikely that the appeal would have acquired the notoriety it did. When preparing the news briefing for the WCC agenda, the African organizing committee elected to print the letter written by Yakunin and Regel'son in its entirety. This action ensured that instead of being buried in a subcommittee, all the participants in the meetings of the WCC would read the letter. Printing it likewise determined that the problems Yakunin and Regel'son raised would become part of the WCC's proceedings.[7]

In their appeal, Yakunin and Regel'son began by making their case within the framework of the WCC's principal mission by appealing to its ecumenical ideals.[8] They spoke to the feeling of brotherhood and the commitment to the love of Jesus Christ, which prepared Christians for genuine unity. It was within this context that the two writers placed the tragic story of the Russian Orthodox Church, which had suffered an enormous human tragedy under the abusive antireligious policies of the Soviet government. In the name of Christian love, Yakunin and Regel'son appealed for selfless help. They referred to a similar plea made by Patriarch Tikhon in 1921, in the midst of a great famine that ravished the Russian countryside. "Not to your ears, but to the depths of your hearts," Patriarch Tikhon had cried out, "let my prayer convey the suffering cry of millions of human beings doomed to death from starvation; let me bring it home to your conscience, to the conscience of all humankind."[9] Yakunin and Regel'son's clarion call went out not to address physical starvation, but the spiritual suffering of a people denied the right to worship, a people whose lifeline had been cut off by the antireligious policies of the Soviet government. The appeal echoed the cry of the Russian people, Michael Bourdeaux has written, "with all its spiritual power welling up from generations of suffering—to be heard in a totally new way by hundreds of delegates, many of whom had previously thought of the Russian Orthodox Church in terms of somewhat ominous figures—with whom communication was difficult—circulating at ecumenical gatherings."[10]

In a statement that would eventually prove important to Yakunin's and Regel'son's future, their appeal recalled an international protest led by Christians everywhere against the Soviet government's actions that had exacerbated the famine of 1921–1922. The international outcry, they claimed, led by Anglican, Catholic, and other faiths, had a decisive impact on Soviet behavior. Outside pressure had resulted in the release of Patriarch Tikhon from prison, an event that had large significance for the Orthodox Church.[11] Patriarch Tikhon they regarded as a martyr in the defense of the Orthodox Church against efforts to destroy it, and they maintained that Russian believers had never forgotten his legacy.[12] Similarly, they would always remember the support of the WCC.

Moving to the present, Yakunin and Regel'son noted that, heretofore, world attention had focused on issues other than religious repression in the Soviet Union. Their appeal made it difficult for members of the WCC to ignore any longer the fate of religious believers in that country. First, Yakunin and Regel'son exposed the intolerance Orthodox Church leaders had exhibited toward other faiths, their devotion to the government's nationalistic agenda, and, above all, their unquestioning submission to the political authorities of the Soviet Union. For example, when the Soviet government's foreign policy shifted from the Cold War to détente, the church, too, fell in line with the government's approach.

Second, despite the Soviet state's frequent claims to the contrary, Yakunin and Regel'son provided a catalogue of specific actions it had taken to suppress religious belief. The specificity of their charges, offered not as parochial instances, but as widespread, disparate cases, painted a picture of violence that made denial of these hard. Paradoxically, in 1961, the same year the Russian Orthodox Church joined the WCC, the Soviet government initiated a wave of antireligious terror and forced the closure of a large number of churches, monasteries, and theological institutions. A year later, at the Twenty-Second Party Congress, the Soviet leadership promised that the current generation of Soviet people would live in a country devoid of religious belief. It was extremely important, Yakunin and Regel'son asserted, that "Christians all over the world learn about their confessing brethren, wherever the victims of persecution reside and whatever their denomination may be."[13]

Yakunin and Regel'son's observations about psychiatric hospitals in the Soviet Union were among their most important revelations. They requested international inspection of these "torture chambers," where psychiatrists regularly prescribed shock therapy for religious believers and dissidents, thinking it would "cure" them of their so-called irrational behavior. Psychiatrists used electrical shock as a weapon against "freedom of thought and conscience." "There we encounter a threat to humankind as dangerous as nuclear bombs and bacteriological warfare," the two writers claimed.[14] They also cited the American psychiatrist Dr. Robert Coles's warnings about the effects on people placed in these "psychiatric torture chambers": "Such people know what it means to be abandoned and deserted. In their perplexity, they often ask themselves whether they are not already in hell, at this very moment. For them heaven remains a vision just as for a thirsty man in a desert. Somebody must save them."[15]

The two writers offered specific recommendations to the Nairobi Assembly. Foremost among them was the need to awaken to the suffering of their Russian brethren. They again appealed to the universal sense of brother- and sisterhood that, they maintained, lay at the core of Christianity.[16] They emphasized the importance of circulating information about the suffering victims of religious persecution in newspapers and magazines and on radio and television, as well as in a special mass-circulation bulletin focused on the plight of confessors of Christ all over the world. Most important, they called on the WCC to take up the issues they had brought to the delegates' attention. Speaking to the delegates' sense of shame, Yakunin and Regel'son asserted that an egotistical indifference to the suffering of Christian confessors had too long characterized the meetings of the WCC. The two writers called upon the delegates to overcome their disinterest and to hear again Christ's call to care for the poor and the suffering of the earth.[17]

Several features added to the power of the appeal. It was written in eloquent language that spoke to the mission of the WCC, which made it nearly impossible for the assembly to ignore the document's call for action. Moreover, it spoke in the language of Christianity, articulated how best to witness to the call of Christ in the modern world, and proposed how to advance the spiritual unification of Christians all over the world through human rights and religious liberty.[18]

Scorned, ridiculed, and ostracized from their community, both psychologically and religiously, believers in the Soviet Union needed to feel part of a world Christian community. They could not themselves reach out to other people, but would have great joy if members of the world community reached out to them.[19] Yakunin and Regel'son offered simple, practical suggestions for how individual churches might respond.[20] They asked for prayer, personal contacts, sharing of information, international protests, support for the persecuted, and fraternal concern for people who wished to emigrate.

The appeal Yakunin cowrote to the delegates in Nairobi also marked the widening scope of his public statements. The 1965 letters had addressed Soviet leaders in the government and the church. A decade later, still suspended from serving as an active priest, he sought a wider audience, casting the grievances in a much larger framework and connecting them to universal claims. The lone exception to this broader perspective appeared in a previous letter, in which he and Regel'son addressed fellow Christians in Portugal. Surveying Portuguese politics, they warned that the country presently faced a situation not unlike what Russia confronted in the era of the 1917 Revolution, when it had broken from its traditional culture. This process had let to "spiritual, national, and political decay."[21] They cautioned Portuguese Christians about falling into a similar trap and implored them to become actively involved in politics.[22] Yakunin began to cast his thinking in larger, more universal terms than before. He took an ecumenical approach, and in his Nairobi appeal, he reached across denominational lines, alluding to the suffering not only of Orthodox Christians but also of Muslims, Jews, Baptists, Pentecostals, Jehovah's Witnesses, and Catholics. "We believe," he and Regel'son wrote, "that it would be the right thing if churches made an effort to support Confessors of all religions, as well as all fighters for freedom, human dignity, and the preservation of God's image in man."[23] Their plea went further: "Are not Christians more than anyone obligated to lead the implacable struggle against such a diabolical assault on human personality?"[24] Denied political support in his own country, Yakunin turned to the outside world for help. Yet pragmatism did not constitute the only reason for his decisions. Ecumenism also played an important part in his thinking, his growing view that the isolation of the Orthodox Church had hindered its creativity and its need for dialogue. Readings and discussions in the Christian Seminar had encouraged such an approach, and they constituted one of the sources on which he had drawn. Reaching across religious boundaries soon became a key element in his political actions and represents one of the first attempts by an Orthodox priest to take this ecumenical approach.

When it appeared in the assembly's daily newspaper on November 25, 1975, the appeal caused a great deal of backroom conversation among delegates, particularly those from Western Europe. It also put the Soviet delegates in an extremely awkward position. To them, it came as a surprise and created a political dilemma. As representatives of a country whose government officially declared itself atheistic, Soviet delegates had always confronted the difficult task of simultaneously professing themselves emissaries of Jesus Christ. Facing the charges made in the Yakunin–Regel'son "Appeal," they now had to defend their government, while responding to specific claims of injustices and persecutions of religious believers for practicing their professed faith.

The Soviet delegation's response came on November 28. Metropolitan Yuvenalii (Vladimir Kirillovich Poiarkov), the chair of the Moscow Patriarchate's Department of Foreign Relations, wrote the reply to the claims Yakunin and Regel'son had made. Yuvenalii had impressive credentials. Born in 1935 in the city of Yaroslavl into a family of priests, the forty-one-year-old Yuvenalii was a well-educated, highly respected metropolitan who had rapidly risen within the leadership of the Russian Orthodox Church.[25] He was ordained to the priesthood in 1960, the same year the church selected him to be a member of the Russian delegation to attend the first European Ecumenical Youth Assembly, held in Lausanne, Switzerland. Afterward, he remained to study in the WCC's Ecumenical Institute in Bossey, Switzerland, thus giving him contacts that would be useful to him in his later career.[26] After completing his course of study, he had traveled extensively in Western Europe, often participating in conferences devoted to building ecumenical relationships between different denominations. In 1965, Patriarch Aleksii I appointed him deputy chair of the patriarchate's Department of Foreign Relations. In 1972, he became chair, replacing Metropolitan Nikodim, who had become ill. Yuvenalii was a widely experienced, knowledgeable, and well-known member of the church hierarchy who played a large part in the shifting of foreign policy within the church from the Cold War to peace and ecumenical politics.

Metropolitan Yuvenalii's written response to the assembly represented a masterstroke of "walking a thin line" between two disparate points of view. Obviously, he had to clear his response with the KGB, which exercised a tight hold on all Soviet delegations sent abroad. He could not totally whitewash the internal conflicts within his country without earning the disapprobation of WCC delegates. His response, therefore, required judicial judgment, and it was certain to provoke a heated reaction.

At the beginning of his reply to the Yakunin–Regel'son "Appeal," Yuvenalii disparaged the character, as well as the motives, of the two writers. Yakunin, he claimed, was an inveterate troublemaker, a renegade within the church who had earned the opprobrium of both the leadership and the rank-and-file loyal servitors. "He has been in conflict with his own church for some time," Yuvenalii wrote, referring to Fr. Gleb's previous troubles with the authorities following the letter he and Nikolai Eshliman had sent to the patriarch in 1965. Fr. Gleb's cohort, Lev Regel'son, a layperson, had long been known for his opposition to ecumenism, Yuvenalii claimed, as evidenced by a statement he wrote "to the Local Council of the Russian Orthodox Church in 1971, in which he criticized the ecumenical activities in the theological field of the Moscow Patriarchate's representatives." In his statement, Regel'son asserted that "ecumenism and all connected with it is a danger for Orthodoxy and must be seen as a heresy of our day."[27]

Despite the harshness of his opening rhetoric, Yuvenalii's tone softened. He made several surprising admissions about the shortcomings of Soviet officials: "We do not disguise the fact that there do arise problems in the life of the church, resulting from the infringement of the laws concerning religious communities, both by local representatives of the State authorities, and by members of church communities."[28] In addition, he expressed regret for the transgressions of the laws: "We do not condone the violations of these laws, whether on the political plane, or any other."[29] He neither sought to excuse the violations nor attempt to justify them.

Nevertheless, Yuvenalii asserted that the Council for Religious Affairs, which operated under the Council of Ministers, had made great strides in working on these infringements, and he asserted that its work had proved highly beneficial to the well-being of the country. Foreign visitors to the Soviet Union could clearly see the opportunities for religious believers to worship freely, to enjoy all the amenities of the state, and to appreciate the respect for their religious activities so long as their actions did not violate the legal separation of church and state. Foreign visitors repeatedly had found little evidence of religious persecution.[30] Yuvenalii called the rumors that frequently circulated in the Western press about religious persecution to be wildly exaggerated accusations, and he declared them extremely harmful to resolving his country's internal problems.[31] By implication, he placed the charges that Yakunin and Regel'son advanced in the category of these distortions, which misrepresented the long-term course his country was taking: "At the same time, we cannot but note the fact that our society is evolving in the direction of ever-increasing development of democratic principles. The church has found its level in this process, and contributes to it to the extent that it is possible for her to do so."[32] Yuvenalii thus tried to make Yakunin and Regel'son's appeal appear to be a minor issue. The Soviet state was not perfect, which he well recognized, but it was moving along the path toward the pursuit of democratic ideals. He hoped the WCC delegates would disregard the problems Yakunin and Regel'son had brought to light.

On the same day that the WCC's organizing committee received Metropolitan Yuvenalii's response, it also received a letter from Russian Baptist delegates. They wrote on behalf of the All-Union Council of Evangelical Christians and Baptists in the Soviet Union. Evangelical Baptists, they pointed out, had deep roots in Russia, having existed there for more than a hundred years, and presently represented more than half a million believers. Ostensibly, their letter expressed support for the government's policies. The letter, however, confirmed what Yakunin and Regel'son had claimed about the persecution of believers. It referenced a group of schismatic Baptists who wanted nothing to do with the All-Union Council, preferring to remain separate and true to their faith and outside government control. The motto of these schismatic Baptists was the "Persecuted Church Is the Saving Church."[33] Electing to remain separate from the state and refusing to comply with state laws on registration, they often suffered arrest and conviction.[34]

Although the issue of religious liberty in the USSR raised heated discussion in the back rooms and hallways of the WCC, two weeks passed before, on December 8, the problem finally arose in the assembly sessions. That it eventually did so was almost by accident. The opening for its discussion followed a report of the working Committee on Disarmament and the Helsinki Accords when Dr. Jacques Rossel, a Swiss Protestant delegate, moved to incorporate the following statement in the concluding paragraph of the committee's report: "The WCC is concerned about restrictions to religious liberty particularly in the USSR. The Assembly respectfully requests the government of the USSR to implement effectively principle number 7 of the Helsinki Accords."[35] This statement moved the claims made in the Yakunin–Regel'son appeal to the center of the WCC's agenda. It also targeted the Soviet Union's violations of the Helsinki Accords. The proposal forced the WCC to consider taking a strong stand on religious liberty, which it had hitherto been reluctant to do.

Rev. Richard Holloway of the Episcopal Church of Scotland immediately seconded the motion. As might have been expected, Russian delegates strenuously opposed it.[36] A period of confusion followed, likely caused by uncertainty among the delegates over whether they were voting to close the discussion or to end the session.[37] After this proposal for closure failed to receive the required two-thirds majority, the discussion continued, with Dr. Ernest Payne, an English Baptist, urging that the amendment be sent back to the committee for more deliberative consideration. He hoped that the result would lead to a wider level of consensus. Payne's suggestion was approved, and that evening, the Committee on Disarmament and the Helsinki Accords held an open hearing. The records reveal that a large number of delegates attended. Late in the evening, a small group of committee members were assigned to draft a final statement.[38] The next day, December 9, the committee members filed their draft proposal, saying that they had deliberated into "the small hours" before arriving at a recommendation that they had unanimously approved. Although it called attention to "alleged infringements of religious liberty," the revised statement contained no mention of the Soviet Union. It read: "The Assembly requests the General Secretary to see to it that the question of religious liberty be the subject of intense consultations with the member churches of the signatory States of the Helsinki Accords and the first report be presented at the next Central Committee meeting in August 1976."[39] After the reading of the revised statement, Dr. Rossel and Rev. Holloway withdrew their original amendment. An extensive, often heated discussion ensued, in which the Soviet delegation announced that its members would abstain from any subsequent vote. Professor Vitalii Borovoi spoke on behalf of the Russian Orthodox Church and reiterated the wish to engage in conversation that "deepened our understanding of, and to apply, human rights, including religious liberty." On this issue, he explained the Soviet delegation's intention to abstain: "We were always ready, and at this present moment, declare our readiness to participate in open, brotherly, and equitable discussion of these problems which are of prime importance for us all. We are prepared for frankness, for dialogue, and for co-operation. But we were unpleasantly disappointed by the prevailing atmosphere which surrounded the discussion of these questions at the Assembly, an atmosphere compounded of haste, nerves, emotion, and divisiveness."[40] The proposed statement from the committee was then put to a vote, and it carried by "an overwhelming majority," with four negative votes and many abstentions.[41]

The Aftermath

The discussion of religious liberty and human rights did not end in Nairobi; the questions Yakunin and Regel'son raised continued to resonate long after the WCC's meetings concluded in December. On March 3, 1976, the Holy Synod of the Moscow Patriarchate sent a letter addressed to the general-secretary of the WCC, Dr. Philip Potter, and to the chair of the WCC's Central Committee, Archbishop Edward Scott, that sharply criticized the WCC's resolution. The synod's letter argued that, in preparation for the assembly, no representative of a socialist country had participated. Further, in the assembly's discussions, socialist representatives had rarely had the chance to speak, while their Western counterparts had dominated the sessions. The synod wanted an explanation for why the leadership had pushed forward its own agenda.[42]

The conflict between these opposing forces over religious liberty would become even more strident in the ensuing months. During that time, the WCC received many letters from clergy and religious believers in the Soviet Union claiming that they enjoyed religious freedom and praising the opportunity to practice their own faith traditions. Throughout 1976, they also excoriated Yakunin and Regel'son for creating a false picture of the Soviet Union and castigated them for "this type of slander" against the Soviet system (figure 4.1).[43] Conversely, persecuted people also sent letters, testifying to the closure of churches and the prohibition of many of their religious activities.

The leadership of the WCC continued to wrestle with these conflicting issues despite an abundance of evidence it received supporting the case Yakunin and Regel'son had originally made. Even so, the leadership welcomed the participation of the Soviet and East European representatives in its meetings,

FIGURE 4.1. Fr. Gleb Yakunin, summer of 1976. Courtesy of the Keston Center for Religion, Politics, and Society, Baylor University, Waco, Texas.

and it did not want to precipitate their withdrawal. Concurrently, the WCC wanted to hear the cries of the persecuted, voices it could not easily ignore and to which it needed to respond with compassion. The struggle to resolve these dilemmas sparked several meetings: the first, in late July 1976, in the resort town of Montreux, Switzerland; the second, from August 10 to 18 in Geneva. The former, called the Helsinki Colloquium, included representatives from Eastern Europe and the Soviet Union. It fostered a great deal of conversation among the attendees, but in the end, it resolved little.[44]

Attended by 130 people, including a large delegation from the Soviet Union, the second meeting convened with a great deal of anticipation of a resolution. In his final report to the participants, however, Dr. Potter avoided reaching an ultimate conclusion. The existing conflicts over human rights and religious liberty, he said, could be solved only "in the context of mutual trust, mutual respect, and mutual caring and support."[45]

As one might have expected, Dr. Potter's report did not fulfill the hopes or desires of Western European or American delegates, who had long sought to clarify the WCC's position on religious liberty and connect this issue to human rights. In the end, the leadership of the WCC tried to bridge the excessive disparate interests and beliefs. It feared offending different parties, and thus it satisfied none of them. The leap of judgment it had to make was too great, the danger of creating permanent fissures in its membership too risky, and its desire to forge unity among its members too deeply rooted for it to take a resolute stand.

The controversy over religious liberty did not dissipate in the months after the delegates returned home from Geneva, because the issues it had raised were too important. They involved the self-image of the countries competing for international prominence during the Cold War, when the strength of a nation's internal coherence served as an important measure of national power. Moreover, the charges brought by Yakunin and Regel'son concerned the difference between truth and delusion. In the Soviet Union, Great Britain, and the United States, the claims made by Yakunin and Regel'son rapidly became contentious matters of public concern. They altered the perception of the Soviet Union, particularly in matters of religion. The issues they raised and the debate that followed in the WCC also had wider ramifications in political circles both within and outside the Soviet Union.

Rocking the Boat

In Moscow, the reaction was swift and condemnatory of how certain political factions in the Nairobi Assembly had treated representatives of the Soviet Union.

Metropolitan Nikodim, the second-highest-ranking member of the church hierarchy, spearheaded the defense of the state's policies. Yakunin must have known that church officials would stand behind the Soviet state. As the British historian Jane Ellis notes, the church had sided with the state, rather than with the clergy's desire to speak out for church autonomy a decade earlier in response to the letters Yakunin and Nikolai Eshliman sent to the patriarch.[46] Patriarch Aleksii I, in 1965, like Metropolitan Yuvenalii in Nairobi, had chosen not to rock the boat in the interest of preserving what few privileges the church possessed.

At the Nairobi Assembly, the delegates elected Metropolitan Nikodim president of the WCC; he was well-known among them for his major role in supporting the ecumenical movement and advancing Soviet goals within it. Raised in the aggressive atmosphere of Stalin's Russia, he did not see the church as an autonomous institution and favored the total subordination of the church to the state. In February 1976, Metropolitan Nikodim gave an interview with the English-language newspaper *Moscow News* in which he presented his views—and by extension, those of the church hierarchy—of the events that had taken place in Nairobi.[47] Some groups in the leadership of the previous WCC, he asserted, had sought to make the "persecution of religion" in the USSR and in other socialist states a primary issue in the Nairobi meetings, as a means of denigrating them: "Certain circles indirectly connected with the Nairobi staff, tried to create an Anti-Soviet atmosphere at and around the Assembly, speculating on certain factors pertaining to the understanding and interpretation of the problems of human rights and religious freedom."[48] Although some delegates approved of the claims that Yakunin and Regel'son had made, the large majority, Metropolitan Nikodim said, appeared unconcerned; rather than rely on conjectures made by the two discontented Russians, most of the delegates, he maintained, took a more "objective approach," relying on the testimonies of religious believers throughout the Soviet Union and socialist countries elsewhere.

In his interview, Metropolitan Nikodim portrayed the issues advanced by Yakunin and Regel'son as politically motivated. "Reactionary forces in the West," he said, aspired to "cast a shadow on the Soviet Union and other socialist countries." Nikodim described their ultimate aim as an effort to undermine the peace process to which the Soviet Union had committed itself. He argued that the Soviet Union had signed the Helsinki Accords in order to promote world peace, which certain political interests in Western Europe and the United States did not support. They planned, before the Nairobi sessions began, to disrupt the proceedings by deliberately plotting to raise an issue that was not on the program's agenda.

Metropolitan Nikodim characterized Yakunin and Regel'son as two biased, opinionated individuals who had a superficial, misconceived view of the relationship between church and state. In his defense of the state, Metropolitan Nikodim's own understanding of this relationship became evident. Although he was a church leader, he perceived the church as little more than a body of believers without any legal standing. It had no claim to equal partnership with the state. Its authority was always limited: it operated within its own sphere of interest, and nowhere did those interests take precedence over those of the state. As loyal citizens of the country, believers should not, for any reason, either challenge or transgress the laws established by the state. This understanding, he said, corresponded to the common view of the truth—that is, "the Russian Orthodox Church is carrying on its activities in parishes, divinity schools, and monasteries absolutely unhindered, within the limits, naturally, of the existing laws of our country."[49]

In his public statement, Metropolitan Nikodim disregarded both the relevance of canon law and the sanctity of individual conscience. Growing up during the early Stalin years and being educated in the Moscow Ecclesiastical Academy, like many other church officials of his generation, he identified the prosperity of the state with the well-being of the Orthodox Church. As he emphasized in his interview, those who claimed to be victims of religious persecution were people who, in reality, had violated state laws. Nikodim cited the many examples of visitors to the Soviet Union who testified to the flourishing state of the Orthodox Church; they told a different story, he said, from the one that Yakunin and Regel'son had fabricated.[50]

The publication of the interview with Metropolitan Nikodim is curious. Its appearance in an English-language newspaper and its timing, shortly after the Nairobi meetings, raise questions about the political motivations underlying the metropolitan's accusations—and perhaps also the pressure he felt. He wrote primarily to an international, rather than a Russian, audience. Since the appeal had been written by an Orthodox priest and a layperson, rather than by two people outside the church, the charges they made had to be taken seriously. The accusations of Yakunin and Regel'son, made in an international setting, required a severe response. As Jane Ellis notes, the publication of the interview with a high-ranking church official offered clear evidence of the church hierarchy's need "to disown publicly the 'two dissidents.'"[51]

What Is to Be Done?

In England, the issues raised by Yakunin and Regel'son touched off a lively, contentious, many-sided debate. In some quarters of the British establishment, bringing forth the question of religious freedom at the time appeared unwise.

Détente was still in its infancy, and the Soviet Union's engagement with England and others in Western Europe needed to progress further, without the threat of Soviet withdrawal over religious liberty. Foreign relations officials generally agreed with Pope Paul VI's *ostpolitik*, the importance of keeping open political doors to the East, rather than closing them over problems like the persecution of religious believers. Such difficulties represented internal matters, in which Western countries should not become entangled.[52] What, then, was the most appropriate course of action to take?

The question invited much discussion that was sometimes heated. The East-West Relations Committee of the British Council of Churches, under the skilled guidance of Rev. John Arnold, a Russian speaker, debated the issue. Arnold invited speakers from all sides to participate and hosted an open exchange of views about the meaning and scope of religious liberty. The committee's main goal was to strengthen the channels of communication between governments and religious believers in East and West. It viewed the cultivation of these relationships as the best way to deal with contentious matters.[53] Elsewhere, however, not every group looked with favor upon organizations that reached out to persecuted individuals in the Soviet Union and Eastern Europe and interpreted these efforts as politically motivated intentional distortions of realities in the Soviet Union. Erich Weingartner, of the WCC's affiliated Commission of the Churches on International Affairs, published a report on *Human Rights on the Ecumenical Agenda*, in which he argued that the Western focus on religious liberty and human rights in Eastern Europe represented a weapon that intensified the Cold War.[54] Christians who engaged in such actions, according to Weingartner, participated in "pious denunciations from a safe distance" which "are not only ineffective ... but mask a certain hypocrisy."[55] Why, Weingartner asked, did the United States and Great Britain devote such extensive attention to religious persecution in the USSR, while they showed much less concern with equal violations of human dignity in apartheid South Africa and American massacres in Vietnam?[56] Other prominent church leaders refused to accept the accusations of religious persecution that Yakunin and Regel'son cited. They asserted that these accounts deliberately distorted the realities of communism. For example, the Rev. B. O. Fielding Clarke disparaged Yakunin and Regel'son with the following words: "I *do* regard the letter of the dissidents to the World Council of Churches in 1975 at Nairobi not only as Anti-Soviet propaganda, but as an attack on the whole position of Patriarch Pimen and of the Russian Church as regards the State."[57]

In England, however, one organization dedicated itself to being what it called the "voice of the voiceless."[58] Founded by Canon Michael Bourdeaux, Leonard Schapiro, and Peter Reddaway, Keston College served as a significant research institution that monitored religious persecution in the communist world. Supported primarily by private donations, Keston engaged in a wide range of research related to religious liberty and church-state relations. It published a journal, *Religion in Communist Lands*, edited by the Russian specialist, Xenia Howard-Johnston (Dennen), which featured articles by leading international scholars, as well as samizdat publications from the Soviet Union.[59] Although occasionally accused of being an instrument of Cold War politics, Keston's contributions to opening up a wider public discussion on religious liberty, human rights, and the problems identified by Yakunin and Regel'son were undeniable.

Not only in England but also in the United States the persecution of religious believers in the USSR attracted a great deal of interest. The House of Representatives in the US Congress convened meetings on the subject, delegating further study to the Committee on International Relations. The committee, in turn, appointed two subcommittees to hold special hearings. On June 24 and 30, 1976, the Subcommittees on International Political and Military Affairs and on International Organizations of the Committee on International Relations met jointly to hear from experts and make recommendations on how the US government should proceed. The issues raised by Yakunin and Regel'son in Nairobi, the persecution of individual believers, and the alleged violations of the Helsinki Accords combined to make them major issues in how the US government viewed its relationship with the Soviet Union.[60]

Donald M. Fraser, a Democratic congressman from Minnesota, presided over the hearings, which heard from leading experts on the Soviet Union. They included Bohdan R. Bociurkiw, a professor in the Department of Political Science at Carleton College; Yanis Smits, chair of the Council of Churches of Evangelical Christians and Baptists and a former prisoner in the Soviet Union; John Dunlop, a professor in the Russian, East European, Eurasian Studies Department at Oberlin College; and Alexei A. Kiselev, a professor in the Slavic Department at the University of Pittsburgh, who represented the Committee for the Defense of Persecuted Orthodox Christians.[61] The subcommittees and Committee on International Organizations, therefore, heard both from top scholars and from people who had intimate experience with the subject under investigation. The case of a Soviet citizen, Georgi Vins, stood at the top of the agenda. His example fit well into the framework that Yakunin and Regel'son had outlined in their appeal.

In the mid-1970s, Georgi Vins became a well-known name in the United States. He was the son of an American Baptist missionary of Russian origin, Peter Vins, who had once pastored a church in Pittsburgh that had a large number of Russian immigrants. While there, he heard a call to do missionary work in Russia, and, in 1926, he left the United States for Siberia. There, a year later, he married Lydia Zharikova, and in 1928, she gave birth to their son, Georgi.

During Stalin's assault on religion in the early 1930s, the Soviet authorities revoked Peter Vins's American citizenship, arrested him, subsequently freed him, and then arrested him again. In 1936, he was executed. Following her husband's death, Lydia Vins took Georgi and his siblings to Kyiv, where she raised them alone. There, Georgi completed his schooling, specializing in electrical engineering, and while working in Kyiv, he fell in with a group of Baptists. In 1962, although he had no formal theological training, Georgi Vins was ordained as a Baptist evangelist. His ordination took place during Nikita Khrushchev's antireligion campaign, which compelled religious organizations that remained open to follow stringent state requirements and prohibited parents from teaching religion to their children. Vins refused to comply, maintaining that Christ's commandments superseded the laws of the state.

Vins became the pastor of a breakaway Baptist congregation that met secretly in the forest outside Kyiv. Passionate, a dynamic speaker, and a pastor who demonstrated warmth and care for his people, Vins rapidly gained a reputation as a tireless spokesperson of the "initsiativniki," or "Reformed Baptists," which had separated from registered Baptists and refused to comply with the requirements for registration and other state commands.

Vins also drew the scrutiny of the KGB. In May 1965, the Reformed Baptists held a large demonstration outside the offices of the Central Committee of the Communist Party in Moscow in protest of the laws restricting the church. Arrests followed, and when Vins and two other leaders went to police headquarters to inquire about the fate of the protesters, the police arrested them, too, and a trial followed, with Vins receiving a three-year prison sentence. After serving his prison term, Vins resumed his pastor's role, again holding underground services, meeting in the fields and forests near Kyiv. He became a major voice speaking for "freedom of conscience," as guaranteed in the Constitution, and instituted a long series of appeals in defense of prisoners in the Soviet Union. In March 1974, he was again arrested, which prompted a vigorous protest on Vins's behalf by the human rights activist Andrei Sakharov, who called for support from the World Council of Churches. The WCC was slow to respond. Vins was tried in Kyiv in January 1975 and sentenced to five years in prison, to be followed by five years of internal exile. After the trial, Baptist women in Russia created the Council of Prisoner's Relatives which publicized Vins's case around the world. He became, in the historian Felix Corley's words, "the Soviet Union's most famous religious prisoner."[62]

In their appeal to the Nairobi Assembly, Yakunin and Regel'son referred to Vins's case. They cited the international support for Vins and how the Reformed

Baptists' advocacy for the cause had inspired them and given them hope that sympathizers would pursue a similar course with others who freely practiced their religious beliefs.[63] The case of Georgi Vins presented the congressional subcommittees with an immediate, compelling example of an assault on religious liberty, illustrating the precise charges that Yakunin and Regel'son had made in Nairobi. For the subcommittees' members who had little knowledge of the Soviet Union, the key issue concerned the context in which the Soviet government acted. They sought to better understand the motivations and rationale governing its religious policies.

At the beginning of the hearings, the chair recognized Representative John H. Buchanan from the state of Arkansas, who had introduced a bill in Congress demanding Georgi Vins's release from prison. Representative Buchanan announced that the bill had gained support from more than one hundred members of Congress, who called for the Soviet Union to respect its vow of commitment to religious liberty.[64] The United States, he emphasized, needed to use "all the moral persuasion at our command" to enhance the rights of citizens as guaranteed in their Constitution.[65] To that end, the subcommittees should seek to understand not the words of leaders but the realities of the Soviet Union.

Following Buchanan's introductory remarks, the chair called Professor Bociurkiw as the first witness. A native of Western Ukraine, Bociurkiw earned his doctoral degree in political science at the University of Chicago. A distinguished scholar and teacher, he was foremost an expert on church-state relations, domestic politics in the Soviet Union, political dissent, and the Ukrainian Autocephalous Church (1921), whose legitimacy the Russian Orthodox Patriarchate refused to recognize. He placed his statement to the subcommittees in the framework of how he understood the actions of the Soviet state. He argued that the Communist Party ought to be interpreted not so much as being a secular and rational authority, but as "occupying a position once reserved for an established religion and church."[66] The governing apparatus represented, in Bociurkiw's view, a "state church" with its own set of beliefs, doctrines, rituals, and codes of proper conduct. The party politicized its faith and saw the world exclusively through the lens of that faith.[67] Turning Marxism into a dogmatic faith, he argued, constituted the only way in the Soviet Union that the leaders could consolidate and maintain their hold on power. This "state church" evolved into a political-religious order that sought control over the values and beliefs of its citizens. It waged war on other belief systems that fell outside the Soviet political-religious order, because other faiths challenged or repudiated the legitimacy of this order.

Although Bociurkiw did not specifically call critics of the established church "heretics," his words suggested that Soviet political leaders considered dissenting views as heretical. The leaders viewed Russian Orthodoxy and other faiths as hostile ideologies that obstructed the political-religious order they wanted to create, and thus as threats. They could not totally destroy the Orthodox Church and other religious bodies, but they could force them to register with the state, and through registration, they could control the behavior of these diverse religious bodies. Leaders did not tolerate groups that refused to comply by taking an independent road. Thus, in the Soviet Union, as the perceptive Orthodox writer Anatolii Levitin-Krasnov pointed out, a "strange paradox" existed: "a state church within a system of an atheist state," a situation in which the government acted as the protector of the state church against its own freethinkers and dissenters.[68]

According to Bociurkiw, church dissenters fell into three generations, each of which had its own distinguishing characteristics. The oldest emerged in the 1920s among groups that formed around Patriarch Tikhon, and then later among priests who refused to accept Metropolitan Sergei's declaration of loyalty in 1927. The middle generation of dissenters came into existence following World War II; the government labeled them "bourgeois nationalist" or "anti-Soviet." The youngest generation arose in opposition to Khrushchev's extensive antireligion campaign from 1959 to 1964. The last group benefited from Stalin's earlier revival of the church as well as the loosening of some restrictions on thought after Stalin's death.[69] Preeminent among the dissenter priests was Fr. Gleb Yakunin. The letters he and Nikolai Eshliman sent to Patriarch Aleksii I and Chairman Podgorny, and, a decade later, the letter he and Lev Regel'son wrote to the Nairobi Assembly represented direct challenges to the ideology and practices of the Soviet regime. In the eyes of the authorities, the freedom of religion Yakunin and his associates advocated threatened to undermine the existing political-religious order. In response, as Bociurkiw noted, the state and church authorities swiftly retaliated.[70]

In his analysis of trends in politics and religion, Bociurkiw missed the opportunity to discuss the groups of young people who gathered in Moscow, Leningrad, and other cities in the 1970s. Dissatisfied with the ideology of the state and the practices of the Orthodox Church, they sought a new moral center for themselves. As described in chapter 3, the existence of these groups and the rapid spread of their writings deeply worried the state authorities, who fervently worked to suppress them.

Next, the subcommittees called Professor Dunlop to testify. A specialist in the politics of religion, Dunlop had only recently begun his academic career.

Unlike Bociurkiw whose approach concerned the ideological framework of the Soviet state, Dunlop focused on the laws. He offered a wide-ranging, factual account of the Soviet state's efforts to "extirpate all religious 'survivals' from the Russian earth."[71]

Although the Soviet Constitution of 1918 had decreed the separation of church and state, the understanding of this division, Dunlop maintained, differed from its usage in the United States. In the Soviet Union, the laws had a hidden agenda in which they might only have seemed to protect the church from state encroachment, but in reality, they enabled the assault on all religious institutions. The 1918 legislation put an end to all parochial schools, church-sponsored homes for the elderly, church-funded hospitals, and parish libraries, all of which the government determined were hostile to the population.[72] This legislation served as a prelude to what soon turned into massive assaults on monasteries and convents, closures of Orthodox Churches, and executions of bishops and priests. As Dunlop noted, they were what Yakunin and Regel'son had emphasized in their "Appeal" to the Nairobi Assembly and their March 6, 1976, letter to the WCC general-secretary Philip Potter, in which they emphasized the discrepancy between a literal reading of the laws and "lawlessness under the guise of law."[73]

Dunlop's testimony about the obstacles to belief highlighted a central argument Yakunin and Regel'son had made earlier. According to the two writers of the Nairobi "Appeal," state policies severely restricted the opportunities for the intellectual growth of the Soviet citizen. These policies confined the mind to a narrowly defined framework. In his presentation, Professor Dunlop expanded on the practical consequences of these policies. In the educational system, in which the entire curriculum was based on "scientific atheism," students who questioned the premises of this paradigm or advanced an alternative way of thinking suffered a severe reproach, including ridicule from teachers.[74] People who desired to enter the priesthood also had little opportunity to receive the education they needed. In a country that once had thriving theological institutions, most of them had closed; only two ecclesiastical academies and three closely monitored seminaries remained, thus severely limiting the future theological capacity of the Russian priesthood. All these were consequences of the state's commitment to extirpating religion.

The congressional subcommittees spent the remainder of the sessions hearing from other witnesses. They included Janis Smit, a Latvian Catholic priest who had recently emigrated because, he said, "the Soviet government prohibited his pastoral activities," and David D. Klassen, whom the Soviet police had arrested four times and confined for ten years in prison and psychiatric clinics. Both former Soviet citizens gave personal accounts of their struggles with the authorities. In Smit's case, his troubles developed with the state's control of the Union of Evangelical Christians and Baptists, which prevented the "restoration of Christian and Biblical normalcy in the life of the church."[75] Like Smit, Klassen asked the US Congress to give moral support to the plight of religious believers in the Soviet Union. Although they did not refer directly to Yakunin and Regel'son's appeal, their testimony confirmed the charges of state persecution that Yakunin and Regel'son had made. Smit and Klassen made passionate appeals for the help of the United States government, claiming that such assistance offered the only hope for them and other Soviet citizens who suffered for their religious beliefs.

The statements of all the spokespeople the subcommittees summoned invited questions about how the United States should best respond as well as about the long-term health of the Orthodox Church in the Soviet Union. First, did the United States or any other country have the right to interfere in the internal jurisdiction of the USSR? Professor Bociurkiw argued that they had earned this right when the USSR abrogated the international agreements it had signed. Certain moral issues such as human rights constituted universal and inalienable rights, to which the USSR had committed itself. Did these agreements, Bociurkiw asked, have one meaning for international public relations and another meaning for internal practices?[76] Second, did the development of détente require overlooking the violations of human rights and religious liberty? Members of the subcommittees agreed that these policies should be connected rather than perceived separately. Progress in détente with the Soviet Union needed to correspond to support for human rights and religious liberty, and the United States ought to demand their convergence.

Third, and perhaps most important, since the late 1920s Orthodox leaders had made many compromises, rationalizing their collaboration with government officials as necessary to preserve what they could of their faith. It had been said sarcastically that Orthodox clergy "hold no secrets from God and no secrets from Soviet authorities."[77] Therefore, they resorted to distortions of the truth, to "lying" to their flock, they maintained, "for Christ's sake."[78] What consequences did these compromises have for the well-being of the church as an institution? As Professor Bociurkiw said in his report, the distortions undermined trust in the official church, and when people saw what they did or the profligate lifestyles of members of the church hierarchy, they lost faith in one of the church's most important attributes—its integrity.[79] He reiterated the argument Yakunin and Regel'son had made in their letter to Dr. Potter on March 6, 1976: "It is not surprising that, seeing the apparent helplessness of Christianity in the face of the militant and advancing spirit of violence and falsehood, many Christians are saying even now: 'Who is like unto the beast?

and who is able to make war with him? (Rev. 13:4).'"⁸⁰ Falsehood had weakened the church's capacity to defend itself against state persecution. By distorting truth, church officials had undermined their moral authority.

Members of the congressional subcommittees knew that they had little power to affect change. Yet they vowed to maximize their concerns about the difficulties of religious believers in the Soviet Union.⁸¹ They pledged support for Voice of America and Radio Liberty, radio outlets that the two former Soviet prisoners said were extremely important as news sources of inspiration to many Soviet citizens. The subcommittees' members also learned that congressional interest in religious believers provided encouragement to people who suffered from state persecution.⁸² The members voiced agreement with the resolution that called for the release of Georgi Vins from prison.⁸³ The hearings brought greater recognition of the predicament of religious believers in the USSR, and they exposed the moral challenges that violations of international laws entailed.

Although neither Fr. Gleb Yakunin nor Lev Regel'son were physically present at the congressional hearings or at the WCC Assembly in Nairobi, they closely followed the proceedings of both. They saw even more clearly than ever the importance of information about specific cases of state abuses and violations of the laws. Yakunin knew well that, in pursuit of his goals, he confronted a powerful political machine whose own use of the media presented a major structural obstacle. How to bring to light concrete evidence of violations of freedom of conscience and to give them wider publicity became daunting tasks. Most important, the WCC meetings and US congressional hearings brought home to him an issue that needed much more attention: the conflict between the laws and the religious-political ideology of the state, laws that served not as a cover for government oppression, but as instruments for moral authority and social justice. In Fr. Gleb's case, the confrontation between these indomitable forces would become the central focus of his life.

CHAPTER 5

Gleb Yakunin, Henry Dakin, and the Defense of Religious Liberty

On a cold, gray afternoon in late December 1976, Fr. Gleb Yakunin and two of his associates held a press conference in a Moscow apartment. The purpose of the meeting was to announce the formation of a small group they called the Christian Committee for the Defense of Believers' Rights in the USSR. They proclaimed that the organization had no political goals whatsoever.[1] Its sole purpose was to better the lives of religious believers, and it aimed neither to violate nor subvert, but to act within the laws of the state. Foreign and Soviet journalists attended the press conference that afternoon. It also attracted the attention of the KGB, which, for more than a year, had been monitoring Fr. Gleb's activities. He had already provoked new KGB suspicions the previous year by the letter he and the physicist Lev Regel'son had written to delegates of the World Council of Churches. The creation of this new committee, despite the priest's public claims, invited the further watchfulness of the security police.

Although Fr. Gleb asserted the Christian Committee's benign, noncontroversial intentions, they could easily be interpreted as political. Members of the committee aimed to document violations of human rights in the USSR. At a time when local government officials often arbitrarily applied the laws, acts of recording and publicizing those infractions, in the eyes of state officials, amounted to political pursuits. As its charter read, the Christian Committee intended "to gather, analyze, and distribute information," to advise religious believers of their rights, to appeal to the government when those rights had been violated, and, fundamentally, to help with "strengthening Soviet laws on religion."[2] If conducted well, the collection, analysis, and distribution of information promised to open a wide window on the concrete realities of religious life. No longer would the government control the narrative about freedom of religion. A different picture thus had the potential to emerge.

The Christian Committee's work raises several basic questions about the intended audience for its work and whether it had in mind state officials, the rumor mills of provincial Russia, or a much wider, even international public. Should it seek the latter course, the Christian Committee would have to establish a network of sympathetic people who would help make their desires into realities. In December 1976, such a network did not exist. Until his arrest on November 1, 1979, Fr. Gleb's committee collected a massive amount of information about the those had been persecuted and disinherited. To members of the World Council of Churches, who had taken Fr. Gleb's words lightly at the Nairobi meeting in 1975, the committee's materials challenged their earlier conceptions and led to a rethinking of freedom of conscience and its repressors. In pushing his endeavors further, Fr. Gleb had the support of his young family, which in 1976, in addition to his wife Iraida, included two children, Mariia and Aleksandr (figure 5.1).

Russian historians often emphasize the significance of the Christian Committee in the reawakening of Russian religious consciousness. Mikhail Vital'evich Shkarovskii's seminal history of the Orthodox Church in the twentieth century cited the committee as a major example of the "flourishing Orthodox dissidence" in the late 1970s.[3] Dimitry Pospielovsky noted the committee's collection of data on religious persecution that circulated in samizdat, some of which made its way to the West via Western correspondents.[4] The British historian Jane Ellis emphasized the special role the committee played in defending religious believers; it was the one body that tried to protect them against state persecution.[5] These studies provide valuable insights into the workings of Yakunin's committee and place them in the context of the Soviet era. But they do not tell the full story of Yakunin's work and how the information the committee gathered became widespread. This historical background gives greater depth to a story heretofore scantily known.

First, the identity of the committee's leaders further exemplified the religious awakening then developing among certain members of Russian society in the 1970s. The founders consisted of Fr. Gleb Yakunin, Hierodeacon Varsonofi Khaibulin, and Viktor Kapitanchuk, the latter an Orthodox layperson. A brief word about each of them will help explain their commitment. In 1976, Fr. Gleb Yakunin, the Christian Committee's chief spokesperson, was forty-

FIGURE 5.1. Yakunin and family, mid-1970s. From left to right, daughter Mariia, son Aleksandr, Yakunin, and wife Iraida Georgievna. Courtesy of the Keston Center for Religion, Politics, and Society, Baylor University, Waco, Texas.

two years old. Among intellectual circles around Moscow, he already had a growing reputation as a defender of religious liberty. Hierodeacon Varsonofi Khaibulin served on the committee for only a year before his transfer to a parish in the Vladimir region, at which time Vadim Shcheglov replaced him.[6] Viktor Kapitanchuk was a thirty-two-year-old chemist who worked in an art restoration institute in Moscow. Earlier, while a student, he had visited Fr. Aleksandr Men's parish in the nearby town of Tarasovka and had become a regular participant.[7] Kapitanchuk's friend Tat'iana Lebedeva described him as an extremely intelligent person who had "little concern with church ceremonies, but much interest in how to understand faith, and he raised many questions about it."[8] He served as secretary of the Christian Committee.

Vadim Shcheglov was a forty-six-year-old layperson when he joined the committee after Khaibulin's departure. Shcheglov, a mathematician, was employed by the Ministry of Health. He had not grown up as a religious believer and, as a young man, had scant concern with matters of faith. But his entire life changed after his fortuitous reading of a book written by Metropolitan Anthony (Bloom) of Sourozh. No longer did he remain a passive observer of state persecution of religious believers.⁹ In the Christian Committee, he found like-minded associates who voiced similar concerns about what they considered a primary human right.

Second, the Christian Committee's creation had a close relationship to the origins of another significant organization formed earlier that same year in Moscow. On May 12, 1976, at the home of Andrei Sakharov, Elena Bonner (Sakharov's wife), the physicist Yuri Orlov, and fellow human rights activists announced the inception of the Moscow Helsinki Monitoring Group. The goal of their group, Orlov proclaimed, was "to inform the heads of the signatory states, as well as the world public, about direct violations of the Helsinki Accords."[10]

In Point 7 of what is known as the Helsinki Accords' Final Act, all signers of the diplomatic accord committed to "respect human rights and fundamental freedoms, including freedom of thought, conscience, religion or belief, for all without distinction as to race, sex, language, or religion." The group of Russian dissidents saw the statement on human rights as an opportunity to hold the Soviet government accountable. Members of the Moscow Group invited Soviet citizens to notify them about abuses that interfered with "their fundamental freedoms" as stated in the Helsinki Accords which the Soviet Union had signed in 1976.[11]

Yuri Orlov sympathized with Fr. Gleb's efforts to address religious persecution, and the two became friends. Orlov had reached out to Fr. Gleb and asked him to join the Moscow Group, but the priest declined, telling Orlov he hoped to create a parallel organization that focused specifically on freedom of conscience.[12] Although the Helsinki Accords advocated freedom of conscience and thought for all regardless of their religious beliefs, race, sex, or language, Fr. Gleb saw freedom of conscience as the basis for all other human rights. From it came freedom of thought and speech and the core principle of human dignity.[13] When the state violated spiritual freedom, it also abused the core of human identity and purpose. This was a belief that may well have come from Nikolai Berdiaev's *Philosophy of Freedom*, which Fr. Gleb admired and to which he returned repeatedly throughout his life.[14] Although the Christian Committee remained an independent organization, it had close coordination with the Helsinki group, channeling materials to Sakharov and supporting his work.[15]

The leadership of the Christian Committee consisted exclusively of Orthodox members, yet it announced its intention to speak for all religious believers in the Soviet Union, seemingly a contradiction between its membership and its stated purposes. In explaining this discrepancy, Yakunin addressed the church's guilt. Throughout much of its history, he said, the Russian Ortho-

FIGURE 5.2. From left to right, Lev Regel'son, Fr. Gleb Yakunin, and Viktor Kapitanchuk, mid-1970s. Courtesy of the Keston Center for Religion, Politics, and Society, Baylor University, Waco, Texas.

dox Church viewed itself as superior to other faiths; it had a long tradition of trying to suppress non-Orthodox denominations. The time had come for the church to rectify its prejudicial behavior (figure 5.2). Fr. Gleb and his associate Viktor Kapitanchuk, as well as others, including Lev Regel'son, needed "to redress these historical wrongs and come to the defense of believers of all denominations," a responsibility Yakunin viewed as an obligation.[16]

The committee's files contained a large number of letters from grassroots religious organizations and people, many of them addressed to Patriarch Pimen. They beseeched the reigning high priest of the church to hear their cries of distress; many others, coming from all over the Soviet Union, told the stories of individuals and families whose appeals to local courts about grievances had not met with what they considered to be just responses.[17] Originally, many of the documents assembled by Yakunin's committee circulated in samizdat in the Soviet Union. Taken as a whole, they represented an uncoordinated, chaotic assortment of letters and petitions. The Christian Committee's contribution was to put the documents together into a full set of materials that told a story of religious life and the struggles to preserve freedom of conscience in diverse communities throughout the country. In some cases, Yakunin's committee appealed to the relevant authorities to redress the grievances, but it also sent these materials across national boundaries. They ultimately reached California in the United States, where they were published and circulated in parts of the Western world in multiple copies, which surreptitiously reentered the Soviet Union. In the United States, they found an unusually entrepreneurial publisher who exhibited a willingness to venture beyond his familiar environs to forge a relationship with Yakunin's committee in Moscow. He was Henry Dakin of San Francisco.

Henry Dakin and Breaking the Boundaries of the Cold War

At first glance, Henry Saltonstall Dakin, a San Francisco entrepreneur, appeared to be an unlikely candidate to forge a relationship with Fr. Gleb Yakunin. A soft-spoken, gentle, middle-aged father, he had earned a reputation as an innovative, forward-looking professional who prized people, took risks, and looked beyond the everyday circumstances of life. He sought to better the world, and he had confidence that with hard work and creativity, this goal could be achieved.

Henry Dakin and Gleb Yakunin were about the same age, the former born on December 6, 1936, in Los Angeles, and the latter two years earlier, in Moscow. Both men had a keen interest in the sciences—Dakin in physics, Yakunin in biology—and they had lifelong interests and curious, inquisitive minds that ranged widely across numerous fields. Each left home for university education. Dakin attended Harvard University, where, in addition to his physics major, he developed an interest in the Soviet Union and took elective courses in Russian history and literature.[18] Yakunin, as described earlier, studied at a zoological institute in Irkutsk, Siberia, before going home to Moscow to prepare for the priesthood. After graduation, Dakin returned to California, where he went to work at the Lawrence Berkeley National Laboratory in San Francisco in the growing field of health physics.[19]

Both Dakin and Yakunin faced severe personal difficulties shortly after beginning their careers. In 1966, Patriarch Aleksii I's suspension of Yakunin from the priesthood had severely cut short his future plans. Dakin confronted traumatic personal tragedy. On Christmas Day 1966, the private plane carrying Henry Dakin's father and mother, his older brother and wife, and four of his brother's five children crashed in Baja, California, killing all eight family members.[20] The air disaster left Henry Dakin bereft of most of his family, the touchstones of his existence and the sources of support on which he had heretofore relied. The catastrophe irrevocably changed the course of his life.

"Henry believed that the only good purpose of money was to put it to good use," and "he never valued money for its own sake," his sister Susanna said.[21] Dakin had no interest in expanding his inherited fortune, but his inheritance enabled him to pursue new directions in his life. Opening an office on Washington Street in the Pacific Heights area of San Francisco, he involved himself in cutting-edge projects that spanned the fields of philosophy, psychology, and technology. He attracted young scientists and entrepreneurs, many of whom had little capital but whom Dakin perceived as having innovative minds, people who needed support to put their ideas into practice. "I have a feeling Henry blundered into what he was doing about fourteen years ago, when he began giving a haven to creative-waifs who had no money or place to go," observed Willis Harman, a Stanford University professor and director of the Institute of Noetic Sciences in the late 1980s.[22]

Dakin cut an imposing figure intellectually, but not physically. He was of medium height and build with a thick head of hair, which turned silver in his middle years. "He liked to laugh, which he did often," his daughter Adriana later described. "He had a dry sense of humor, enjoyed physical activity," and loved to play with his three daughters. "He often took us with him to his office, and allowed us to play on the technological equipment. He loved his work, but he found time for us."[23] Intellectually, Dakin had a brilliant mind and a passion for learning, which he retained all his life. He had a "ceaseless wonder for things new and unusual," said a close friend and collaborator, and he "provided essential and often hidden support for individuals who demonstrated those same qualities."[24]

Henry Dakin believed the future required the building of relationships that brought people of diverse backgrounds, skills, and interests more closely together. Politically, he lived at a time when nations and individuals were rigidly separated, a time marked by the peril of nuclear confrontation and military conflict. Scientifically, in contrast, Dakin worked in an Einsteinian universe characterized by the rapid disintegration of boundaries once held to be immutable. How to bring similar ways of thinking from the sciences to politics and to relationships between people fascinated him.

In the late 1970s, the threat of nuclear annihilation had reached a crescendo, heightened by harsh rhetoric emanating from both American and Soviet political leaders, who appeared unable to resolve the issues that engulfed their citizenry. "It was then," recalled Jim Hickman, who worked with Dakin, "that Henry became convinced of the power of individuals, not working through cumbrous bureaucracies, to more effectively deal with dilemmas" confronting the two countries. "He thought that individuals had to take responsibility for the fate of the world."[25]

International contacts, as Dakin later said, offered the chance to "break down walls," because "there is mental suffocation that comes from not having contact with the rest of the world."[26] He thought that direct communication between people offered the most effective means of overcoming boundaries, sharing information, and creating the conditions for world peace.[27] In the 1970s, Dakin began publishing materials from Soviet scientists, especially physicists and those in the burgeoning fields of physics and parapsychology. He learned about samizdat, the unofficial self-publishing industry that had rapidly developed in the Soviet Union since the late 1960s. Samizdat had opened a clear pathway to the ideas and aspirations of the Russian people, who found a means of self-expression that circumvented the government, as Dakin, too, found a new channel for disseminating information.[28] The documents of Fr. Gleb Yakunin's Christian Committee for the Defense of Believers' Rights stood at the top of Henry Dakin's nascent publishing activity.

The documents, however, first needed to reach Dakin's San Francisco office. As it did in the case of other materials issued in samizdat, the Soviet government did not sanction publication of the Christian Committee's materials, so they could not be transported through official channels. They had to come via a backdoor network. The Christian Committee had couriers who transported the documents across the borders of the Soviet Union to Western Europe, where they were mailed directly to Dakin's office in San Francisco. The people who courageously risked their own arrest included Natalia Solzhenitsyn, the former wife of Aleksandr Solzhenitsyn; the human rights activist Natalia Khodorovicha; and foreign tourists.[29] Committee members copied the materials on 35mm negative microfilm for transport, and Dakin agreed to publish the documents within three weeks of delivery.[30]

From 1977 to 1980, the years of the Christian Committee's existence, Henry Dakin's Washington Street Research Center published twelve volumes of these documents. Dakin printed them in Russian, with the exception of the third volume, which represented a compendium of selected documents translated into English. Each volume had a summary in English of every document it contained. Taken as a whole, the materials created an intimate portrait of religious life in the Soviet Union that had rarely existed on such a local level since the Russian Revolution. As will be shown later, these publications depicted the arbitrary, often illegal activities of government officials in numerous towns and villages, generally in contravention of the Soviet Constitution. They provided concrete testimony about violations of the international human rights standards that the Soviet government had pledged to uphold. They also offered another side to religious life that readers might not have expected to see.

Abuses of Power

The Christian Committee's files contained many letters beseeching Patriarch Pimen to hear their cries of distress. They discussed abuses of power coming from outside their parishes, but it is also striking to find here letters describing wrongdoing emanating from within the parish. In February 1977, a few months after the committee's creation, a series of letters and petitions from a community in Ukraine, in particular, offered a poignant example of such misbehavior. The story was related by parishioners of the Church of St. Nicholas, in the town of Nikolaev (in southern Ukraine), describing instances of illegal harassment and asking Patriarch Pimen "to help us find justice and truth." They began by relating an incident that took place on November 11, 1976, when "the police, treating us like brigands, burst into the church, cut off the locks everywhere with a blowtorch, and . . . accused the former church assembly of stealing 14 thousand rubles" from local authorities.[31]

The files coming from the Nikolaev Church portrayed a series of actions that had destroyed trust within the parish community. The parishioners attributed most of the disturbances to the behavior of their new head priest, Fr. Pyotr Stryzhik, who had arrived to serve them two years earlier. According to parishioners of the Orthodox Church of St. Nicholas, Fr. Pyotr failed to minister as a caretaker of the parish and a holy father to his flock, but instead acted as someone who looked upon the Orthodox community as his own patrimony. He demanded extra payments from congregants, falsely claiming that they went to paying the church's registration fees. In reality, however, he "put the money in his own pocket."³²

Parishioners described a litany of other abuses attributed to Fr. Pyotr: theft, threats, embezzlement, beatings, curses, embarrassing outbursts against older women, public insults directed at servitors of the church, and immoral acts that he conducted both within the church and on the streets of Nikolaev. When parishioners complained, Fr. Pyotr said, "I am the boss [*khoziain*], and what I wish to do, I will do."³³ The local town representative of the Council for Religious Affairs, identified as Chunikhin, served as Fr. Pyotr's protector. The two formed a close alliance that made any attempt of the parishioners to defend themselves against their priest's barbaric behavior extremely difficult. Chunikhin told members of the parish who complained that if Fr. Pyotr were removed from the parish, he intended to close their church. Upon learning of their plans to write to the authorities in Kyiv or Moscow, Chunikhin replied that he feared neither Kyiv nor Moscow, and despite his threats to put the complainants in jail for five years, they persisted.³⁴ When the parishioners prepared an appeal to higher authorities, the archbishop of the diocese intervened. He ordered them to desist and then, to intimidate their leaders, excommunicated eleven members of the parish, eight of them women.³⁵

Yet the parishioners of St. Nicholas refused to capitulate. They appealed to the Regional Central Executive of the church, and, following that, petitioned the People's Court of the Central Region. Both bodies ignored their requests. In addition, the local government-sponsored radio station and newspaper, *Iuzhnaia Pravda* (Southern Truth), disparaged the parishioners' loyalty, morality, and "political" motivations." The author of the newspaper article branded the parishioners of St. Nicholas Church as religious fanatics who had little regard for church unity. He asserted that they had turned the church into what the local archbishop called "a den of brigands."³⁶ As it turned out, nearly everything appeared allied against the parishioners of St. Nicholas, as if the diocesan and local authorities, the court, and the media had conspired to prevent their pleas from gaining a sympathetic hearing.

Having exhausted all available channels open to them, the parishioners sent two letters to Patriarch Pimen, in which they described many occurrences of harassment in their church community.³⁷ Significantly, the writers of these letters appeared to understand that Pimen had no ability to rectify their grievances. Their words seemed to express either sympathy for him or, more likely, the helplessness of his plight, given the political restrictions under which he operated. Nevertheless, they needed him to hear their pleas and what they hoped would be the path he would take: "Your Holiness," their appeal read, "we know that we cannot ask for your help. We know that it will not be forthcoming, but we ask for one thing only—that you not cover up the lies and hypocritical actions before the whole world. Before the world, it is necessary to make war not with beautiful words, but with the realities. . . . Against the lies, it is necessary to fight. We must not cover ourselves in lies but dress ourselves in the truth. . . . Let the atheists cover themselves in lies. We will stand with the truth."[38]

The patriarch offered no response to the letters. Fr. Gleb and his associates on the Christian Committee, however, heard their cries. The materials in this case served as a major part of the information gathered about the harassment of religious believers, a significant segment of the larger story about truth and falsehood that they wanted to tell.

Fr. Pyotr Stryzhik's degradation of the Russian Orthodox Church in Ukraine did not represent a solitary example. The Christian Committee files included a similar account of profligacy that took place in the Osh community of Tashkent. The Osh parishioners had a head priest, Leonid Demianovich Aleksenko, who for nearly a decade had served in the local Orthodox Church exhibiting behavior that violated nearly every norm of the moral teachings of the church. The Osh parishioners described his brutish actions, drunkenness, and callous treatment of members of the community, especially of older women, whom he regarded with disdain.[39]

The Osh parishioners' letter to the patriarch described numerous acts of Fr. Leonid, which they claimed betrayed the sacrosanct traditions of their church: "At New Year's, during the last four years, our priest, Aleksenko, dragged four-meter-tall fir trees into the church sanctuary, placed them immediately in front of the altar, decorated them with all kinds of baubles, and wired them with bright lights. Everything about them shined and sparkled in the church, while the people who were praying said to themselves, 'Next, we'll probably have a carnival, with dancing, in the church.'"[40]

When inebriated, Aleksenko violated every principle of his sacred oath. His boorish behavior, as members of the Osh community described it, extended beyond the church to his family and to the town. "Our Aleksenko can hold his own against any alcoholic churl on a side street off the market square."[41] They portrayed him as having a corrupt and unprincipled family life, quarreling incessantly with his wife and beating her so that when he is drunk, "she flees their home, leaving the children behind to endure his wrath and abuse."[42] The Osh parishioners had tolerated him long enough: they proposed the defrocking of Fr. Leonid and his transfer to a job in an industrial plant where perhaps he would be able to reform his dissolute behavior. But if this was not possible, they requested that the church move him from their parish to a small, remote town where he would "be able to put less money into his pocket. To put it more simply, our Aleksenko would dry out more quickly in the fresh air."[43]

In their description of Fr. Leonid Aleksenko's behavior, the Osh petitioners intentionally employed extremely harsh language. Some of their complaints about their priest—his public drunkenness, boorish behavior, abuse of his family—should not be taken literally. These accusations exemplified what the historian Stephen Kotkin labeled "Bolshevik speak," in which supplicants, in order to be heard, adopted the language of Bolshevik anti-religious propaganda to express their grievances.[44] Fr. Leonid, however, had likely violated certain norms of the parish and deeply offended the members, and they wanted his removal. In voicing their resentments, the Osh petitioners sought to present themselves as true Soviet citizens, loyal to the state, while simultaneously identifying themselves as religious believers. As did other members of the rural population, in their minds, they saw no difference between being a "Soviet citizen" and being a "religious believer."[45]

Additional examples of the church's appointed leaders reveal the harsh, inhumane qualities of priests' leadership roles. In the Pskov-Caves Monastery, one of Orthodoxy's most venerated treasures, Archimandrite Gavriil, recently named head of the monastery, had created "an oppressive environment for the brethren." According to the nun Anastasiia Kleimionova, Archimandrite Gavriil made the monastery an unwelcome place for pilgrims. Rather than welcome them, he deliberately scorned and turned them away. "We are crucifying our Lord once more; the Mother of God weeps over our iniquities," she asserted in her letter to Patriarch Pimen.[46]

Numerous photographs in the *Journal of the Moscow Patriarchate* show that, in 1970s and 1980s, the majority of worshippers in the Russian Orthodox Church consisted of older women, the famous "babushki"—humble, long-suffering, and among the most poorly educated people in Soviet society.[47] Viewing themselves as protectors of church tradition, they responded with suspicion and outright resentment toward younger priests, newcomers to their parish, who attempted to change the rites of service or introduce new approaches.[48] In their criticisms of Frs. Pyotr Stryzhik, Leonid Aleksenko, and Archimandrite Gavriil, however, their outrage expressed something else. Parishioners were furious that their church no longer provided a sanctuary from social ills and preserved practices they considered inviolable. The images their priests presented undermined the trust and respect for an institution the parishioners viewed as sacred.[49]

Whether the letters and petitions of these and other church communities represent anomalies or more widespread phenomena remain difficult to determine. Yet they evoke questions posed by the Russian historian and essayist Evgenii Barabanov: whether the church itself had a large hand in turning people away from religious belief; and, closely related to this, whether the actions of some religious leaders were among the main instruments that promoted atheism.[50] In their attitudes and behaviors, certain priests did a great deal to convince people that the church was morally bankrupt. Describing the priesthood in general, Yakunin, too, called the interior of church life a "tragic phenomenon."[51] When people came to the church seeking help with the deepest concerns of their lives, they rarely found what they sought. The materials of the Christian Committee provided evidence that Orthodox leaders, according to Barabanov, might have done as much to undermine trust and respect for the church as the prosecutorial agencies of the Soviet state.[52]

Stories of Struggle

Despite the cases of profligate behavior described above, a large number of Orthodox priests served with dignity, remaining true to the mission, tending to the spiritual needs of their flocks, and exhibiting compassion for older people or those with disabilities. Even under pressure from the political authorities, they fulfilled their responsibilities—celebrating the liturgy, providing a sanctuary against the harsh circumstances of life, and paying homage to the beauty and richness of the Orthodox heritage. The materials collected by the Christian Committee contain a wealth of diverse stories of individuals and groups of believers in the former Soviet Union.

These stories depict spiritual quests pursued by individuals and groups of people at great personal cost to their well-being and that of their families. They also offer accounts of their desire for justice, a wish to overcome the large discrepancy between what they perceived as their constitutional rights and what they witnessed in their lives. It was this disparity that Yakunin's committee sought to document, despite the Moscow Patriarchate's and the Soviet government's repeated denials of their veracity. The published materials recount many tales of individuals, the challenging circumstances they encountered, and their struggle to make freedom of conscience a reality. Three cases illustrate these themes: one describing the experience of a Russian Orthodox priest, a second involving the education of children in Lithuania, and a third concerning a recently married young woman in Taganrog.

Lev Konin, the second priest in the Orthodox Church in the city of St. Petersburg (then Leningrad), had had a difficult, trouble-filled life. Born in the Ural city of Ekaterinburg (then Sverdlovsk), the son of a secondary-school teacher, he first studied at a technical institute. There, at the age of sixteen, in 1961, he ran into trouble for the first time after he made some disparaging comments about Khrushchev's twenty-year program to achieve communism in the Soviet Union.[53]

The institute's director expelled him. Afterward, he entered a pedagogical institute, where three years later, in 1964, after witnessing the rector of the institute pocketing the monthly stipends of students, he revealed what he had seen. In a school assembly, in front of the other students, the rector humiliated him. This time, his punishment was more severe than before: the pedagogical institute, in coordination with the local authorities, had Konin committed to a psychiatric hospital. The diagnosis of the hospital specialists was that he suffered from "a paranoid syndrome," which provoked, they said, "delusional and irrational behavior"—that is, behavior that did not conform to the Communist Party's ideological goals.[54] He remained in the psychiatric hospital until July 1965, undergoing "injections and shock treatments" and was released, he said, "when the doctors feared that I would soon die."[55]

Konin's hospital stay did, however, have a positive result. For the first time, he recounted, he began to think seriously about his life's purpose. After his discharge, out of curiosity, he went to the only Orthodox Church in Sverdlovsk, an experience that ultimately led to his desire to be baptized. In the winter of 1965, he said, "I memorized the texts of prayers and read all the atheistic literature and the little spiritual literature that could be found in the city—Dostoevsky, Leskov, separate issues of old journals—and I also began study of the German language," reading and study that persuaded him to seek enrollment in the St. Petersburg Ecclesiastical Seminary.[56]

Konin's life had finally set out on a stable course. In January 1973, he was ordained as an Orthodox priest. He married, started a family, secured a house, and received an appointment as second priest in the Nikolskaia Church in the suburbs of St. Petersburg. After his turbulent earlier years, he felt confident that his personal and professional life had taken an upward turn. But then came a bombshell that shattered his sense of well-being: someone wrote a denunciation about him, and he was removed.[57] Beyond temporarily serving in a Pskov diocese, for the next four years, he did not hold a regular church appointment. In March 1977, a story in the newspaper *Vechernii Leningrad* (Evening Leningrad) brought up new allegations. The newspaper, without offering any evidence, claimed that Fr. Lev was working as a Swedish agent and "deemed him to be a terribly dangerous element of society."[58] The following month, the KGB arrested Fr. Lev and confined him again to a psychiatric hospital.[59]

After his release, he wrote an appeal to the Christian Committee requesting their help in seeking justice. The justice he desired entailed adherence to the Constitution of the USSR, which sanctified the rights of Soviet citizens against capricious, illegal treatment by state authorities. In concert with his appeal, he called for an end to the "psychological torture-chamber," which, he argued, had no place in a just society.[60]

The pursuit of social justice extended to other spheres of life beyond the Orthodox priesthood. In Lithuania, members of the Catholic Church, inspired by Yakunin's committee in Moscow, created a similar organization, the Catholic Committee for the Defense of Believers' Rights. Expressing identical goals, it closely coordinated with Yakunin's group. Its aims included protecting the rights of children.

In September 1978, the Soviet Union hosted an international conference in Moscow devoted to the theme "Towards a Peaceful and Happy Future for All Children." At the conference, which was attended by human rights activists from all over the world, the participants pledged "to defend children from violence in all of its forms."[61] A consensus emerged among the participants about the responsibilities of all nations to guarantee through the laws that children would be protected against all kinds of force.

In Lithuania, the Catholic Committee closely followed the agreements made at the Moscow conference and saw an opportunity to reopen the question of childhood education. In the Lithuanian Soviet Socialist Republic, the Ministry of Education decreed that "from the very first class," the primary goal of pedagogy at all levels must be to inculcate in each schoolchild and in all extracurricular activities "a scientific worldview, in order that each child will grow up as a militant atheist."[62] How was it possible, the Catholic Committee wanted to know, for the state to combine this compulsory goal with the rights of the child, especially with the documents signed in Moscow titled "Towards a Peaceful and Happy Future for All Children?"[63]

The Catholic Committee cited a specific case in which a teacher in Belarus visited the family of one of her students during the summer holidays. While there, she taught the children several prayers and the rudiments of Christianity. An informer learned of her actions and had her arrested, after which the police imposed upon her a monetary fine. A month later, the police charged her with violating the Criminal Code of the Belarusian SSR and placed her in a jail cell "together with the drunks and venereal prisoners."[64] The entire judicial process in this town, the Catholic Committee wrote, demonstrated that children in this republic had "only a single right—to be atheists."

As Fr. Gleb's Christian Committee in Moscow repeatedly asserted, the Catholic Committee in Lithuania emphasized the large gap between actual practices in everyday life and the international agreements the Soviet Union purported to uphold. Compulsion as a means of molding citizens into compliant beings contradicted Soviet public claims about the upbringing of children. The Lithuanian committee members argued that the greatest violence done to children entailed taking away their freedom to worship according to the dictates of their souls. Only by adherence to freedom of conscience, this fundamental human right, could children develop the capacity to create for themselves "a peaceful and bright future."[65]

The third case in the trilogy of disputes concerned a young mother, Tati′ana Ivanovna, who lived in the seaport city of Taganrog on the northern shore of the Sea of Azov. Her story concerned a dispute between a husband and wife and how the authorities, in violation of the laws, discriminated against religious believers.

In 1977, twenty-three-year-old Tat′iana married Sergei Ivanovich Sorokin, a worker and member of the Communist Party. The birthplace of the Russian playwright Anton Chekhov, Taganrog, in the 1970s, had become one of the most important industrial and scientific centers of southern Russia. Although her husband did not want children, she testified, the following year she gave birth to a son. The birth of the child exacerbated difficulties that had already emerged in the marriage. The couple did not have much money, and Sergei Sorokin often came from work drunk, at which time he would berate and sometimes beat his wife. Having few defenses against her husband's abusive behavior, Sorokina sought solace in reading the Gospels and praying for help. Her behavior, which ran counter to her husband's views of what their marriage should be, infuriated him. In July 1978, five months after her baby's birth, her husband forcefully took the child from her and moved back home with his parents. She went to his parents' home, she said, "asked for my baby back, but was driven away, insulted, and struck by my husband."[66]

Sorokina took the only course of action open to her: she filed suit in the district court to reclaim her child.[67] In the court proceedings that followed, Sorokina, desperate to recover the most important part of her life, pled her case as a mother who wished to raise her child and had the capacity to do so responsibly. Her husband argued the reverse, claiming that his wife had not worked since June, resided in a private apartment, and lacked the proper means for the child's upbringing. Asked by the judge to explain his capability for raising the child, Sergei Ivanovich testified that he had a regular job, had adjusted his working hours in order to care for his son, and had the ability to provide everything the child needed. But a key component in the husband's testimony appeared to be his contention that his wife had joined "a sect of Baptists-Pentecostals, to whose meetings she brought the child as well." He claimed he had taken the child away because he "did not wish to have the child brought up in the religious spirit."[68]

The district court denied Sorokina's suit, as did the Rostov Regional Court to which she next appealed. In both instances, the official verdict, which awarded custody of the child to the father, justified the decision by asserting

FIGURE 5.3. From left to right, Varsonofi Khaibulin, Viktor Kapitanchuk, and Fr. Gleb Yakunin, founders of the Christian Committee for the Defense of Believers' Rights in the USSR, 1976. Courtesy of the Keston Center for Religion, Politics, and Society, Baylor University, Waco, Texas.

that the father had all the economic means to give the child a normal upbringing. Although the courts made no mention of Sorokina's religious belief in issuing their verdicts, at every level this played a significant role in the court's denial of the mother's claims. At the first hearing, in the district court, Procurator Riabova, upon learning that Sorokina was a religious believer, expressed outrage and called her an "animal" who "belonged in the woods." According to Sorokina, "they said that they would take my child away because I believed, but in the court decision, they wrote down that it was because I was not working and had no place to live."[69] The father's forcible removal of the child from the mother's care without first going through the proper channels constituted an illegal act. Yet in siding with the father, the courts disregarded this unlawful deed.

In founding the Christian Committee for the Defense of Believers' Rights in the USSR, Varsonofi Khaibulin, Gleb Yakunin, and Viktor Kapitanchuk pledged to bring to light examples of state violations of Soviet citizens' constitutional rights (figure 5.3). Other examples contained in the files of Yakunin's Christian Committee provide specific testimony concerning the persecution of religious believers. In Ukraine, after confessing that she had converted to

Christianity, Valeriia Petrovna Bondarenko, a twenty-five-year-old mother of two, suffered immediate reprisals. Mocked, scolded, and threatened with the loss of her children, she also lost her job and was divorced by her husband. A letter to the Christian Committee from Anna Paul recounted the hardships her family endured following the arrest of her husband, a dentist, in Kochetov, a village in the Briansk district of western Russia. Charging him with disseminating religious propaganda and teaching their children about the Bible, the local court sentenced him to two and a half years in jail and suspended him from his dental practice for an additional three years. Anna Paul appealed her husband's loss of work: "We have three young children—ages from one to seven—and elderly sick parents," she wrote, "and without his income, we lack the means for our survival."[70]

In a communication directed to General Procurator Rudenko, Riazan' Baptists protested the indifference of local authorities to the plight of a fellow believer, Galina Afanas'evna Ivashura who, after confessing her belief in God, suffered several kinds of indignities. Her husband, a police officer, took away from her care their four-year-old son. Pregnant with another child, when she was in the hospital, the police chief installed a fellow police officer in her apartment, leaving her with only one room, yet required her to pay rent for the entire apartment.[71] In a letter addressed to Christians of the Whole World, the Christian Committee, and the Council of Prisoners' Relatives, young Baptist people living in the Zakarpattia district of western Ukraine recounted a gathering of their friends in the forest for prayer and a "peaceful worship service," when about two hundred people from the police and KGB descended upon them. The authorities seized their religious literature, musical instruments, and personal items, before ordering the youth onto a bus, arresting five of their leaders, and imposing fines and forced labor on the rest of them. In addition, the letter writers referred to similar recent attacks against fellow Baptists in Kharkov, Briansk, Omsk, the Central Asia region, and other cities in the Soviet Union.[72]

The documents published by Henry Dakin do not offer a complete picture, especially of religious believers in parishes that operated under the solicitous care of devoted priests, although they, too, functioned under great pressure from state authorities. The Christian Committee's purpose, however, never intended to offer a comprehensive account. The intimate look at abuses coming from outside and within church communities gave much greater depth to the claims he had made in the letter Yakunin and Nikolai Eshliman sent to the patriarch in 1965 and his appeal to the Nairobi Assembly in 1975. They provided the factual evidence for a report Yakunin soon made about the efficacy of the church.

Yakunin's Report

On August 15, 1979, shortly before his arrest, Yakunin issued a major report that represented his overall assessment of the findings drawn from the publication of the Christian Committee's documents.[73] Jane Ellis called Yakunin's paper probably the most important single document issued by the organization.[74] Every aspect of the patriarchal structure had been surveyed, including the patriarch and the church episcopate, the clergy, parish council, parishes, monasteries, seminaries and academies, financial management, and publishing. Yakunin's report analyzed each part and its effectiveness in addressing the spiritual needs of the Russian people. Based on factual evidence, his examination made one other contribution: it lifted the veil on the inner workings of the church previously concealed behind the veneer of political assertions.

A common thread running through every part of the report consisted of the dominating influence of the state in suppressing creativity. Nearly fifteen years earlier, the letter he and Nikolai Eshliman had sent to Patriarch Aleksii I voiced a similar complaint. Yakunin's 1979 report demonstrated the progression of his thinking and also showed how the church had changed, becoming even more stultifying and ineffective than before. In 1965, he and Eshliman had expected a political and religious springtime that would usher in a new administration and new thinking, marking the end of Khrushchev's irrational policies. "Today," Yakunin wrote in 1979, "an icy darkness" enveloped the church, which had chosen to become docile and complaisant, completely under the control of the authorities.[75] "In Russia, at the present time," Yakunin wrote, "an awakening of religious consciousness is taking place. Those who are reaching out for religion, who are coming to it, only yesterday were atheists."[76] He spoke of this growing consciousness, after many years of hibernation, as a springtime. Neither the church nor the government understood the significance of this awakening, he asserted. The government's ideological commitments had left it blind to present realities, particularly the thirst for new ways of thinking among young people.

Yakunin's report portrayed an authoritarian mentality that pervaded every part of the church's official structure. One could not expect action from either the patriarch or the episcopate, both of which were dependent on civil authorities. Fear and intimidation characterized the upper hierarchy of the church, whose dependency left them enfeebled and enslaved. But even in lower "tiers" of the church hierarchy—the clergy, monasteries, seminaries and academies— government control pervaded the entire atmosphere. Living under constant intimidation, priests elected to play it safe; to confine their services to rituals; to eschew interpretation of the Gospels, the sacraments, and key biblical texts;

and to refrain from going beyond the narrowest possible limits of their duties.[77] He cited the first encyclical of the newly elected Pope John Paul II, in which he defined the primary goal of Christ's Church as the redemptive service of humanity.[78] Yakunin claimed that in its quest to serve the state, the Orthodox Church had lost sight of its fundamental mission.[79]

In *The Captive Mind*, Czesław Miłosz defined the compliant personality as one who accepted what his superiors said, submerged his identity in the New Faith, and willingly gave up his own creative spirit.[80] Yakunin's description of the patriarch, episcopate, and clergy exemplified nearly every aspect of this mentality. For its own purposes, the state had made them dependent functionaries. The state's quest to "extinguish religious life" meant that in relation to the clergy, "the worse the priest, the better." Thus, the authorities turned a blind eye to corruption, as in the aforementioned case of Pyotr Stryzhik, who, according to Yakunin, did not represent an isolated example. "Each diocese," he wrote, "contains immoral priests who are supported by local authorities, because their presence aids the cause of religious propaganda."[81] A large gap existed between the Soviet people who sought help from the church and what they found there.

Despite the dark portrait it painted of the Moscow Patriarchate and its gloomy prognostications for leadership and reform, the report still held out hope. This expectation did not lie within the official agencies of the church, but outside them. Most of all, Yakunin's optimism resided in the young people and the quest for a spiritual renaissance. He had seen this aspiration in the Christian Seminar, whose energy and dedication he had witnessed firsthand. In their expressions of communal love, compassion, and their desire for knowledge, they had created a communal atmosphere that stood diametrically opposed to the "pharisaical mentality" Yakunin found within the Moscow Patriarchate. "The government does not persecute the Moscow patriarchate," Yakunin wrote, "but the religiously active young people, thus attesting to the fact that it is precisely among them that Russia's true meeting with Christ is taking place."[82]

According to Yakunin's report, the most promising movements took place, by necessity, in those that operated independent of governmental control. The more talented and energetic the priest, the more independent he was.[83] He offered two examples of such priests: Frs. Dmitrii Dudko and Aleksandr Men, whose willingness to step outside the docile, compliant framework in which other parishes operated attracted large numbers of young people.[84] He cited the earlier examples of "catacomb priests" who, refusing to pledge their allegiance to the Soviet state, functioned independently of its stultifying controls.

Perhaps most surprisingly, Yakunin's report held up as models unregistered Catholic, Baptist, Pentecostal, and Adventist parishes, which, despite state prohibitions, taught the young people. Although they operated illegally, they chose to pursue their own pathways, to teach their children, and to develop thriving communities. Orthodox parishes, he believed, should pursue a similar pattern. He proposed that Orthodox believers follow a dual track in which some parishes would remain inside the state-regulated structure while others would take the risk of functioning illegally.[85] In addition, he suggested a significant change in the Orthodox Church's jurisdiction, a change that would not have earned the favor of the Moscow Patriarchate. Canon law dictated that a local church organization did not have the right to operate on the geographical dominion of another. Recent circumstances, however, required another look at this principle. In the United States, for example, the Moscow Patriarchate had parishes located on the territories of the American Autocephalous Orthodox Church. The American Orthodox Church (AOC) had its origins in Alaska and was founded by Russian Orthodox monks. After the purchase of Alaska by the United States in 1867, the arrival of Russian and East European immigrants in the last decades of the nineteenth century led the Orthodox Church to spread out into other regions of the country. In 1970, the Moscow Patriarchate granted autocephaly to the AOC, formally recognizing the status it had held since the Russian Revolution. Governed by its metropolitan, located in Washington, DC, the AOC retains full communion with the Moscow Patriarchate.

If, Yakunin proposed, suffering churches in the Soviet Union were permitted to come under the jurisdiction of the AOC, it would significantly "render them brotherly help." Additionally, as he maintained, "it would deepen the exchange experience," which the Moscow Patriarchate encouraged elsewhere in the church hierarchy.[86]

Whether such ideas represented realistic possibilities when Yakunin advanced them remains questionable. To expect the Moscow Patriarchate to regard them favorably appeared extremely unlikely. Nevertheless, they were imaginative and forward-looking, and they signified the kind of thinking that Henry Dakin would have admired, since these ideas crossed over boundaries that limited human contact. In an effort to justify his proposal, Yakunin quoted Christ: "The Sabbath is for man, not man for the Sabbath."[87] Practical needs justified breaking the law when the act was intended to benefit people and lift a heavy burden. The patriarchate presented obstacles that stood in the way of the country's religious renaissance.[88]

The publication of the Christian Committee's materials was significant for additional reasons.

First, during its four-year existence, Yakunin's committee sent Dakin 419 documents, amounting to more than 2,600 pages of materials. The Christian

Committee's charter had promised to speak for all denominations, and the materials the committee forwarded to Henry Dakin held true to this commitment. Although 154 of the documents related to Russian Orthodox individuals or bodies, the remainder comprised a wide assortment of denominations, ranging from Catholics to Reform Baptists, Pentecostals, True and Seventh Day Adventists, and others.[89]

When the Russian Orthodox Church joined the World Council of Churches, Metropolitan Nikodim (Rotov) of Leningrad and Novgorod, a strong proponent of ecumenism, had led the effort. His report, "The Russian Orthodox Church and the Ecumenical Movement" (1968), presented at Uppsala University, signified a major change in the church's desire for rapprochement with the Catholic Church.[90] Metropolitan Nikodim's advocacy of the ecumenical movement primarily related to international relations. He specifically had in mind the desire for reconciliation with the Catholic Church, Christian unity, and support for the peace movement. Yakunin's Christian Committee had a goal much different from Nikodim's. While it, too, wanted reconciliation with the Catholic Church, the committee had a much broader focus. It aspired to overcome the long-standing enmity of the Russian Orthodox Church toward other faiths. Its support for freedom of conscience did not end with Russian Orthodoxy. Yakunin and the Christian Committee embraced a practical ecumenism that the Russian Orthodox Church had not heretofore experienced.

Throughout much of its history, Yakunin and his associates reiterated, the Russian Orthodox Church had viewed itself as superior to other faiths; it had a long tradition of trying to suppress non-Orthodox denominations. The time had come when the church needed to rectify its prejudicial behavior. The Christian Committee, therefore, owed to others the duty "to redress these historical wrongs and come to the defense of believers of all denominations," a responsibility it viewed as an obligation.[91]

This practical ecumenism also appeared in the letter Yakunin and his associates wrote to the Ecumenical Patriarch of Constantinople Dimitrios I. On Christmas Day 1977, Dimitrios I appealed to heads of state and churches everywhere to proclaim the new year the Year of Religious Freedom. The committee's letter offered a devastating critique of the Moscow Patriarchate in its transformation from a spiritual body that supported religious believers into a political institution that buttressed the Soviet state. The Christian Committee appealed to Ecumenical Orthodoxy to "raise your voices, that Christian love with brotherly criticism and exhortation will arouse the pastoral conscience of our Hierarchy, will awaken in them the courage to confess their faith, without which spiritual freedom is impossible."[92] In addition, the Christian Committee sent three letters to the pope, the first sent in the interim after the death of Pope

John Paul I in September 1978, and the other two to the new Polish pope John Paul II. They sought the pope's help with and understanding of the plight of religious believers in the Soviet Union. They expressed the wish for the pope to join forces with them in supporting freedom of conscience in East and West.[93]

Second, the Christian Committee's materials bore witness to a spiritual thirst, especially among young people, a thirst that the state, through various means, attempted either to deny or to suppress. These methods included the political manipulation of the courts and the use of psychiatric incarceration, both of which the published materials confirmed. Yakunin also castigated Patriarch Pimen for his seeming indifference to the religious awakening that was taking place, particularly among the young Russian intelligentsia. Yakunin's "Report" claimed that the patriarch existed in a "golden cage," ignorant of the needs of the people.[94] Rarely venturing outside the narrow confines of his insulated world, the patriarch met the desire for knowledge with either dismissal or apathy.[95]

Third, the publication of the Christian Committee's documents aspired to draw public attention to the persecution of religious believers not only in the Soviet Union but also internationally. The committee countered the narrative promulgated by Metropolitan Nikodim in 1976 at the World Council of Churches about the flourishing condition of the Russian Orthodox Church. According to Yakunin, however, Metropolitan Nikodim and others in the church hierarchy had created a distorted image with little relationship to actual realities.

In disseminating falsehoods, Yakunin argued, Nikodim had done something even more insidious. He had "given unconditional approval to the legislation obligating Christians to participate in the realization of the Communist ideal: the creation of a society of worldly prosperity in which there is no place for religion, and the raising of a consciousness in which there is no place for God."[96] The documents of the Christian Committee challenged that ideal. Speaking from the grassroots of Soviet society, the documents of the Christian Committee told a story much different from the official narrative.

Fourth, upon its creation, the Christian Committee proclaimed that it had five major goals. The first of these, and probably its primary goal, was the "collection, study, and distribution of information."[97] Yakunin and his collaborators understood an often repeated principle: Knowledge equals power. Whoever controls the flow of information controls the source of power. "The lie has long been a tradition in the official declarations of the Moscow Patriarchate," Yakunin and his committee members wrote, and the lie conceals the truth.[98]

Fifth, having lost trust in the patriarch's ability and willingness to address their concerns, Fr. Gleb and his associates sought to build a new network of authority outside the old. In contrast to the traditional hierarchical network, the new arrangement was decentralized. Aided by new technologies—cassettes, self-publishing, and digital printing—Yakunin and his colleagues reached beyond the hierarchical structures of power. They attempted to shift what the US political scientist James Rosenau termed a "state-centric" to a "multi-centric world."[99] Forging a relationship with Henry Dakin served as one of several fresh channels that Fr. Gleb Yakunin and others used to gain support.

The significance of the collaboration between Yakunin and Henry Dakin's Washington Street Research Center cannot be overstated. The issuance of the committee's documents and other materials that emanated from the Washington Street Research Center represented early efforts at desktop publishing. Henry Dakin believed in the power of telecommunications to transform human relationships.[100] Like Keston College in England, Dakin's center gave religious believers in the Soviet Union a voice, connecting their outcries from provincial towns and villages of the Soviet Union with a much larger audience. Their voices enabled an opposing narrative to gain traction versus the official account. In creating these new relationships with Dakin, Yakunin's Christian Committee, perhaps inadvertently, countered the state's goal of creating a harmonious, unified social order based on an all-embracing ideology.

The relationship between the Moscow priest and the San Francisco entrepreneur challenged the traditional political order in an additional way. In the following decade, Henry Dakin would become a prominent leader of the person-to-person diplomacy movement, which helped defuse the politics of the Cold War.[101] He invited prominent Russian and American political leaders and scientists to the Esalen Institute, the retreat center in Big Sur, California, where they engaged in conversation and developed personal relationships.[102] "In 1988," Henry Dakin's spouse Vergilia recounted, "a Russian delegation arrived in San Francisco. Gleb Yakunin was among its members, and he came to our home. I shall never forget Henry's excitement in meeting him face-to-face."[103] The earlier collaboration between Yakunin, Regel'son, and Dakin marked the first stage in breaking down what had once seemed impenetrable barriers.

In the late 1970s, Soviet leaders knew of the dangers that the Christian Committee posed to the established political and religious order. Their response lay immediately ahead, and it would have severe consequences for Yakunin.

CHAPTER 6

"I Thank God for the Fate He Has Given Me"

In many ways, the late 1970s were years of accomplishment and triumph for Fr. Gleb Yakunin. He developed a devoted following in a coterie of young people who saw in him a crusader for social justice. He sent copious amounts of information to the West, which centered on documents about specific injustices that demanded attention. He believed himself to be on the cusp of a religious reawakening in the Soviet Union that was predicated on revealing large cracks in the state's relentless assault on religious beliefs. He had a young family whose adoration for him was unceasing, even in difficult times, and he, in turn, deeply loved his wife and three children. And he was fulfilling what he believed to be his primary purpose: service to a church whose leadership rejected him and to a suffering people who wanted to practice their faith without state interference.

But if these were years of achievement, they were also years of hardship and adversity. Fr. Gleb and his colleagues on the Committee for the Defense of Believers' Rights remained under the suspicious eye of the KGB. As the victims of three house searches by the security police in 1979, Yakunin's family lived in fear that he would be charged with criminal activity.

Conspiracy theories have been an integral part of political life in Russia and the Soviet Union. Fostered by certain factions in the government, conspiracy theories identify specific groups or individuals who aim to subvert the social order and overthrow the government. Governments generally sponsor conspiracy theories to strengthen public order and focus attention on so-called public enemies. In his classic work *In Pursuit of the Millennium*, the historian Norman Cohn finds that the rise of apocalyptic thinking takes place during times of great social and economic conflict, when social groups feel adrift.[1] Similar tensions underlie the spread of conspiracy theories, especially when ideological underpinnings of the social order are threatened. The actions of Yakunin's Christian Committee for the Defense of Believers' Rights and the religious reawakening of Soviet youth in Moscow, Leningrad, and other cities imperiled a centerpiece of Communist Party ideology. Anxiety over these movements reverberated in KGB communications.[2] Unwilling to tolerate the further development of such activities, the authorities planned an immediate response.

On April 13 and 20, 1977, a two-part article appeared in the popular newspaper *Literaturnaia gazeta* (Literary Gazette), which struck a hard blow at Yakunin and his associates. Written under the byline of one Boris Roshchin, it carried an ominous title, "Svoboda religii i klepki" (Freedom of Religion and the Slanderers).[3] Whether Roshchin actually existed is questionable; the name of such a person had appeared earlier in articles designed to besmirch the reputations of certain people whom the government had targeted for criticism. Most likely, "Roshchin" served as the pen name for a KGB operative or as a composite name for several agents. The article's main purpose aimed at castigating several leaders of the religious reawakening in Russia and labeling them as dangerous enemies. The article particularly targeted Fr. Gleb.

Roshchin set his accusations within the framework of a conspiracy directed against the Soviet state. Although Yakunin and his associates professed to be Orthodox and claimed to have a religious mission, Roshchin argued that their activities had nothing to do with religion. Rather, their actions were entirely political and their primary motivation was state subversion. Yakunin and his associates conspired with "foreign centers of reactionary propaganda exploiting the ignorance of people in the West," misrepresenting religious freedom, and calling for outside interference in the legal processes of the Soviet state.[4]

In his assertion about "reactionary centers" in foreign countries, Roshchin cited one main example: the publishing enterprise of the San Francisco entrepreneur Henry Dakin. Roshchin accused Gleb Yakunin and Lev Regel'son as being in Dakin's employment. He quoted from one of Regel'son's letters to Dakin: "It is important to have such a collection [of documents] published in English. I entrust you with the authority to conduct all the necessary negotiations and to sign contracts in my name, observing all the usual practices adopted in the West for such publications."[5]

By referencing this letter, which the police had uncovered in Regel'son's correspondence, Roshchin hoped to portray Yakunin and Regel'son as petty parasites whose chief motivation was personal enrichment gained by surreptitiously providing materials to a hostile agency in the United States. Roshchin, it should be noted, made no attempt to describe the contents of the documents that Yakunin and Regel'son had transmitted. He depicted these materials simply as commercial instruments that spread "falsehoods discrediting the Soviet regime."[6]

Roshchin's article included severe criticism of others in addition to Yakunin and Regel'son, and claimed they had gone astray: Aleksandr Ogorodnikov, Fr. Dmitrii Dudko, and Anatolii Levitin-Krasnov. He presented each one as a vile human being who lacked integrity, spread false teachings, and indefatigably slandered the Soviet state. Roshchin depicted Levitin-Krasnov, a prolific essayist who had recently emigrated to Switzerland, as an associate of émigré publications hostile to the Soviet regime. He portrayed Ogorodnikov as a misguided, undisciplined, failed former student who was also a parasite in the Soviet state. Roshchin labeled Fr. Dmitrii a pastor who poisoned the minds of Soviet youth and lacked any loyalty to his homeland. Each of these people Roshchin castigated as essentially dishonest, corrupt, and dangerous. But what ran throughout his malicious presentation was an effort to criticize their influence on the young. In hindsight, Roshchin's article offered a forecast of how the Soviet police soon intended to act.

It would have been out of character for Fr. Gleb Yakunin not to respond to the article in *Literaturnaia gazeta*. The attack on him personally did not trouble him as much as the misrepresentation of facts and the moral justification that the author used for his attack. On April 27, Yakunin called a press conference to which he invited Russian and Western correspondents. Convened in the Moscow home of Fr. Dmitrii Dudko, the meeting began with Fr. Gleb's emotional statement in which he emphasized the significance of the article's appearance and its timing. We Christians, he said, "are not surprised by the attempt to define us in a moral and spiritual sense—which is one of the features of the article. This method has been used continually over the last sixty years in antireligious propaganda during the struggle against religion. The historical roots of this method of slander and lies emanated from the first centuries of Christian existence, when it was used in the Roman Empire to instigate the heathen mobs against Christians."[7]

Declaring that neither he nor other members of the Christian Committee for the Defense of Believers' Rights could be broken by scurrilous attacks in the press or by police arrests, Yakunin asserted their willingness to suffer for a cause they considered just. He made clear that he and the others would not submit to threats by the police, and he made his case by references to Soviet history. Since the 1917 Revolution, the government had succeeded in destroying many aspects of Russian culture, but it had not succeeded, Yakunin said, in vanquishing religious believers. Despite intensive, nearly continuous efforts by the government, the faithful had survived and were even stronger than ever, and this, he said, gave him hope.[8] He also admitted that he was buoyed by support from outside the Soviet Union: "If the repression of the movement for the defense of human rights and spiritual values causes protests all over the world, then repression against Christians, especially those who defend the interests of the church, causes a stronger reaction from the brothers in faith, fellow believers, and all Christians. Such persecution only causes a stronger religious revival, which is a result completely contrary to the aims of the oppressors."[9]

Most important, at the press conference, Yakunin addressed what he called an ideological "crisis" developing in Moscow and Leningrad, which had begun to spread into the provincial cities of the Soviet Union. "The violence directed at the clergy and their flock, which we observed in the twenties, has now disappeared," he said.[10] To deal with this change, the government concocted fantasies, Yakunin argued, conspiracy theories based on fear, in an effort to revive the atmosphere of the 1930s, in which the police accused dissenting individuals of engaging in espionage and terrorism.[11]

The case Yakunin made against his attackers had both strength and weakness. The strength lay in his attempt to establish facts and call out fanaticism, based on charges of espionage and terrorism, which lacked concrete evidence. In addition, he spoke correctly and passionately about the growing search among Soviet youth for new ways of thinking about human purpose and community life as well as the increasing interest in religion. He could also point to the large outpouring of people who attended the recent Easter services.[12]

The weakness concerned his optimistic conviction that he lived on the cusp of a powerful religious awakening in Russia. He remained certain that the wave of new recruits to student circles represented a transformational moment. He was a hopeful person who repeatedly saw new possibilities and promising beginnings, although he often overestimated their widespread support. He also underestimated both the power of the Soviet government to stifle the leading voices of this religious movement and the desire of hard-liners in the government and conservatives in the Orthodox Church to preserve the status quo.

As noted earlier, it would be two years before the KGB arrested Fr. Gleb. In the interim, between the article in *Literaturnaia gazeta* and his arrest, Yakunin continued his work on the Christian Committee; the next two years proved to be extremely productive, despite warnings from the KGB that he needed to curtail his work (see chapter 5). Knowing that they likely faced arrest and imprisonment, Yakunin and his associates recruited other members to take their place. Boldly announcing that the government would not shut down the committee, Yakunin said that trust was far stronger than threats of force and that the committee had several members prepared to step in at any moment when called upon.[13] On December 29, 1977, he announced that Vadim Shcheglov had become a member of the committee and was told that he had "a mandate, if the police arrested the committee's founding members to release the names of others—and there were many—who wished to join, and to make them members."[14]

Although Yakunin did not announce their names, at least three other people had agreed to join the committee. None would become active members until after Yakunin's arrest. Although they were few in number, the identity of two of them suggests the existence of priests within church circles who sympathized with the committee's goals. The first of these, Fr. Vasilii Fonchenkov, the forty-seven-year-old son of an old Bolshevik family, had rebelled against his family's values at the age of eighteen and become a Christian. After graduating from the Moscow Theological Academy, he had held a position in the Department for External Church Relations, and in the late 1970s, he taught courses at the Moscow Theological Academy and the Theological Seminary, at the latter on the Constitution of the USSR. The second member was Fr. Nikolai Gainov, a forty-four-year-old native from the Yaroslavl region. After working in a factory, he had spent time in the Soviet army before converting to Christianity. Gainov entered the Moscow Theological Seminary in 1960, and upon graduation four years later, he was ordained a priest; in the late 1970s, he served as a parish priest in a village near Moscow.[15] Neither Fonchenkov nor Gainov saw the work of the committee as something hidden from the state. They participated in order to bring actual state practices in line with state laws, with Fr. Vasilii expressing the desire that his involvement not jeopardize his teaching position at the academy or seminary.[16]

Given the large number of arrests the KGB made between 1976 and 1979, it is surprising that the police waited so long before moving against Yakunin. Yakunin wondered, too, at his April 27, 1977, press conference. He thought the hesitancy could be explained by the fear that the arrests of those who defended the church would only strengthen the religious revival then taking place in the country.[17] Another explanation might have been the belief that his arrest would provoke a severe response from Christian organizations abroad similar to the strong support that the persecution of Pastor Georgi Vins had elicited earlier.

Another explanation for the delay is perhaps even more convincing. Yakunin and his associates had not broken any state laws. They had not held any public demonstrations, threatened violence, or violated the public order. Instead, they had simply insisted that the government uphold its own laws, its written constitutional responsibilities.[18] Searching for an ostensible legal reason justifying Yakunin's arrest, the police could find none. They had only one remaining recourse: to bring a political charge.

Disputing the Party

Until 1977, the laws of the Soviet state and the ideological aspirations of the Communist Party overlapped, although occasionally they came into conflict, and when divergences took place, Soviet courts had to reconcile them. The 1977 Constitution (known as the Brezhnev Constitution) aimed to clarify the relationship between the state and the party by asserting that the social and political goals of the party took precedence over all other activities in the Soviet Union. Thus, the highest moral and legal claims of the individual were determined by a minority party. Unlike the two earlier Constitutions, in 1924 and 1936, the 1977 Constitution, for the first time, conflated the Communist Party with the state and left no doubt about the party's supremacy: "The leading and guiding force of the Soviet society and the nucleus of its political system, of all state organizations and public organizations, is the Communist Party of the Soviet Union. The CPSU exists for the people and serves the people."[19]

Invited to respond to the draft copy of the new Constitution, many citizens wrote to President Brezhnev, and the Christian Committee did likewise. In its letter to Brezhnev, the committee pointed out the dangerous precedents established by the new Constitution. For the first time, the committee emphasized, the document no longer separated the state and the party, but instead merged the party's ideological platform with the national laws. For the church, this move had disastrous consequences, the Christian Committee correctly argued:

> A believer cannot agree with the Constitutional legalization of compulsory godlessness for the whole of society. In fact, the Preamble and Article 6 of the Draft set out the theses of the party program, which have now been elevated to the status of national law. Therefore, the borderlines between the Party and the state are obliterated, and the Soviet citizen's passport becomes a communist's party card. The Draft of the new Constitution, turns the Soviet state, by a legal document, into an ideocratic-totalitarian state.[20]

The party newspaper *Pravda* printed a large number of letters sent by Soviet citizens, but it did not publish the letter from Yakunin and his associates.[21]

Shortly afterward, on behalf of parents whom the laws prohibited from providing religious instruction to their children, the Christian Committee reached out to the BBC, Voice of America, and Deutsche Welle and asked them to broadcast programs for children in Russian.[22]

On November 1, 1979, the police arrested Gleb Yakunin in his Moscow home and transported him to the Lefortovo Prison, the home of the KGB. As previously mentioned, on the same day, the police also arrested the prominent human rights spokesperson Tat'iana Mikhailovna Velikanova (1932–2002). Like Yakunin, despite threats from the police, she had not ceased her work as an editor of the main vehicle for publicizing human rights abuses, the prominent samizdat newspaper *A Chronicle of Current Events*. And also like Yakunin, the prospect of imminent arrest had neither cowed her nor prevented the international distribution of her publications. Since 1970, when she began to write for the samizdat bimonthly publication *A Chronicle of Current Events*, she collected and publicized violations of court procedures and civil liberties by political authorities throughout the Soviet Union. She became a champion of the defenseless, an unfettered voice for people who had no other recourse against the arbitrary use of state power, and, according to a close friend, a person "who is steadfast and fearless in her unequal fight with evil."[23] Andrei Sakharov described her as the embodiment of the "moral inspiration of the human rights movement, its purity and force, and its historical significance."[24] Velikanova's arrest by the police on November 1, 1979, sought to still her voice and restore the silence.

The arrests of Yakunin and Velikanova were not unrelated. Both set the stage for other notable arrests that soon followed. Yakunin and Velikanova each had a long history going back to the 1960s of protests against the regime. They viewed their causes as moral efforts to protect the sanctity of individual rights and human dignity against arbitrary power. To agents of the police state, both of them threatened the principle that the party, not the laws of the state, constituted the "leading and guiding force of the Soviet society."[25] Their arrests left their families behind, in Yakunin's case his wife Iraida and three children, Mariia, Aleksandr, and Anna (figure 6.1).

The arrest of Fr. Gleb Yakunin on that same November day struck a blow at the heart of the religious liberty movement. Like Velikanova, he had broken the silence and revealed falsehoods about the frequent claims concerning religious freedom. His voice, like hers, transcended national boundaries, reaching out to supportive organizations in the defense of individual rights. His was a searing voice that came from an uncommon source—not from secular society, but from within the Orthodox Church. As the previous pages have repeatedly shown, Yakunin had also turned his critical eye on the church, observing with disdain its

FIGURE 6.1. Yakunin's family, in a photo taken soon after his arrest in 1979, from left to right, daughter Mariia, son Aleksandr, daughter Anna, and Iraida Georgievna. Courtesy of the Keston Center for Religion, Politics, and Society, Baylor University, Waco, Texas.

complicity with the government and its refusal to stand up for the persecuted. In recent years, he and his associates had displayed little hesitation in trying to fill part of the void left by the church hierarchy's reluctance to speak.

Velikanova's trial took place August 26–29, 1980, immediately after the closing ceremonies of the Moscow Olympics. Charged with anti-Soviet activities and cooperation with the West to the detriment of her own country, the outcome of her trial was predetermined from the outset. Remembering the farce that she had witnessed at other trials, Velikanova refused to participate in her defense and remained mute throughout the proceedings. She received a severe sentence of four years in a prison camp and five years' internal exile in the far north (figure 6.2).

As stated earlier, Fr. Gleb Yakunin waited nearly nine months for his trial and for his fate to be determined, a month longer than the Soviet legal standard between arraignment and trial. During the interim, the police moved quickly to terminate the activities of other outspoken defenders of religious liberty and human rights. On December 24, they arrested Fr. Gleb's colleague Lev Regel'son in Tallinn, where he had gone into hiding to avoid apprehension. On January 15, 1980, Fr. Dmitrii Dudko was arrested at his church in

"I THANK GOD FOR THE FATE HE HAS GIVEN ME"

FIGURE 6.2. Tat'iana Velikanova in exile, 1984. Courtesy of the Keston Center for Religion, Politics, and Society, Baylor University, Waco, Texas.

Grebnevo, a village 19 miles east of Moscow, where the church had reassigned him. On January 22, the police took Andrei Sakharov into custody and exiled him to Gorky (Nizhnii Novgorod), 260 miles east of Moscow.[26] On March 12, the KGB arrested Yakunin's associate Viktor Kapitanchuk.

During these early months of 1980, the police moved against former members of the Christian Seminar. On January 8, a Soviet court tried Tat'iana Shchipkova, the Smolensk teacher and prominent member of the seminar, sentencing her to three years in a labor camp. The state charged her with "malicious hooliganism" for an incident that took place during the search of her apartment when she refused to relinquish a book and struck a police officer after he twisted her arm.[27] On January 8, the KGB arrested two other leading seminar members: Viktor Popkov, a Smolensk worker, and Vladimir Burtsev, a Moscow technician. Neither man had broken any laws, but they were arraigned under a false charge of "forgery" and tried jointly in Smolensk on April 8 and 9. The presiding judge sentenced each of them to eighteen months in a labor camp.[28]

Yakunin's arrest had thus taken place during a wave of police attempts to obliterate groups to which he was connected. His arrest did not pass unnoticed within the Soviet Union, where some of his strongest supporters resided.

On November 4, an open letter signed by twenty-three people and published in samizdat expressed sympathy for him and praised the Christian Committee he founded. "In a society where atheism is the state's ideology," the authors wrote, "the Committee represented the first real association of Christians to defend religious freedom."[29] Also in November, four leading Catholic priests in Lithuania issued a document expressing gratitude for "Fr. Yakunin's work and his contributions to breaking down the hostility between denominations," and appealed to the authorities to release him from custody. More than three hundred Catholic Lithuanians signed the statement.[30]

Outside the Soviet Union, several groups joined the protests. In England, Michael Bourdeaux and Keston College publicized the plight of Fr. Gleb, defending his activities on behalf of the oppressed and lauding his courage in the face of unrelenting pressure from the church and the state. On March 9, 1980, the Church of England sponsored an Interdenominational Service of Prayer on behalf of Gleb Yakunin, Dmitrii Dudko, and Lev Regel'son. The service took place in the historic St. Martin-in-the-Fields Church at the corner of London's Trafalgar Square. Featuring readings from sermons, letters, and interviews of the three men, the event praised their role in defending Christian values and their suffering as a consequence. A central part of this gathering was a Russian Orthodox Service of Intercession conducted by Metropolitan Anthony Bloom.[31] St. Martin-in-the-Fields symbolized the encounter between God and all humanity, a theme emphasized in the ceremony on March 9.

Although Cold War politics might have played some small part, most of the protests fell outside the purely political realm. Organized by members of the clergy and church groups, they recalled the ideals expressed by Yakunin and Regel'son in their Nairobi "Appeal" to heed the cry of persecuted humanity in the name of Christian solidarity.

Concern about Yakunin rapidly spread beyond Great Britain. On January 23, in Montreal, seventy-five people participated in a protest vigil in front of the USSR Consulate, where they prayed for the health and release of Frs. Gleb Yakunin, Dmitrii Dudko, and also Lev Regel'son. At the vigil, three priests chanted a prayer of intercession (*Moleben*) alternately in Slavonic, English, and French.[32] On Sunday, February 24, 1980, in New York, a massive demonstration took place in defense of persecuted Christians in the Soviet Union in which supporters spoke passionately about their incarcerated brethren.[33] On February 26, 1980, in Switzerland, more than nine hundred ministers, professors of theology, and students of diverse confessions signed a letter to President Brezhnev. They asked for the release of Fr. Gleb Yakunin and all those imprisoned who had participated in the Christian Seminar and cited Yakunin's "Appeal" to the Nairobi conference.[34] On March 13, in Paris, the Russian émigré newspaper *Russkaia mysl'* published an article calling for increased protests from Western countries. The Soviet hierarchy, the anonymous author asserted, had assumed that little public outcry would come from other countries and that the arrests would soon be forgotten. Recalling "how highly Solzhenitsyn had valued Fr. Gleb" earlier, the letter writer hoped that Solzhenitsyn would come to Yakunin's defense from his secure perch in the Vermont woods. "It is impossible without pain to speak about the fate of Fr. Gleb," the author wrote, and he pleaded for continued support both from inside the Soviet Union and abroad.[35]

The winter and spring of 1979 to 1980, indeed, was a difficult period for Fr. Gleb Yakunin. He remained in the Lefortovo Prison, housed in a windowless, unheated cell, most of the time in solitary confinement. On the outside, the Soviet Union became ever more deeply mired in the war in Afghanistan, and in Moscow, preparations were well underway for the international Olympics, the first Olympic Games held in a Slavic-language-speaking country, and the public's attention focused largely on those events. During these months, Yakunin faced constant interrogations and threats. From his interrogators, he learned of the arrests of his friends and associates, news that he found excruciatingly hard to bear.

Fr. Gleb's troubles were exacerbated by the news of the surprising confession of his longtime friend and fellow priest Fr. Dmitrii Dudko. Dudko had stood by Yakunin on several occasions when other government and church officials had attacked him; Yakunin admired Dudko's courage and his appeals to the young people who flocked to his unique sermons and open discussions. But on January 20, 1980, five days after his arrest, Soviet national television carried live a tearful, heart-rending apology from Fr. Dmitrii in which he expressed sorrow for his previous actions. He now recognized his errors, he lamented, and knew they had harmed the Soviet people. This broadcast, which drew worldwide attention, has received extensive coverage elsewhere and needs little elaboration here.[36] It bears noting that Fr. Dmitrii most likely underwent severe mental and physical torment in the days leading up to his television appearance. His confession had a major psychological and spiritual impact on the Russian intelligentsia and on the legion of followers who had admired his stand for principle and truth. Yakunin had called him one of the few talented, universally respected priests active in the Soviet Union.[37] The confession undermined that image.

Dudko's act of contrition intensified the pressure on Yakunin. The police would have considered it a major coup to extract a similar act of repentance from Fr. Gleb, which would have had a complementary devastating effect on the "religious revival," particularly among the young, in whom he had placed so much hope. In addition, he knew that the arrests of Lev Regel'son and Viktor Kapitanchuk, factored into the case the police planned to build against him. They, too, confronted lengthy, painful questioning about their relationship with Yakunin. Moreover, as KGB interrogators commonly did, they used information gleaned from them to increase the pressure on him. Extracting an admission of guilt and remorse from Fr. Gleb Yakunin, as the KGB had supposedly done with Dudko, would simultaneously destroy two of the most prominent proponents of religious freedom in Russia. As the historian Nicholas Ganson convincingly argues, however, an attempt to cast Dudko's "confession" in *political* terms is to misrepresent his motives.[38]

All spring and most of the summer, Yakunin wrestled with the question of how best to proceed. He well knew that a plea of repentance would free him immediately from imprisonment. It would also allow him to provide support for his family, who otherwise faced certain deprivation as well as the taunts and insults of neighbors and classmates as the wife and children of a state villain. "Those months were particularly difficult for us and for him," said Iraida Yakunina.[39] In addition to the other problems his family faced, they underwent a third search of their apartment. The police turned their household belongings upside down looking for two items that they intended to use against Fr. Gleb: materials related to the organization of the Committee for the Defense of Believers' Rights and a book written by the Russian journalist Mark Popovskii, *The Life and Times of Archpriest Voino-Iasenetskii and His Circle* (*Zhizn' i zhitie Voino-Iasenetskogo arkhipiskopa i khiruga*). Following the Soviet censor's rejection of the book, Popovskii had published it in Paris.[40] On the eve of the unexpected police visit, a friend had delivered a copy of the book to Iraida Yakunina's apartment. She hid it under the piano, where the police, who examined nearly everything they owned, by some miracle "never thought to look."[41]

As Fr. Gleb's wife, Iraida Yakunina was allowed only sporadic visits to the Lefortovo Prison. Each time, she found Fr. Gleb in a joyous mood, even though she knew he was suffering. "He always questioned me about myself and the children, and he inquired about all of us in detail," she recounted.[42] He gave little outward sign of the inner turmoil over the agonizing decisions he had to make, the relentless pressure he had to endure from his interrogators, or the lengthy time he spent in solitary confinement. But as the date approached for Fr. Gleb's trial, the KGB concocted a plan to secure his confession of guilt and repentance. Before the hour of Iraida's scheduled visit, KGB officials asked to meet with her. When she arrived at the prison, the officials escorted her into a small room. Courteous and seemingly solicitous about her welfare, they asked Iraida about her children and their future prospects. They carefully laid out the legal case and accusations against her husband. They told her of the likely consequences, including the material deprivations the family would continue to face. The officials then presented a different scenario, a much more pleasant portrayal of the future—of Fr. Gleb's return to them, of a normal family life, and of children who would have their father with them as they grew up. Such possibilities required only Fr. Gleb's public act of contrition and repentance. The KGB officials encouraged Iraida to present this case to her husband, and they relied on her to do so.[43]

The full details of the ensuing meeting between Iraida and Fr. Gleb are unknown. As always, they discussed the children's welfare, her own well-being, and news of the day. It is highly likely that Iraida discussed the conversations she had with the KGB officials preceding the visit with her husband. Fr. Gleb rarely, if ever, considered his personal comfort, but he had great concern for the welfare of others. He told Iraida that he had recently wavered a great deal on the question of what to do, but was leaning toward accepting the KGB's offer. Obviously, a decision had to be made, and the two of them discussed the options that lay before them and their future consequences. But it was Iraida Yakunina who, according to Fr. Gleb, made the decisive assertion: she advised her husband that he must never betray his fundamental principles. She told him that the hopes of a great many people depended on his remaining a person of moral integrity.[44]

The Trial Begins

Monday, August 25, 1980, began as a sunny, clear day in Moscow. The weather was slightly warmer than normal for a late summer morning, and in the parks and public gardens that endowed the city with greenery, foliage throughout the capital had not yet begun to change colors. Nevertheless, change was in the air. In this city of a little more than eight million, large numbers of people had begun their return from summer dachas to prepare for the fall and the annual beginning of the school year on September 1. For most Muscovite families, transition from the slower pace of summer was underway.

Politically, however, tension and uncertainty about the future characterized the upper echelons of the Soviet government. The army's venture into Afghanistan eight months earlier had not resulted in a quick victory, and it had become increasingly clear that a protracted standoff might lie ahead.[45] But at the moment, the most immediate worry came from a situation rapidly developing on the country's northwestern border. Less than two weeks earlier, some seventeen thousand nonunion Polish workers, protesting rising food prices and expressing their objection to other grievances, had gone on strike and taken control of the Lenin shipyards in Gdańsk. In the following days, workers in other factories joined the movement, proclaiming their right to strike and to form an independent, self-governing trade union. On August 25, the workers, led by Lech Walesa, began calling their trade-union movement "Solidarity."[46] In Moscow, on the same day, the Politburo set up a special commission, chaired by Mikhail Suslov, the party's chief ideologist, "to pay close attention to the situation unfolding in Polish People's Republic" and to recommend "measures needed to be taken by Soviet leadership."[47] Worried that the strikes might spread across the Soviet border, the Politburo soon made plans to move military forces to the northwestern frontier.

On August 25, the day the government had set for Fr. Gleb's trial, a small crowd of his relatives and supporters as well as members of the foreign press gathered outside Moscow's city court waiting for permission to enter the building. The public announcement had proclaimed that it would be an "open trial." When police officials unlocked the courtroom doors, however, they refused entrance to supporters and journalists, saying that the courtroom had already filled to capacity. They allowed admittance to Fr. Gleb's wife, Iraida, but all others were told that they could not be accommodated and that they should go home. Lord Baron Carrington, the British foreign secretary who had the assignment of representing the British government, was denied entrance. Those supporters who remained witnessed four KGB officers who were escorted to seats in the courtroom; all of them had participated in house searches or interrogations of various Christian Seminar members.

In organizing the trial, the police left little either to chance or to the opportunity for Fr. Gleb to use the proceedings for his own benefit. They packed the courtroom with students and workers, the "people's representatives," who had no sympathy for him. Iraida Yakunina was permitted to secure a defense lawyer for her husband, but she had not succeeded in doing so and consequently had to rely on a court-appointed counsel, L. M. Popov, a less than mediocre trial attorney. The prosecutor, Procurator G. I. Skaredov, had issued summonses to eleven witnesses. They included Yakunin's associates Viktor Kapitanchuk and Lev Regel'son, both of whom awaited their own trials in the Lefortovo Prison; Viktor Popkov, a participant in the Christian Seminar; A. I. Osipov, a professor at the Moscow Theological Academy; Fr. Superior Iosif Pustoutov, head of postgraduate studies at the Moscow Theological Academy; Feliks Karelin, a former friend of Yakunin's; a churchwarden; a financial administrator; and several of Fr. Gleb's acquaintances, with whom he was alleged to have had extremist conversations. The court did not permit Yakunin to call any witnesses.[48]

The judge assigned to hear the case, Valentina G. Lubentsova, had a history of presiding over trials of prominent dissenters. A seasoned, tough, rigid person, she had first presided at the trial of the Moscow Seven in 1968. She had handed down particularly severe sentences to the young demonstrators who had protested the Soviet army's actions against the Prague reformers. She had also heard the case of Vladimir Bukovsky, the Russian-born, British human rights activist, who played a prominent role in the Soviet human rights movement. Most recently, in May 1978, Lubentsova had presided over the trial of Yuri Orlov, at which she had refused to allow him to call witnesses to speak in his own defense.[49] There, again, she displayed her severe manner, inflexibility, and ruthlessness. Her appearance at Yakunin's trial did not bode well for the defendant.

As the trial began, Judge Lubentsova read the state's charge against Yakunin: his alleged violation of Article 70 of the Criminal Code of the RSFSR. Used repeatedly against individuals who dissented from the laws of the state, Article 70 prohibited the publication, dissemination, or possession of literature with an anti-Soviet message.[50] She then read the indictment. Lubentsova cited numerous letters and appeals that Yakunin had allegedly composed, most importantly, an "Appeal to the Fifth Assembly of the World Council of Churches" and an "Appeal to Christians in Portugal." Judge Lubentsova asked for Yakunin's response. He replied, "Not guilty."[51]

On the first afternoon of the trial, the public procurator Skaredov called to testify three individuals who knew Yakunin well, two of whom had worked closely with him. Skaredov had summoned all three from their cells in the Lefortovo Prison. First, the judge turned to Yakunin and asked whether he had taken part in the writing and distribution of the above-mentioned letter and appeals. "Yes, I took part," Yakunin responded. The procurator then called on Lev Regel'son and inquired about his connection with the materials cited in the indictment of Fr. Gleb. He admitted that he had participated in the composition of several of them. But he especially wished "to underscore, however, that during the writing of the documents, Fr. Gleb always pointed out the reasons for their composition: their importance to religious believers and to the defense of Orthodoxy, and he opposed inserting in them any political assertions."[52] The procurator next summoned Viktor Kapitanchuk and asked him about his work with Fr. Gleb on the Christian Committee for the Defense of Believers' Rights. Kapitanchuk admitted that he had taken an active part. The procurator then asked him whether he acknowledged that "these documents contained slanderous and deliberately false fabrications that discredit the Soviet social and state system." Kapitanchuk replied that he did not acknowledge this claim.[53]

The third witness summoned by the prosecutor had been a very active participant in the Christian Seminar. The police had arrested Viktor Popkov nearly two years earlier, and the court had sentenced him to punishment in a labor camp, where he had already spent a year and a half. The primary reason the procurator summoned Popkov related to an alleged meeting with a British member of Parliament, David Atkinson, who, during a trip to Moscow, had made contact with Yakunin and several other religious activists, including Popkov. Asked whether Fr. Gleb had attended the meeting with Atkinson and other members of the British delegation, Popkov responded that Yakunin had played a leading part in the conversation. When questioned, Popkov recounted that he had seen Yakunin give Atkinson a small packet, although he had no idea of its contents.[54] In responding to the procurator's questions, Popkov simply told the truth, but the questions to which he responded helped build the procurator's case that Fr. Gleb's loyalties were not to the Soviet state.

The next day, Procurator Skaredov further developed the main lines of his attack on Yakunin. He called nine witnesses, among them Aleksandr Il'ia Osipov and Fr. Superior Iosif Pustoutov. Both men had been present in Nairobi as members of the Soviet delegation when the World Council of Churches received the "Appeal" sent by Yakunin and Regel'son, and both willingly testified to its impact on the Nairobi Assembly. A self-assured, well-spoken, religiously conservative teacher, then at the beginning of a long academic career, Osipov specialized in the history of theology. He tended to downplay as insignificant voices that did not conform to his views of history or theology.[55] He dismissed the influence of the "Appeal," claiming that it had little impact on the session to which he had been assigned. When pressed by the prosecutor to state his views on the document itself, he said he considered it "antigovernment."[56] The state prosecutor then summoned to the stand Fr. Superior Iosif, who took an approach different from Osipov's. He had not attended the Nairobi Assembly as a representative of the Moscow Patriarchate, but as a private person. The "Appeal," he said, had produced a negative response from some of the delegates, whom he called "uninformed" about the true situation in the Soviet Union, and it had undermined the Soviet delegation's standing in the Assembly.[57] He considered the document written by Yakunin and Regel'son to be slanderous and biased. It had distracted the Assembly from pursuing much more important matters, such as "the unity of World Christians, the struggle against racism and the danger of war, disarmament, and a just settlement of the Middle East crisis."[58]

During the remainder of the second day and continuing into the third, the procurator called witnesses who testified about Fr. Gleb's character and his "deleterious actions" concerning the Soviet state. Interestingly, Feliks Karelin, with whom Fr. Gleb had once enjoyed a close relationship, turned out to be a severe critic: he labeled the documents Yakunin had written as efforts to undermine the Soviet government and the Constitution.[59] Other witnesses made scurrilous attacks on Fr. Gleb, claims without any supportive evidence: of his receiving money from Solzhenitsyn, making insulting remarks about the KGB and Soviet leaders, harboring hatred for the authorities, betraying the Soviet people, and engaging in the illicit trade of icons for personal gain.

Although the trial proceedings were deadly serious, they also had farcical moments and unanticipated developments. A Fr. Krivoi from the city of L'vov, assigned to besmirch Yakunin's moral reputation, accused him of once drinking two bottles of vodka, whereupon Yakunin retorted: "Over what period of time?"[60] Another witness, Aleksandr Shushpanov, churchwarden of the Nikolo-Kuznetskaia Church in central Moscow, who had served for many years in the Moscow Patriarchate's Department for External Church Relations, was known to Fr. Gleb as a KGB agent. The procurator had prepared him to testify about Yakunin's contacts with the West. When Shushpanov entered the courtroom, he immediately began shouting, nearly in a frenzy, that Fr. Gleb "was an abettor of imperialism and an anti-Sovietist and that he belonged in the dock."[61]

This was not the only incident that failed to remain entirely on script. Several other witnesses did not deliver the testimony that the procurator expected. The head priest at the last church Yakunin had served reported that Fr. Gleb had never given him any documents to read and that he had not observed anything illegal in the accused's behavior. In another unexpected incident, the procurator called to testify E. B. Zagryazkina, who worked as the financial administrator in a church Fr. Gleb had served for many years. The procurator had carefully prepared her, and in pretrial testimony, she had expressed her willingness to cooperate. But when called to the stand, she changed her mind. Praising the respect that many priests and believers had for Fr. Gleb, she wanted to add some personal words about him. Zagryazkina said that "in all her life, she had never met such a decent, honest, good, brave, and moral man as Fr. Yakunin."[62] Judge Lubentsova asked her about her testimony in the pretrial investigation, in which the witness had mentioned Fr. Gleb's role in buying and selling church valuables. The judge continued to press Zagryazkina on this issue, but she refused to provide any evidence.[63]

As court opened on the fourth day, Judge Lubentsova pressed forward in an attempt to conclude the trial. She had heard enough to render a verdict, and she denied the request of Yakunin's defense attorney's to summon Fr. Dmitrii Dudko, whose name had come up several times in the proceedings. The judge called for the procurator's closing statement. The court had fully proved, he said, the guilt of Fr. Gleb, whom he called a criminal, an enemy of the country and the church, a degenerate, and, referring to the testimony of Fr. Krivoi, a drunkard.[64]

Fr. Gleb then had the opportunity to make his final speech. He asked the judge whether the "court and the public here were interested in the facts that motivated me to act in defense of the human rights of Christians?" Judge Lubentsova cut him off and replied that the court had no interest. She told him instead that he could make a final plea for mercy, an offer he rejected. While Judge Lubentsova likely expected his remorse or perhaps a lengthy, tearful proclamation of his innocence, to her surprise, she heard neither. Gleb's final speech consisted of only one sentence: "I thank God for the fate he has given me." The court sentenced him to five years in strict-regime camps and five years in exile. As Judge Lubentsova pronounced the court's decision, television cameras recorded the scene for showing later that evening on the news.[65]

On August 28, following the trial's conclusion, a small crowd outside the Moscow city courthouse stood by helplessly. As a green van pulled slowly away, the prisoner's weeping aunt threw pink gladioli against its darkened back window.[66] Several in the crowd tried to comfort the prisoner's disconsolate wife, the mother of his three children. Inside the police van, Fr. Gleb Yakunin took a final look at his loved ones gathered nearby on the street. He did not know whether he would ever see them again.[67]

In retrospect, the internal dynamics of Fr. Gleb Yakunin's trial illustrate the conflict between law and ideology. "The court is not interested," the wording of Judge Lubentsova's reply to Yakunin's offer to speak to the motivations underlying his actions testified to the court's lack of concern with getting to the truth as well as its predetermined view of what the trial's outcome had to be. The prosecutor's lack of concern about legal standards, the reliance on claims without supporting evidence, the general nature of the indictment without reference to underlying legal statutes, and the behavior of many of the witnesses are evidence of the court's ideological interests. The preplanned course of the trial and the assumption of Fr. Gleb's guilt aimed to satisfy these interests. An article published a few days later in the trade union newspaper *Trud* applauded the trial's outcome: "The criminal got his just desserts. Those present in the hall, including workers and engineers from several Moscow enterprises and building sites, workers from scientific institutes, and personnel of state institutions met the court's decision with approval."[68]

"I thank God for the fate he has given me." The one-sentence summation uttered by Fr. Gleb at the trial's conclusion conveyed a meaning different from a political message. In these words, Yakunin referenced a significant touchstone in the Russian Orthodox tradition. They evoked memories of individuals who confronted royal authority and willingly suffered the consequences. Whether he had them directly in mind was unlikely, but the spiritual values they represented were present in his farewell statement. The image of fate recalled the great luminary of the early Church Gregory of Nazianzas (Gregory the Theologian, 325–390), one of the three fathers of the Russian Orthodox Church, who lived in an era marked by violent clashes between Christians and pagans.[69] This father of the church, whom Fr. Aleksandr Men celebrated, was a lifelong seeker whose suffering caused him intense personal pain, but led to his greatest poetic achievements.[70] Yakunin's statement also expressed the self-suffering values of Russia's first canonized saints, Boris and Gleb (d. 1015), who accepted voluntary suffering and death in imitation of Christ. Hearing the court's verdict, Yakunin understood its consequences and the suffering that awaited him.

CHAPTER 7

The Outcast

The sentencing of Fr. Gelb Yakunin did not go unnoticed either in the Soviet Union or in Western Europe. In response, two different narratives quickly developed. The first offered severe criticism of the court proceedings and underscored the values that Yakunin represented. The second aimed at defending the court's decision and portraying him as an arch-villain. The two narratives provided vastly dissimilar interpretations of Fr. Gleb's activities and how their motivations should be perceived.

After the conclusion of Yakunin's trial in late August 1980, as in the case of Tat'iana Velikanova, human rights organizations in the Soviet Union immediately protested what they viewed as a "judicial farce." In Velikanova's case, Elena Bonner, wife of the exiled dissident Andrei Sakharov, returned from visiting her husband in Gorky to take part in a public vigil outside the courtroom.[1] On the day following Yakunin's trial, on August 29, a petition signed by Sakharov and forty-six other supporters, titled "Who Is Guilty?" protested the court proceedings in the trials of Yakunin and Velikanova. The charge of "Anti-Soviet agitation and propaganda," causing the "weakening of Soviet power . . . through the dissemination of slanderous fabrications for the same purpose, are lies," the petition read.[2] The petitioners called out the injustice of the sentences in both trials. They spoke for the defendants, proclaiming the purity of their motives in emotional but decisive language, describing "two flawlessly honest people doomed to serve long terms in prison and exile, separated from their families, because they wrote the truth; the truth is objectionable to those who fear it, and truth is what those persecuted here stand for."[3]

A similar defense of Fr. Gleb came from a Moscow monk who signed his name simply as the Orthodox monk Innokentii. Innokentii wrote as a severe critic of the legal processes that had taken place in Yakunin's case. His paper, which he composed and distributed in samizdat soon after Yakunin's trial ended, was titled "The Reprisal" (*Rasprava*). In it, he excoriated the state for holding Fr. Gleb for ten months in the Lefortovo Prison while the police undertook a so-called investigation of his activities. This turned out not to be an "investigation" at all, but an effort to subject him "to psychological pressure designed to break his will, spirit, and resistance, to destroy his personality, and, in this way, persuade him to make a public confession of self-condemnation and recantation."[4]

Innokentii asserted his view that several claims made against Yakunin were false narratives concocted by the state. Like Sakharov, he disputed the charge that Yakunin had violated the laws and undermined the state's legal order. Yakunin had spoken the truth, and for telling the truth, the Soviet government had prosecuted him. Further, in his support for the laws, Yakunin had conducted a struggle "not against the government, but against lawlessness, deceit, arbitrary power, and wanton violations of religious rights and freedom."[5] For these, the authorities considered him a dangerous criminal. To protect their own power, which the author identified with lawlessness, the governing authorities punished the person who called out their transgressions.[6] Innokentii's paper posited what he saw as the fundamental conflict between fantasy, wrapped up in an ideological distortion of social order, and harsh realities, evidenced by concrete facts.

Like the petition composed by Sakharov and his supporters, the monk Innokentii addressed a higher order of morality than the court proceedings had shown. Both documents emphasized the importance of truth to a flourishing civil society. Both defended the accused against the malicious falsehoods of those in power. Sakharov appealed to a "just order" embedded in laws and adherence to the truth. Innokentii, on the other hand, framed his argument in what he called the "rebirth and stabilization of humanity," the standard, he maintained, found in Orthodox Christian morality.[7] In the place of egoism, pride, deception, killing, and the love of power, this moral ideal had its foundation in "Christian freedom, charity, and love."[8] It was the moral ideal, he argued, that Yakunin had fought to preserve.

Both Sakharov's petition and Innokentii's "Reprisal" created a strong narrative in defense of Fr. Gleb Yakunin. Condemning the legal processes that had condemned Fr. Gleb, they found the harsh sentences levied against Yakunin and

Velikanova unjust. "Their relatives, their friends, and all those who value the honor of our Motherland are proud of them and will always be proud of them," wrote Andrei Sakharov.[9] In the eyes of government officials, however, this narrative could not be allowed to stand. They created a much different account of the proceedings that led to the verdicts, particularly in the trial of Fr. Gleb.

On the day Yakunin's trial concluded, TASS, the official Soviet news agency, issued its version of his sentencing. TASS justified the outcome as consistent with Part 1 of Article 70 of the Criminal Code, which defined criminal acts as propaganda and agitation aimed at weakening the Soviet state.[10] The prosecutor had proved that Yakunin had fabricated, reproduced, and widely distributed materials aimed at undermining the Soviet Union. But the TASS correspondent's news summary also went further, portraying Yakunin as dangerous to the social order, guilty of establishing criminal connections with ideological centers abroad whose major purpose aimed at the internal subversion of the Soviet Union.

Perhaps the most damning indictment in the TASS correspondent's narrative consisted of his assertion that Yakunin's activities had nothing to do with religion.[11] The writer of the report dealt mainly with psychological and personal factors in which commercial and political gains underlay Yakunin's motives. The court established, he claimed, that Yakunin skillfully bought and sold icons, books, and precious metals and stones for his own profit, that he did little in service of the church, and that he had cleverly cultivated an image of selflessness that concealed his real interests. TASS referenced one of the main witnesses, Aleksandr Shushpanov, who had served alongside Fr. Gleb early in the priest's career. Yakunin had betrayed the church, Shushpanov said: "At first, I considered him a very religious person, but the longer I served with him I came to the conclusion that his primary interest lay in accumulating political capital for himself, through the use of religion."[12]

In its efforts to defend the court's decision publicly, the TASS account contained several misleading and false statements. The TASS story cited testimony from two of Yakunin's closest associates, Lev Regel'son and Viktor Kapitanchuk. Both men testified to working with Yakunin; both, according to this official account, confessed to knowing their actions were harmful to the Soviet state, with Kapitanchuk going further and naming foreign organizations to which all of them had deliberately allied themselves. Finally, the TASS correspondent maintained, Yakunin himself had confessed to taking part in acts "hostile to the Soviet Union," tearfully asking for forgiveness and saying that he "would never again engage in such actions."[13]

The significance of the government's account was that it provided the context for other, later accounts of Gleb Yakunin. Less than a week later, a lengthy article titled "Which 'Father' Did Gleb Serve? written by Soviet journalist Leonid Kolosov, appeared in the mass-circulation newspaper *Trud* (Labor). The article contained many inaccuracies, including the assertion that Yakunin's trial was an "open process."[14] Kolosov rarely mentioned Fr. Gleb's service as a priest, focusing instead on what he considered—and several witnesses in the trial referred to as—Yakunin's commercial activities, buying and selling icons, silver and other precious metals, rare books, and jewels. This was the person Western propagandists called a "leading fighter for religious liberty in the Soviet Union." Kolosov mentioned two British visitors to Moscow, David Atkinson, a member of the British Parliament, and David Beak, his assistant, both supporters of Yakunin, who advised him about how best to attack Soviet ideology. In the same vein, the *Trud* journalist cited the trial testimony of Viktor Kapitanchuk, who invoked the name of Henry Dakin: "I fully admit that, after establishing criminal relations with Dakin, the editor of the 'Washington Street Research Center' through Yakunin and Regel'son, during 1977–79, we regularly sent him, through illegal channels, materials that I and the above-named individuals had prepared, materials of a tendentious nature, containing slanderous inventions for mass distribution. . . . I know that these documents were used by various Anti-Soviet centers and organizations, including the so-called People's Labor Alliance, the editors of the journal *Posev*, 'Radio Liberty' and others in their hostile activity against the Soviet state."[15] These articles in the Soviet press cast Yakunin not as a committed servitor of the Orthodox Church, but as a rogue figure whose primary interest lay in self-aggrandizement. But the articles had another significant purpose: to warn Orthodox clergy about making connections with foreigners and what the possible consequences were.

While Soviet journalists criticized Yakunin's connections to Henry Dakin and others as associations designed to subvert the Soviet state, these efforts warrant a different interpretation. As mentioned earlier, Henry Dakin had a strong interest in cultivating people-to-people relationships that transcended national political bureaucracies, which, he believed had produced frozen, outworn confrontations.[16] Yakunin, too, although operating from a different set of values, had a major desire to forge bonds with people of different nationalities in a common struggle against nearly universal problems. In these attempts, Yakunin and especially Lev Regel'son held views they had encountered earlier in the student seminar in Moscow.[17] Facing harsh, often unyielding government power, seminar members wrote to their brothers and sisters in the United States, during the darkest days of the Cold War and the nuclear threat, seeking to establish common ground and to emphasize their shared humanity. In a letter addressed to "Young Americans," composed in late November or early December 1979, seminar participants expressed their desire to reach across physical boundaries. They wrote, "We would like to tell you that, in response to this call, there is another that is growing and rising to meet it, coming from the depth of our existence. It began with a desperate protest of our human nature against the total power of the lie."[18] The principle of "all-unity," which seminar members derived from the Russian philosopher Vladimir Solov'ev, conceived of everything in the natural world, the social world, and the spiritual realm as interrelated; this unity, Solov'ev had written, comprised one of the foundational principles of Christianity.[19] Earlier, in their "Appeal" to the World Council of Churches, Yakunin and Regel'son had emphasized this fundamental principle in calling for the delegates' support for persecuted religious believers in the Soviet Union and elsewhere. They pleaded for churches to move beyond their narrow "egotistical indifference towards other people's suffering" to defend freedom of conscience wherever such action might be required.[20]

In Western Europe and elsewhere, strong but diverse reactions almost immediately followed the verdict in Gleb Yakunin's trial. In London, 3,500 members of clergy of numerous faiths signed a petition demanding the release of Yakunin and others who had led the struggle for freedom of conscience. The petition, presented to the Soviet Embassy, expressed the conviction that "their arrest and present imprisonment have come about solely as a result of their faithfulness to the Gospel."[21] In Oxford, Michael Bourdeaux and his colleagues at Keston College, who had supported Yakunin for several years, pledged to stay in touch with him.[22] In Frankfurt, Anatolii Levitin-Krasnov, having emigrated six years earlier, wrote a lengthy piece for the émigré journal *Posev* in which he portrayed Yakunin and others as leaders of a burgeoning democratic movement. He called them "heroes of the spirit" in the Soviet Union.[23] In Sydney, the Orthodox Church of Australia issued an appeal for letters of moral support and letters of protest from church leaders and members of Parliament to be sent, respectively, to Iraida Yakunina and Patriarch Pimen.[24] These petitions, letters, and other writings offered evidence that Yakunin's plight would not be soon forgotten.

Incarceration

As expected, in the days following his trial, Yakunin appealed for a commutation of his sentence, asserting that he had not violated any laws. Meanwhile, he remained incarcerated in the Lefortovo Prison while awaiting the results of his appeal. Months passed, an unusually long time for a review, which normally required only a few weeks. Finally, after six months, he learned that the courts had denied his appeal.[25] In March 1981, Yakunin left Lefortovo Prison for transport to a forced labor camp, the notorious Perm-37, where the state sent "political prisoners" deemed dangerous to the Soviet political and social order.

Perm-37 represented one of three labor camps—Perm-35, -36, and -37—that were part of a vast chain of the gulag, which Stalin created in 1930. As the numbers of people accused of crimes against the state mushroomed in the late 1920s, Stalin put them to work. He built a massive network of labor camps that eventually stretched from the Ural Mountains across Siberia.[26] The Perm settlements made up a minor segment of this chain. Founded in 1946, the three Perm sites originally served as logging camps in the dense forests to the east of Perm, where workers felled trees and floated them down the Kama and Chusovaia Rivers to the Volga to collection sites from which they were distributed to construction locations throughout the Soviet Union.[27] All three of the Perm camps lay near the village of Kuchino, about sixty miles east of Perm; travel to the camps from the city required a four-hour bus ride across rutted roads marked by frequent potholes.

After Stalin's death in March 1953 and the general amnesty that soon followed, the Perm camps fell into disuse. But their abandonment proved short-lived. During Khrushchev's rule, they served as places of incarceration for former state security officers. In 1972, under the administration of Leonid Brezhnev and the KGB chief Yuri Andropov, the purposes of Perm-35, -36, and -37 again underwent change. They became the primary sites to which the state sent "politicals"—human rights activists, people of influence from the republics who supported independence, religious visionaries, and rebellious writers and publishers.[28]

Yakunin arrived at Perm-37 labor camp in the early spring of 1981, when the worst of the winter had passed, but the air remained frigid and deep snow covered the entire settlement. The site presented a dilapidated, godforsaken appearance. Several rings of barbed-wire fences encircled the camp. A heavy metal gate allowed admittance, and inside were several rows of ramshackle, poorly constructed wooden barracks that were unpainted and poorly heated. A high wooden fence surrounded the compound, with several watchtowers rising above the fencing. Upon arrival, a prisoner would be issued a bug-infested woolen blanket, a pair of leather boots, and a thin gray uniform.[29] Here Gleb Yakunin would spend the next four and a half years of his sentence, enduring winters in which the temperature often reached 40 to 50 degrees below zero and the summers were infested with mosquitoes and had daytime temperatures in the 90s. His fellow inmates included writers, poets, religious believers, and former demonstrators for civil liberties whom the state considered in opposition to the regime.[30] Incarcerated in Perm-37, too, was the human rights activist Yuri Orlov, whom Yakunin had known in Moscow.

The police designated Perm-37 as a high-security camp, which meant it was not as stringent as the neighboring maximum-security outpost, Perm-36, several hundred yards away. The restrictions and treatments in Perm-37 did not match the extreme cruelties of Stalin-era labor camps; nevertheless, the guards could be harsh and their demands onerous. Yet Perm-37 camp authorities did allow the limited receipt of mail, an occasional visit by a relative, and printed materials, but only those published in the Soviet Union. On April 29, soon after Fr. Gleb's arrival, camp authorities allowed him a visit from his wife, Iraida. The visit gave her the first glimpse of her husband since his trial the previous August. "He is very thin, and is having health problems because of high blood pressure," she reported to the Keston News Service. "He has not been assigned to one specific kind of work in the camp, but is constantly moved from task to task. His hair and beard have been shaved off."[31] The same news service noted that on May 4, Fr. Gleb participated in a one-day fast that Yuri Orlov had planned to coincide with a world conference in Madrid, convened to review the compliance of various governments with the Helsinki Accords on human rights.[32]

Here, as in labor camps elsewhere in the Soviet Union, prisoners' relationships with the guards required constant negotiation. As the journalist Anne Applebaum has written, guards exerted pressure on prisoners to become informers, to renounce their former lives, or to break their will.[33] Prisoners, in turn, sought to manipulate guards into rewarding them with extra privileges, food, or release from onerous duties. A sympathetic guard might be willing to post a letter to a spouse or a friend, while a hostile guard could easily add to the burdens the inmate faced daily. The rules governing life in the camp were not fully known by prisoners, and they were applied arbitrarily, leaving inmates uncertain of their standing and fearful of what lay immediately ahead. This lesson Yakunin would quickly learn.

A contemporary of Yakunin's who served in Perm-37 at the same time penned a detailed description of life and work in the labor camp. The authorities, he wrote, allowed prisoners to spend up to five rubles in the camp commissary—more like a stall—which opened only once each month.[34] The camp paid prisoners a meager amount for each day's labor, of which 10 percent was deposited and the monthly sum accumulated in a camp logbook. The rules for Perm-37 required each person to do physical labor every day, excluding a day of rest on Sunday, regardless of the prisoner's physical condition or age. Often, camp authorities enlisted a prisoner to perform unofficial work that went unpaid.

In the event, however, that someone violated the rules, the authorities deducted a certain unspecified sum from the person's total amount in the fund. If the violation was severe, authorities had the right to deduct the whole sum. Perm-37 had a work plan for the month, a production quota, and if prisoners failed to fulfill their allotted share of the plan, they were fined.[35] This, too, happened often. Only on occasion, therefore, did a prisoner accrue the five rubles to spend at the commissary. "What would five rubles buy, if a person had that amount? It was enough to purchase two cans of jam, a month's supply of unfiltered cigarettes, and sometimes a few small items," a fellow prisoner wrote. "If a person had several violations on his record, the individual could be denied any purchases."[36]

The authorities in Perm-37 designed these restrictive camp practices of penalties and rewards as a means of controlling the inmates. They allowed little recourse for those who opposed camp practices to fight back without incurring severe consequences, but this did not mean that a person had to be submissive.[37] Yakunin offered an example of the refusal to compromise on an action he viewed as an assault on his personhood. Upon his arrival at Perm-37, camp authorities removed all his possessions, including the religious literature he had brought with him. Despite his repeated pleas for the return of these items, the authorities refused, asserting that they could not allow such publications in the labor camp. Undaunted by their refusal, Yakunin wrote to the Perm Regional Procuracy, whose reply on May 28, 1981, adamantly refused his request, stating, "There is no provision in the law for the possession and use of religious literature by condemned persons."[38]

Refusing again to accept the procuracy's verdict, Yakunin went further. He wrote two appeals, both of which were smuggled out of the camp and posted elsewhere. The first he addressed to President Leonid Brezhnev and signed it from "Gleb Pavlovich Yakunin, incarcerated under Article 70 of the Criminal Code of the RSFSR." He reported that camp authorities had taken from him his Bible, Psalter, prayer book, and a church calendar; all of these materials the Moscow Patriarchate had published legitimately, and he asked for their return. Yakunin's appeal also mentioned fellow prisoners Aleksandr Ogorodnikov in Perm-36 and Vladimir Poresh in Perm-35, who had endured similar confiscations. The actions of the camp authorities, he argued in inflammatory language, were "unprecedented in history; even in Nazi chancelleries, the fascists did not seize Bibles and the New Testament from the clergy and religious believers."[39] Yakunin's appeal was signed by sixteen inmates of Perm-37, including Yuri Orlov.

The second letter, addressed as "An Appeal to Western Christians," Yakunin sent to Keston College in England. Significantly, he did not sign his "Appeal" as a prisoner in a labor camp, but as a priest and member of the Christian Committee for the Defense of Believers' Rights.[40] In it, he requested the prayerful support of Christians everywhere on behalf of those whom the state had sentenced to lengthy terms for their religious beliefs. He specifically mentioned Ogorodnikov and Poresh; both they and he, Yakunin wrote, offered concrete examples of state persecution, which representatives of the Moscow Patriarchate had vehemently denied at the Nairobi Assembly. Each of them had not only faced persecution for their beliefs, but the authorities' confiscation of their religious literature denied them even the right to read the Bible. Yakunin noted that he had written in protest to the appropriate state bodies, but his protests "resulted in refusal or [had] been ignored completely."[41] His remaining recourse was to reach out beyond the governing institutions in his country and "appeal to you, dear friends, and to all those believers who do not remain indifferent to the lot of persecuted Christians to support imprisoned believers who are demanding that the Soviet authorities cease to violate their right to freedom of conscience."[42]

In his "Appeal" to Western Christians, Fr. Gleb cited fasts begun by Ogorodnikov and Poresh. "Now, it is my turn," he said, and announced his intention to begin a hunger fast on September 16, if camp authorities continued to deny him access to his Bible.[43] Furthermore, he proclaimed his desire to "draw attention to the crude denial of the right to freedom of conscience to inmates in Soviet prisons and camps." Having exhausted every internal venue to protest what he believed violated rights of conscience, Yakunin turned to the only avenue available to him: communicating personally with citizen supporters outside the Soviet Union. Somehow, he had confidence they would hear his pleas for help.

Historically, hunger strikes initiated by well-known leaders of social movements have drawn world attention to the causes for which they struggled. The most famous examples were the fasts of Mahatma Gandhi, which he offered as a sacrifice on behalf of the "suppressed brethren and sisters" in India.[44] Cast in similar language, Yakunin viewed his coming fast as an effort to draw the Western world's attention to people deprived of liberty, confined in labor camps, where they were "condemned to spiritual starvation."[45] When he began his hunger strike on September 16, Keston College followed his movements as closely as possible through information leaked to its contacts in Moscow. Keston reported that ten days after Yakunin's hunger strike began, other camp inmates, including Yuri Orlov, had joined him in staging fasts to "demonstrate their solidarity with him."[46] In light of his already weakened physical condition, Fr. Gleb's body could not withstand a prolonged fast, but, determined to continue his protest until the authorities relented and returned his Bible, he stayed the course. On September 26, camp officials, concerned about Yakunin's rapidly deteriorating health, ordered him to be fed intravenously. They arranged for his temporary transfer to Perm-35, which had a small hospital where he might receive better medical care.[47]

It is unknown precisely when Yakunin ended his hunger strike. He returned to Perm-37 in early 1982, and Keston College later reported that he then had access to his Bible.[48] Despite this concession, however, neither his harsh treatment nor Western interest in his fate dissipated over the next two years. In the second half of the year, camp authorities sentenced him to four months of solitary confinement in the camp's internal prison, where his food ration consisted of only fourteen ounces of bread daily and, on every second day, a small bowl of soup. They forbade him to receive any correspondence, allowed him no extra warm clothing, and, without a bed, left him to sleep on the cold floor of his cell.[49] The stated reason for his punishment was his engagement in "religious agitation" among the young who were serving time in the camp, but the more plausible unofficial explanation was that Fr. Gleb had revealed the identity of a person who earned special favors by regularly reporting on fellow prisoners to camp authorities.[50]

Yakunin survived the next two years in Perm-37 enduring the mocking taunts of the prison guards, the perpetual threat of further punishment, and the physical demands of an intensive work schedule. Any extra time at his disposal he spent writing, beginning a long poem whose contents will be discussed in due course. He was perhaps buoyed by news of several awards for bravery and civic service in New York and in London, but even these were tempered by worries about the condition of his wife and children in Moscow.[51] In late 1984, Fr. Gleb Yakunin's five-year prison term that had begun at the end of his trial in 1979, came to an end, and he prepared to begin the next stage of his sentence, his five-year term of forced internal exile.

Exile

While Yakunin might have found relief in his release from Perm-37, any solace he experienced was short-lived. The state security police assigned Fr. Gleb to a village in the harshest, coldest region of the inhabited world, the Republic of Yakutia (Republic of Sakha). Located in northeastern Siberia, Yakutia is Russia's largest republic, with a land area of 1.2 million square miles; it is the basin of Siberia's mightiest rivers—the Lena, Kolyma, Indigirka, and Yana—which flow northward into the Arctic Ocean. The average temperature in January is –46 degrees F, but the nights and early mornings often reach –50 to

–60 degrees F; Yakutia has recorded the lowest temperatures in the Northern Hemisphere. The republic produces the most prized diamonds in the world and provides one-quarter of the world's supply of these precious stones. The Sakha people, an indigenous Turkish tribe, originally inhabited Yakutia; in the 1980s, they composed about one-third of the population, making a living from mining, fishing, herding reindeer, and hunting fox, ermine, and squirrel. In the twentieth century, the republic became a favorite location for the police to send political dissidents. In exiling Fr. Gleb Yakunin to this remote region, the police ensured that, for the immediate future, his voice could not be heard.[52]

Yakunin was posted to the distant Siberian village of Solnechnyi, in the southeastern corner of the republic. Travel to Solnechnyi presented a major challenge, since the railroad did not pass nearby. To reach the village, a person had to fly to Yakutsk, the capital city, then negotiate with the pilot of a small plane to fly to a town closest to the village, and, upon arrival, take a bus, and from there hitch a ride with a lorry or, failing that, walk the remaining distance.[53] Yakunin's arrival in late January presented another impediment: it coincided with the most severe time of year. Although details are lacking about this difficult situation, upon his arrival in the village, he somehow managed to obtain temporary lodging with a local inhabitant and to wait for warmer weather before securing a more permanent accommodation.

Yakunin was skilled at improvising, and late that spring, he began to construct a small hut for himself, although he lacked the necessary materials to secure it against the cold winds that swept through the village (figure 7.1). To earn money, he obtained work in a carpentry shop in the village, making minor repairs for local people and eking out meager pay that barely enabled him to live.[54] That summer of 1981, his wife Iraida and two of his children, Mariia, the eldest, and Anna, the youngest, anxious to see him after these many months, traveled the vast distance to be with him. Iraida reported that he worked mostly as a common laborer, doing odd physical jobs, including grave digging.[55] The presence of his wife and two children undoubtedly lifted his spirits.

The visit of his wife and children, however, also sharply reminded Fr. Gleb of the suffering that they, too, had endured. Whether financially or psychologically, the daily struggles and well-being of his family bore constantly upon them. Earlier, he had learned that his wife had fallen seriously ill and had to take a leave from her job, a misfortune that left the family without her salary.[56] Already lacking the financial cushion to survive during a crisis, they did not have adequate food and clothing for the long Moscow winters. How the members of Yakunin's family managed to live during these extremely difficult circumstances required considerable ingenuity. It also took a great deal of help

THE OUTCAST   149

FIGURE 7.1. House in Siberian village in which Yakunin lived in exile, 1985–1987. Courtesy of the Keston Center for Religion, Politics, and Society, Baylor University, Waco, Texas.

from friends, especially from a remarkable person named Lidiia Iosifovna Zdanovskaia.

Lidiia Iosifovna was Fr. Gleb's aunt and the wife of Anatolii Levitin-Krasnov. A resourceful, strong, and humble person, she was also a parishioner of the Moscow church where Fr. Viacheslav Vinikov, a close, lifelong friend of Fr. Gleb's, served.[57] When a friend was in need, she stepped in. In the 1960s, because of his critical writings, Levitin-Krasnov ran into trouble with state authorities, which prohibited him, a single man living in a communal apartment, from entering Moscow. Because he lacked a private residence, which otherwise would have enabled him to live in the city, Lidiia Iosifovna offered to marry him, and she took him into her own apartment in Moscow. Whether they actually lived as husband and wife is uncertain, but in 1974, after his emigration to Switzerland, she spoke of him as her "husband," and he, in his memoirs, referred to her as his "beloved wife."[58] In the 1980s, during these trying times for the Yakunin family, Lidiia Iosifovna cared for the children and helped to raise them. She provided constant support to all of them, without which their very survival would have been doubtful.[59]

In significant acts of heroism, Aunt Lidiia also reached out to Yakunin in Siberia. In the late summers of 1985 and 1986, she filled two large suitcases

150   CHAPTER 7

with food and flew to Yakutsk. There, she engaged a helicopter pilot to fly her to the village where Yakunin lived. The pilot helped her stow the heavy suitcases on the plane, and when they landed, he unloaded them for her, leaving her only to find Yakunin's small hut. She had worried he would not survive the brutal winters and had confided her concerns to a friend. Her friend assured her of Fr. Gleb's strength and capacity to endure this challenge, but Aunt Lidiia had to make certain, and her delivery of food was her endeavor to help. She stayed with him into the autumn. "When the first freeze came, she awakened in the morning to find herself covered with frost, which had drifted in through the cracks in the walls."[60] Only then, having fulfilled her mission, did Lidiia Iosifovna return to Moscow.

Facing the cold, loneliness, and isolation of the village in distant Yakutia, Yakunin had to dig deep into his own inner resources to endure the hardships he faced. As others before him had experienced, personal isolation became one of his greatest challenges. But just as he had managed earlier in Perm-37, he did not give in to these life-threatening difficulties. He needed to find a means of connecting to a world larger than his own immediate circumstances. In the labor camp, and particularly in exile, he turned to poetry as spiritual and emotional sustenance. Poetry gave him a way to replenish his storehouse of ideas and to relate to others beyond the daily exigencies of physical life. Above all, poetry became a means of stimulating his imagination and bringing to the surface memories that lay buried in his consciousness.

A "Golden Treasury"

Poetry has a "very special place in this country," wrote Nadezhda Mandel'stam, the wife of Osip Mandel'stam, one of Russia's greatest twentieth-century poets. Poetry, she said, "is a golden treasury, in which our values are preserved; it brings people back to life, awakens their conscience and stirs them to thought."[61] While serving in the labor camp, and later in exile in remote Siberia, Yakunin wrote poetry in an attempt to reflect on Russia's past and to project a vision for his country's future. This awakening of conscience and stirring of thought characterized the verses Fr. Gleb conceived from the depths of Perm-37. In them, he returned to his aspirations as a younger man and to his hopes of being part of a reformation within the church. He wanted to contribute to this reformation and its attendant practices of redemption and healing, which formed key elements of his poetry. They were, he believed, more important than ever in Russia's present condition. He wrote a long narrative poem, much of it while in Siberian exile, a personal, probing account of the ideals for which he fought with such passion and determination. The poem, he said repeatedly, contains his theology, his hopes, and his perspectives on humanity.[62]

Yakunin titled his poem "Eulogy of a Simple-minded Fool of God: In Honor of God, the Universe, and the Homeland."[63] In neither the labor camp nor exile did Yakunin have the essential scholarly resources to write a narrative poem. He would work on it for many years afterward, and he told his readers that in the process of writing it, he went through many periods of depression and anxiety, thinking that he would not be able to complete it.[64] Ultimately, however, the long poem was finished, most likely in the 1990s. But the original conception and the main ideas belong to that earlier period, during his years of imprisonment and exile when his oldest daughter, Mariia Glebovna, believes he wrote the best parts of his narrative poem.[65]

The Russian literary scholar Elena Volkova, who has written a fine introduction to Yakunin's work, described the poem as written in the genre of "idiotic primitivism," a "form of writing popular in the late seventeenth and early eighteenth centuries."[66] As Volkova points out, Yakunin's work is filled throughout with popular speech and images, the language of the street, and a play on words, "characteristic of the 'dark' unchained language of 'holy fools,' who like children, loved to play with shapes and gestures."[67] The purpose of these so-called holy fools was to "unmask delusions" and forecast the future. It was Yakunin's attempt to "unmask delusions" that had led to his arrest earlier and his sentencing to the labor camp and exile. Although he broke no law, he did aim to expose hypocrisy and to champion human dignity, goals that proved deeply threatening to the captive mind. These themes run throughout his poetry.

"Eulogy of a Simple-minded Fool of God" treats a wide range of topics. The poem discusses the conditions of the labor camp and the cold, hunger, and isolation the author had to endure, as well as the extreme cold and dense fog of the Siberian village. But the poem is also Yakunin's spiritual testimony and includes long, lyrical verses about nature, the skies, the seas, and the earth, with reference to the book of Genesis and the creation of the world, the wisdom of the Creator, and his compassion for human beings.

In the wide range of subjects that Yakunin's poem addresses, one theme is threaded throughout, and it applies to every part of his life and theology. He emphasized the need for human beings to be open to the world—to the beauty of nature and to creative activity.[68] Too often, Yakunin stated, the church closed itself off from the world, and it had much richer fare to offer than the materialist philosophy of the Soviet state and its claims of victory over religious belief: "And in celebrating victory / atheism summons everyone to a dinner / but its poverty is revealed by its one-course meal."[69]

Fr. Gleb displayed a dynamic view of world history, in which the entire cosmos was in movement, constantly evolving toward something different from the past: "The whole world lives and evolves, / and it moves under a banner, / under a shadow bearing the inscription / "Progress." / This phenomenon / (the creative method)—/ does not undermine my faith."[70] Like Fr. Aleksandr Men, he conceived of an evolving, unfinished universe, a major thesis of Men's multivolume magnum opus, *Istoriia religii*.[71] Christianity remained incomplete, and people who claimed to have a complete knowledge of the truth were mistaken, because it, too, was in process. Yakunin's poem underscored this view: "The development of the earth is a clear fact / and didn't give me a heart attack."[72]

Since the world's creation was an ongoing process in Yakunin's view, the person participated in this continuous creation. The Creator had not made human beings to be slaves, but because God had endowed humans from birth with a divine spirit, they were made to be creative beings in order to contribute to the betterment of all humanity and to the eventual perfection of the universe: "We have this rare gift, / that the Supreme Authority gave us."[73] Yakunin repeatedly emphasized the connection between creativity and faith and he found it to be a major theme in the teachings of the Gospels. Yet the church in the twentieth century had failed to emphasize this connection, turning its back on the world and on the sciences. In the place of creativity, the church had promulgated an anti-Christian message, locking the door on society and wrapping itself in a pagan cult of empire, power, and collaboration with the police. Yakunin severely condemned this captive spirit and its allegiance to false claims about other human beings and about life in general. His faith required him to speak the truth, regardless of the suffering it might bring in its wake: "Lies / I will not utter / From my mouth / And from my writing. / Listen—/ You will listen to tears."[74]

If the Orthodox Church lay silent under the weight of its transgressions, its ill-begotten present faults, it still had the potential to be a major living presence in Russian life. Yakunin believed strongly in Orthodoxy's inner strength and its capacity to speak profoundly to the Russian people. He had unwavering faith in its potential to break through the stultifying mentality that pervaded it. "But still—can she not be resurrected? / We are yet awaiting the spiritual events to take place in her."[75]

Yakunin told his readers that he wrote his narrative poem as a manifesto, a clarion call to action that he hoped would contribute to this spiritual awakening. Recent circumstances, particularly the spiritual awakening among young people, convinced him that his country was on the verge of an inner transformation. For the Orthodox Church to play a significant part in this transformation would require repentance, healing, and different ways of thinking—needs that his poem expressed in the form of a prayer. "O God? We are paralyzed! / We have frozen! / For a higher purpose / heal us / in your own invigorating way."[76]

In "Eulogy of a Simple-minded Fool of God," Fr. Gleb also expressed his abiding love for Russia. Despite its faults, his country possessed spiritual resources that he believed allowed it to construct a promising, holistic vision for its future. Among the main sources of inspiration were its great religious leaders and writers, to whom Yakunin paid homage. They included Boris and Gleb, the twelfth-century saints whose passive suffering in the face of violence stood out as models of behavior; St. Sergius of Radonezh, the spiritual leader of medieval Russia and Russia's patron saint; the great nineteenth-century elder St. Seraphim of Sarov, whose acts of charity became renowned among the Russian people; and the early twentieth-century patriarch Tikhon, who, at great cost to himself, refused to compromise with the Bolshevik government. Yakunin also emphasized the profound impact of the philosophical/theological writers of the late nineteenth and early twentieth centuries—Vladimir Solov'ev, Nikolai Berdiaev, Sergei Bulgakov, and Viacheslav Ivanov—who initiated the Russian Religious Renaissance. While their influence had been limited in time, they had "pushed back the darkness: / rehabilitated the / humanistic beginning, / and from freedom, the human being began to stir."[77]

Similarly, Yakunin believed it was critically important to rediscover the "revelatory voices in Russian literature," beginning with Maksim the Greek and continuing with Denis Fonvizin, Alexander Radishchev, Nikolai Gogol, Mikhail Saltykov-Shchedrin, and Nikolai Pomialovskii. These visionary writers showed that members of the Russian clergy always talked about God, but, in reality, their behavior demonstrated how little the teachings of the Gospels resonated in their lives.[78] Such revelatory voices, Yakunin pointed out, had not subscribed to the state's ideology; instead, they had challenged the principles on which that ideology rested. They depicted another side of social life, its poverty, the beggars, and marginalized people who struggled against nearly devastating obstacles to retain their sense of human dignity. The works of Nikolai Gogol served as an example: "Before Gogol's eyes / Did not pass by without seeing / (How many beggars there were), / (How much pain existed everywhere!)."[79] All the cultural giants Yakunin named in his poem underscored the importance of the freedom to speak, think, and write to Russia's future well-being.

In addition, as he had in his early years as a parish priest, Yakunin remained critical of the hypocrisy that he witnessed in large parts of the clergy. The years he spent in Perm-37 and Siberian exile did not lessen his disdain for behavior that undermined the sacred mission of the Orthodox Church. His references to Gogol and other Russian writers and artists aspired to bring to public attention a long-standing caste system that perpetuated social injustices. Through their creative works, the writers he referenced had provided a signal service to their homeland. Their emphasis on freedom of thought, their capacity to look beyond static norms, and their courage to challenge unexamined beliefs, in Yakunin's view, had made significant contributions to Russia's moral strength. Even in the depths of his Siberian exile, these voices continued to speak to him. The church needed to purify itself, seek repentance, and embrace the creative spirit with which the Creator had endowed each person.[80] Russia's greatest cultural and religious writers emphasized this connection between creativity and faith, and the future of Christianity in Russia depended on restoring this relationship.

A twist of fate, even less anticipated than those he had experienced earlier, would soon alter the course of Yakunin's life. A remarkable change of events moved him from a remote village on the extreme periphery of Siberia to a position near the center of Russia's political controversies.

CHAPTER 8

Return

The years Fr. Gleb spent in the Perm-37 labor camp and, afterward, in a remote village in northeastern Siberia coincided with some of the most significant events in twentieth-century Russian history. On February 9, 1984, Secretary-General Yuri Andropov, Brezhnev's successor as party leader, died. His replacement, the septuagenarian Konstantin Chernenko, ascended to power on February 13, 1984. In poor health and lacking energy and vision, he was essentially a caretaker who ruled for only a little more than a year before his death on March 10, 1985. His successor on March 11, 1985, fifty-three-year-old Mikhail Gorbachev, understood and almost immediately signaled the need for fundamental reform of the Soviet system. On December 10,1986, he called the exiled human rights leader Andrei Sakharov in Gorky and told him that he was free to return to Moscow. The Soviet leader soon amnestied individuals who had been incarcerated for political reasons. Granted amnesty in early 1987, Yakunin returned to Moscow and immediately took up the causes to which he had previously committed himself. He would find the political and religious landscape he reentered to be both promising and treacherous.[1]

In his narrative poem, "Eulogy of a Simple-minded Fool of God," Yakunin said that his seven-year sentence and exile had not changed him.[2] Whether he wrote this line during or after his two-year stint in a remote corner of Yakutia or afterward is uncertain, but he returned to Moscow with similar goals to those he had before his incarceration. In a much different political environment, the wily art of negotiation and compromise, rather than direct confrontation with political and religious authorities, generally yielded better results.

Months after coming to power, the new Soviet leader Mikhail Gorbachev introduced the program he called perestroika, his revitalization plan to reform the Soviet economy and society. As outlined by the British political scientist Richard Sakwa, between 1986 and 1991, perestroika went through several phases, beginning with an effort to strengthen the economy and make more rational decisions about investments. The next phase featured debates about democratizing the Soviet system and bringing to light issues that previously existed beyond the boundaries of public discourse, followed by the transformation of the economic and political structures and the coup of August 1991. The final phase, from late 1991 to 1992, witnessed the disintegration of the Soviet Union.[3]

Yakunin's return to Moscow took place during the second phase of these revitalization efforts, which began with discussions at the Nineteenth Party Congress in January 1987 about loosening up the socialist system and promoting "openness and transparency" in all phases of Soviet life. What was needed, Gorbachev emphasized, was not only political advancement, but "a new intellectual breakthrough."[4]

If Fr. Gleb confronted a much different political setting post-confinement than he had witnessed earlier, he also encountered a profound change in the government's view of the church. From the outset of his accession to power, Gorbachev recognized and addressed concerns about the erosion of the moral values of the Soviet people. What we must have to succeed, he said, "is greater order, greater consciousness, greater respect for one another, and greater honesty."[5] Concurrently, Gorbachev reversed policies that had long characterized the Soviet government's treatment of the Orthodox Church. In late 1987, the Soviet leader announced the return to the church of two historic monasteries: the Tolga Presentation of Mary, Mother of God nunnery, near the city of Yaroslavl, and the Optina Presentation men's hermitage in the Kostroma Diocese. Both monasteries had faithfully served the Russian people during times of difficulty, and the latter also enjoyed a reputation as a chief source of inspiration for some of Russia's greatest cultural figures, including Nikolai Gogol, Ivan Kireevskii, Ivan Turgenev, Fyodor Dostoevsky, Vladimir Solov'ev, Leo Tolstoy, and many others.[6]

The return of these historic religious centers forecast other changes. On April 29, 1988, Gorbachev invited the now older Patriarch Pimen and five leaders of the Holy Synod to meet with him in the Kremlin. Held in the Great Catherine Hall, this historic event heralded a major change in the status of the Orthodox Church, signaling a much different view of religion than had existed during most of the Soviet era. Gorbachev rescinded a fundamental goal of Marxism-Leninism: to obliterate religious beliefs and practices. He told the patriarch that "believers are Soviet people, workers, and patriots, and they have the full right to express their convictions with dignity."[7] In preparation for the coming celebrations of the millennium of Orthodox Christianity in Russia, Gorbachev also underscored the common history shared by the Russian people and the Orthodox Church and his expectation that this historical bond would continue into the country's future.[8]

Gorbachev's earlier meeting with Patriarch Pimen and the millennium celebrations of Orthodox Christianity in the summer of 1988 precipitated major changes in the status of the church in Russian society. Although the alterations did not immediately overturn decades of ridicule and harassment of the church in public consciousness, they marked the beginning of a vast shift in public attitudes toward one of the cardinal features of Soviet ideology. The atheist goals, proclaimed from the beginning of the Soviet state, suddenly underwent a dramatic reversal. As the state reformed its views on religion, the church quickly regained the physical structures it had lost earlier. In 1988, the church opened 809 new Orthodox communities; in the following year, their numbers grew to 2,564.[9]

The rapid opening of new parishes created major problems of staffing them with qualified pastors. The church's need for well-qualified priests presented Fr. Gleb Yakunin with a golden opportunity when he returned from exile. Despite his suspension by Patriarch Pimen, Yakunin had never relinquished his position as an Orthodox priest, and he immediately sought an appointment to a church parish. This position allowed him to serve the church during an increasingly volatile and rapidly changing period, while also offering support for his family. Moreover, he had long believed that the reawakening of Russian society required rebuilding connections with the treasures of Russia's past. The poetry he wrote during his incarceration and exile had stressed the importance of recovering and building on this mostly forgotten religious heritage.[10] His reintegration into parish life would enable him to contribute to a need he considered essential to strengthening the Orthodox Church and reconstructing his country's identity.

Shortly after the millennium celebrations, Yakunin applied for a position in the church, and the patriarchate assigned him as head priest of a small church on the outskirts of the city of Shchyolkovo, a short distance to the northeast of Moscow, on the Kliazma River. Household silk-weaving craft enterprises had developed here, and over time, they had evolved into silk manufactories.[11] Shchyolkovo was the home of five churches once renowned for their architectural beauty and the thriving parish communities that sustained them before their closure during the Soviet era.[12]

Fr. Gleb began his tenure in the small St. Nicholas Cathedral. The church's origins dated to the mid-sixteenth century, although in 1727, a fire had destroyed its original wooden structure. The present stone church was constructed in 1836, with an elegant bell tower adorning its front edifice.[13] At the time of Fr. Gleb's arrival in 1987, St. Nicholas Cathedral was the only functioning church in a city of fifty thousand people. Although it may have seemed an eternity since he last actively served as a priest, he was well-schooled in the correct order and the complex requirements of the Orthodox service, and he immediately fell into the traditional role of the parish priest. "If one did not know his past," wrote a young journalist assigned to write a story on Yakunin, "it would seem that he [had] always served here, forever submerged in this peaceful and disciplined church world." Sympathetic to his plight, the journalist reminded her readers that the "journey Fr. Gleb had traveled to get here was one of painful difficulties."[14] His arrival coincided with a large infusion of new churchgoers. Many came out of curiosity, wanting to taste the fruit that the state had considered anathema for so long. But Fr. Gleb also found that large numbers came in search of something more satisfying than Soviet schools had prepared them to experience. Asked to explain the rapid growth in the numbers of newly arrived parishioners, Fr. Gleb offered the following explanation: "In the last half-year, most of those who came to my parish were adults, who asked to be baptized. This, apparently, was related to the crisis in the official communist ideology, the lack of success in what state leaders have called the development of socialism. People arrived in despair; they no longer believed in the capacity of the government system to bring them personal well-being. Human beings are essentially spiritual beings—they do not live by bread alone. In reality, by their nature, they are searching for spiritual health, for new ideals."[15]

At the same time that he served his parish community, as throughout his adult life, Fr. Gleb kept a watchful eye on the political direction of the country. Local affairs had never fully satisfied his craving for something more substantial, more connected to the fate of the church as a whole and its role in Russian society. Since his student years, he had believed it was necessary for the church to overcome its inward focus and speak to social and moral problems, as the Russian Orthodox essayist Evgenii Barabanov urged. The clergy needed to help the people "overcome the fetters of lies, the lack of faith, and the [church's] connivance with the political authorities," as Barabanov advised.[16] The church, Barabanov argued, had to recover its own moral traditions, which would enable it to break the chains of subjugation and give it the opportunity to free a compliant, mentally enslaved people.

In 1989 and 1990, Yakunin's public reputation underwent a reversal compared to the perception of him a decade earlier. In the late 1970s the official government press had excoriated him, calling him an enemy of the Soviet state, whereas he was now viewed in a positive light. Having returned from the labor camp and exile, incarcerated for exposing the falsehoods and corruption of the patriarchate, he had reentered a society turned upside down. The journalist Natal'ia Pavlova, writing in one of Moscow's popular newspapers, highlighted the human rights leader Andrei Sakharov's praise of Yakunin and the Orthodox priest's willingness to "speak truth to power."[17] Another journalist, reporting in Novosibirsk's most prominent newspaper, placed Yakunin "on a parallel with Andrei Sakharov and Anatoly Marchenko."[18] Such accolades and his reputation as an outspoken advocate for reform placed Yakunin in a position to speak more broadly than his priestly service in a provincial city might otherwise have allowed. In spring 1990, while continuing to serve his St. Nicolas Cathedral he stood for election to the new Congress of People's Deputies of the Russian Federation.

Intended to loosen the stranglehold of the heavy-handed bureaucratic system, elections, a primary feature of perestroika, aimed at imparting greater dynamism into policy making. The initial two elections—the first in 1987 to local soviets and the second in the spring of 1989 to the new Congress of People's Deputies—represented major stages in the development of competitive elections in the Soviet Union. The third election, on March 4 and March 18, 1990, took place at a turning point in the Gorbachev era. Richard Sakwa points out that the election on March 4, 1990, and its second round on March 18 represented significant developments in democratic politics in the Soviet Union. Unlike other republics, Russia kept its two-tier legislature and elected a Congress of People's Deputies with 1,068 members. The Congress then selected a smaller Supreme Soviet, which dealt with parliamentary issues. Russia had truly entered a time of transformation, and this election came at a precipitous time, when democratic politics and debate over the wholesale remaking of the country had become central parts of this process.[19]

This Congress had significant "long-term importance" in "the shaping of a distinctively Russian political identity," Sakwa wrote. "The vessel of democratic politics was no longer the USSR but 'Russia,' or as the democrats tended to put it at the time, the 'country.'"[20] These developments, in turn, further brought the question of Russia's identity and history to the forefront of public debate.

In the months preceding the 1990 elections, Yakunin and others voiced concerns about the Orthodox Church's capacity to play a significant role in Russia's transformation from a formerly closed society to an open one and whether its previous servility to the political authorities hindered it from thinking creatively.

In November 1989, a small group of senior Orthodox officials and laymen expressed similar worries. They wanted a more honest discussion about the church's ability to adapt to the moral changes on which the success of perestroika depended. In late November and early December 1989, they convened a small conference to debate these issues. The organizers defined their goals as seeking to bring to fruition the "regenerative processes in church life," to establish "healthy standards" for how the church should relate to the state, and to discuss how the church might best rebuild its internal structures.[21]

The leaders of the conference invited Fr. Gleb to make the opening presentation. He and other critics had called for the church to examine its history and its complicity with the communist government, believing that confrontation with the past offered a first step in the church's rebirth.[22] Before it could contribute to the development of religious consciousness in Russia, Fr. Gleb said, the church needed to confront its own past behavior: its collaboration with the Soviet authorities, its complicity in spreading lies, and its unwillingness to protect the downtrodden from the assaults of the state. An honest assessment of these deficiencies would go a long way, Yakunin insisted, toward healing the wounds that the church had inflicted upon itself.

In 1989, Yakunin served as leader of the Church and Perestroika movement formed during the church millennium to examine the moral condition of the country.[23] In line with one of the key goals of perestroika, the movement explored the question of whether the church was prepared to contribute to the transformation of Russia. Yakunin believed that an honest look at the church during the Soviet period—the problems the church confronted, the moral decisions its leadership made, and the consequences of those choices—would help prepare it for the future role it needed to play.[24] He wanted to dispel the mythological version of the past and take a close look at the practical realities of the times, believing that they held moral lessons for Russia's present. His views came close to what the American historian James Sheehan meant by history as a moral science. According to Sheehan, "history works best when it stays closest to the contours of ordinary life, where people must face the painful choice between compliance or resistance, greater or lesser evils, inflicting or suffering harm."[25]

Although dialectical materialism dominated the instruction in Soviet schools, the Russian historians Pyotr Vail and Aleksandr Genis have pointed out that students had also been exposed to the writings of Plato and Aristophanes, Cervantes and Shakespeare, Boccaccio and Pushkin. As a result, as Vail and Genis noted, the moral values mentioned above had inadvertently been ingrained in the mental framework of many students.[26] According to Vail and Genis, Russia's democratic reformers in the late 1980s and early 1990s exemplified these humanistic values in their actions. Moreover, certain moral ideals were embedded in the works of Russia's own literary giants, specifically in Pushkin, Gogol, Dostoevsky, Tolstoy, and Chekhov, whose writings emphasized honesty, compassion, truth-telling, and self-sacrifice.[27] In the Russian Orthodox Church itself, St. Gregory of Nazianus (325–389), one of the three Fathers of the church, exhibited the same attributes in both his personal life and his poetry.[28] Yakunin and his democratic colleagues had a plethora of rich resources on which to draw. The problem now concerned how to inculcate these moral principles in the public sphere and everyday lives of citizens.

In his electoral campaign, Fr. Gleb spoke repeatedly of the need to strengthen the moral climate of the country (figure 8.1). Although the process still had a long distance to travel, the electoral campaigns and the open discussion of major social issues signified that this educational venture had begun. His political campaign emphasized the need for a "religious renaissance, moral guidance, and spiritual education," without which, he reiterated, "we will not succeed in raising the level of [the country's] morality." He then issued a charge that cut to the heart of his political campaign: "It is necessary for us not to be afraid to speak truth to power in our world. An authoritative voice is necessary—especially in a time of cataclysms and shocks. And the church must play this role."[29] To Yakunin, taking an honest look at Soviet history and repenting of the church's

FIGURE 8.1. Yakunin campaigning for office, early 1990s. Courtesy of the Keston Center for Religion, Politics, and Society, Baylor University, Waco, Texas.

complicity in the telling of lies represented vital steps in that direction. In publicly expressing these views, he was clearly treading on extremely sensitive grounds. These notions would raise questions about guilt and collaboration that the leaders of the church might have preferred to leave dormant.

A Democratic or an Authoritarian Order?

In late spring and summer of 1990, the Soviet Union confronted a massive transformation of its political and social life. In nearly every corner of public life, a lively debate ensued over how the state should move forward and what role the church would play in the future rebuilding of Russia. "Who is bold enough to predict with any degree of accuracy when we shall be able to stabilize the situation and begin to live in a civilized, humane, and democratic society," a well-informed, moderate member of the Communist Party wrote in late July 1990. "And finally, who can explain why the path to a rule of law often lies through the jungles of anarchy and lawlessness, shootings and fires, blockades and strikes?"[30]

During those same spring and summer months, two events took place that significantly affected Yakunin's future. First, on May 3, 1990, seventy-nine-year-old Patriarch Pimen (Izvekov), who had served as the head of the Russian Orthodox Church since 1971, died. His replacement, sixty-one-year-old Aleksii II (Ridiger), was enthroned on June 10, at a time when the resurgence of the church was well underway. More energetic and forceful than his exhausted and passive predecessor, the new patriarch promised major changes in the church's status and policies. A former parish priest, Aleksii II viewed the revitalization of the parish and the religious education of the Russian people as among the church's highest priorities. "The greatest wound inflicted by the Communist dictatorship," he said, shortly after his enthronement, "was lack of spirituality."[31] "All other evils," he noted, "were the result of the systematic and total eradication from the souls and consciousness of the people of the very notion of spirituality." Spiritual consciousness, he maintained, formed the common basis of humanity.

But if the new patriarch's early messages promised the resurgence of the church, as well as hopes of building closer connections to the Russian people—actions Yakunin endorsed—other aspects of Aleksii II's portfolio offered more troublesome prospects for what might lay ahead. His education, life as a priest, and rise within the church hierarchy had taken place during the Soviet period, experiences that shaped his world outlook. He had ascended to the patriarchy as a compromise candidate. Having served as bishop of

Tallinn for nearly three decades, and for the previous five years as bishop of Leningrad and Novgorod, the new patriarch had made many concessions to the political authorities.[32] Yet he also expressed a willingness to change with the times, learn from the past, and meet the spiritual needs of the Russian people during times of rapid change and economic instability. In helping to rebuild the church after seven decades of oppression, he knew he faced a formidable task.

Second, only a few months after the new patriarch's enthronement came the shocking murder of Fr. Aleksandr Men, Yakunin's spiritual mentor and longtime friend. Several months before his murder, Men had taken part in a symposium in Germany titled the "Individual and Mass Consciousness."[33] In the opening address to the symposium, the well-known Kyrgyz novelist Chinghiz Aitmatov spoke about mass systems of belief as the bedrock on which totalitarian governments were built. Aitmatov worried about present trends in the Soviet Union. "We are going through a difficult period, a time of troubles, which is assaulting our self-image," he said. "Many in our society want to put an end to this discourse" and revert to a less anxious time, when the state told people what to think.[34]

During the discussion following Aitmatov's presentation, Fr. Aleksandr spoke about the dignity of the individual, which, he noted, could not be separated from a person's spiritual well-being. Mass thinking, he emphasized, invariably led to the degradation of the individual and to a general impoverishment, which Fr. Aleksandr likened "to amputating the foot or hand from the body" or divorcing one from one's own spiritual essence.[35] Recognizing and strengthening this reciprocal relationship and overcoming the attractions of mass society, Fr. Aleksandr said, presented Russia with a pathway forward. Affirming the dignity of the human being offered Russia the opportunity "to build a new paradigm" that would serve the country well in the future.[36] His remarks at the symposium reiterated the importance of "freedom of conscience" as a fundamental human right, which Fr. Gleb Yakunin similarly viewed as essential to the development of an open and democratic society.

Fr. Aleksandr's unexpected death and the failure to discover the culprits made it more important than ever for the state to protect the sanctity of the individual. This required stronger laws that affirmed the right to freedom of conscience, laws that safeguarded people from state incursion into their spiritual beliefs and actions. The creation of such a system necessitated not only new ways of thinking about the laws but also an investigation into the Soviet past and why the government had so willfully violated freedom of conscience.

In the early 1990s, when religious belief had taken on new meaning in the Soviet Union, how might the political system provide future protections against government intrusion? What obstacles needed to be removed in order to guarantee freedom of conscience? These were serious, controversial issues confronting the legislative arm of the government, and they greatly concerned Fr. Gleb Yakunin. Having successfully won a seat in the Russian Congress of People's Deputies in the spring of 1990, he soon found himself in the middle of an effort to address these questions on several fronts.

Remodeling the State

Until 1989, the 1929 Law on Religious Associations governed the laws on religion in the Soviet Union. By this statute, the state allowed religious gatherings to take place only within buildings located on the grounds of a church registered with the government. The law had prohibited churches from conducting various activities, including reaching beyond the narrow confines of those establishments, engaging in charitable activities, teaching religious subjects to children at home, publishing and distributing religious materials, and proselytizing one's faith beyond the physical boundaries of the grounds of the church itself. Some people breached these restrictions, but by doing so, they faced arrest and prosecution that often resulted in long prison sentences.[37]

Given the new status of the church and perestroika's attempts to revitalize religious beliefs, the Congress of People's Deputies of the Soviet Union proceeded to write a new law on freedom of conscience in 1989. Deputies knew the task was urgent in these new conditions, but finalizing a draft of the law went slowly.[38] After much discussion, debate, and revision, the Soviet Congress of People's Deputies completed its task, and on October 9, 1990, a new law on Freedom of Conscience went into effect, extending its coverage to the entire Soviet Union.[39]

Meanwhile, following the general elections in the spring of 1990, the newly formed Congress of People's Deputies of the Russian Federation commenced work on its own law on freedom of conscience. A newly created and loosely organized group calling itself the Russian Christian Democratic Movement spearheaded this effort.[40] Three people made up the leadership of the movement, two priests and an Orthodox layperson: Fr. Gleb Yakunin, Fr. Viacheslav Polosin, a prominent Orthodox pastor, and Viktor Aksiuchits, a layperson and coeditor of the religious-philosophical journal *Vybor* (Choice).[41] Knowing they were in competition with the Soviet committee, Yakunin, Polosin, and Aksiuchits rushed to finish their task.[42] On September 24, 1990, they produced a first draft for presentation to the Congress of People's Deputies of the Russian Federation, whose delegates, for the most part, received it enthusiastically.

After going through several rounds of amendments, the Congress of People's Deputies of the Russian Federation officially adopted the new law on October 25, more than two weeks after the Soviet law went into effect. The Russian law was similar, although in some ways, it was less restrictive than the Soviet version. Crucially, both the Russian and the Soviet laws offered radically different conceptions of the church and the state than those of the preceding sixty-one years.

In the short term, the simultaneous existence of the two different laws created an ambiguous, confusing situation about which law had precedence.[43] The dilemma, however, would soon be resolved by two circumstances: the Russian Republic's growing power and authority and the eventual demise of the Soviet Union. Nevertheless, the conceptions of religious freedom and the independence of the person warrant brief consideration and a comparison of each of the statutes.

Pre-1990 Soviet law, as the legal scholar Harold J. Berman has written, played a parental and educational role. Its purpose was to "guide, discipline, and protect."[44] It treated the individual less like an autonomous human being with autonomous desires and ideas and more like a dependent member of a collective in which the citizen was part of an uncompleted social order. The new Soviet law had a different purpose. In 1988, the chair of the Council for Religious Affairs, likely reflecting Gorbachev's thinking, said that the government had to rectify the wrongs of the past, particularly the treatment of religious believers.[45]

Having learned from the mistakes of Soviet history, both the Soviet and Russian laws defined the individual as an independent being capable of following their own desires and beliefs, allowing each citizen to decide their "own attitude towards religion" and to "confess any religion" or "not to confess any religion."[46] In asserting this legal claim, both laws repudiated the policies on religion that had served as centerpieces of Soviet ideology.

The 1990 Soviet law declared the "equality of all citizens independently of their relationship to religion" (Part 1, Article 6). It thus rescinded the previous claim that the party represented the most enlightened, leading group in society and gave much wider scope to the individual's formulation of his or her religious beliefs. The law removed the source of this authority from the Communist Party and placed it in the citizenry, firmly stating that the "government, its agencies, and its officials are not to interfere in questions belonging to citizens in their relationship to religion" (Part 1, Article 8).[47]

Previously, the term "freedom of conscience" (*svoboda sovesti*) was understood in a contradictory fashion. At times, as the legal scholar Giovanni Codevilla notes, in Soviet jurisprudence, "freedom of conscience" had meant the freedom to believe or not to believe; at other times, the term had signified the obligation of the citizen to free oneself from religious prejudices.[48] For many decades, in order to foster this freedom *from* religion, the state had permitted the publication and dissemination of atheistic materials only. In Soviet constitutional law, "freedom of conscience" thus had a double meaning: the 1977 Soviet Constitution reaffirmed a citizen's right to believe or not to believe, but it expressed the citizen's responsibility to overcome what the party conceived as superstitious, irrational religious thinking.

Both the newly written Russian and Soviet laws removed the ambiguity, giving citizens the right to hold and develop their own religious beliefs.[49] In the Soviet version, however, "freedom of conscience" did not apply to everyone; it specifically applied only to citizens of the Soviet Union; the Russian law did not make this distinction.[50] Moreover, the Russian law affirmed this right in a much broader context than did the Soviet law: "Citizens of the Russian Republic, foreign citizens, and stateless persons may enjoy the right to freedom of religion individually, as well as in concert with each other" (Part 1, Article 3).

By abrogating the party's preeminent position in Soviet society, the 1990 Russian law, like its Soviet counterpart, resulted in a radical social and political reshuffling. The state, not the party, had sovereignty. No longer did the law forbid parents to raise their children in their own religious beliefs; it allowed them to provide religious instruction in the home. Further, the 1990 Russian law proclaimed "the right of every citizen to freely choose, profess, and disseminate one's religious and atheistic beliefs or not to profess any, and to act in accordance with their beliefs, subject to the laws of the state" (Part 1, Article 3).[51] The most important Christian festivals of Christmas and Easter, both of which the former Soviet calendar had not observed, became national holidays. The Russian law affirmed the right of citizens "to receive, acquire, and use religious literature and to participate in religious rites" in a variety of settings, including the military, medical facilities, children's homes and orphanages, institutions for older people, those with disabilities, and prisoners ("as well as in pre-trial detention and penal isolation cells.")"[52]

In their members' discussions, in both the Soviet and Russian legislatures, education quickly became one of the most hotly debated topics, and the two bodies took different roads. The issue concerned how the nation's schools might be transformed to fit the democratic aspirations of the Gorbachev era. The Soviet law no longer required teachers to incorporate an atheistic worldview during regular school hours; it prohibited the teaching of either religious or atheistic ideals. It also required teachers to express neutral attitudes toward these subjects and forbade them to express their personal beliefs.[53]

The 1990 Russian law took a different, less restrictive position. The law reaffirmed the secular nature of the educational system, but it allowed both religious and atheistic classes to be optional offerings in state schools. As part of the regular curriculum, schools could provide "informational classes on religion, but the performance of religious rites in these classes were to be strictly prohibited."[54] As one might expect, the new law had a dramatic effect on classroom instruction and school textbooks. As the state implemented the new law, teachers throughout the school system fundamentally had to adjust to these new ways of thinking, changes that they could not have easily implemented.

In allowing the Orthodox Church to recover from a history of repression and to assert its capacity to engage Russian society, the committee that prepared the 1990 Russian law had to strengthen the church's economic stability. Since the late 1920s, the church had no right to own its buildings and landed property. In previous antireligion campaigns of the Stalin and Khrushchev eras, the police had confiscated sacred objects, precious stones, and religious art, some of which state agents had destroyed and others they had transferred to museums.[55] The question of how to strengthen the church's weak physical capacity was a major issue, and it had large future implications for the church and the state.[56]

The 1990 Russian law restored religious organizations' right to own property, acquire property on their own account, and develop land for their own purposes (Part 3, Article 26). An entire section of the new Russian law, which dealt with property and financial rights, gave religious organizations ownership of their buildings, cultural objects, religious artifacts, icons, monetary donations, and "all other property necessary for their activities" (Part 3, Article 26). Some thorny issues concerning property rights would soon emerge, but for the immediate future, the new Russian law offered the church the chance to regain its economic footing.[57] The law provided only a legal framework, not a detailed plan, for this physical recovery; it left related issues unresolved in a field certain to provoke heated controversy.

In his opening presentation of the new draft law to the Russian parliament, the committee's chair, Fr. Viacheslav Polosin, reminded the deputies of the history of church and state relations since the revolution and the state's brutal attempt to extirpate religion from the consciousness of the Russian people. In 1917, he reminded the deputies, Russia had almost 100,000 Orthodox priests; in 1939, their number had fallen to roughly 500. In 1917, the country had 120 bishops; in 1939, only 4 remained. In 1918, the Bolsheviks shut down all Orthodox ecclesiastical establishments.[58] Stalin labeled his Second Five-Year Plan (1933–1937) an "atheistic plan," which sought to remove the word "God" from the Russian vocabulary. By 1936, Russian priests no longer had legal status, but were "outside the law" and considered parasites. Polosin also asked the deputies to recall that since 1929, the state had forbidden the church to reach out to those in ill health, help people in their local communities, and collect funds for the poor. Khrushchev's massive closure of Orthodox Churches, following their reopening during and after World War II, continued the Soviet state's long-term goal of destroying religious beliefs.

Fr. Viacheslav Polosin told the deputies that they had the choice between two different conceptions of state policy. The first was the Stalinist conception, which, in its official declaration of the separation of the state from the church, in effect meant the government's sovereignty over the church. Such thinking had precipitated the violent assault on the church and its priesthood. The second conception, Polosin said, could be found in the draft law that he, Yakunin, and Aksiuchits had prepared and that lay before them. It needed their support and it underscored the new law's fundamental guarantees against state power. Most important, by clearly defining the rights of believers, the proposed law provided strong protections against the state's infringement of those rights. Furthermore, Polosin emphasized, the draft law provided legal status to religious organizations upon which the state could not legitimately infringe. While he may have oversimplified the choices laying before the deputies, Polosin underscored the seriousness of the present moment. The passage of the proposed new law by the Parliament on September 15, 1990, by a vote of 152 to 16 in support of its adoption, with 20 deputies abstaining, signified enthusiastic support for the second conception Polosin had outlined.[59]

As a member of the committee that wrote the original draft, Fr. Gleb Yakunin spoke immediately after Fr. Viacheslav Polosin. The proposed new law offered the church an opportunity to make itself more outward-looking and dynamic at every level of its operations. "From the point of view of juridical ethics," Yakunin said, "perhaps the law is incomplete, but from the point of view of its content, after many decades, this is the first law in our country that is truly democratic, truly protective of the rights of freedom of conscience, and is in full accordance with the human rights articulated in the Helsinki Accords."[60] The law, he claimed, upended the history of church-state relations in the Soviet Union and potentially prepared the way for a momentous step forward.

The passage of this law signified much more than a legislative act, Yakunin told the deputies; it constituted new ways of thinking, promising to free the citizen from the mental servility that characterized the Soviet era. He expressed faith in the capacity of the Russian people, who, once freed from bonds of servitude to the state, would unleash their democratic spirit. But for this process to gain momentum, Fr. Gleb believed a moral and spiritual revolution was essential. Given the previous history of the Soviet Union, Fr. Gleb's faith in an inherent democratic spirit revealed a certain naiveté about the prerequisites of democracy, and this failure to understand the strength of opposing forces exposed one of his weaknesses. He consistently held out hope in people and their capacity to change, to seek the truth, and to develop a better society than the one presently holding them back.[61] After reading the draft of the law, a deputy from a Moscow district expressed a similar faith in the potential outcome: "We are taking a step to return Russia to its true heritage and civilization, to place emphasis on the moral and spiritual development of the country, and to liberate Russia from the hold of a totalitarian regime over the thought of humanity."[62]

Fr. Gleb knew well that mental and spiritual liberation from the tyranny of a despotic regime depended on more than the passage of a new law. Such liberation also required a fresh look at the reasons underlying the party's control over the mind, an understanding of the historical forces that precipitated "mastery over the human spirit," as Czesław Miłosz referred to the flight from reason to illusion. A tyrannical government appealed to reason, Miłosz noted, while at the same time, it embraced and propagated a collective magic, a collapse of the boundaries between truth and fantasy.[63] What had led to this cataclysm? In Yakunin's view, the historical factors needed elucidation in order for Russia to transition from a tyrannical society to a more democratic one.

More than a decade earlier, Yakunin had written an essay that was published and circulated in Russian samizdat, "In Service to the Cult (The Moscow Patriarchate and Stalin's Cult of Personality)" (*K sluzhenii kul'tu* [*Moskovskaia Patriarkhiia i kult' lichnosti Stalina*]). In 1989, the essay was republished in a volume of essays, *On the Road to Freedom of Conscience* (*Na puti k svobode sovesti*), where it attracted a large readership. In his essay, Yakunin explored some of the foundations of this mental captivity, whose chains of bondage Russians needed to break. "Never, in fact, has its subject—the Moscow Patriarchate and Stalin's cult of personality—been so topical as it is today," he wrote.[64]

Yakunin's "In Service to the Cult" covered a wide range of subjects related to his main theme, which was the connection between the hierarchy of the Russian Orthodox Church and the adoration of Stalin. In identifying the sources of the "cult," Yakunin put in first place the slavish devotion of the leaders of the Russian Orthodox Church to authoritarianism. The patriarch had repeatedly showered Stalin with praise, as exemplified by the patriarch's extravagant, worshipful testimony on December 21, 1949, at Stalin's seventieth birthday celebration. Patriarch Aleksii I assured the Soviet leader of the church's profound devotion and allegiance that had never faltered over the many years of Stalin's rule. He begged the "Great Leader" never to doubt the love of the church and its servitors and the sincere gratitude the people felt for the Soviet leader, who "had selflessly devoted his life" to the "freedom and well-being of the people."[65] In his official letters, the patriarch glorified the Soviet leader with various epithets: "Supreme Leader," "Leader of Genius," "The Great Head of Our State," "Great Builder of the People's Happiness," and "Wise Leader of the People's Well-Being."[66] These words, Fr. Gleb wrote, conveyed much more than political loyalty and praise; they expressed a religious awe and reverential feeling of devotion that the patriarch consistently bestowed on the Soviet leader.

How could this be, Yakunin asked, when the same Soviet leader had put to death many thousands of Orthodox priests, murdered nearly all Orthodox bishops, killed large numbers of believers, and plundered their churches? At the time that he wrote his essay, Yakunin found the same sacrificial devotion in the homage paid by church leaders to Leonid Brezhnev, the Soviet head of state from 1965 to 1982. Even more broadly, this sacred fidelity characterized the entire leadership of the church, a phenomenon that Yakunin's essay attempted to explore, and the reason for its persistence in Russia's religious culture. He saw the "cult" as a sickness, which first had to be diagnosed and, subsequently, extirpated.

Part of the reason for the "cult" was historical. Yakunin believed that the church had started making compromises in the decade following the revolution, when it faced an extremely difficult situation. Although he praised Patriarch Tikhon, the newly elected and revered church leader in the early 1920s, for his truthful and courageous stand in defense of a suffering people, Yakunin traced to Tikhon's time the origins of a long list of compromises perpetuated by church leaders. Yakunin simplistically attributed blame to Patriarch Tikhon, but too easily glossed over the complexities of that early period, as well as Tikhon's repentance near the end of his life.[67] Fr. Gleb was more convincing in his depictions of subsequent leaders and their boundless capacity for pretension and lies. Beginning with the ascension of Metropolitan Sergei in the late 1920s, many of these phenomena were useful to the state, and they fit Stalin's pathological phobias. But they poisoned the church's integrity and compromised its need always to tell the truth. Yakunin maintained that church leaders promoted lies not simply because of fear of destruction and the desire to save the church from extinction, but also because of their wish to recover "symphoniia," this Byzantine concept of state power in which the church served as the government's partner, not as its chief critic or a subservient body. Church leaders failed to "comprehend that the 'symphonic' era was gone forever. They faced a new type of state—one fundamentally hostile to the church—and relations with it required an entirely different direction. The leaders of the church did not see that the contemporary position of the church had become quite similar to its situation in the early years of Christianity."[68]

According to Yakunin, by the late 1930s, the strategy of the state had undergone a change. No longer did the Soviet government seriously consider itself a revolutionary order; the slogan "Workers of the world unite" boldly printed at the top of Soviet newspapers was generally ignored. In practice, the government replaced earlier ideological promises with nationalistic ideas and policies, which became stronger with the onset of World War II. In resurrecting it from near extinction in 1943, Stalin saw the church as a means of bringing the Russian people together around his nationalistic vision. According to Yakunin, the "renaissance" of the church during the war evoked in the patriarchate the belief in a miraculous occurrence, "willed by God," after terrible years of isolation in the desert. Divine Providence had intervened, and, in this historic event, Stalin took on the mantle of "Deliverer." Church leaders referred to him by new appellations such as "Wise One," "God's Deliverer," and the "God-given Supreme Leader." The patriarch, in turn, received special privileges—awards, decorations, medals, and other social distinctions that he and his closest hierarchs quickly learned to savor.

Yakunin's essay is most insightful in its analysis of the psychological effects on the leaders of the church, which their relationships with Stalin produced. In his many meetings with leading hierarchs of the Orthodox Church, Stalin made a strong personal impression on them. Their growing reverence for him had a profound psychological effect on their vision for the future. Seduced by Stalin and the nationalism he espoused, leaders of the church began to think of him as a "new Constantine," and of Moscow as the "city of Constantine," the chosen city, which, in its splendor and beauty, would lead Russia's revival towards unparalleled "power and glory." The spectacular celebrations during the eight-hundred-year anniversary of the founding of Moscow (1947) promoted this vision in the minds of Orthodox leaders. Yakunin cited an article written by the Orthodox priest Mikhail Zernov, published in the *Journal of the Moscow Patriarchate*, as exemplifying the Church's messianic outlook:

> But Moscow, the ancient, 800-year-old Moscow, at the same time eternally young and beautiful, mightier than ever, still glows with the gold of the Kremlin's cupolas. Its glory grows more and more prominent in the world, *surpassing the glory of the most glorious cities of all times and of all nations.* . . .
>
> We believe that until the end of time shalt thou be the great stronghold of faith, truth, and liberty.[69]

Yakunin included other examples of these messianic hopes centered on the city of Moscow in this anniversary year. For example, according to Bishop N. A. Khar'iuzov, "the ancient capitals of other states—Paris, London, Venice—did not experience everything that Moscow went through during its eight-hundred-year history. Their development was gradual, evolutionary, while the development of Moscow took place by leaps-and-bounds. This historical feature has left a corresponding imprint on the people of our homeland. Many times, it was thought that our people were on the edge of death, but always after the difficult experiences, they became stronger, more persistent, and more robust."[70]

This messianic vision addressed both the past and the future, and it tied the Russian Orthodox Church ever more closely—politically and spiritually—to the Russian state. Ideologically, "Red Moscow" was again proclaimed as the "Third Rome," whose star shone in bright contrast to the decrepit see of Constantinople and degenerate Rome. This was a delusion, but, Yakunin argued, it had long-lasting effects. It promoted among many church leaders a deepening antipathy toward Catholics and, more particularly, toward the West. The delusion also led to a disregard for Russia's religious martyrs of the twentieth century, "whose blood had turned Russia crimson." Their humble, sacrificial service to the Russian people stood in sharp contrast to the worship of power that the church hierarchy had embraced. Moreover, Russian martyrs offered rich sources of "spiritual and moral wealth" for the church, which still retained their memory; their lives and teachings contained the "promise and hope for the church's true rebirth." The church's seeming indifference to these holy martyrs offered clear proof, Yakunin said, of its spiritual apathy about one of the richest sources of moral regeneration in the church's treasury.[71]

His belief in the significance of the holy martyrs to the church's future development did not constitute a recent phenomenon. In 1975, Yakunin, Viktor Kapitanchuk, and Lev Regel'son wrote to Patriarch Pimen, making an "Appeal for the Glorification of Russian Martyrs in the USSR."[72] They sent the letter on the fiftieth anniversary of the death of Patriarch Tikhon, whom they praised for his courageous support for freedom of the church and the church's separation from the Bolshevik government. This "gentle and formidable" patriarch stood as a prime example of the "light of Truth" during a time marked by falsehood and deception.[73]

The letter writers proposed canonization for six additional church leaders who sacrificed themselves for their faith. They included Metropolitan Pyotr, the steadfast church leader who, in the late fifteenth century, had spoken truth to power and suffered the consequences; Metropolitan Veniamin of Petrograd (d. 1922), a self-sacrificing confessor who, in the great famine of the early 1920s, raised money for the suffering people, while refusing to comply with Bolshevik efforts to confiscate church treasures; Metropolitan Kirill (Smirnov, d. 1937), who worked tirelessly to restore the church's spiritual unity, after its split in the late 1920s; Bishop Arseni (d. 1945), the visionary priest, teacher, and missionary who devoted his life to service and to succor for the poor; Bishop Afanasi (Sakharov, d. 1962), a spiritual giant, teacher, and preacher, who, after the Russian Revolution, fought for the preservation of the church and, while serving time in the Gulag, gave spiritual comfort to those in pain; and Seraphim of Sarov (d. 1833), one of Russia's greatest saints, beloved by the people and widely known for his contemplative prayers, love for people of all ranks, spiritual advice, and the simplicity of his life. According to Yakunin and his associates, none of these ever compromised the church, unlike Metropolitan Sergei (Stragorodsky) and later members of the church hierarchy, whose alliance with the Soviet government did great harm to the Orthodox Church, its integrity, and its role as a servant to the people. Suffering greatly for their faith, each of the martyrs presented an image of the church as "courageous, self-sacrificing, free, and filled to the brim with beauty and truth, an image sorely needed in a "world becoming increasingly secularized."[74] The themes running through the lives of each of the martyrs they mentioned was their service to people in need and their opposition to violence. The memory of these sacred martyrs stood as the diametrical opposite to the "cult of power," a memory that the present leadership of the church sought to extinguish.

In the early 1990s, the issues Yakunin raised in his essay on the cult of power remained very much alive. Remnants of the church's participation in the cult of Stalin continued to define its leadership. To find the true church, religious believers had to break through "the mounds of lies, deceit, and slander" that plagued the recent history of the Orthodox Church.[75] In his essay, Yakunin called for the church to repent publicly of its past behavior, which he believed essential to the recovery of its sacred mission. Unless the church purified itself, Yakunin maintained, it was incapable of providing the kind of moral leadership the country required for its rebirth. The Moscow Patriarchate had to take a truthful look into its history in the twentieth century and summon the courage "to peer into the abyss of [Russia's] moral and spiritual degradation" to which it had contributed.[76] It was essential that the patriarchate open the closed pages of its past in the twentieth century. It needed to admit to and ask forgiveness for placing the appetite for power and privilege at the top of its agenda, relegating its sacred teachings to a secondary position.

Whether leaders of the church had the willingness and fortitude to address their complicity with political power in 1991–1992 remained an open question. The act of looking more deeply into the Soviet past threatened to invoke historical ghosts that to some church leaders had best be left hidden. Fr. Gleb

Yakunin was willing to push forward in an attempt to free the church from its servility and from its reluctance to open itself to self-examination. In the process, his actions were certain to provoke controversy. As in the past, he neither feared the consequences nor worried about the antagonisms that such an inquiry invited.

CHAPTER 9

Lifting the Cover

In the 1990s, Fr. Gleb Yakunin was not unique in believing that moral and religious issues lay at the center of Russia's future identity. The initial step to recovering the church's true purpose required exposing the lies and betrayals that had corrupted it in the past. In this effort, Fr. Gleb offered strong support, and was joined by another powerful voice, an outspoken critic of the church's behavior with an equally courageous personality, Zoia Krakhmal'nikova. Although the two were never close friends, they expressed similar views about the course the church ought to take.

Someone looking at her portrait when she was a young woman would not have imagined Zoia Aleksandrovna Krakhmal'nikova (1929–2008), with her shoulder-length black hair, brilliant smile, and friendly face, to be a rebel. Born and raised in Ukraine, she fell in love with Russian and Ukrainian literature at a young age and hoped to become a writer. She matriculated at the prestigious Gorky Institute of World Literature in Moscow, where she earned high marks, before going on to postgraduate study. Afterward, Krakhmal'nikova entered the profession to which she had long aspired, the career of a writer. She became a member of the Union of Soviet Writers, acquiring the necessary credentials for publication in the leading literary journals, to which she successfully sent her articles. In 1971, three years after her graduation, she married another writer, Feliks Svetov, who had followed a similar career path. The two of them settled into a secure and promising family life in Moscow, where she, in particular, acquired a reputation as a talented author of articles, books, and translations and earned an appointment in the Academy of Sciences Department of Philosophy.[1]

Krakhmal'nikova was restless, however, and not completely satisfied with her life and the ambitious direction she had taken. Although somewhat older than members of the young Soviet generation that had begun to question Soviet ideology and to search for meaningful alternative worldviews, she and Svetov had similar yearnings. In 1974, they accepted Christianity, a decision that led to her dismissal from the writers' union, expulsion from the Academy of Sciences, and a ban on her publications in government journals.

These setbacks nevertheless did not mean the end of her writing life. In 1976, Krakhmal'nikova resurrected the prerevolutionary journal *Nadezhda* (Hope), whose subtitle she inscribed as "Christian Reading." The journal, which she published in samizdat, carried articles on church history, the writings of the Church Fathers, and pastoral thoughts, stories, and poems. Rather than publish the journal anonymously, she signed her name to every issue. On August 4, 1982, Krakhmal'nikova was arrested and charged with anti-Soviet agitation and propaganda. After spending a year in the Lefortovo Prison, she was tried and sentenced to five years of exile in a village near the border of Mongolia. In 1987, during the Gorbachev era, the authorities offered her clemency.[2]

Upon her return to Moscow, Krakhmal'nikova resumed her publishing life. Like Yakunin, she strongly believed that the moral underpinnings of a new society required a truthful look into the history of the church in the twentieth century. Like him, she decried the church's silence during the decades when the party persecuted large numbers of religious believers, and she believed that healing could not take place until the reasons behind the church's silence were uncovered. Not everyone in the leadership of the church welcomed this call for a truthful look into the past, in fear, she wrote, "that such an act will uncover both the abyss and the depths of horror, the moral degradation, criminality, predatory behavior, and corruption, which are hidden under the mask of piety."[3]

Deeply religious, unafraid of state reprisals, and democratic at heart, Krakhmal'nikova joined Yakunin in his distaste for hypocrisy (figure 9.1). She did not accept the excuse of church leaders that they could not speak out because they remained "captives of the state," an excuse that Yakunin had decried for many years. Krakhmal'nikova exposed the hypocrisy of the patriarch's excuse even more graphically:

> As I was taking my first steps towards the church, I often heard in response to my questions about the silence of the more experienced and

FIGURE 9.1. Fr. Georgii Edel'stein and Zoia Krakhmal'nikova, 1990s. Courtesy of the Keston Center for Religion, Politics, and Society, Baylor University.

more "deep rooted" of the church people and the Patriarch and bishops: "They are held in captivity." Not once, however, did I see handcuffs on Patriarch Pimen, not once did I see a convoy accompanying the patriarch or the bishops, not once did I see him emerging from a "paddy wagon," but with amazement I observed how they blessed the crowds, who bowed before the wheels of a black "Chaika" or "ZIL-111" in which our church hierarchs rode around in comfort.[4]

The chance to delve more deeply into the darkest corners of Soviet history would soon become a reality. During the heady August days of 1991, when the old guard of the Communist Party and the KGB attempted to overthrow the Gorbachev government and regain authority, Fr. Gleb played an active part in helping to diffuse the power of the opposition movement. After narrowly escaping arrest by the KGB, he was one of a handful of Orthodox parish priests who came to the defense of the newly elected Yeltsin government. Dressed in his priestly regalia, he stood in the road before an oncoming column of tanks that threatened to disperse the crowd defending the White House, home of the Russian Parliament.[5] Standing on the balcony of the White House, he addressed the crowd, urging them to defend Russian democracy. "Take courage and fulfill your duty as citizens," he told them, "God will help you and will help Russia."[6] He had confidence that the young soldiers commanding the tanks and members of the militia gathered around the crowd would hear the ancient call of the church; walking among the barricades defending the massive building, Fr. Gleb offered blessings to scores of people. He fearlessly championed the promise of a new beginning for the Russian government and the Orthodox Church.

After the failed August coup attempt, Yeltsin's government abolished Directorate "Z" of the KGB, the unit charged with watching over domestic political developments. Soon to be known as the Fifth Department of the KGB, it had closely monitored Russian dissidents and others suspected of disagreeing with state policies and failing to comply with the party's goals. On August 24, 1991, only a few days after the failed coup, Yeltsin issued a series of presidential decrees that required the transfer of KGB archives and those of the Communist Party to the Russian government.[7] The Supreme Soviet of the Russian Republic thus took control of both archives. Although not all of these valuable documents were turned over, on grounds that they contained classified operational intelligence, they became more accessible to researchers than at any time in the Soviet period.[8] They opened up a whole panoply of formerly closed resources that the KGB and the Communist Party had considered off limits to outsiders.

Following the abolition of Directorate "Z," President Yeltsin formed a commission to investigate the leaders of the coup and the KGB's involvement in planning and executing the attempted coup, naming Lev Aleksandrovich Ponomarov as head of the commission. A brilliant physicist and mathematician, the slender, black-haired, dignified Ponomarev had taken the place of Andrei Sakharov in the Congress of People's Deputies after Sakharov's death in 1989, and the following year, Ponomarev easily won the seat on his own account. He was a founding member of Democratic Russia, a loosely bound group of people who assisted in the transformation from Soviet rule to a more open and democratic society.[9] In turn, Ponomarev selected three people to investigate a special section of the archives, Directorate "Z's" Fourth Department, which dealt with the Orthodox Church and other religious organizations. The investigators included two Orthodox priests, Fr. Gleb Yakunin and Fr. Viacheslav Polosin, the latter to serve as chair.

Fr. Polosin (1956–) graduated from the philosophy department at Moscow State University before going to work for the Orthodox Church and, shortly afterward, he graduated from the Moscow Theological Seminary. After his ordination as a priest in 1983, Fr. Polosin served first in Orthodox parishes in Central Asia, before the Soviet authorities deported him for his alleged lack of proper respect for government officials and his refusal to comply with state orders. He returned to active service in June 1988, during the church millennium, and was appointed to a newly opened, crumbling church in the Kaluga region. In 1990, Polosin participated in the founding of the Russian Christian Democratic Movement, became interested in politics, and ran successfully for election to the Congress of People's Deputies. A strong supporter of Boris Yeltsin, he served on the president's inauguration committee.[10]

The third person appointed to the parliamentary commission was Aleksandr Iosifovich Nezhnyi, a young journalist and author whose articles in the late Soviet period were among the first to present the church in a positive light, and quickly attracted a large readership. A strong proponent of freedom of conscience, Nezhnyi severely criticized the Bolshevik's persecution of religious believers, which he described in detail in his writings. Nezhnyi was the only member of the commission who did not serve in the Congress of People's Deputies, but in selecting him, Ponomarev appointed a talented writer who was certain to present the investigation into the archives in a sympathetic way.[11]

When the long-closed files of the KGB were opened, it gave members of the parliamentary commission the chance to peer into a world of personal networks connecting the KGB and the church. The files contained materials on church agents of the KGB, how these agents were used to gather foreign intelligence, KGB efforts to manipulate public opinion, and how the state sought to control thought. The archives, therefore, offered a look into not only history but also the shaping of the political framework in which the church and other religious organizations functioned.[12]

As he began his work, Yakunin knew that admittance into the KGB archives represented a rare opportunity. Not knowing how long this privilege would last before political interests forced their closure, he worked tirelessly. Here was the chance to reveal, with concrete evidence, one of the most closely guarded secrets of the Soviet period, the collaboration between the church and an agency determined to destroy it. Nevertheless, he faced several immediate difficulties. He quickly learned that the files were in near total disarray. Documents were misfiled, some were incorrectly labeled, others were missing. Uncovering the stories concealed in the archives would require time and prodigious effort, but Yakunin was determined. He refused to let the obstacles he confronted deflect from his main purpose, which was to find and document the networks that had inflicted such pain on religious believers.[13]

Before his dismissal in 1989 from his post as chair of the Soviet Council for Religious Affairs, Konstantin Kharchev admitted the KGB's complicity in the affairs of the Orthodox Church.[14] Yet the scope and depth of the organization's influence—which Yakunin and his commission members discovered in the archives—touched on some of the most sensitive issues before the investigative body. These issues concerned how much the public should be told about the church leaders who had betrayed their sacred oaths. Would full disclosure irrevocably tarnish a key institution, a pillar of social stability, at a time when the new political order was only in its infancy? After more than seventy years of severe persecution by the Soviet state, could the church endure another crippling blow to its legitimacy, particularly at a time when it had only begun to recover its status?

Such questions set off a lively debate, both in certain parts of the church and among other members of Russian society. Shortly after the investigative commission began its work, some of its findings were leaked to the Russian press. In February 1992, the journal *Stolitsa* held a roundtable discussion in its editorial office to debate the conundrums associated with publishing this information. The participants included two prominent representatives of the Moscow patriarchy, several church dissidents, a few laypeople, and the journalist Aleksandr Nezhnyi. In the discussions, the representatives of the Moscow patriarchy urged the parliamentary commission to move forward but to exercise extreme caution: "We have a matter that is unique and also tragic before us," they said. "In the history of the Christian Church, it is not easy to find an example when a similar fall from grace is so fully revealed, and the ulcers are exposed. Therefore, it is necessary to exercise restraint and very soberly approach the phenomena that are now becoming public. They are tragic for the people and for the church itself; it is necessary that we understand the extremely complex situation this is for the servitors of the church. Not all of them, we think, became collaborators with the KGB."[15]

From the outset of the commission's work, Ruslan Khasbulatov, the chair of the Supreme Soviet of the RSFSR, faced intense pressure from conservative and nationalist groups, both within the Parliament and in society, to curtail or at least limit the commission's investigations. He especially worried about the public release of the findings, particularly how they might place an irremediable stain on the Orthodox Church's reputation. Never comfortable with the probe into the KGB archives, Khasbulatov, in February 1992, terminated the parliamentary commission's access. His decision to end the investigation took place shortly after Patriarch Aleksii II came to see him, and in a closed-door meeting attended by the patriarch and Evgenii Primakov, head of the state intelligence service, Khasbulatov acted.[16] Despite the curtailment of their work after only four months, however, the commission members had succeeded in uncovering many KGB transgressions into the life of the church that they had long suspected and could now prove.

Public Disclosure (and Its Dilemmas)

Shortly before the closure of the archives, Viacheslav Polosin published an article in the newspaper *Izvestiia* that provided an introductory account of the revelations that would soon follow. Speaking about his experiences on the investigating commission, he said he had discovered that the KGB's involvement in church affairs extended far beyond what he had imagined. Earlier, in 1991, he noted, he had found a letter written by Vladimir Lenin, soon after the Bolsheviks' accession to power, about the party's plans for infiltrating the church. Fr. Viacheslav had uncovered Lenin's document in the files of the KGB, and it revealed the Bolsheviks' long-term strategy: "An honest priest is a thousand times more harmful than an immoral one, because his [wrongdoing] is a thousand times more difficult to expose," Lenin wrote, near the beginning of the campaign to suppress religion in Russia.[17] He followed up this statement with another, written in 1921, near the end of the Russian Civil War, instructing the security police (Cheka) to recruit church leaders for jobs in the new administration. He recommended that the police employ bribes, threats, and other inducements in order to identify people of weak character and exploit them for political purposes. The goal, Lenin wrote, was to convert the church leaders into "eternal slaves of the Cheka."[18] Seventy years had passed, Fr. Viacheslav noted, yet the police still employed the same methods in their efforts to compromise the leadership of the Russian church and ensure their compliance with the policies of the Soviet state:

> It would seem that the document is seventy years in the past. But it remains, to this day, the key to understanding the essence of the secret services' contributions to ideological security. Over all these years, the security police's methods have not changed, except that they have become more sophisticated. Over time, the selection of believers has become more sophisticated and resulted in the practice of sending agents to infiltrate religious organizations in order to recruit members. . . . In the end, the state must admit before millions of our believers that it had become an instrument of a misanthropic force which, introducing the fourth dream of Vera Pavlova, plotted to transform a free person into an "eternal slave."[19]

In recent decades, this ideological dream, Polosin wrote, had weakened among the Soviet people. The state had attempted to replenish it by employing "agents in cassocks," the term he used to describe members of the church hierarchy who worked for the police. Had the time not come, he asked, for the secular state to provide a legal foundation for the establishment of religious tolerance that prevented the state from interfering in the affairs of "any religious confession, without exception?"[20]

The motivations underlying Yakunin's fervent labors in the archives remain a matter of conjecture. Revenge served as a possible explanation. By temperament and character, however, Yakunin, rarely, if ever, sought retaliation against those who caused him suffering; he was more likely to forgive than to look for retribution. "My father never viewed individuals as enemies, even people who offended or harmed him" recalled Mariia Glebovna, his daughter, "their actions, in his view, were dictated by the circumstances in which they found themselves."[21] A much stronger causal factor had its origins in his religious convictions. He believed that the church had to cleanse itself before it could begin to heal. The church's collusion with the KGB had to be clearly defined and factually proved as the most appropriate means of identifying the people who, in the present, continued to work with the security services.

Yet in the process of discovery, several major problems emerged. Before its dissolution in 1991, the Council for Religious Affairs had destroyed some of the documents in the archive. Yakunin was not able to find the red books of the KGB, which specifically identified the real names of the church officials who collaborated with the security police.

Despite the absence of missing documents, Yakunin learned that the KGB issued code names for its church collaborators, and, in addition, had given code names to individuals the agency deemed especially dangerous to the party's goals. In his first interview after his participation in the fact-finding commission, in early January 1992, Yakunin revealed the code names of church leaders who regularly reported to the KGB.[22] In reports to their superiors, KGB officers identified their sources only by these names, never by their church appellations, in this way concealing the identities of their collaborators. In an interview, Yakunin disclosed the code names most prominently featured in the reports: "Adamat," "Abbot," and "Antonov" commonly appeared. Other names from farther down in the church hierarchy also came to light, but, crucially, these three names featured in reports describing international trips.

The indication that these collaborators had traveled abroad offered the principal clue to the identity of these church leaders. Comparing their code names with mention of their international trips and other activities published in the *Journal of the Moscow Patriarchate*, Aleksandr Nezhnyi discovered the identities of the people behind the masks. In the popular magazine *Ogonek*, he published their real names. "Adamat" referred to Metropolitan Yuvenalii of Krutisk and Kolomna, the prominent former chair of the Department for External Church Relations; "Abbot" signified Metropolitan Pitirim of Volokolamsk and Iurev, chair of the publishing department of the Moscow Patriarchate;

and "Antonov" was Metropolitan Filaret of Kyiv and Exarch of Ukraine.[23] "This was one and the same person," Nezhnyi wrote, "but with two faces, a double and a shapeshifter."[24] They were among the most influential figures in the church leadership: each served as members of the Holy Synod, the powerful governing body of the Russian Orthodox Church.

In their research into the KGB archives, Yakunin and his colleagues discovered additional code names, among them an agent the KGB referred to as "Drozdov," whose identity, at first, remained a mystery.[25] Shockingly, they learned that it represented the newly elected patriarch Aleksii II (Aleksii Mikhailovich Ridiger, 1929–2008). The selection of his code name was not accidental: at the Theological Academy in Leningrad, Aleksii had elected to write his thesis on the famous metropolitan of Moscow Filaret Drozdov. Ordained as priest in his native Estonia, Aleksii had risen rapidly in the church hierarchy, from his graduation from the Leningrad Theological Academy in 1953 to his appointment as metropolitan of Tallinn and Estonia in 1968, at the comparatively young age of thirty-nine.

Such a rapid rise required KGB approval, thereby creating the potential for compromise through association. Some church officials, however, expressed doubt about the future patriarch's complicity, even after his exposure, rationalizing that perhaps an overly zealous agent padded his monthly reports by writing in the metropolitan's name.[26] Although much of the proof appeared circumstantial, the weight of the evidence suggests efforts to collaborate with the security police. For example, in an extremely sensitive case in March 1983, Agent "Drozdov" was sent to quell a disturbance in the Leningrad region. A KGB official reported the following to his superior:

> In December of last year, a group of monks from the Pskov Caves Monastery expressed their disagreement with regulations in the monastery and complained to Patriarch Pimen about the superior of the Pskov Caves Monastery.
>
> By actions of agents "Drozdov" and "Skala," educational work was conducted among the monks of the Pskov Caves Monastery.
>
> As a result of the agents' recommendations, the monks who initiated the disturbances were transferred to other parishes in the Pskov diocese (4 persons), 2 individuals were left in the monastery, and 4 persons were dismissed from the Pskov diocese.
>
> At the present time, the situation has returned to normal.
> [signed by] Comrade Zotov[27]

To cite another example: in 1988, upon the initiative of its chair, Viktor Chebrikov, the KGB presented an honorary citation to Agent "Drozdov" for his meritorious service.²⁸ The Russian investigative reporter Yevgenia Albats, author of the most authoritative study of the KGB's collusion with the church, noted that the KGB's award to Agent "Drozdov" (Metropolitan Aleksii) signified services that went much beyond the act of "pacifying monks."²⁹ As the Russian public learned, many more revelations would soon come to the surface.

Major Targets

Fr. Gleb Yakunin and his colleagues' archival research uncovered a mass of information concerning the KGB's efforts to control and manipulate all levers of thought within the body of the church. As the country approached the 1988 millennium celebrations, KGB anxieties about what it perceived as "anti-Soviet" centers of opposition intensified. In early 1984, an agent's report read: "An analytical report has been prepared on the situation in the monasteries of the Russian Orthodox Church (ROC) with suggestions for activating agent-operational work among the monks."³⁰ In the same month, "Material has been prepared for publication in the bulletin of the 5th Directorate on inadequacies in the matter of counter-intelligence security of the religious schools of the ROC."³¹ The growing interest in religion among the population and the rapid weakening of Soviet ideology heightened the KGB's concerns.

In the KGB files, Yakunin discovered his own name and those of two others cited as potential threats to the social and religious order of the Soviet Union. The two whose actions the KGB closely monitored, in addition to Yakunin, included the layman Aleksandr Ogorodnikov and Yakunin's friend Fr. Aleksandr Men. They were also given code names and labeled as subjects to be watched closely.

The KGB referred to Ogorodnikov by the code name of "Aptekar." In April 1987, he had returned to Moscow from prison, and later that year, married a theater and art critic, Paulina Bogdanova. They had an infant child, born in May 1988, at a time when Ogorodnikov had already resumed his energetic past activities, reaching out to critics of the Soviet government, holding frequent meetings in his apartment with Western correspondents, and, at every opportunity, testifying to widespread religious persecution in the USSR. His behavior did not comport well with government officials, particularly in the beginning weeks of the millennium celebrations, when large numbers of foreign journalists and religious leaders visited Moscow. The KGB moved against Ogorodnikov in the summer of 1988 when he left Moscow to visit Lithuania. Rather than strike him directly, the KGB sought to disrupt his family by putting enormous pressure on his wife and threatening to take away their new-born son unless she left her husband. When Ogorodnikov returned from his trip, he learned that Bogdanova had filed for divorce and locked him out of the apartment, leaving him without a residence permit in the city.[32]

The KGB called Fr. Aleksandr Men by the apt name of "Missionary." Troubled by the large crowds that gathered for the services and Men's growing reputation as a powerful public speaker during perestroika, the security police tightened their surveillance of his activities. They were especially concerned about the discussion circles for young families that Men had begun organizing in Moscow in 1979. As a KGB agent reported in January 1986, the agent had initiated "the process of checking on the illegal gatherings of youth in a private flat in Moscow. The persons taking part in these gatherings have been identified. They included M. V. N., K. A. V., M. L. D., as well as T. I. Sh., who is the link with the object 'Missionary.' The persons listed above have come under study."[33]

No evidence indicates that Fr. Aleksandr ever collaborated with the KGB. Yet some of the people who came to his church were controversial and did not always behave with proper decorum, which further attracted the attention of the security police. Fr. Aleksandr repeatedly had to answer for them, as well as for his own activities. In 1986, according to a KGB report, "The agent 'Nikitin' traveled to see 'Missionary' in the Zagorsk district, where he concluded a series of conversations with him."[34] The report was signed by Colonel Vladimir Sychev of the KGB's 4th Department. Colonel Sychev supervised the surveillance of Fr. Aleksandr and played a leading role in developing a case against him, purporting to depict him as a person disloyal to the Soviet state.[35]

Yakunin had never doubted the security police's hatred of him as well. And now, in researching the KGB files, he saw it well documented. In January 1977, an agent of the 4th Department spoke with pride about the success in "continuing to break up a group of reactionary-minded churchmen (Yakunin, Fr. Dmitrii Dudko, and a layperson [Lev] Regel'son) and their hostile activity against the church and the state."[36]

More recently, in June 1987, the security services had attempted to dissipate the international support Yakunin had garnered during his years in prison and Siberian exile. The KGB began an "operation" to portray him as a radical and religious fanatic whose religious and social views had little popular support. A report submitted by Agent V. N. Timoshevskii to his superiors described a KGB counterattack on Yakunin and his desire for a more open Russian society:

> We aim to establish a campaign with the foreign media to transmit information about the religious extremist Yakunin and like-minded people in Moscow, whose "appeals" to the authorities demand the liberalization of religious life in the Soviet Union. We held a press conference for

Soviet and foreign correspondents, with the cooperation of Metropolitans Yuvenalii and Filaret. These priests of the Russian Orthodox Church objectively enlightened the correspondents about the real situation of the church and freedom of conscience in the USSR.[37]

Speaking of Yakunin and his "liberal" friends, the secret police sought to break up the circle of "extremists" who recklessly aspired to undermine the country. Rather than seek their imprisonment, this time the KGB endeavored to isolate them by ordering the Council for Religious Affairs to reassign one of the most outspoken members of Yakunin's group to a rural parish in the distant Kostroma region of Russia.[38] The KGB files also revealed that the one of the tasks of the journal *Slovo*, which began publication in the summer of 1988, was to publish articles aimed at "unmasking the anti-social character of the activity of the priest Yakunin."[39]

As Yakunin and the other members of the parliamentary commission learned about the targets of the KGB's domestic agenda, they also uncovered the agency's international objectives. They discovered that the domestic and international spheres of operations were interconnected. A special focus of KGB attention concerned the World Council of Churches (WCC), in whose international gatherings the leadership of the Russian Orthodox Church had actively participated. The archives revealed that all the official members of the Russian delegation to these meetings had KGB connections.

The Soviet delegates to the WCC had several major objectives, uppermost of which was to present a positive image of the Soviet Union and to shape the topics at the top of the WCC's agenda. Metropolitans Nikodim, Filaret, and Yuvenalii, three of the most prominent and active Soviet representatives at the WCC's international meetings, repeatedly attempted to keep the focus of the organization on nuclear disarmament, racism in the United States, and world peace, and away from questions of religion and freedom of conscience. Yakunin had personally witnessed such efforts in 1975 in the Soviet delegation's response to his and Lev Regel′son's letter to the WCC on religious persecution in the USSR.

In addition, members of the Orthodox delegation had the task of assessing the personal nature of WCC leaders. A KGB report from January 1973 proudly asserted the success of one of its operations: "Agents of the KGB 'Magistr' and 'Mikhailov' were sent to Thailand and India to participate in the work of the WCC. The agents had a positive influence on the work of the Council, offered information of operational interest to the WCC, and also collected information on the personal character of individual figures."[40]

Moreover, the agency played a key role in planning conferences hosted by the patriarchate in Moscow, whose main purpose was to present a positive image of religious tolerance in the Soviet Union.[41] A prime example concerned the carefully orchestrated visit to Moscow of the general secretary of the WCC, Dr. Philip Potter. The West Indies-born Potter served as head of the WCC during some of its most turbulent years, from 1972 to 1984, and cultivating his friendship became a goal of the security police. In February 1973, upon receiving an invitation from Patriarch Pimen, General Secretary Potter traveled to Moscow as a guest. The entry in the KGB's ledger recorded the results: "Agents 'Sviatoslav,' 'Adamat,' 'Mikhailov,' and 'Ostrovskii' exerted a favorable influence on him." They also "obtained information about the activity of the World Council of Churches, which has operational interest."[42]

Moral Regeneration?

In his poetry and public statements, Fr. Gleb Yakunin had repeatedly emphasized the importance of Russia's moral regeneration to his country's ultimate spiritual and cultural revival. Like Zoia Krakhmal'nikova, Aleksandr Men, and others, he strongly believed in the importance of recovering the revelatory voices and human values that served as spiritual guides to that effort.[43] The revelations from the KGB archives, however, suggested both the importance and the difficulty of this task, especially when leading members of the church hierarchy had been deeply engulfed in corrupting the church's sacred mission. Most of the individuals mentioned earlier, with the possible exception of Patriarch Aleksii II, served as examples of this inner corruption. Yet the question remained of how far down within the structures of the church such corruption had penetrated and what the political consequences of this duplicity were.

The archival revelations especially brought to light the egregious behavior of the powerful Filaret, metropolitan of Kyiv and Ukraine. One of the most intelligent and ambitious members of the church hierarchy, Metropolitan Filaret (Mikhail Antonovich Denisenko), in 1990, was considered a leading candidate to replace the deceased Patriarch Pimen. Born in 1929 to parents who lived in the Donbass region of eastern Ukraine, he committed his life to the church at an early age and he had an impressive church career. He graduated from the seminary in Odesa and then the Moscow Theological Academy and had risen extraordinarily fast within the church, becoming a bishop at the age of thirty-three and head of the entire diocese of Kiev and Ukraine at the age of thirty-seven.[44] The KGB files that Yakunin and his colleagues accessed revealed that Metropolitan Filaret had served as a trusted representative of the church at international conferences as early as 1967. He had already become a KGB informant by then, whose code name, "Antonov," repeatedly appeared in reports of these conferences.⁴⁵

In late 1991, in a scathing two-part article published in *Ogonek*, Aleksandr Nezhnyi wrote an exposé on Metropolitan Filaret.⁴⁶ In Ukraine, he wrote, the powerful Filaret oversaw the jurisdiction of his diocese with a stern, uncompromising hand that brooked little dissension.⁴⁷ Yet in his personal life, Metropolitan Filaret displayed a much different standard of behavior, which Nezhnyi uncovered in numerous letters that provided a detailed picture of corruption and hypocrisy. "The family life of the metropolitan long ago had ceased being a secret," read one letter to the Moscow Patriarchate.⁴⁸ In violation of the church's canon law, he lived with his housekeeper, an uneducated common woman named Evgeniia Petrovna Ronionova, who bore him three children, all out of wedlock. Evgeniia Petrovna dominated the household, and, in violation of canon law, extended her authority beyond the family to the diocese. "She often participated in the selection of church personnel, intervened in the ordination of priests," and decided which letters that arrived at the metropolitan's office reached his hands.⁴⁹ On the streets of Kiev, people often greeted her as "Your Holiness [*blazhenstvo*], Evgeniia Petrovna."⁵⁰ She lived in luxury, which she also bestowed on her three children.

In his account of the metropolitan and his household, Nezhnyi, sympathetic to the church, had no reason to belittle its leaders. In this case, however, the realities, drawn from archival materials, were at variance with the ideals Nezhnyi harbored in his mind. In 1992, he returned to his theme, expressing surprise that his earlier exposé of Metropolitan Filaret had elicited little response. Nezhnyi had expected to see Filaret either quietly retire from his position or face canonical action from his superiors; yet he remained in his position while Evgeniia Petrovna carried on as before. Nezhnyi learned that the metropolitan had excommunicated three monks who had testified about corruption in his administration and prohibited discordant priests from taking communion.⁵¹ After the earlier articles had come out, Metropolitan Filaret and his mistress hosted a large banquet, the journalist learned, at which she had railed against and threatened the "slanderers" of His Holiness.⁵²

Nezhnyi found the duplicity of Metropolitan Filaret to be the most disturbing aspect of his behavior. The metropolitan's relationship with the KGB compromised the integrity of the church, a theme to which the journalist returned at the end of his 1992 article, writing sarcastically: "When his Holiness was born his parents named him Mikhail; when he became a monk, he was given the name Filaret; the KGB gave him a third name. I propose that believers from now on call His Holiness, 'Comrade Antonov.'"⁵³

Focused on the difficult tasks of rebuilding the church and proud of their newfound status after the end of Soviet power, the church hierarchy had little desire to see further revelations of complicity with the KGB. Several months after the closure of the KGB archives to further embarrassing investigations, church leaders thought their situation had stabilized and that the crisis had blown over. But on April 24, 1992, came what Russian historian Sergei Bychkov called "a clap of thunder in a clear sky."[54] The cause was an interview given by Archbishop of Vilnius and Lithuania, Khrizostom (Martishkin) to the journalist Mikhail Pozdniaev, which was published in the newspaper *Russkaia mysl'*. Titled "I Was an Agent of the KGB, but I Was Not an Informer" (*Ia byl agentom KGB, no ne byl stukachem*), the archbishop's interview offered a stunning account, coming from one of the most respected leaders in the Russian Orthodox Church.[55]

The interview took place shortly after a meeting of the Archbishops' Council on the situation unfolding in Ukraine. Ukrainian leaders wanted political separation from Russia, and they pressed for the independence of the Ukrainian Orthodox Church as well. Because of this major development, the council relegated the topic of complicity with the KGB to a committee for study. The lack of concern troubled Archbishop Khrizostom, who voiced his displeasure before the council in the following words: "Among us, and especially among our priests, there are a great many unworthy, amoral people. Their amorality benefits by the absence of a church court, a situation that the KGB has used. The KGB has protected them from us, in order that we could not punish them, as the canons of the church required."[56]

In his interview, Archbishop Khrizostom said that the KGB had given him a pseudonym, the code name of "Restorer." Using his code name, he conscientiously carried out his assignments, trying simultaneously to pursue his commitments to the church while fulfilling what the KGB called his patriotic responsibilities. He observed, however, firsthand, how some church servitors abused their positions, which he tried to point out in making his required reports, but to little avail. He had little hesitation about voicing evidence of these abuses:

> If I spoke badly about anyone in my reports, it was about the enemies of the church, about KGB agents embedded in the Body of the church. I knew all of them, because they did not care who knew. They did not need to be calculated, but, by their deeds and actions, it was immediately clear which ones of them were real agents. That is why I always spoke badly about them in interviews with the KGB. I made these contacts when I was

already a bishop—but we have real KGB people in the church who have made dazzling careers; Metropolitan Methodius of Voronezh is an example. He is a KGB officer, an atheist, a vicious person, imposed on the church by the *gabeshniki* [a slang term for KGB operatives]. The Synod is unanimously against such a bishop, but we were forced to take such sin on ourselves; and then, how he took off! He became a metropolitan, and, as chairperson of the Economics Department, for nearly ten years, he controlled millions in church funds. He never liked independent, honest priests, never protected them, and tried to drive them away.[57]

In a subsequent biographical statement, Archbishop Khrizostom recounted that he had served as a bishop for a decade, from 1974 to 1984. All this time, as the KGB pressured him, he worked as an agent. He provided details of what the agency ordered him to do, including writing accounts of international trips, encounters with foreign emissaries, activities of church organizations, and assessments of people who might serve as KGB contacts. Concurrently, on his own, and often to the displeasure of his superiors on the Council for Religious Affairs, he ordained many priests who had a higher education, including those of Jewish heritage, the latter in violation of state laws. They included the controversial priest Georgii Edel'stein. "He came to see me [and said] twenty-two bishops previously refused to ordain me, and you will likely do the same. He is Jewish by nationality, an intellectual, a man with a higher secular education, who, in the past, worked as a teacher." His pathway to the priesthood was blocked. "I ordained him, and for the next five years I protected him; no one touched him. There were many such examples."[58]

The archbishop's lax policies and behavior often incurred the displeasure of the authorities, especially the members of the Council for Religious Affairs. Eventually, they sent him into exile to Irkutsk for the maximum term of five years. In 1989, he was released and sent to Lithuania. As archpriest, he declined to support Soviet efforts to suppress Lithuania's move for independence. A year later, he said, "Precisely because of the Lithuanian question, I broke with the organs of the KGB."[59]

Archbishop Khrizostom wanted to see the investigation into the KGB's activities continued. Unconcerned about his own name in the files, he believed it essential that the council open the books and seek the truth; after receiving the information, the church should then study its collaboration with the KGB intently and fully. The church had to take on this responsibility because to remain silent, in his view, offered the worst possible outcome. Already, he said, "a frenzied campaign has developed around this issue, of course, with the goal of destroying the church. Who appears most outraged by the contacts between the

Orthodox Church and the KGB? Yesterday's atheists, yesterday's KGB, who, using their authority, forced us to cooperate."[60] These longtime enemies of the church stood to benefit most should the church refuse to accept responsibility for cleansing itself. Archbishop Khrizostom implored his fellow members on the Archbishops' Council to take seriously the forthcoming recommendations of the parliamentary commission. "We have no right to ignore this issue," he said.[61] Whether they would choose to accept his admonition remained an open question.

Separating the Wheat from the Chaff

Archbishop Khrizostom's distinction between an agent of the KGB and an informer suggests that the church's collaboration was more complex than many writers on this issue admitted. As an agent, the archbishop never fully cooperated with the police authorities, and he tried to manipulate his position to support people for whom the Council for Religious Affairs demonstrated little respect. His efforts at taking independent actions eventually led to the state's disfavor. Given the intense pressure on bishops and priests, one has to assume that cooperation with the KGB took various forms that greatly depended on the character and values of individual bishops and priests as well as the situations they faced. Asked the share of priests who cooperated with the KGB, Fr. Georgii Edel'stein estimated it to be 100 percent.[62] Asked the same question, Fr. Gleb Yakunin put the figure at 20 percent.[63] These estimates, however, fail to reveal the depth and scope of complicity. Some of the clergy had little interest in politics and, under extremely difficult circumstances, quietly went about their responsibilities, serving their parishioners as efficiently as possible. They responded in diverse ways to state demands for reporting on individuals they baptized. No evidence exists, for example, that Frs. Aleksandr Men, Dmitrii Dudko, or Boris Talantov complied with the state's requirements. At the grassroots level, the Orthodox Church was extremely diverse, as John Burgess has demonstrated for a later period, whether in church activities, political beliefs, or commitment to the state.[64] Khrizostom (Martishkin), Archbishop of Vilnius and Lithuania, testified that the Voronezh parish had "independent, honest" priests, but Metropolitan Methodius "drove them out."[65]

Others, however, bent with the wind, or, if personally ambitious and seeking advancement and privileges, succumbed to the pressures and personal advantages that came with working for the KGB.[66] Such was the case of a major tormentor of Fr. Gleb Yakunin.

The revelations in this particular case suggest how the KGB held out the "spice cake" in recruiting agents and giving them certain targeted assignments. The mechanisms of control exerted by the security services were also divulged. These matters were addressed in an interview with a former KGB agent, Archpriest Aleksandr Shushpanov, published in February 1992 in the newspaper *Argumenty i fakty*. Readers may recall that Archpriest Shushpanov served as a main witness for the prosecution during the trial of Gleb Yakunin more than a decade prior, when he had accused Yakunin of being anti-Soviet. The interview is significant for two reasons: it provided concrete personal corroboration of the conclusions reached in the forthcoming parliamentary commission's report, and it revealed the government's strategy in the prosecution of Fr. Gleb.

Asked to recount his recruitment by the KGB, Archpriest Shushpanov described an unfortunate incident that befell him soon after his graduation from the theological seminary. For many years, he said, he had dreamed of working in the prestigious Department for External Church Relations of the Moscow Patriarchate. When, at last, he managed to land a job as a translator in the department, he described his overwhelming joy. Shortly after he began working in the department, an acquaintance approached him and requested help for a former dissident, Vladimir Bukovsky. Following his recent release from prison, when Bukovskii returned to Moscow penniless and seeking work, Shushpanov sympathized with Bukovskii's plight and agreed to help. He gave Bukovskii several translations that the department had assigned Shushpanov to complete. He paid for this work out of his own pocket, after which he turned in the completed translations as his work. At first, he said, this arrangement went smoothly, but then, in his words, "everything fell apart: Somehow they [the KGB] tracked this down. Everything went according to script. They kicked me out of the Department for External Church Relations, and, for a half-year, I bounced around unemployed. Then, one fine day, they called me into KGB headquarters and offered to restore my position. In exchange, they told me, 'You have to go to work for us.... Alas," he lamented, "I did not allow the cup to pass me by."[67]

The assignments the agency gave Shushpanov were also carefully planned. After enrolling him in a special course of study, KGB officers taught him how to do searches, make arrests, and conduct surveillance. Next, as a translator in the Department for External Church Relations of the Moscow Patriarchate, he had responsibility for accompanying foreign delegations on their visits to the USSR. His KGB supervisor required all the translators to "submit detailed reports about the visits and where we took foreigners, whether to a store or to the toilet."[68]

Archpriest Shushpanov described an intricate, surreptitious network designed to conceal the work of the department in its relations with foreign delegations. He delivered his reports to a KGB officer who rented a room in the downtown Tsentral'naia hotel. For the "extra" services that went beyond his normal work in his department, he was well rewarded. "I regularly received a second paycheck and not for an insignificant amount," he said. "The department manager personally delivered this additional payment to me, and I always signed by my code name 'Aramis.'" Shushpanov followed the same process every time he accompanied a foreign delegation.[69]

As he progressed in his work, Shushpanov received an assignment that, he confessed, tormented him for years afterward. He did not speak of his performance in the trial of Fr. Gleb, but of certain activities preceding the trial in which he took part. Most likely, he considered everything part of the prosecution of Fr. Gleb. He described the attempted "unmasking" of Yakunin as follows:

> I worked mainly spying on a well-known religious activist, the former religious dissident and priest Gleb Yakunin. I not only followed him, but also developed the conspiracy the security police planned to use against him. The KGB wanted to develop a case against Yakunin as a spy. It prepared an operation, the essence of which would be catching him delivering confidential information to the protestant chaplain at the American embassy in Moscow, Michael Spengler. During the contrived meeting between Yakunin and Spengler, the KGB planned to arrest him as a spy, and denounce Spengler and label him a persona non grata. Thank God, this operation—not without my help—collapsed.[70]

In his interview, Shushpanov did not divulge the circumstances that precipitated the failure of the plot. Perhaps, in advance, either Fr. Gleb or Rev. Spengler suspected the conspiracy and did not meet; Yakunin was well attuned to such efforts. In making his public confession, Shushpanov might have intended to exonerate himself by claiming that KGB officers forced his participation in the plot. Yet his testimony suggests sincere remorse for his complicity in acts aimed at severely hurting certain targeted people. Years later, his guilt in helping build the case against Yakunin continued to trouble him. Finally, he went to see Yakunin and "told him everything." Shushpanov said that he asked Yakunin for forgiveness, and Fr. Gleb "forgave me." Shushpanov hoped that "the Lord God will also forgive me."[71]

Having gathered similar revelations and other materials, in March 1992, the parliamentary commission issued its final report. The account was written and signed by the commission's chair, Lev Ponomarev, who also recommended ways to prevent such abuses of power in the future. The report claimed to be based on factual evidence without ideological biases. Given the disputatious political atmosphere of the 1990s, the commission's conclusions were certain to be controversial.

Ponomarev highlighted several of the major findings that Yakunin, Polosin, and Nezhnyi's investigation had uncovered about the KGB's power over religious organizations:

- The agency exercised control over the church's emissaries who travelled abroad, where they were expected to promote the peace-loving aspirations of the Soviet Union.
- Members of the clergy had the responsibility to collect information about the chief actors at international meetings.
- By the recruitment of agents in leadership positions in the church and in other confessions and the appointments and transfers of priests throughout the country, the KGB directed the social views of the clergy.
- The KGB had the responsibility to prepare criminal prosecution of recalcitrant priests and believers. In 1982, for example, criminal courts had sentenced 229 clergy and sectarians for punishment and sent eighteen others into exile. These same documents named more than 2,500 individuals considered as "hostile elements" among the Soviet population.[72]

The commission's report, however, went further in analyzing the political and social conditions that had given rise to these practices, exploring the making of government policies toward the church, which had, from the outset a "duplicitous character":

> On the one hand, the government proclaimed freedom of conscience and, since 1918, issued legal acts designed to provide this freedom. They acknowledged the rights of believers to form religious associations and perform religious rites, within the limits of the laws. They granted freedom of religious activity to various confessions.... On the other hand, under the cover of democratic slogans and the declaration in the laws about the freedom of conscience, the government concealed another, much different, secret policy, aimed at the total subjugation of the life and activity of religious associations. In secret, the goal of the Communist Party of the Soviet Union (CPSU) aspired to eradicate religion by the use of administrative and forcible means.[73]

The report traced the processes through which these double-edged policies developed in the late 1920s and 1930s "within the bowels of the Central

Committee of the CPSU, which issued laws and regulations aimed at harming the church, reducing its authority, and circumscribing its activities."[74] Throughout the next two decades, the 1940s and 1950s, the Central Committee served as the main "'kitchen,' which 'cooked up' all the state's policies on religion." But in the 1950s and continuing afterward, the primary agency that carried out these policies, working out in detail "everything concerning religion, was, indisputably, the KGB."[75] Because its agents worked close to the everyday life of citizens, it had the most complete information about the men and women who practiced religion. "The possession of information is power," Ponomarev wrote, "and it is no wonder that the KGB functions as a 'government within the government.'"[76]

Most important, the commission's report attempted to expose the deleterious effects of the KGB not only on the church, but also on communal mentalities throughout the country. The system of control, organized and conducted by the KGB, created what Ponomarev called a "completely unique situation in the history of religion and the church. First, it deprived some of the most respected and revered ministers of worship from taking an active part in the life of the community, since they were always in danger of being transferred to peripheral regions of the country or forced to enter monasteries." Second, those members of the clergy "most inclined to compromise, servility, or indifference to the fate of the church were assigned to positions of leadership," where "they became obedient performers of the will and desires of this 'secret police' of the Central Committee of the CPSU."[77]

At the time of the report's writing, the commission had responsibility for looking toward the country's future, seeking to construct a framework for a more dynamic and trustworthy system of governance. The report wanted the Supreme Soviet to put safeguards in place to prevent the abuses of power from recurring. To that end, the commission advocated the passage of legislation preventing members of religious organizations from participating in the operational activities of the security forces. It proposed that religious bodies include in their canonical laws a prohibition against secret collaboration with government organs. The Russian government, the commission emphasized, must ensure that all of its agencies comply with the principle of separation of church and state.

In addition to the violation of the Constitution and the laws of the Russian Federation. near the end of the report, Ponomarev emphasized an imminent danger that resulted from the "transformation of religious organizations into KGB agent centers." During times of political instability, this transformation had the potential to institute anti-constitutional actions. This is precisely what happened, he said, on August 21, 1991, at the height of the attempted coup to overthrow the Russian government. The powerful Metropolitan Pitirim (Nechaev), one of the three senior bishops of the church and publisher of the *Journal of the Moscow Patriarchate*, paid a visit to one of the ringleaders of the coup, Boris Pugo, the Russian minister of internal affairs. The visit by such a high-ranking church official, "acting outside the law, in effect, proclaimed the state criminal Pugo, as the [incoming] President of Russia." The commission considered it essential for the Supreme Soviet to pass legislation and ensure the separation of church and state to prevent such circumstances form ever recurring in the future of Russia.[78]

The revelations from the KGB archives and the commission's report raised a whole series of controversial issues, none more important than the question of what the church was and what it should be. How should the church respond to the parliamentary commission's investigations and discoveries? Additionally, what impact did they make on Russian society?

Some, like Deacon Andrei Kuraev of the Moscow Patriarchate, rejected the claim that the church had willfully betrayed its ideals.[79] It had not become a state church, whose primary interest lay in pursuing power in a rapidly changing society.[80] The church's singular objective lay in advancing the spiritual well-being of the Russian people. Others, such as Fr. Viacheslav Polosin, argued that church leaders who were complicit in fostering evil acts should be held accountable under the guidance of Patriarch Aleksii II. The patriarch should seek to recover the church's "symphonic" relationship to the government, giving its leaders moral counsel, serving as a partner in advancing the people's welfare, and helping the government unify the Russian people.[81]

Fr. Gleb Yakunin, like Zoia Krakhmal'nikova, had reached the conclusion that the Russian Orthodox Church had to seek a new beginning. It needed to take an honest look at its history of compliance with an atheist state and separate the wheat from the chaff. He shared Krakhmal'nikova's contention that the church, since 1927, had practiced a brand of "political Christianity," by prioritizing servitude to the government over servitude to Christ.[82] Like Krakhmal'nikova, Yakunin believed that the church required a clean break from the secular power, because only then could it free itself from the duplicity and falsehoods that stained the history of the Russian church in the twentieth century.

In the end, however, the Russian Orthodox Church refrained from probing too deeply into its collaboration with the KGB. Not only would such further study invite serious questions about the decisions the church had made but also it would implicate current leading members of the Holy Synod, the governing body of the Orthodox Church. These powerful interests had cause to stifle additional inquiry into their complicity in perpetuating an unjust and immoral system. Moreover, as Archbishop Khrizostom stated in his interview, the newly elected Patriarch Aleksii II faced intense pressure from factions within the church who limited his capacity to act according to his own desires.[83] In addition, the revelations from the archives did not meet with the broad public outcry that Yakunin and others might have expected. By late 1992 and early 1993, the attention of the great majority of Russian citizens focused on immediate daily needs and the economic difficulties that the dissolution of the Soviet Union had precipitated.[84] Many citizens had little inclination to blame church leaders since they regarded personal compromises as a common feature of Soviet life.[85]

Yakunin well knew that issues concerning Russia's future hung in the balance at this point. To suppress the church's collusion with the KGB would hinder its ability to make a clean break with the darker features of the Soviet past and obstruct one of the foundational pieces of a democratic society. In Yakunin's view, the church's independence from the state heightened its creative capacity, its ability to build social trust, and its potential to contribute to an open society that recognized the equality of all religious confessions, rather than fostering intolerance and violence. To the Russian sociologist of religion Sergei Filatov, these attributes were extremely important for his country's future. What the church needed most was "democracy" and "new ways of thinking," he said. The leadership of the church, however, "is made up of extremely conservative people, who are lacking in new ideas. The most interesting priests are beneath them, hidden from view, and reticent to speak out, but they are there, patiently doing their pastoral work."[86] In any other institution, the revelations from the KGB archive would have led to a shake-up at the top of the hierarchy, Filatov maintained, but the Russian Orthodox Church experienced no such upheaval and soon continued as though oblivious to the disclosures. Rather than responding to democratic forces developing from below, the inactions of church leaders, in general, contributed to authoritarianism in the church's governing structures.[87]

Despite the church's reluctance to confront the explosive revelations from KGB files, those revelations set in motion a chain of events that had long-term significance. In Ukraine, the disclosure of Metropolitan Filaret's complicity strengthened the hand of the recently formed Ukrainian Autocephalous Church, a competitor of the Ukrainian Orthodox Church.[88] In addition, the Russian Church Abroad, headquartered in the United States, became extremely active in Russia, rapidly expanding its appeal. These circumstances would have a significant impact on the future course of Fr. Gleb Yakunin's life.

CHAPTER 10

Priest and Politician

In the years 1992 through 1997, Russia continued its transition from the Soviet Union to an independent state. In terms of political stability, the period had significant peaks and valleys. These years included the consolidation of power under President Yeltsin's leadership, separatist conflicts over the province of Chechnya, terrorism, economic dislocation, a nationalistic political culture, and the resurgence of an increasingly powerful KGB (FSB). These and other changes in Russia's political framework scrambled the country's identity. Whether the changes would lead to a new political order remained an open question. "It seems that the Russian people need the protection of the state, but they do not want to serve it," observed the Russian sociologist Yuri Levada, director of the nongovernmental Levada Center in Moscow.[1]

In these years, the fundamental theme in Fr. Gleb Yakunin's life concerned his conflict with the Moscow Patriarchate. It was not a new clash, as this book has attested. But in the 1990s, his disagreements with the patriarchate reached a crescendo and led to a complete break between the priest and the church itself. Yakunin had never compromised his belief in speaking the truth, and his dislike of the hierarchy's willingness to support the political power of the state led him to take extreme positions, perhaps too extreme for his own well-being. In the 1990s, he exhibited both of these strengths and weaknesses, for which he would pay a large personal price.

The 1990s began with two developments that set the stage for Fr. Gleb's actions and his thoughts about how the Orthodox Church should move forward. The first concerned the explosion of interest in religion among the Russian population. The dissolution of the Soviet government and, in the late 1980s and early 1990s, the revelations about the Soviet system left a large ideological space that many political and religious groups rapidly endeavored to fill.[2] The end of the Soviet era raised a series of additional questions whose answers remained uncertain. As the Russian state sought to remake itself, what remnants of the massive Soviet secularization program would shape the future? What religious denominations would enjoy the greatest success and speak most effectively to the Russian people? As the Russian Orthodox Church regained its status as Russia's traditional religion, what political and social role would it play?[3]

It is incorrect to assert that the Russian people lived in a religious and political vacuum, as Western analysts have often claimed. A large number of indigenous groups had functioned for many years, despite the government's persecutions. They made for a wide assortment of religious perspectives and faiths operating across the religious landscape, making Russia one of Europe's most religiously diverse societies.

The second development that had a large bearing on Yakunin's life concerned the regeneration of Russia. A national rebirth had already begun in the 1980s. Even before the escalation of Mikhail Gorbachev's perestroika, this national rebirth reached a crescendo. Nationalist groups proliferated; they offered a sense of psychological and social stability during a time when Russians, unmoored from their previous ideological bearings, sought new means of support. Further, during a time of uncertainty about the future, state officials viewed the church as a prime vehicle for enhancing national unity. Increasingly, in the mid-1990s, government officials connected the reconstruction of the Russian state with the revival of the Orthodox Church. "Which Russia will be inherited by our grandchildren depends on us," Patriarch Aleksii II said, "and it is only on the basis of the Orthodox religion that the Motherland can regain its magnificence."[4]

Not only Patriarch Aleksii II but also government leaders perceived the Orthodox Church as a primary source of moral authority. The church replaced the previous code of morality taught during Soviet times that required ultimate loyalty to the Communist Party. The regeneration of the Russian state, as the Russian writers Aleksandr Kyrlezhev and Konstantin Troitskii observed, went hand in hand with the "ascendancy of the church in social consciousness, which, in turn, connected to the country's historical experiences and offered a way of overcoming the feeling of national decline. To move beyond the Soviet past meant—in part—to resurrect the destroyed church, assist in its revival, return its possessions, and, by these means, atone for the sins of sacrilege and apostasy."[5] The revival of the Orthodox Church and its promotion in Russia's social consciousness also opened the door to diverse forms of Russian nationalism. They ranged widely across the political spectrum from those who equated the reconstruction of the Russian nation with opening the country to Western political and economic ideas, on one extreme, to radical fundamentalists who advocated closing the country to outsiders, restoring the monarchy, and putting to death the proponents of ecumenical ideas, on the other.[6]

In the months before the end of the Soviet Union, numerous groups and individuals had begun looking to the future. Fr. Gleb Yakunin and several of his associates in the Russian Congress of People's Deputies envisioned the beginning of a new era fundamentally different from the Soviet past. In 1990, three members, Fr. Gleb Yakunin, the writer Viktor Aksiuchits, and Fr. Viacheslav Polosin, founded the Russian Christian Democratic Movement, modeled in part after similar political bodies in Western Europe. Others, including Fr. Georgii Edel'stein, soon joined the group (see figure 10.1). Although their Western counterparts had derived their main ideas from the social philosophy of nineteenth-century Roman Catholicism, the Russian movement drew from a different base. It looked to Russia's own philosophers and theologians of the early twentieth century.[7] The Russian Christian Democratic Movement (RCDM), therefore, operated within a different framework than did its kindred political groups in the West. Although Yakunin left the movement in 1992, the core principles on which he helped establish it remained central to his aspirational goals throughout the next decade.

Fundamental to his thinking and his worldview, these principles also helped shape the course he pursued. Although he had embraced several of them in the past, the five principles contained in the founding document of the Russian Christian Democratic Movement constituted his vision of how Russia should construct its future.

The movement's most basic principle underscored the priority of developing a "religious-political renaissance of the individual, society, and nation."[8] Accomplishing this goal required an unqualified rejection of the communist ideology, which had based the entire social order on an atheistic and materialistic view of the world. According to the founding document of the Russian Christian Democratic Movement, placing everything in the service of a radical and godless doctrine of power had served as an ideology of destruction. Aspiring to construct a new world and a new way of being, this former ideology, in practice, had injected into Russian society the "spirit of malice" as a means of destroying the spiritual roots of life. Communism, as the document read, "did not seek to destroy [Russian] civilization so much as to destroy the

FIGURE 10.1. From left to right, Fr. Georgii Edel'stein, Fr. Gleb Yakunin, and Viktor Aksiuchits, early 1990s. Courtesy of the Keston Center for Religion, Politics, and Society, Baylor University, Waco, Texas.

spiritual beliefs of the human being." To achieve this goal, Soviet communism replaced the God of Christianity with the god of material prosperity. The party lived with an illusion, because human fulfillment could not be achieved in this way; "step by step Communism aspired to destroy and re-forge everything on which was imprinted the godlike nature of the creativity of humankind."[9] In such a society, a person died young, although not from a physical death, but rather from the "destruction of the soul in life itself."[10]

The second principle of the RCDM concerned Christian politics. Having expressed determined opposition to the communist past, Yakunin, Aksiuchits, and Polosin contrasted the Christian view of national policy to its Soviet predecessor: "The freedom of the human personality, the value of each person separately, the priority of the interests of the person over any theory of social development—here are the chief characteristics of the Christian world understanding.... In the eternal and not the temporary capacity of the human personality lies the source of the principal difference between the Christian and the neo-pagan communist."[11]

In making this claim, Yakunin and his colleagues did not draw a sharp line between the eternal and the earthly. Following the great nineteenth-century Russian philosopher Vladimir Sergeevich Solov'ev, they emphasized that Jesus

Christ had united the two spheres.[12] He had not turned his back on the world, as had leaders of the Russian Orthodox Church in the twentieth century, but embraced it. A fundamental duty of a Christian was to improve personally and then reach out to one's neighbors and strive for their well-being. Such a process would begin with the internal moral improvement of the individual and then, after fully inculcating love and compassion into one's inner being, reaching out to the world. The reformulation of laws and institutions in the direction of Christian truth, rather than through the protection of selfish motives, would be one means of completing the task that Yakunin and other leaders of the RCDM had in mind.[13]

The Christian thus had the moral duty to serve other people, selflessly and in the spirit of love, through politics and reform as well as social activities. This service had to begin, the founders of the RCDM repeatedly underscored, with the "internal, moral, and spiritual transformation of the human being."[14] They warned against radical political change, as their communist predecessors and other political activists had promoted. Their long-range program advocated the reverse—a slow, gradual, systematic process of development that took into account the social and economic conditions and the education of the Russian people. Political change ought to be "guided by the cold wisdom of experience over any kind of passionate enthusiasm based on blind and false faith."[15] In making this assertion, the founders rejected the many times in the history of Russia when passion had ruled and reason had been left by the wayside.

Third, as a central long-term goal, the RCDM aimed to build what it called a free society and a democratic government. The movement's leaders considered this as "our moral duty," but they also realized the difficulty of the task. They understood that the construction of such a society, given Russia's history of the past seventy years, could not be completed over a short period. Thus, they labeled this principle "creative democracy," signifying the whole process of laying the groundwork for the free society and democratic government they had in mind. As a beginning step, it was essential to have an educational system free of ideology that provided knowledge and valued independent thinking. Next, the people had to understand and appreciate the meaning of freedom. Freedom did not consist of the "unleashing" of one's desires. It could not be imposed by external forces, but had to come from within—from developing internal connections, teaching self-discipline, holding oneself accountable to the laws, and knowing the limits of the laws. Freedom required a "high level of legal awareness," and if such an understanding of freedom did not exist, then "'democracy' led either to anarchy or despotism."[16] The leaders of the RCDM maintained that the communist regime had crushed the skills essential to a democracy. These skills had to be painstakingly cultivated by the educational process in order to prepare the people for the kind of independent judgment a creative democracy required.[17]

Fourth, a fundamental principle of the RCDM concerned its emphasis on "personalism." The concept owed a great deal to the writings of the Russian philosopher Nikolai Berdiaev and the French Catholic philosopher Jacques Maritain.[18] Both philosophers viewed the human being as a free personality whose primary responsibility lay in service to others, in care for one's neighbors, and in putting such an obligation above the fulfillment of one's own needs. This focus on a person's responsibility to make the world a better place and fulfill God's plan for humankind distinguished "personalism" from "individualism."[19] The church's rejection of the world, Yakunin maintained, had led to Russia's tragedy in the twentieth century; if the Orthodox Church followed the same path in the future, it would lead to "an even more terrible tragedy."[20]

The Christian Democratic ideal stood in stark contrast to the communist ideal of building a "heaven on earth" in some remote future. It was no accident that the latter had become "a place of prisons, psychiatric hospitals, and a system of the total suppression of personhood, and the endless oppression of people."[21] In contrast, the Christian Democratic ideal proclaimed the unique value of each person and the recognition of "two spheres of life" (the heavenly and the earthly) while calling for the absence of violence and a demonstration of love for the entire human community. The leaders of the RCDM did not aspire to make Christianity into a state religion; rather, they hoped to infuse the above-mentioned Christian ideals into laws, state policies, social organizations, and economic relationships. In practical terms, the RCDM's approach advocated freedom of speech, respect for the sanctity of the person; the development of civil society; freedom of assembly; the renunciation of violence between classes, nationalities, and religious denominations; the abolition of the Council for Religious Affairs; and "the ideals of love, kindness, and *sobornost'* [conciliarity] in all spheres of human activity"[22]

Yakunin and the other founders of the RCDM called the fifth philosophical principle "enlightened patriotism." It was a term opposite to the nationalism that Soviet leaders had promulgated since the Stalin era and that Yakunin had seen reemerging in various forms at the end of the Soviet period. As a political principle, nationalism proclaims that a common culture serves to unify all members of a society; in its extreme form, it forces all people in a given country to identify with a common culture viewed as superior to foreigner cultures.[23] Yakunin and his associates viewed "enlightened patriotism" much differently. They defined it as "love for one's native land," which required a sober look at one's own people, both their achievements and their deficiencies. When problems were identified, enlightened patriotism sought to heal them through reason and repentance. At its core, enlightened patriotism was the "consciousness and recognition of as well as personal responsibility for one's history, culture, customs, and spiritual heritage."[24] Enlightened patriotism had an additional dimension, which the founders of the RCDM defined as the "rebirth of universal sensitivity, sympathy, and the openness of the Russian people." It signified a "selfless, sacrificial patriotic consciousness that avoided the temptation of self-delusion."[25]

Instead of enmity, it expressed respect for other cultures. Moreover, enlightened patriotism conveyed belief in the creative strength of the Russian people who, once fully liberated from the stifling yoke of Bolshevik tyranny, were capable of building a new and better Russia. At the conclusion of their founding document, the leaders of the RCDM cited the poet Alexander Pushkin and his enduring faith in the Russian people and quoted the following lines from his epic poem "Poltava":

> But in her lust for retribution,
>   Having endured the blows
> of late,
>   Rus took up arms. And as
> a hammer
>   Shatters glass, she forged steel blades.[26]

The principles expressed in the founding document of the RCDM served as a basis for a debate within the church between Fr. Gleb Yakunin and Patriarch Aleksii II over opposing views of Russia's future. The Russian Orthodox Church was composed of different factions and perspectives, and the patriarch's views did not necessarily convey the dominant ideas about the country's future course. As the proclaimed leader of the Russian Orthodox Church, his public pronouncements, however, carried a great deal of weight, both internally and internationally. Since Fr. Gleb Yakunin and Patriarch Aleksii II did not share the same political platform, and they held vastly different positions of authority, an antagonistic relationship soon developed between the head of the Russian Orthodox Church and his chief critic. To a significant degree, their dissension evolved over differing conceptions of the role of the church in Russian society.

The Debate

Fr. Gleb Yakunin

By 1992, Yakunin had served for four years as head priest in the town of Shchyolkovo. It had been five years since his release from exile in Siberia and more than a decade since he had faced the intense daily pressure from the KGB's scrutiny of his activities. Like many of his contemporaries, he continued to find challenging the adjustment to a political environment much different from the one he had known for most of his life. In 1992, he also faced a personal dilemma. As a participant in the new Russian Parliament, he had found political activity appealing. It offered the rare opportunity to integrate his religious ideals directly into the political arena in order to advance the principles he had articulated earlier as a leader of the Russian Christian Democratic Movement. In a dispute with other RCDM leaders over support for a new All-Union treaty to solidify the Soviet regime as well as their desire to turn the movement into a political party, he had left the movement in late August 1991. Yet he wanted to be involved in politics, although he did not know how he might best serve. In this uncertainty lay his personal dilemma.

As a priest in Shchyolkovo, according to his daughter Mariia, Fr. Gleb had found a great deal of personal fulfillment. He had been extremely successful, she said, and she had repeatedly witnessed the personal relationships he had built with the members of his parish. She cited the testimonies of the parishioners, especially the priest Dmitrii, who served with him: "When he [Fr. Gleb] heard confessions, a long line formed before him, although other priests were also available. The people eagerly came to his worship services and confessions. His celebration of the liturgy was heartfelt. Whenever he returned from his duties elsewhere, parishioners were invariably happy to see their pastor and treated him with much affection."[27]

Earlier, Fr. Gleb had criticized the Orthodox Church many times for its failures to reach out to people in the community, thereby leaving a large abyss between the church and Russian society, of which the Bolsheviks had taken advantage. As a priest, Fr. Gleb attempted to break down the walls between his church and the local community: "He was attentive to each person, gave them helpful advice, and built their trust, and his parishioners, seeing his steadfastness, did trust him." Mariia Glebovna witnessed firsthand her father's work as a pastor:

> Fr. Gleb led many people to the faith, even those in the community who had once professed to be militant atheists. People saw in him a person who did not spare himself in selfless service to God. He never feared hardships, nor taking risks, nor enduring persecution. In the difficult years of the early 1990s, when all kinds of possibilities began to open up, his sermons instructed people on how to live. He gave practical advice to many families, in which he tried to cultivate Christian qualities of brother and sisterhood that helped the community live together in peace and care for one another.[28]

Because of his political activities, which led to repeated confrontations with the government and the Moscow Patriarchate, people rarely remembered that Fr. Gleb had been an ordained Orthodox priest. The political dimension of his life inadvertently created a one-sided view of his personality and major commitments. Nevertheless, in the early 1990s and throughout his career, Fr. Gleb firmly believed that he served Orthodox Christianity. "Few people talk about him as a priest," said Mariia Glebovna; in addition to his political activism, "people should know that there was another dimension to him."[29]

In 1992, facing the prospect of standing for elections to the Russian Parliament, Fr. Gleb had to make a crucial decision about his future: whether to continue serving as the priest in Shchyolkovo or to stand for office. At the time, he was recognized as arguably the most prominent religious dissident of the former Soviet Union, a principled and fearless opponent of the former Soviet regime, and a supporter of the Russian president Boris Yeltsin. As mentioned earlier, the previous August, he had stood with Yeltsin on the platform and called for the Russian people to reject the communist past, believing that Boris Yeltsin intended to carry the country in a democratic political direction. At the end of 1991, as the Soviet Union disintegrated, a delegation of scientists from the nearby town of Chernogolovka paid a visit to Fr. Gleb. The members of the group told him that they trusted and respected him, and they encouraged him to run for office from the district. Chernogolovka is a town located some twenty-seven miles northeast of Moscow. In the 1970s, it had served as the main scientific research center for the Soviet Academy of Sciences.[30] Whether the visit of the delegation determined the path Fr. Gleb ultimately took is unclear, but it had a significant influence.[31]

Politically, Yakunin had to convert his personal principles into a specific strategy. The development of a flourishing society, he believed, called for a reformulation of the entire paradigm of Russian life. The change that he envisioned required the moral reconstruction of Russian society into one that built trust in individual citizens as well as between the citizenry and the government. Trust, he believed, could not be gained without bringing the Orthodox Church, which had been relegated to an oppressed position in the Soviet state, into a central place in Russian life. Its dramatically increased prominence, however, should not resemble the Orthodox Church of the past, but rather a radically different church built on repentance and humility. The church that he envisioned should draw on the best of Russia's heritage—on compassion for the outcast, openness to the world, tolerance for dissenting views, separation from the government, and close adherence to the teachings of Jesus Christ. The perspectives came from Fr. Gleb's interpretation of the Gospels and the writings of the early Church Fathers, notably St. John Chrysostom, on whom the

Russian Christian Democratic Movement had also drawn.³² St. John had denounced abuses of power by the ecclesiastical and political authorities of his time. He had also maintained that Christ had come into the world not to reject it but to save it. The church, as Fr. Gleb emphasized, needed to follow his example and reach out to those who were suffering, downtrodden, and poor.

In addition, as the RCDM had stated, Yakunin emphasized the central importance of the independent mind, free of the self-confining ideological framework of the Soviet state. Education, therefore, would play a fundamental role in the development of Russian society.³³ The Russian educational system had to promote freedom of thought and develop autonomous individuals who thought for themselves and questioned both state and ecclesiastical power, while promoting civic consciousness and a sense of responsibility for the whole society. An urgent need, therefore, was the abolition of all ideological organs that had thrived in the past, the party organizations that had dominated the upbringing of young people and narrowed their mental capacity.³⁴ The mind had to be free from its captivity to official organs of the state and allowed to follow its own proclivities in service to the world.

Yakunin understood freedom of conscience, freedom of thought, and the development of civil society as interrelated goals. Both a flourishing Orthodox Church and a flourishing society should value the equality of religious faiths. As the 1990 law on freedom of conscience became a hotly debated topic in the Russian Parliament from 1993 to 1995, Yakunin was unwilling to compromise on the provisions of the original law, and he had President Yeltsin on his side.³⁵ Neither sympathized with political blocs that advocated the necessity of restricting the religious rights of several non-Orthodox confessions.

To his disappointment, however, by the mid-1990s, Yakunin had become increasingly convinced of the Moscow Patriarchate's inability and unwillingness to reform itself and to provide the moral leadership he believed essential to Russia's regeneration.³⁶ He believed that the Orthodox hierarchy, rather than leading the country to a new and healthier condition, constituted an impediment to the process of national renewal. The leadership of the Russian Orthodox Church, he maintained, had not freed itself from its previous loyalty to Soviet agencies. It retained the negative psychological attributes of the former Soviet Union in its extreme nationalism, its enmity toward the West, its defensiveness, and its suppression of dissent. His comments were harshly critical; they signified impatience and indignation in response to the hierarchy's behavior toward him, which will be discussed in due course.

In 1995, Fr. Gleb wrote two letters to President Yeltsin in which he disparaged the leadership of the Orthodox Church for its ultraconservative and irresponsible actions. He wrote the letters in despair, but also in anger, and they contained acrimonious accusations of the patriarchate's unwillingness to meet the spiritual and social needs of the Russian people. Writing to the Russian president, he rejected the patriarch's claim that the church should have a privileged position, arguing that it had forfeited that status earlier in the twentieth century when it had allied itself with the Soviet atheist government. Since then, the patriarchate had "fashioned a myth" that the church was the only institution in Russia whose legacy and special position went back a thousand years. In its present form, Yakunin charged, the "Moscow Patriarchy was the creation of Joseph Stalin in 1943; it was the child of the Central Committee of the Communist Party of the Soviet Union and the MVD [Ministry of Internal Affairs, the forerunner of the KGB]."[37] Rather than promote democracy, he said, the Moscow Patriarchate had helped foster a new sickness in Russia: it had become "a natural reservoir for the growth of Stalinist fundamentalism and authoritarianism." This "post-Stalinist church hierarchy and its government supporters," Yakunin charged, served as the "main incubators for the growth of fascism in our country."[38]

Fr. Gleb's unsparing words about the Moscow Patriarchate overly generalized a dangerous trend then on the ascendancy. In the 1993 elections to Parliament, Vladimir Zhirinovsky and his Liberal Democratic Party showed surprising strength, winning 23 percent of the vote and coming in first in sixty-four of eighty-seven regions of the country.[39] A flamboyant Russian nationalist, Zhirinovsky combined militarism and populism in a new political style that many Russians found appealing during a time when their country's place in the world had suffered a large setback. In the next two years, Zhirinovsky's national appeal continued to rise, leading many Western journalists to view his popularity as evidence of an emerging fascism that threatened Yeltsin's presidency.[40] Fr. Gleb's letters to the Russian president, linking the church hierarchy to this threat, oversimplified the complex situation in which the church leadership found itself.

Patriarch Aleksii II

In the 1990s, the Russian Orthodox Church faced unparalleled opportunities and extremely difficult challenges. In the immediate aftermath of the Soviet Union's demise, Russia became a fertile field for foreign missionaries, as Presbyterians, Methodists, Pentecostals, Seventh-Day Adventists, Roman Catholics, and Southern Baptists arrived in large numbers. Many of them did not speak Russian and had little knowledge of Russian history and culture.[41] Well financed, often with superb technological skills, they gained access to Russian media and spread their messages widely. Some of these groups brought medical supplies and printed materials, which provincial regions of Russia sorely needed. The presence of these newly arrived religious organizations posed a threat to their impoverished Russian counterparts, who struggled to expand their own activities in a rapidly changing society.

In addition, in the early 1990s, foreign sects entered the country, aspiring to attract young people to their cause. They included organizations such as the Rev. Sun Myung Moon's Unification Church of the United States, Scientology, and Aum Shinrikgo (Aum Supreme Truth) from Japan. Fringe groups that had operated underground during the Soviet period emerged into the open, where they operated freely. These included the Great White Brotherhood (Velikoe beloe bratstvo), the Church of the Last Testament (Tserkov' poslednego Zaveta), and the Center of the Mother of God (Bogorodichnyi Tsentr).[42] The patriarch expressed dismay at the proliferation of these groups for the threat they posed to Russia's regeneration. "They undermine the foundations of our life," he said. He singled out the Great White Brotherhood and the Center of the Mother of God which "have special influence on the young. I have had occasion to meet such young people; they left the impression on me that they were under the influence of some kind of hypnosis."[43]

Challenged from all sides in the competition for Russian souls, the Orthodox Church confronted daunting tasks. The most serious of these difficulties, however, were internal. The Russian people, even the best educated, had little knowledge of biblical literature and religious teachings. The church had a paucity of Bibles and biblical literature; it also had an enormous shortage of well-qualified priests. Between 1988 and 1997, the number of functioning Orthodox Churches grew from 6,800 to more than 17,000. In the same period, the number of monasteries increased from 18 to more than 300, and the number of theological schools expanded from 5 to more than 65.[44] After decades of government repression of the Orthodox Church, this increase in the number of newly opened and functioning church institutions constituted one of the signal achievements of Patriarch Aleksii II's tenure. Once more, open churches dotted the Russian landscape, their gleaming cupulas standing out above the trees, and their bells a ringing presence in the daily lives of the Russian people. Yet, after decades of ruin, few of these churches had adequate resources to restore their sanctuaries, rebuild their edifices, and attract competent priests and teachers. They had to depend on government grants or donations from local congregations for these funds. During a time of rapid inflation, however, when most people struggled to survive, such funding would be especially difficult to raise.

Installed at the end of the Soviet Union, Patriarch Aleksii II knew that he faced severe problems. If Fr. Gleb believed the church's top priority ought to be its leaders' repentance for collaboration with an atheist government, Patriarch Aleksii II envisioned it as the Christian education of the Russian people. To him, the seven decades of assault on all religions had nearly obliterated their knowledge of Christianity, leaving them ignorant of its teachings. Many conceived of these teachings as the opposite of their actual substance. Not only did the church lack sufficient numbers of priests, but because of the closure of theological academies, many of the priests who were available lacked the necessary training to carry out their tasks of ministering to the people. In the provincial town of Akulovo, where Fr. Aleksandr Men first served, the head priest had spent most of his career as an accountant, had little theological education, and conducted the service strictly by the book because he was unable to venture outside the rigid order he had memorized earlier.[45] The result was an unimaginative, unattractive situation that all too often characterized churches in the countryside.

In the first years following his election as patriarch, Aleksii II stressed the importance of overcoming the psychological attacks of the Bolsheviks on the religious consciousness of the Russian people. On September 15, 1993, in the Siberian city of Irkutsk, he spoke about the fundamental need facing the country: "Our task," he said, "is to resurrect faith in the hearts of those who, over the course of many years, had it driven out of them."[46] Given the turmoil in which Russia presently found itself, reinstilling this faith would not be easy to accomplish, but the church had to accept this difficulty as a "cross it had to bear for the good of the Fatherland."[47] The patriarch, therefore, connected the Orthodox Church's spiritual responsibility to Russian patriotism, both of which were necessary to rebuilding the country's core foundation.

Like Yakunin, Aleksii II considered the moral reconstruction of Russia essential to its future well-being. He, too, viewed social trust as fundamental to fostering trust between individuals and their neighbors as well as to generating confidence in the governing authorities.[48] Unlike Fr. Gleb, however, he did not claim that this trust derived from a clear and consistent system of laws; it came about through a religious sensibility that knew the difference between right and wrong. Trust also required, the patriarch said, "an openness towards other people," a willingness "to understand that they see the world and its problems differently and what may be the cause of our disagreements."[49] This openness, the sensitivity to Indigenous peoples, and the capacity to see beyond the interests of the self, the patriarch maintained, came best through the teachings of the church and other religious traditions. When the church regained its strength in post-Soviet Russia, it would have the capability to provide this service. On this point, Yakunin fundamentally disagreed. His disillusionment with the church was unwavering; he did not have confidence in its leadership, thanks to its past compromises with the Soviet government and the KGB.

The discussion of capability points to a major disagreement between Yakunin's views and those of the Russian patriarch. After difficult decades of suppression, the church, according to the patriarch, needed time to regain its bearing and to recover central components of its rich heritage. In its present weakness, it needed protection from those who acted to dismember it and benefit from its fragility. "Today is the time to gather stones and not to scatter them," the patriarch said.[50] Most significantly, Aleksii II identified the problems the church faced with those confronting the country, which grew larger "by the propaganda of Western and Eastern pseudo-religious people who glorify the violence that floods our television screens and movie theaters." He decried the West's assault on Russia's intrinsic values, especially what he saw as a "systematic campaign to get people drunk" with alcoholic beverages imported from the West. He also criticized the grandiose promises made by foreign missionaries, and the competition for Russian souls between the church and outsiders who preyed on Russia's weaknesses as it tried to recover its identity.[51] Presently, the church "lacked the means to carry out missionary work at the highest level."[52] To face these challenges, the patriarch wanted the government to limit the incursion of foreign missionaries as well as the cultural assault brought about by Western commercial interests.

But it was Western Baptists and other Protestant groups that most troubled the patriarch. For the sake of national unity, he wanted to curtail their activities, asserting that they wanted to see the Russian people "with an outstretched hand, begging for the humanitarian aid that they had come to offer."[53] These groups exacerbated the divisions that already existed in Russia, Aleksii II said in an address he gave in the Ivanovo Diocese. Russia, he asserted, "must stand on its own legs" and must not fall into the nefarious clutches of those interests that wanted to divide the country.[54] Again, he asserted that the Orthodox Church's interests paralleled the national interests of Russia.

Yakunin fought against this view. He believed it injurious in the long term to limit freedom of conscience, as the patriarch was inclined to do. He accused the patriarch of taking the same path that the leaders of the church had followed in the past: faced with a challenge to its authority, the patriarch pursued a familiar course—to prohibit the troublemaker.[55]

Yakunin supported the Protestants' activities in Russia. He wanted to limit neither their presence in Russia nor their missionary activities. By forcing the church to enhance its social role, the pressure on the Orthodox Church, he believed, would only make it stronger. Operating in an atmosphere of greater openness, the church ought to be able to stand on its own, and he sharply criticized the patriarch's efforts to limit the freedom of exposure to other faiths: "The patriarch is trying to cast us back to a medieval situation. . . . I do not know of one instance in which the Baptists have stolen anyone from the Orthodox patriarch. . . . I am from the Orthodox Church and I believe my faith is the right one, and if my belief is all-powerful and true, I would be ashamed to try to close the mouths of others."[56]

Both Gleb Yakunin and Patriarch Aleksii II confronted the ambiguities and possibilities of developing an open pluralistic society and, in such a setting, how church-state relations should operate. Surveying Russia and its diverse religious traditions, the patriarch recognized their variety. But his appreciation of these diverse faiths did not extend beyond certain confessions that had a long history in the countryside—specifically, Catholicism, Islam, Protestantism, and Buddhism—which he singled out as legitimate. "I do not call on all of us to be Orthodox," he said.[57] Nevertheless, "each person must think about what his/her roots come from," and in tracing those roots, the patriarch identified Russia with Orthodoxy as the bedrock of Russia's history.[58] He said little about other minority confessions other than naming several extremist sects. Yet the patriarch's views were unmistakable: for the sake of national unity, he did not countenance the existence of newly arrived confessions that, he claimed, tore at the foundation of Russia's national life.

"The Church exists to serve God," Patriarch Aleksii II emphasized.[59] The Orthodox Church and its servitors, he pointed out in 1990, "did not have any [political] program for Russia's revival."[60] He asserted that the church had a peacekeeping mission, sought to resolve disputes and to serve as a mediator during conflicts, and opposed the use of violence. As a mediator, the patriarch claimed that the church stood above politics, above the unsavory, often intense partisan conflicts that engulfed opposing political parties.[61] Yet the various services he emphasized had political implications. While he professed that the church separated itself from political struggles and took no political position, its actual behavior spoke otherwise.

Russian federal laws proclaimed freedom of religion and the separation of the church from the state, but many agencies contradicted the laws. Educational institutions collaborated with the church in introducing courses in their curricula on the history of Orthodoxy; the Moscow Patriarchate concluded agreements with the Defense Ministry and the Ministry of the Interior, which gave the church a prominent role in the military and the police. Faced with a paucity of funds, the patriarchate often relied on the Russian government to provide the financial resources to restore newly reopened churches and monasteries, rebuild theological schools, and refurbish the heavy operational budgets of theological academies and seminaries. "Violating, but without changing the laws," Sergei Filatov argued, on an increasing scale in the 1990s, "the government carried out a series of actions directed at giving the Moscow Patriarchy significant rights and privileges, which elevated the church to a high official status."[62]

Prohibiting the Troublemakers

Shortly after the bloody confrontation between the Russian Parliament and President Yeltsin in September 1993, Patriarch Aleksii II chastised priests on both sides of the political battle. Instead of acting as peacemakers, he said, they had fomented violence, in violation of their priestly oath. The patriarch accused them of promoting schism and discord within the church, rather than encouraging unity and harmony. Therefore, he ordered Russian priests to desist from engaging in politics in the future, to withdraw from standing for elections, and to return to their time-honored duties as advocates of peace.[63]

The patriarch's order had immediate ramifications for Fr. Gleb Yakunin. He and the Orthodox monk Innokentii (Pavlov) had filed for the December elections to the State Duma. On October 8, 1993, the Holy Synod of the Russian Orthodox Church issued a special federal decree that emphasized the time-consuming responsibilities of elected representatives, which made it impossible, the decree read, for priestly delegates to fulfill their pastoral obligations.[64] The Holy Synod called on them to uphold the integrity of their priestly calling and exhorted them "not to promote trouble in the church and in social life."[65] A few weeks later, on November 1 and 2, 1993, the Holy Synod invited Innokentii and Fr. Gleb to a special session to discuss their situations. During the meeting, this supreme church body, citing the canon law of the Russian Orthodox Church, ordered the two men to terminate their candidacies in the elections to the Federal Assembly in the Russian legislature. Innokentii agreed to comply with the synod's decision; Fr. Gleb, on the other hand, refused. The Holy Synod, citing Fr. Gleb's disobedience, ordered him defrocked as an Orthodox priest.[66]

On the surface, the Holy Synod's action, in concert with the patriarch, appeared justified, given Yakunin's defiance of their directive. His compliance, however, would have contradicted everything for which he had fought for many years, including his conviction that the church, to its detriment, had played too passive a role in the nation's social and political struggles.[67] Although he drew firm lines between church and state in the political arena, he was reluctant to dismiss the church's voice in the making of state policy. The creation of a just legal system that protected freedom of conscience required wider representation than input from the patriarch and the church hierarchy, given their past complicity with the Soviet administration and the KGB.

Stripped of his priestly rank, Yakunin fought back. Asserting the illegality of the Holy Synod's defrocking him as an Orthodox priest, he filed a criminal case against the Moscow Patriarchate.[68] In January and February 1994, he wrote two open letters to Aleksii II, both of which accused the Holy Synod of acting unjustly. These letters represented a cogent, closely argued case that attempted to indict the church hierarchy for its hypocrisy and illegitimate use of canon law. At the heart of his appeal was the claim that the Holy Synod violated an earlier resolution that was passed in August 1918 by the All-Russian Church Council. Last convened in 1917–1918, during the Russian Revolution, the council represented the supreme governing body of the church. It had restored the Moscow Patriarchate, two hundred years after Tsar Pyotr I had abolished it. The resolution to which Yakunin referred had prohibited the persecution of priests who engaged in political activities, and the Council had rehabilitated a priest (Grigorii Petrov), who had suffered abuse for his participation in the former State Duma.[69] Since the church had never repealed this earlier decision, it remained binding. Moreover, canon law allowed the defrocking of a priest only for severe misbehavior consisting of violations of church dogma or immoral conduct, neither of which applied in his case.[70]

"Your Holiness," Yakunin wrote, "I regard holy orders as too valuable a treasure to give up without a fight: my religious conscience and moral principles will not allow me to submit to your decision, which contradicts canon law."[71] In this and his subsequent letter, he accused the patriarch of having a personal vendetta against him for calling the patriarch and members of the church hierarchy to account and for labeling the hierarchy a "church *nomenklatura*."[72] Both of Yakunin's letters exhibited a fearless, withering attack on the entire Moscow Patriarchate.[73] He accused it of pandering to the nationalistic forces in Russian politics, expressing nostalgia for a "lost 'totalitarian paradise,'" suppressing dissenting voices, and contributing to the moral decay that continued to hinder real reform of the church.[74] While strong in their claims, his words also expressed anger and a determination never to give in to threats and denunciations.

Yakunin's letter to Patriarch Aleksii II was significant for another reason: it concisely laid out his understanding of Russian democracy. He called it the primary road to the church's resurrection, the basic principle that held a key to the rebirth of democratic government within the Orthodox Church. Once again, Fr. Gleb cited the resolutions of the All-Russian Church Council of 1917–1918, which had laid the groundwork for bringing laypeople and the clergy directly into determining the course that the church should take. The council's resolution had thus redirected power from the top of the echelon of the church to the Orthodox community. According to Yakunin, after the Bolsheviks consolidated control over the country, they deliberately concealed the democratic resolutions of the All-Russian Church Council of 1917–1918 from the Orthodox faithful. He accused "the leadership of the Moscow Patriarchate of hiding this information from church and society, since it contradicted the current Regulations [*Ustavy*] of the Russian Orthodox Church," over which the Bolsheviks had exerted a strong influence.[75]

The council's resolutions on power and authority in the church, Yakunin pointed out, rested on the principle of conciliarity (*sobornost'*). It was the opposite of the top-down hierarchical structure of the Moscow Patriarchy, which had been in place since its resurrection by Stalin in 1943. This autocratic structure had placed authority in the hands of the bishops and had given them "absolute power over the people of God," enabling them to appoint and remove the clergy, move them around, and control their behavior—in short, "to enslave people's souls with lies and spiritual terror."[76] Was this why the church had been so reluctant to participate in the democratic transformation of Russia, he asked? He saw the authoritarian mentality as deeply ingrained in the Moscow Patriarchate, which explained why it was so consistently drawn to the methods used in the past as well as to the policies presently advanced by nationalist parties in Russia. The building of a democratic Russia, he asserted, required the church to reclaim the principle of conciliarity, which would remove power from the Moscow Patriarchate and restore it to where it rightfully belonged—in the local community. Conciliarity, Yakunin maintained, would help the Russian people "overcome the legacy of totalitarian slavery" and ensure that no one had "the right to infringe on the conscience or faith of the individual."[77]

Despite the setbacks he suffered at the hands of the patriarch and the Holy Synod, Yakunin continued to promote the conciliar approach to governance. He won his seat in the Federal Assembly of the State Duma in 1993. Although the Holy Synod had forbidden him to wear the vestments and crucifix of the priestly rank, he kept them on, to the chagrin and often the anger of ultraconservative deputies in the legislature.[78] As he had done throughout his life, notwithstanding the misfortunes and severe blows that he endured, he did not relinquish his belief in the rightness of his cause; he held fast to the ideals that he considered essential to the well-being of the Orthodox Church and the future of Russia.

It would be misleading, however, to claim that the resolution of the Holy Synod to remove him from the Orthodox priesthood did not wound him personally. In spite of its flaws, he had committed himself to the church, believing in its core theological principles: love for all humankind, sacrificial spirit, and humility. Yet the resolution of the Holy Synod left him with an abiding sense of rejection. It was manifested in the first letter he wrote to Patriarch Aleksii II in 1993, after the Holy Synod had defrocked him. In his letter, Fr. Gleb referenced the time, nearly thirty years before, when Patriarch Aleksii I had suspended him and Fr. Nikolai Eshliman. In 1965, he wrote, they had been punished after "Patriarch Aleksii I received an order from the KGB and the Council for Religious Affairs to ban us from church ministry. Obedient to the persecutors of the church, he denied us the opportunity to fulfill our priestly duty." After the dissolution of the Soviet Union and the freedom he had to seek out, the punishment was even more severe: "In those remarkable days, only in a nightmare could I have foreseen that in the kaleidoscopic series of events shortly to come—the collapse of the USSR, of communism, of the power of the soviets and the KGB—I would again be repressed; but this time by the free 'good will' of the patriarch and the bishops. And I would be repressed more cruelly than before—by defrocking: even the godless state did not go as far as that."[79]

Yakunin would again be an outcast, but his dismissal only intensified his resolve to fight.

Fighting Back

The tension between the patriarch and reformist elements inside, and, in Yakunin's case, outside the church, soon developed an increasingly sharp edge after his defrocking. First, Yakunin refused to give up his priestly vestments, and his appearance in them during sessions of the Federal Assembly of the state legislature drew increasingly vigorous rancor on the part of traditionalist and nationalist deputies. On Saturday, September 11, 1995, their hatred provoked a wild scene on the floor of the Federal Assembly. Following the reading of a complaint sent by the patriarch proclaiming that Yakunin was continuing to pose illegitimately as an Orthodox priest, the ultranationalist delegate Nikolai Lysenko rushed up to Yakunin and struck at him. Vladimir Zhirinovsky joined Lysenko in berating Yakunin and tearing at his cassock. A liberal deputy, Evgeniia Tishkovskaia, came to Yakunin's defense and attempted to remove the assailants from him.[80] Her efforts further inflamed Zhirinovsky, who, she said, "grabbed me by the hair, pulled me away, injured my hand, and proceeded to choke me."[81] In the melee, Lysenko stripped Yakunin's pectoral cross from around his neck and triumphantly waved it in the air. The entire scene was filmed and was shown that evening on all the major national television networks. This "outrageous vilification," a Russian commentator wrote, amounted to the "slandering and desecration of the cross" in the Federal Assembly by supposed defenders of the church.[82]

Second, the conflict between Yakunin and the Moscow Patriarchate escalated further in the discussion over legislation concerning freedom of conscience. As mentioned above, the patriarch wanted legal restrictions on foreign missionaries, agreeing with the words of Metropolitan Kirill (Gundiaev) of Smolensk and Kaliningrad in his address to the World Council of Churches Conference on World Mission and Evangelism in November 1996:

> As soon as freedom for missionary work was allowed, a crusade began against the Russian church, even as it began recovering from a prolonged disease, standing on its feet with weakened muscles. Hordes of missionaries dashed in, believing the former Soviet Union to be a vast missionary territory. They behaved as though no local churches existed, no Gospel was being proclaimed. They began preaching without even making an effort to familiarize themselves with the Russian cultural heritage or to learn the Russian language. In most cases, the intention was not to preach Christ or the Gospel, but to tear our faithful away from their traditional churches and recruit them into their own communities.[83]

In his criticism of the foreign missionaries who had rushed in after the fall of the Soviet government, Metropolitan Kirill's assessment was accurate. But his judgment about the present threat in late 1996 was overblown. By the mid-1990s, the "totalitarian sects" that had earlier proliferated had failed to attract a following and had largely disappeared. The Russian sociologist of religion Sergei Filatov showed in a detailed study of major religious trends in Russia that the influx of foreign missionaries had not succeeded in sustaining large numbers of converts and had mostly left the country.[84] Humanitarian aid provided by churches in the West continued to offer relief to needy communities in provincial Russia, but there was little evidence that Protestant groups had either flaunted Russian laws or taken advantage of local communities to undermine the Orthodox Church.[85]

Western governments, including the United States and Great Britain, urged the Yeltsin administration to retain the provisions of the 1990 Law on Freedom of Conscience and Religious Associations. They saw it as a progressive law that would align Russia more closely with the democratic, open societies of the West. It would further ensure that the country would not revert to the authoritarian political order that had characterized its past.

Despite the political pressure coming from Western governments, Patriarch Aleksii II maintained that Russia, as a sovereign state, had to seek its own road. It had no tradition of religious pluralism and lacked any historical experience with such a model. Most important, in the present difficult time of the country's transformation, the Orthodox Church served as a source of national stability. Orthodoxy, in the patriarch's terms, formed the core of Russia's religious identity.[86] All these arguments catered to the nationalists' views of the path the country ought to take, and they gave priority to the Orthodox Church as the key element in Russia's process of national rebuilding. The Orthodox Church alone provided a bulwark for strengthening the post-Soviet moral order, in contrast to nontraditional religions whose presence threatened the spiritual unity of the Russian people.

In the contentious political and religious climate of the 1990s, Patriarch Aleksii II faced several competing factions within the church. The unity that he sought depended on his ability to balance these various interests. Although the majority of Orthodox priests occupied the middle of the political spectrum, a reform-minded series of Orthodox communities operated on the more liberal end. On the other side were radically different circles composed of ultranationalists who viewed Orthodoxy as the core of Russia's unique cultural traditions. Represented by the passionate fundamentalist Metropolitan Ioann (Snychev, 1927–1995), the ultranationalists embraced a militant religious nationalism that railed against what they saw as destructive influences—democracy, pluralism, and ecumenism—as a betrayal of Russia.[87] Although the ultranationalists made up only a small fraction of the clergy, they nevertheless had a public presence that exceeded their numbers, which the patriarch could not ignore. His ability to maintain a central position between these competing perspectives within the Orthodox Church would have a large bearing on his success in bringing about the church's revitalization.

Yakunin and other religious reformers, however, understood the restrictions on religious freedom as a fundamental attack on freedom itself. They believed it important to preserve the ideals set forth in the 1990 Law on Freedom of Conscience and Religious Associations, because they provided a linchpin for the future development of a democratic society. To Yakunin and other religious reformers, restrictions on freedom of conscience set dangerous precedents: they violated the 1993 Constitution, undermined ecumenism, bred intolerance toward non-Orthodox faiths and traditions, and severely hindered the chance for religious reconciliation.

Meanwhile, after the church defrocked him, Yakunin underwent a personal crisis. Angered by what he considered the church hierarchy's mistreatment, he made a bold and perhaps reckless move concerning one of the most contentious political and religious issues in the post-Soviet period. After the disintegration of the Soviet Union, Ukraine seized the opportunity to loosen its ties with

Russia. This act met with strong and determined opposition from the Moscow Patriachate, which considered Ukraine an integral, long-established part of the Russian state and the birthplace of Orthodox Christianity in Russia. Committed to keeping intact the territorial integrity of the Russian Patriarchate, Patriarch Aleksii II adamantly opposed Ukrainian independence. After his election as patriarch, he had appointed Metropolitan Filaret (Denisenko) to head the Exarchate of the Russian Orthodox Church in Ukraine. Metropolitan Filaret promised to preserve the Ukrainian Church's traditional relationship with the Russian Patriarchate. In June 1992, as Ukraine began seeking independent statehood, Metropolitan Filaret, looking for his own political advancement, reversed course in his commitment. In an audacious and surprising move, he and Metropolitan Antony of the Ukrainian Autocephalous Church announced the formation of the Ukrainian Orthodox Church-Kyivan Patriarchate.[88] In 1995, when Filaret was made patriarch, it was the capstone of the stunning turn of events that had infuriated Aleksii II, who viewed Filaret's actions as a betrayal.

In 1996, facing his own troubles, Yakunin made a similarly bold move: he transferred his allegiance to the Ukrainian Orthodox Church-Kievan Patriarchate. Soon he received an appointment as "priest of a parish in the vicinity of Moscow," over which the Kiev-Patriarchate had jurisdiction.[89] This step bewildered and disappointed many of his followers. It seemingly contradicted Yakunin's earlier expressed commitment to reforming the Russian Church from within. Given recent events, however, reformist possibilities seemed, to Yakunin, increasingly unlikely, and, defrocked by the church hierarchy, he no longer had either a voice or status within the Russian Church. The Ukrainian Church offered him the chance to serve and regain his priestly position. A political consideration also played a part in his decision, because he knew the Ukrainian Church challenged what he viewed as the self-indulgent arrogance of the Russian Patriarchate.

The disagreements between Yakunin and the hierarchy of the Russian Orthodox Church soon reached a crescendo. Warned earlier by the Assembly of Archbishops to cease wearing his priestly dress and to repent, Yakunin repeatedly disregarded these orders. In reality, however, the fundamental conflicts between Yakunin and the church hierarchy went much deeper than the issues of priestly vestments and contrition. They concerned larger questions of the church's jurisdictional authority and legitimacy. In addition, differences over Russia's future development as a multiconfessional society deeply divided the patriarch and his antagonist. The Assembly of Archbishops, intending to diminish the public effectiveness of his voice and terminate his membership in the Russian Orthodox Church, took a decisive step on February 19, 1997, after having defrocked him three years earlier: they excommunicated Fr. Gleb Yakunin for disobedience to the orders of the church's authorities. In the same session, the Assembly of Archbishops also excommunicated Patriarch Filaret.[90]

In retrospect, looking at the life of Fr. Gleb, Archpriest Boris Razveev portrayed him as "undoubtedly a religious person, but he had an obstinate character; if he considered himself right on this or that question, he held to it totally, and it was difficult to dislodge him. . . . He wanted to be a great dissident and absolutely wished to sit in prison . . . and in the end, he preferred a political career to a priestly position."[91]

Razveev's characterization of Yakunin has prevailed in the official literature of the Russian Orthodox Church. Only in part, however, is this portrayal just: his resolute unwillingness to bow down before any authority whose actions violated freedom of conscience. Yet the description of him fails to capture the complex, multifaceted aspects of Fr. Gleb's ultimate desires. Despite the difficult obstacles he confronted, Yakunin's commitment to truth and the dignity of the human spirit remained consistent. Razveev's contention that Fr. Gleb's fondness for a political career is a repetition of the former Soviet effort to disparage people by accusing them of personal ambition, self-aggrandizement, and fundamental disloyalty to the established political and religious order. As a critic of the status quo and a fervent believer in the capacity of the Russian people to build a democratic society, Yakunin was willing to suffer for that cause. He consistently chose the path that, to his mind, furthered this goal. He separated the church from the state, but he refused to separate religion from politics. The development of a moral and just democratic society, in his view, required their integration.

CHAPTER 11

Hope and the Twisted Road

After his excommunication from the Russian Orthodox Church in February 1997, Yakunin no longer had an official voice in the intersection between religion and politics. Nevertheless, from then until his death in 2014, he remained a living presence in championing a multiconfessional society and a democratic political order based on truth. "Whether by circumstances or choice, Fr. Gleb appeared to be centrally involved in many of the controversial issues that Russia faced in the late twentieth and early twenty-first centuries," said Fr. Mikhail Meerson, who once knew him well. "He had a knack for anticipating the movement of key events in the history of his country in the previous half century, and in some of them he could be found at the forefront."[1] This was the case before Yakunin's excommunication and remained the same afterward.

Fr. Gleb refused to accept the legitimacy of the church's actions in suspending him from the priesthood in 1994 and excommunicating him in 1997. The two events were connected, in that Fr. Gleb disobeyed the patriarch's order to desist wearing the priest's cross and vestments during his suspension. His disobedience served as one of the two principal causes for his excommunication, the other being his relationship with Filaret (Denisenko), the "illegitimate" patriarch of Kyiv. According to the Orthodox historian Dimitry Pospielovsky, beginning with Yakunin's defrocking, the church establishment poorly handled the entire Yakunin affair. Yakunin correctly maintained that the All-Russian

Church Council of 1917–1918 had permitted priests to engage in political activity, and no subsequent council had rescinded that authority. Moreover, defrocking a priest required evidence of heresy or serious moral wrongdoing, neither of which applied to Yakunin.[2]

The rush to judgment in Yakunin's case, the violation of canon law in defrocking him, and the lack of proper procedure stemmed from one major source, Yakunin believed—the desire of the church hierarchy to punish him for his public revelations of the church's connections to the KGB.[3] The hierarchy's suspension and later excommunication of the outspoken priest, however, may have had another explanation: the wish to remove this "thorn in the flesh" because of his continuing criticism of the Moscow Patriarchate. The hierarchy sought to delegitimize his contention that the church leadership had sold its soul. The Moscow Patriarchate, however, did not anticipate the step Yakunin subsequently took in seeking a place in the Ukrainian Orthodox Church under the authority of the Kyivan Patriarchate.

Authoritarianism and Democracy

Russia's future regeneration, in Yakunin's view, required the church's regeneration, yet by the late 1990s, that renewal seemed to be a distant possibility. The promise of the early 1990s had not resulted in the kinds of changes he had envisioned. In particular, three major events had significantly narrowed the potential for Russia's evolution into an open and tolerant society, and had strengthened the social bases of an authoritarian political order.

The 1990 Law on Freedom of Conscience and Religious Associations that Yakunin championed laid the groundwork for a pluralistic society. Believing that the 1990 law provided legal protection for religious minorities, Yakunin mistakenly assumed it would remain in force throughout Russia's period of transformation. Yet, as discussed in chapter 10, the Moscow Patriarchate and various other interest groups had repeatedly hammered away at the 1990 law, complaining that it allowed foreign religious organizations unlimited access to a country struggling to regain its national identity. Shortly after his excommunication, Yakunin initiated a libel case against an official of the Moscow Patriarchate, Aleksandr Dvorkin, who had become a leading spokesperson in support of taking official action against the new religious movements. The suit served as a major test of the legal principles that Yakunin held as sacrosanct.

Born in Moscow (1955), Aleksandr Leonidovich Dvorkin was educated in the United States at Hunter College, St. Vladimir's Theological Seminary, and Fordham University, where he received his doctorate in medieval studies. After graduation, he first worked for Voice of America radio, before moving to Germany, in 1991, to work for Radio Liberty. Early the following year, he returned to Moscow, where he soon landed a position in the newly created Department of Religious Education and Catechisms of the Moscow Patriarchate.[4] After observing firsthand the growing popularity of several new religious groups, he began to look closely at their organization and methods. He became frightened about their appeal to young people and about what he perceived as their dangerous tactics to recruit and maintain converts. Outspoken in warning about their threat to Russia's stability, Dvorkin rapidly earned a reputation as the chief ideologist of the anticult movement in Russia, especially after he wrote, in 1995, a widely distributed booklet titled *Ten Questions for a Recruiter*, published by the Moscow Patriarchate.[5]

Yakunin filed a suit against Dvorkin on the grounds of protecting the "honor, dignity, and reputation" of the religious minorities whom, he charged, Dvorkin had slandered. Dvorkin, he claimed, had wrongfully branded many law-abiding religious organizations as "totalitarian sects and destructive cults." In his booklet, Dvorkin lumped together a large number of religious groups, calling them "totalitarian organizations" that exercised mind control over their members. Constructed around a charismatic personality, they represented a major danger to Russia's youth, he warned, whose inexperience made them susceptible to simplistic teaching. As Dvorkin had written in his brochure, "We are dealing with mafia-like structures, with people bound together by iron discipline and unquestioning obedience to their leadership."[6] Among them, he included Jehovah's Witnesses, the Church of Jesus Christ of Latter-day Saints, the Unification Church, the International Society for Krishna Consciousness, the Church of Scientology, and several others. He proposed their banishment from the Russian state.

Dvorkin's trial took place in April–May 1997, in Moscow. Although he offered little concrete evidence for his assertions, Dvorkin painted a sensationalized portrait of religious groups whose destructive activities, he claimed, threatened Russia's cultural and religious integrity and the foundation of Russia's national life.[7] The new religious groups, he charged, "are characterized by such phenomena as mind control, the perversion of basic ethical principles, and intensive recruitment, in which the recruits are not told the whole truth either about the organization. By virtue of the above properties, these groups practice inhumane and anti-social methods."[8] They spread their destructive teachings across Russia.

As the plaintiff, Yakunin argued that the defendant had grossly overgeneralized and reduced a complex picture to a few assertions. Dvorkin had ignored the many positive contributions that some of the new religious movements had made to the people they served. Yakunin reiterated the importance of freedom of conscience for Russia's democratic society, then only in its infancy. Dvorkin had not provided, he argued, any details about the ideological content or a single confirmable fact about the religious groups he had targeted.[9] The court, however, largely disregarded Yakunin's request for concrete evidence, as well as the defendant's seeming indifference to the 1990 law. In the end, the court ruled against Yakunin.[10]

Dvorkin's writings, the anticult campaign, and the trial had ambiguous consequences. According to the historian Emily Baran, the accusation of "totalitarian methods" and "mind control" put the church in the awkward position of defending freedom of conscience and Russian democracy. In its desire to protect Russia from what it called antidemocratic religious movements, the church had the opportunity to defend democracy and thus move beyond its authoritarian past.[11] Yet it elected not to follow this path and celebrated the trial's outcome instead. The court's verdict had an additional consequence: the desire to protect the Russian Orthodox Church from new religious movements was a harbinger of political decisions that lay immediately ahead. The court's ruling narrowed the potential for a dialogue that Yakunin and others deemed important for Russia's future health and lay the groundwork for the second set of events that contributed to the rebirth of an authoritarian political order.

The second episode concerned the patriarch's repeated efforts to weaken the 1990 law on freedom of conscience. Until the fall of 1997, President Yeltsin had resisted attempts to restrict the activities of foreign missionary groups in Russia. In September 1997, however, he bowed to pressure from the Moscow Patriarchate and nationalist groups that clamored to rescind key parts of the law. Several of the changes that followed bear mention as they contradict core principles that Yakunin viewed as essential to a pluralistic and democratic society.[12] Unlike the 1990 law that forbade religious discrimination, the new law awarded special status to Russia's "traditional religions." It identified these as Orthodox Christianity, Buddhism, Islam, and Judaism, and the new law conferred protected status on each. In the preamble, the 1997 law awarded priority to the Orthodox Church, declaring that the state "recognizes the special contribution of Orthodoxy to the history of Russia and to the development of Russia's spirituality and culture."[13] Various "traditional Christian" organizations, Buddhism, Islam, and Judaism would have full legal rights, but they could expect substantially fewer financial and material benefits from the state. Although all other religious groups would in theory enjoy freedom of conscience, they would nevertheless be required to register annually with local authorities and could not expect any state benefits. Moreover, the 1997 law permitted only "centralized religious organizations, which have been active on a legal basis for no fewer than fifty years" in Russia, to use the word "Russian" in their name.[14] Only the Orthodox Church, therefore, qualified to meet this requirement; this, too, set the Orthodox Church apart from other faiths operating in Russia.

The 1997 Law on Freedom of Conscience and Religious Associations was a great disappointment to church reformers. Zoia Krakhmal'nikova castigated Patriarch Aleksii II and President Yeltsin for the passage of the new law. One should not compromise fundamental principles, she emphasized: "Freedom of conscience . . . cannot be bought or sold, nor should it be exchanged for certain privileges. . . . It is an absolute value."[15] Fr. Veniamin (Novik) lost his position in the Leningrad Ecclesiastical Academy for his outspoken condemnation of the law. The new federal law, he wrote, "recalls the Syllabus issued by Pope Pius IX in 1864 . . . which condemned the rights of foreigners to settle in Catholic countries and forcefully expelled them."[16] Fr. Veniamin maintained that like the Catholic Syllabus, the new Russian law undermined ecumenism and made religious reconciliation nearly impossible to achieve.

Although the 1997 law did not abrogate the primary goal for which Yakunin had fought, freedom of conscience, it considerably narrowed that goal's scope and protections. The newly revised law, in Yakunin's interpretation, had major implications for Russian democracy, for interconfessional dialogue, and for the religious and civil rights of minorities. The church's growing reliance on the Russian government for financial support and privileges also brought the church and the state closer together.[17] Moreover, the patriarch and his allies significantly exaggerated the threat of foreign religious organizations to the recovery of Russia's national heritage. The greater threat to democracy, Yakunin claimed, did not come from foreign missionaries, but from within Russia—from the Moscow Patriarchate and Russian nationalists, who used the imagined threats from foreign groups to their political advantage, charging that the real totalitarian sect in Russia was the Moscow Patriarchate.[18] In taking such an extreme, perhaps unfortunate position, he further tarnished his legacy among traditional Orthodox believers.

These events constituted only part of the dangerous political and social trends Yakunin saw coalescing in Russia. As mentioned previously, he had once enthusiastically backed Boris Yeltsin and stood by him against assaults on his presidency in 1993, but by the second half of the 1990s, Yakunin's support had turned to disappointment. Yeltsin's signing of the 1997 law deepened Yakunin's sense of betrayal and enhanced his perception that the Russian president was personally incapable of advancing much beyond the practices and values of the Soviet past. In coming to power, Yeltsin had promised democracy and unity, but his economic and political policies had led to a top-down leadership style of governance, which, rather than moving toward a democratic society, had fostered the opposite.

The last development constituted the third set of circumstances that fostered authoritarianism. Throughout his priesthood, Yakunin had criticized the concentration of power at the top of the church hierarchy. In his mind, this contradicted the Orthodox principle of *sobornost'* (conciliarity) in which the church community made administrative decisions, and not a few powerful individuals who claimed the right to speak for the entire body. *"Sobornost',"* Yakunin declared, "is democracy within the Church."[19] In such a community, the laity's voices are heard and respected. He referred to the late Middle Ages, when the reforms of Martin Luther had challenged the concentrated power structures and corruption in the Catholic Church and had led to the creation of churches with democratic structures. These reforms abolished the vertical authority arrangements and "eliminated the despotic submission of believers to the ruling hierarchy."[20] In contrast, he said, the Russian Church resembled a monarchy, in which power was concentrated at the top, an anachronism in a society that aspired to be democratic.

Yakunin saw a parallel between the monarchical power structure of the church and the increasingly powerful bureaucratic, top-down governing apparatus of President Boris Yeltsin. Until the church remodeled itself around the principle of *sobornost'*, neither would the government begin developing a democratic structure. Yeltsin had taken a different path, succumbing to the political pressures of lobbyists from the Moscow Patriarchate and other groups that sought power. Yakunin bemoaned the choices the president had made "by surrounding himself with sycophants and swindlers," power seekers who had fostered corruption within the leadership of the Russian state.[21]

In 1999, Yakunin's disappointment deepened, when President Yeltsin, by then in poor health, appointed Vladimir Putin as his successor. The selection of the former KGB officer, in Yakunin's view, represented an ominous choice; it signified the desire to strengthen the "vertical lines of authority" within the governing apparatus. The new leader's lack of moral values rooted in a strong religious identity quickly became evident. In an interview near the beginning of his presidency, Putin voiced little personal regard for either Christianity or the Orthodox Church. When asked about his belief in a higher authority, Putin responded as a "convinced humanist, but only nominally that."[22] Gradually, however, this image began to change, and in the media "soon appeared a portrait of Putin the pilgrim, attending church services, going to a monastery, conversing with monks, and visiting the St. Nicholas Orthodox Cathedral in New York" in November 2001, where a memorial service was held commemorating the victims of September 11.[23] Shortly afterward, he developed a close relationship with Archimandrite Tikhon (Shevkunov), his rumored confessor, who professed the president's conversion to the Orthodox faith and "solemnly witnessed to the exemplary religiosity of Putin himself and all his family."[24] This public declaration of a private matter crossed a sacrosanct line, in Yakunin's view, by politicizing the president's faith.

The connection to Archimandrite Tikhon, an outspoken antidemocrat and fervent nationalist, Yakunin maintained, forecast the authoritarian direction that the president would soon take. The superior of the Sretenskii Monastery in Moscow, Archimandrite Tikhon had little sympathy for either ecumenism or relations with the West. As cohost of the television program *Russia Home*, where he voiced his political commitments, the archimandrite proclaimed: "Censorship is a normal instrument of control in a normal society, and I support its extension into both the religious and secular fields; the entire second chapter of the Constitution of the Russian Federation professing 'the right and freedom of the citizen' is false ... the declaration in the Constitution of freedom of conscience evolves into the freedom of dishonesty."[25]

The interference of state authorities in the inner life of the church continued to trouble Yakunin and, in 2000, the injection of politics into state affairs demonstrated that the state had no intention of separating itself entirely from the religious sphere. This intrusion took place in a celebrated decision about the canonization of priests who had sacrificed their lives for their faith.

A quarter century after Yakunin's plea for their glorification, in the Jubilee Council of Bishops meeting in August 2000, the same body that passed the "Social Conception of the Orthodox Church," voted to glorify more than one thousand Christian martyrs who had lost their lives under the Bolshevik regime.[26] Their number included Tsar Nicholas II and the members of the royal family. Yakunin supported the canonization of the former tsar; when Yakunin was in exile, Elena Volkova recounted, "he designed a draft of an icon of Tsar Nicolas II and his family, a drawing that both his aunt Lidiia and Fr. Viacheslav Vinnikov had seen."[27] Yet Yakunin did not approve of the process by which the canonization had taken place. Without looking further into the circumstances that transpired behind the scene, it would seem that the patriarch carried out the plea that Yakunin and his associates had made years ago. "Fr. Gleb told me," Volkova said, "that Nicholas II and the royal family were canonized because Vladimir Putin called Patriarch Aleksii II and ordered him to do so." Having recently been elected president of Russia, "Putin wanted to be the person who united Russian Orthodox Churches inside Russia and abroad."[28] Yakunin viewed the politicization of the martyrs as a "forced act behind which a spiritual bond with the holy martyrs did not exist." In post-Soviet Russia, this was clear evidence to Yakunin that the Orthodox Church had again lost its way, its capacity to determine its own sacred actions without the state's interference.

Although he had no authority within the Russian Church and no political standing in his society, Yakunin pursued the same path he had followed throughout his life. Despite the obstacles he faced, he did not give up or lose hope. With the possibility of a return to his priestly status under the Moscow Patriarchate forever closed, his position under the Kyivan Patriarchate enabled him to pursue goals he had long held. It gave him an opportunity to develop a parish community different from those that paid obeisance to the Moscow Patriarch.

Priest Pavel Bochkov is the most prolific and reputable scholar of the separatist religious organizations that came into being in post-Soviet Russia. He has identified three different types of church communities that broke away from union with the Moscow Patriarchate:

1. Nationalistic communities, whose religious consciousness consists of a narrow nationalistic worldview. Psychologically, members of this community suppress the mystical spirit of the church and overlook the universal nature of Orthodoxy in favor of the exclusively national nature of the church.[29]
2. Jurisdictional-political communities that protest the government's interference in church affairs and reject political activities conducted by the state in the name of the religious communities. They express strong opposition to the politicization of the church.
3. Revolutionary and reformative communities whose members support modernism and the integration of rational pragmatism, as a means of adapting theology to rapidly changing present-day events.[30]

The Apostolic Orthodox Church that Yakunin helped create belonged to the second type. Its predominant characteristic lay in the claim that political authorities had no legitimate right to involve themselves in the inner life of the parish community, as the previous Soviet government had done. The church was sacrosanct, and in the Apostolic Orthodox Church Yakunin was determined to maintain that hallowed principle.

Originally named the Orthodox Church of the Resurrection (Pravoslavnaia Tserkov' Vozrozhdeniia), the Apostolic Orthodox Church (Apostol'skaia Pravoslavnaia Tserkov') was established in Moscow in January 2000. Archbishop Stefan (Ainitskii), Bishop Kiriak (Temertsidi), and proto-presbyter Gleb Yakunin attended a press conference that announced the creation of this "independent church jurisdiction."[31]

The Apostolic Orthodox Church (AOTs) traced its heritage to the 1920s and the Russian True Orthodox Church or the Catacomb Church, which the Bolshevik government had heavily persecuted. In its founding declaration, the AOTs paid homage to the Catacomb Church, as well as to the "positive liberal reforms" of the "renovationists" of the 1920s.[32] In 2004, the AOTs officially registered with the state, thus making it the youngest schismatic religious organization in post-Soviet Russia.[33]

Several characteristics distinguished the AOTs from similar religious communities in post-Soviet Russia:

- Fundamentally, the AOTs sought independence because of what it viewed as the Moscow Patriarchate's compromises with the state, accommodations that betrayed the church's mission of service to Christ rather than to the government.[34] As Yakunin for many years had believed, the official church's corruption had begun with Metropolitan Sergei's "Declaration of Loyalty" to the Bolshevik regime; the AOTs, like the Catacomb Church earlier, viewed the church's subservience as a fatal mistake.
- The Russian Orthodox Church had failed to seek repentance for either its allegiance to the Soviet state or its relationship with the KGB. The church's silence about its transgressions, and especially the church's unwillingness to look deeply into its sins of commission made true reform an impossibility.
- The AOTs wanted a new beginning, unhindered either by the weight of the church's previous wrongdoings, or its thirst for power and privileges.[35] When the church worshipped those values, it lost its primary purpose: "Idolatry is terrible in the world, when it betrays Christ in the name of the state, the nation, a social idea, or a small bourgeois comfort and prosperity," proclaimed Mother Mariia of Paris [Skobtsova].[36]
- A distinguishing feature, especially in Fr. Gleb's parish, was his incorporation of *sobornost'* at all levels of the church community. In the eleventh century, in the schism with the Roman Church, why had the Eastern Orthodox Church rejected a hierarchical administrative structure, Yakunin asked, only to create "mini Popes" later, thereby reinstating a network of power it had ejected?[37] Instead of administrative authority concentrated at the top of the church hierarchy, the Apostolic Orthodox Church hoped to diffuse authority throughout the community, a democratic reform that the All-Russian Church Council of 1917–1918 had earlier adopted.

- The AOTs recognized Fr. Aleksandr Men's teachings that helped a generation of people find the way out of the confines of Marxist-Leninist thought. A decade after his murder in 1990, the Orthodox Church had not recognized his singular gifts as a missionary to the Russian people. On September 8, 2000, in honor of his unique contributions, the AOTs canonized Fr. Aleksandr.[38]
- The AOTs policy on sexual morality was much more tolerant than in other similar religious organizations. The church did not object to the marriage either of priests or bishops.[39]
- In addition to the integration of *sobornost'* at all levels of the parish's administrative framework, worship services in the AOTs were performed in the contemporary Russian language, rather than in the archaic Church Slavonic. The "renovationists" had once urged such a reform, but the Moscow Patriarchate had rejected it.[40]

Although they did not change the course of the AOTs, these policies soon forced unforeseen problems. Resistance to the powerful sway of the official Russian Orthodox Church proved too strong for some, and by 2006, several parishes had rejoined the much-better-funded and more stable church.[41] In addition, in early January 2007, when Bishop Sergei (Savinykh) married, reportedly for the third time, it created a scandal that resulted in two influential parishes leaving the church's jurisdiction, one in Moscow led by the publicist Iakov Krotov, and a second in St. Petersburg led by the priest Aleksandr Smirnov.[42]

Many of Fr. Aleksandr Men's followers greeted his canonization with gratitude and as a well-deserved, appropriate honor (figure 11.1). But not everyone responded favorably. Fr. Aleksandr's son Mikhail Men was outraged by the audacity of the AOTs: "I look upon this as a provocation directed against all my family . . . by an organized group of people having no relationship to the Russian Orthodox Church."[43] Yakunin, however, held fast to the decision and the rightness of his church's action, arguing that Mikhail Men may have wanted the Russian Orthodox Church to canonize his father, but political support for the consecration of his father did not exist.[44]

The founding of the AOTs, as well as Yakunin's role in it, provoked strong criticism. According to Pavel Bochkov, the AOTs fostered disunity within the larger body of the church, an approach that deliberately undermined the official church.[45] Through their own self-interest, Bochkov claimed, Yakunin and other schismatics turned a cohesive body into an organism marked by conflict, dissent, and hostility. Sergei Bychkov, Yakunin's biographer and longtime acquaintance, voiced similar criticism. Yakunin's efforts to create an alterna-

FIGURE 11.1. Icon of Fr. Aleksandr Men painted for the Apostolic Orthodox Church, early 2000s. Photo courtesy of the author.

tive church, Bychkov maintained, "seemed to me to be alien, strange, reckless, misguided," and harmful to the unity of the larger church body.[46]

Yakunin had a different view. He was adamant in his belief that the Russian Orthodox Church, with its hierarchical model of leadership and rigid bureaucratic structure, had squandered a historic opportunity to regenerate Russia. When questioned about the wisdom of creating a separate church, he responded: "We are accused of creating a schism. But what exactly caused this schism? In the Gospels, it is said: 'If your eye offends you, pluck it out.' And if one eye remains healthy, or one hand is healthy, but the body is rotten, like the Moscow Patriarchate, separate parts of the body—the eye or the hand—may remain alive. Thus, what causes a schism? If the whole church is dying, then it is necessary to break away from it."[47]

In Yakunin's eyes, the policies of the AOTs would have a positive effect on both the church and the country, by breaking down the leader-subordinate mentality that had long predominated.[48] Yakunin's vision of the future advocated a way of thinking different from that in the past. He was extremely critical of the self-effacing attitudes that he found prevalent among the rank and file of the Orthodox Church. Submissive thinking, in his view, was still widespread among large numbers of the Russian population, who commonly viewed priests as the ultimate authorities, godlike in stature and wisdom. Such attitudes were instilled in religious believers from an early age, and they continued long after the monarchical form of government had passed away.[49]

Yakunin cited an example in which one of his parishioners told him that she had gone to confession and asked the priest, how she might "hear what the Lord God has said to me. And he responded, 'What is this Lord God?' 'I am your Lord God. Whatever I say—you must hear and do!'"[50] This was the kind of thinking that had to change, and it had to begin at a young age. What Yakunin called the "cruel suppression of the will" had deep roots in the church. It had to be replaced by the democratic model of *sobornost'*, in which the priest answered to the people, rather than the reverse.[51] *Sobornost'*, he believed, offered the most effective means of dispelling the compliant attitudes that had dominated Russia's past and present.

The AOTs would also be free from the heritage of communism and the Moscow Patriarchate's complicity with the atheistic regime and the KGB. Although small in numbers, the AOTs had the capacity, Yakunin asserted, to appeal to believers and creative leaders who would be attracted to an open and democratic church. To this end, Yakunin aimed to fulfill the promise that the Russian Church had made earlier, but failed to carry out: "In order that it becomes what it must be, the resurrection of the Orthodox Church in Russia is impossible without deep internal reform and a return to the democratic principles of the All-Russian Church Council of 1917–1918. It is necessary to abolish the all-powerful Patriarchate and the Holy Synod, to regenerate the election of the clergy throughout the vertical leadership of the church."[52]

Further, Yakunin now had the opportunity to integrate certain democratic values that he considered essential in a vibrant parish community. In the place of resignation and compliance with the authorities, Yakunin spoke of a new energy and aspiration. Instead of the subjugation of the clergy, he talked about their liberation from state controls. In doing so, he believed he addressed the future, building a religious community that offered a viable alternative to the official Russian Orthodox Church that had cast him out.

To put his plans into action, Yakunin secured space for his parish church in the basement of the Memorial Society's building in Moscow. Already under pressure from the Russian government for its promotion of democracy and law, the Memorial Society welcomed Yakunin as a fellow advocate and offered him accommodations. Operating as he always had as a parish priest, he warmly greeted the people who came to the services, most of whom belonged to the intelligentsia.[53] He did not waver in his conviction, which he repeated on numerous occasions and in different contexts, that Russia's future required the church's transformation from a static to a dynamic body that defended religious liberty and human rights. He hoped that the Apostolic Orthodox Church would provide, in practice, the basic principles for that transformation.

Today the AOTs has parishes in St. Petersburg, Moscow, Voronezh, Volgograd, and Briansk, as well as in Germany, Ukraine, Switzerland, Latvia, and Belarus.[54]

In the first decade of the twenty-first century, the subject of Russia's transformation from a Soviet to a post-Soviet country continued to occupy public attention that went beyond the regeneration of the church, although the church remained important to that endeavor. As President Putin sought to redefine Russia's ambitions and its place in world affairs, international agreements that the state had made earlier came up for review. Among the most important of these was the Universal Declaration of Human Rights, which the United Nations General Assembly adopted on December 10, 1947. Metropolitan Kirill (Gundiaev) of Smolensk and Kaliningrad and the chair of the Russian Orthodox Church Department for External Church Relations, played a major role in this reevaluation. As the successor (in 2009) to Aleksii II as patriarch of Moscow and All Russia and a close collaborator of President Putin, Metropolitan Kirill's position on the Universal Declaration of Human Rights would have a significant bearing on Russia's commitment to the declaration's principles. As a priest and a long-standing proponent of human rights, Yakunin contested Metropolitan Kirill's efforts to reframe these values.

In April 2006, Kirill presented a Russian alternative to the Universal Declaration of Human Rights, which had served as the moral touchstone for human rights around the globe for a half century. The very first article of the Universal Declaration expressed the fundamental tenet underlying human rights: "All people are born free and equal in their dignity and rights." Metropolitan Kirill's alternative "Declaration of Human Rights and Dignity," revised the first article by connecting human rights and dignity to morality. His new version began by proclaiming the following: "The person as an image of God has a special value, which cannot be taken away. It must be respected by each of us, by society and by the government. By doing good, a person acquires dignity. Thus, we distinguish the value and dignity of the person. Value is what is given, dignity is what is earned."[55] On April 6, 2006, at the Tenth Universal Russian People's Assembly, the delegates adopted Kirill's "Declaration."

Yakunin took strong exception to Metropolitan Kirill's formulation and what he termed its "quasi-religious orientation" as well as its potential danger for democracy in Russia. The underlying peril "becomes more understandable," Yakunin wrote, "if we translate the first article in Kirill's 'Declaration' into theological language . . . : According to the teaching of the church, the person is created in the image and through the love of God. The image of God is indestructible in the person by sin, because it has a special value; the likeness of God is distorted by human sin and is restored only by a personal feat by the person walking the path of moral perfection."[56] The Universal Declaration guarantees human dignity from birth; in Kirill's version, it is acquired by doing good. How is "doing good" determined? According to Kirill, the distinction between good and evil is defined by Russia's "religious tradition, which has God as its Primary Source."[57] The words "Russia's tradition," Yakunin said, represented "key words in the metropolitan's rhetoric." They were bandied about often, but they concealed a great deal. If one looks closely at historical reality, Russian tradition "revered the state and the Homeland" much more than it respected the human being and human life. Given these priorities, Russian tradition had neither prized nor defended the sanctity of the person. According to Metropolitan Kirill's "Declaration," "we recognize the rights and freedoms of a person to the extent that they help the ascent of the individual to goodness, protect the person from internal and external evil, and allow the person to be positively realized in society."[58] Yet the question that troubled Yakunin was what agency determined the moral "ascent of the person to goodness?" If the church is the sanctuary of Russia's religious tradition, the interpreter of the good, and the ultimate judge of human dignity, then it fell to the Moscow Patriarchate to determine good and evil and the actions that constituted each of them. Such a future, Yakunin warned, defined a precipitous course for the protection of human rights.

Kirill's "Declaration," placed certain other values on the same level as human rights. These included morality, faith, holy shrines, and the Motherland. Behaviors that insulted any of them, according to the "Declaration," were dangerous and should be condemned. Kirill did not accept the fundamental democratic principle of human dignity as an inherent right that the Universal Declaration had endorsed.

Like Metropolitan Kirill, Yakunin did not separate human dignity from faith, but unlike the metropolitan, he viewed it as far above the reverence for national shrines, morality, and the Motherland. He expressed surprise that Kirill did not understand that the loss of freedom and human rights undermined a person's capacity to choose one's faith and devalued the love of holy shrines. Kirill's "Declaration," Yakunin charged, was written to satisfy the "needs of the day," and it "chopped away at the struggle for rights and freedoms suffered by humanity and the Christian martyrs who are included in their number."[59] Should the Kremlin adopt Metropolitan Kirill's "Declaration," Yakunin feared, it would become known as the "Russian way" and potentially serve as the basis for a new national ideology. Should this happen, he believed, it would undermine the "democratic foundation of Russian society." The Russian National Assembly's adoption of the "Declaration" in April 2006, Metropolitan Kirill's elevation two years later as Patriarch, and his allegiance to Putin's government added to Yakunin's apprehension about the future of democracy.

Metropolitan Kirill's rejection of human rights as a Western European construct would later become a cornerstone of his "Russian World" (*Russkii Mir*) concept, which, as patriarch, he developed into a civilizational moral and spiritual ideal. "Russian World" connected Ukraine, Belarus, and Russia into a common unit, unified by history, culture, and religion that stood in opposition to the decadent West. Reviving the medieval belief in "Holy Russia," Patriarch Kirill ascribed to the Russian nation the sacred mission of protecting "traditional values" against the steadily encroaching secularism of the West with its denigration of religion, its assault on the family, and its homage to LGBTQ rights, marriage equality, and abortion. The church and the state, acting in concert, had the obligation to protect Orthodox civilization from being infected by anti-Christian values that entered through Russia's relationship with the United States and Western Europe. In February 2022, President Putin used this quasi-religious narrative to justify his invasion of Ukraine and to prevent it, he said, from falling into the hands of the West.[60]

The Final Years

Yakunin's anxieties were compounded by an unexpected problem that would have a significant bearing on his own future. In 2008, he began to experience acute physical difficulties, which affected his ability to perform his work at the level he expected of himself. His consultation with specialists about his physical condition led to several tests to determine the causes of his discomfort, and the results of these tests did not bring positive news. Yakunin learned that he was in the beginning stages of the neuromuscular disease amyotrophic lateral sclerosis (ALS, or Lou Gehrig's disease), a progressive neurological disease of the motor nerve cells in which the muscles begin to atrophy and eventually leave a person immobile. The disease has no medical cure and normally results in a shortened life span. When the doctors gave him this diagnosis, they told Fr. Gleb he had a maximum of two years left to live.[61] His physicians, however, had little knowledge of the fire that burned in Yakunin's heart. While he curtailed some of his activities, he continued to perform his priestly responsibilities.

In these final years of his life, Yakunin neither terminated his political pursuits nor ceased his criticism of the Moscow Patriarchate. He attended nearly every political protest from 2009 to 2011, during which time they became increasingly prevalent in the streets of Moscow. He supported the three young women of the musical group Pussy Riot, whose performance of a "Punk Prayer" on February 21, 2012, in the Cathedral of Christ the Savior of the Russian Orthodox Church in central Moscow, created a religious and political uproar.[62] Patriarch Kirill hastened to label the young women's performance as "the work of the devil," a scourge on everything the Russian people held sacred. "Those people don't believe in the power of prayer," the patriarch charged, "they believe in the power of propaganda, in the power of lies and slander, in the power of the internet and mass media, in the power of money and weapons."[63] Despite the frequent accusations of their blasphemy, sacrilege, and debasement of sacred space, the three women, in Yakunin's eyes, represented authentic folk heroes. In reality, their "Punk Prayer" essentially protested the Moscow Patriarchate's alliance with Vladimir Putin's presidency, Patriarch Kirill's moral authority, the male dominated historical memory of the church, and the Orthodox Church's support for violence and social injustice. Believing they were wrongly demeaned, Yakunin defended the women of Pussy Riot. He asserted that they spoke truth about Putin and the leadership of the church whom, he said, had "chosen service to Putin, instead of to God."[64] He wrote several poems praising the women's courage, vision, and prophetic critique of power. In his poem, "Although Lenin Is Dead, He Has Not Vanished Yet," Yakunin paid homage to what he viewed as the truth of their message:

And now it's a new madness
to strengthen the country with a ruddy mummy

That, which Vladimir Vladimirovich [Putin] wants to keep a secret,
will turn the spiritual into a frail replica of itself.

Presently, many people believe, like you and me,
that Pussy Riot was right.[65]

On August 17, 2012, the three women were convicted of "hooliganism motivated by religious hatred" and sentenced to two years of imprisonment. Their conviction neither lessened his respect for them nor weakened his belief in the rightness of their cause. He continued to assert their heroism in speaking truth to power, despite the condemnation that they had to endure from the Orthodox Church leadership and important segments of the church's followers.[66] Soon, however, Yakunin's own health issues would limit his capacity to speak publicly in support of such causes.

In September 2013, Sergei Bychkov recalled that he saw Fr. Gleb at the funeral of Fr. Nikolai Gainov, an old and dear friend, who, in the 1970s, had served with Yakunin on the Christian Committee for the Defense of Believers' Rights. After the burial, a group of old acquaintances gathered in the home of the deceased and reminisced, as they lamented the loss of their friend, relived the past, and invoked the memories of the causes for which they had struggled. Missing their deceased friend, the small group assembled that early autumn afternoon represented a final remnant of the courageous individuals who constituted the conscience of religious liberty in the former Soviet Union. Looking back at the gathering that afternoon, the elderly members of a group of individuals who had struggled mightily for human rights, Bychkov knew that he had witnessed a significant moment in the history of his country. Soon after that event, Bychkov said, Fr. Gleb fell from his bicycle and severely injured himself.[67] The fall compounded the physical difficulties from which he already suffered and likely hastened his death.

Throughout 2013, Yakunin's neurological illness rapidly progressed. At first, he gradually lost the feeling in one of his fingers before it spread to other fingers, and then to both of his hands. As a result, by early in the following year, he fully lost the use of his hands and could not lift a cup to his mouth without help. Still, he continued to serve in his parish, moving gingerly, yet with a mind that remained sharp and clear.[68] In mid-November 2014, he suffered a major neurological attack that required hospitalization. All the major organs, except for his brain, had shut down by then. He was placed in intensive care, where he remained for the next month and a half. "We were allowed to visit him," his daughter Mariia said, and "he was able to receive communion."[69] "These weeks were incredibly difficult," she recalled. Her father suffered a great deal, interrupted only when the hospital staff permitted the visits of a few friends,

FIGURE 11.2. Mariia Yakunina and her husband Aleksei Belov at home in their studio, 2018. Photo courtesy of the author.

who came to pay homage to him (figure 11.2). On December 9, he was in significant decline, the effects of his illness seriously affecting the intake of oxygen into his lungs. The following day, the hospital staff transferred him to the intensive care unit and connected him to a ventilator.[70] A once powerful body that always displayed energy and resolve slowly lost its capacity to live. Fr. Gleb died on December 25, 2014, at the age of eighty.

Abiding by his earlier request, the family did not hold Fr. Gleb's funeral in a standard Russian Orthodox Church, but in the Andrei Sakharov Center, a place that had come to hold special significance for him. He was buried in the northern region of Moscow, in the modest Piatnitskoe cemetery, a final resting place selected by few members of the former Soviet elite.

Gleb Yakunin is commonly labeled a religious dissident. But, as this book has argued, the designation offers only a partial description of his life. As an Orthodox priest and religious activist, Yakunin became a prime defender of religious liberty, an advocate of social justice, a spokesperson for the outcast and marginalized members of Russian society, and a champion of human rights. His long quest to contribute to a renaissance in the Russian Orthodox Church was predicated on the belief that it would lead to healing the gap between the church and the spiritual needs of the Russian people. The church's overwhelming focus on ceremonial prescriptions, he maintained, may have protected it from a destructive assault by the state's security services, but, as the Orthodox layperson Boris Talantov noted, for the young people who would shape Russia's future, such an emphasis had little relevance to their lives.[71] Yakunin, too, believed it imperative that the church speak with a stronger voice.

The thread that appeared throughout Fr. Gleb Yakunin's life was hope. Despite the severe hardships he endured, he never lost hope in the creativity of the Russian people, in Russia's future possibilities, and in the capacity of human beings, if given the opportunity, to bring about fundamental change. The hope he expressed emanated from several wellsprings, not least of them an inherently positive view of humankind. In addition, hope derived from Fr. Aleksandr Men's strong influence on Yakunin's personal and theological development. Men opened up for the young Yakunin an understanding of Christianity as a liberating, yet unfinished religion, much different from the stolid, closed system of belief that he had previously known.

Hope in the future enabled Yakunin to survive the difficulties he faced and to overcome and move beyond them. He never lost hope in the arc of history, a confidence that also had deep roots in his Orthodox faith. "Our Lord, God, from my point of view," he testified, "very rarely interferes in human history, and in the beginning, God acted invisibly, and the Holy Spirit acts and helps the people through an individual or [through a group of] people. In some special moments in history, God acts immediately. Especially clearly is this found in the Old Testament, although rarely in the New Testament of the Bible."[72] Having such hope, Yakunin did not succumb to the mental captivity that he witnessed around him in much of Russian society. This mental captivity, he believed, perverted the capacity to imagine something different. Feeding on lies and illusions, it disparaged truth and what Yakunin conceived as fact-based realities. Such a readiness to accept lies and illusions, in Yakunin's view, as well as in the eyes of Viktor Popkov and Tat'iana Lebedeva, former members of Moscow's Christian Seminar, constituted key elements that fostered authoritarianism (figure 11.3).[73] In his letters of protest, his creation of the Christian Committee for the Defense of Believers' Rights, his exposure of the Orthodox Church hierarchy, his legislative work, his poetry, and his service as a priest, Yakunin endeavored to shatter the fear of thinking for the self. He wanted to break down the barriers and the illusions, constructed by those in power, which prevented human beings from fulfilling their God-given potential.[74]

Fr. Gleb Yakunin was not the only Russian citizen who fought for intellectual and personal freedom. Other voices described in this study, including Zoia Krakhmal'nikova, Tat'iana Velikanova, Fr. Sergei Zheludkov, Boris Talantov, Lev Regel'son, and Fr. Aleksandr Men, joined him in this struggle. Nearly all of

FIGURE 11.3. Viktor Popkov and Tat'iana Lebedeva, 2018, former members of the Christian Seminar in Moscow, 1970s. Photo courtesy of the author.

them, with the exception of Velikanova, came out of the Orthodox Church or were closely related to it and drew from its heritage in justifying their actions. They represented a small but significant coterie of people who viewed their faith as a liberating force and as one of the foundational stones of democracy, rather than as a restrictive and submissive component of an authoritarian political order. Taken as a whole, they dispute the common view that Russians, by tradition and disposition, are inclined to support a closed, autocratic governmental system. "The history of Russia," the cultural historian Irina Karatsuba has proclaimed, "is not only the history of despotism, Stalinism, and suppression of the individual. It is the history of struggle and resistance, in whose number is also Christianity."[75]

Unafraid of change, the members of this group pressed hard for reform. Yakunin, in particular, was critical of the status quo and disparaged the hierarchy of the Orthodox Church for embracing the existing state of affairs. The memoirist Nadezhda Mandel'stam recounts how, in Soviet society, people loyal to the Soviet regime, as well as many others, resisted social and political change. Fearing instability and an unpredictable future, they greatly preferred the certainty of the present to the unreliability (or capriciousness) of change: "What we wanted was for the course of history to be made smooth, all the ruts and potholes removed, so there should never again be any unforeseen events and everything should flow along evenly and according to plan. This longing prepared us, psychologically, for the appearance of the Wise Leaders who would tell us where we were going. And once they were there, we no longer ventured to act without their guidance and looked to them for direct instructions and foolproof prescriptions."[76]

This, Mandel'stam notes, is one of the salient characteristics of a totalitarian society. Such anxiety about the future, Yakunin also discovered, served as a hindrance to the kind of reforms that he envisioned. Society's reluctance to conceive of an imaginary future fundamentally different from the present made it difficult to instigate the democratic reforms that he had in mind. That is why he pushed so hard in the 1990s and thereafter to change ways of thinking, a process that had to begin early in a person's education.

Relegated to near obscurity by the Russian Orthodox Church, by the time of his death Gleb Yakunin was unknown among most of the Russian population. (figure 11.4). Political events of the second decade of the twenty-first century have commanded the center of public attention, as the battles that had shaped religion and politics at the end of the twentieth century receded from national attention. But to individuals who had fought alongside Fr. Gleb for religious freedom in the last decades of the Soviet era and the first years of the postcommunist period, Yakunin's contributions to a more tolerant and

FIGURE 11.4. Fr. Gleb Yakunin in the last years of his life. Photo courtesy of the author.

open Russian society commanded considerable acclaim. Lev Ponomarev, who served with him on the Parliamentary Commission to investigate the church's connections to the KGB, said that his friend and collaborator "was convinced that life changes only for the better. He was a warrior."[77] To the leading human rights activist Valerii Borshchev, Yakunin exemplified incredible courage and steadfastness to his ideals. "I went to see him in 1984," Borshchev recalled, "precisely on the day before he left the labor camp for Yakutiia. It was December [when he arrived] there—in the dreadful cold and depressing surroundings. Yet he was optimistic and energetic. When he returned to Moscow in 1987, he immediately became active. I am amazed by this man!"[78] To Mariia Riabikova, a friend and member of the Apostolic Ukrainian Church,

> His service was always celebratory, truly joyful. But the most important thing was the steady increase in joy, a celebration up to the time for the Eucharist. I experienced the liturgies that he performed as celebrations, and I wasn't the only one who had this feeling. After all, the liturgy reveals the drama of the living relationship between a person and God, which is brought together in the mystery of the love of the cross. This is the meaning that has always been conveyed. Life for him was also a liturgy, a battlefield where the victor was always Christ.[79]

To Heleen Zorgdrager, a Dutch theologian at the Protestant Theological University in Amsterdam, who served as a visiting professor at Ukrainian Catholic University in Lviv, Ukraine, from 2005 to 2013, Yakunin's life was "a light shining in the darkness of totalitarian regimes and brutal repressions. May his courageous testimony of righteousness and Christian love be a comfort and inspiration, now and forever."[80]

When I began this book, I considered Gleb Yakunin primarily, if not exclusively, a religious dissident. He was, however, much more than this appellation conveyed, and his significance extended beyond his opposition to the Russian state's persecution of religious believers. His critique of power—political and religious—principally aimed at breaking down the barriers that divided people of diverse ideological commitments and whose rigid separation, he believed, fostered war, oppression, and hatred. Religion, as he witnessed firsthand, fostered violence, but in his case, he found it to be a source of creativity and love that led him to recognize a common humanity. A Russian patriot rather than a nationalist, a spokesperson for truth rather than a conveyer of illusions, a believer in personal freedom rather than the comforts of the captive mind, he maintained his hope in the future rather than submitting to despair in the present. Gleb Yakunin devoted himself to making this a better world, and he dedicated his life to that endeavor.

Acknowledgments

The idea for this book began long before the recent publication in Moscow of three books on Fr. Gleb Yakunin. I owe, however, a large debt of gratitude to their authors for their contributions to parts of Fr. Gleb's story that, previously, were obscure to me. All three scholars, Elena Volkova, Sergei Bychkov, and Georgii Rovenskii knew Fr. Gleb for many years, witnessed personally his accomplishments and misfortunes, and fervently believed that his significance for the history of the Russian Orthodox Church, the Soviet Union, and postcommunist Russia remained unrecognized. The near simultaneous publication of all three works in 2021 is curious. As a partial explanation, the passage of time since Yakunin's death in 2014 allowed adequate opportunity for reflection and perspective. Additionally, the political turmoil in Russia in the second decade of the twenty-first century made it difficult to write about contemporary history. Yet Yakunin's life and the subjects that concerned him speak directly to some of the most contentious issues of the present, especially the meaning of truth and the growing threat of authoritarianism. Fortunately, the publication of the three books took place only a few months before the Russian military assault on Ukraine, which would have made their issuance difficult to conceive.

My gratitude extends especially to Volkova, who many years ago introduced me to Fr. Gleb. After his death, I was fortunate to have had several interviews with her on various aspects of his life that helped shape the beginning of this book. She shared his political views with me, but it was her openness about him as a person, his ideals, and his commitments to serving persecuted members of Russian society that I found most informative.

Similarly, I wish to thank Canon Rev. Michael Bourdeaux (d. 2021) for his passionate interest in the Russian people and Russian culture. Like Fr. Gleb Yakunin, whom he admired, he gave voice to the persecuted, as well as those who, under great pressure from the authorities, held fast in their ideals. The numerous books and articles that Canon Bourdeaux published revealed layers of Russian society that remained hidden to outsiders.

I appreciate the opportunity to work in the Keston Archive, housed in the Center for Religion, Politics, and Society at Baylor University and its vast holdings of primary source materials. The archive's stimulating atmosphere adds to its charm and to the benefits of doing research there. I thank Larisa Seago, the archive's curator, for her extensive knowledge of its holdings and for help in assembling many of the documents for this book. Even from afar, Ms. Seago assisted in locating rare materials relating to the Russian intelligentsia and to Yakunin's Christian Committee for the Defense of Believers' Rights in the USSR. I thank Kathy Hillman, the director of the Keston Center, Tanya Clark, the associate editor of *Journal of Church and State*, and Jeffrey Archer, the dean of University Libraries, for their assistance in various ways to my work on this book.

Parts of the present book were presented at the international conference on "Reinventing Religion: The Rise of Religious Sensibility in the Late Soviet Union (1960s–80s)," hosted by the University of Basel, June 10–12, 2021, and at the annual meeting of the Keston Institute in London, November 5, 2021. I greatly profited from the discussions at both events. The international conference organized by Barbara Martin offered an opportunity to consider Yakunin's relationships beyond Russia, which, in the end, proved important in developing his connections to the American entrepreneur and publisher Henry Dakin. Xenia Dennen, the director of the Keston Institute in Great Britain, and the Keston Council hosted the latter presentation, which encouraged me to think more broadly about Gleb Yakunin's global significance. In 2018, an informal conversation with Ms. Dennen about the need for a biography of Yakunin inspired the earlier conceptualization of this book. I thank Xenia Dennen, Barbara Martin, Nadezhda Beliakova, and participants at both events for the contributions they made to this book. I am grateful to the late Jane Ellis for her work on the Russian Orthodox Church and on Fr. Gleb's activities, which provided extremely helpful background for this study. In addition, Alyona Kozhevnikova's personal knowledge of peoples in the human rights movement enriched my understanding of the opposition to Soviet power.

I thank Mariia Glebovna Yakunina, Fr. Gleb's oldest child for her insights into Fr. Gleb as a person and as an Orthodox priest. I shall not forget the long conversation we had, midway through my research, about her father, his activities, and their impact on her family. The conversation took place in her studio, surrounded by large, brilliantly colored icons that she and her husband, Andrei Belov, painted. She and her husband are generous and open people, and she provided details about her father that I could not have known otherwise. During the COVID-19 pandemic and afterward, Mariia Glebovna responded by email to many queries concerning her father. In Moscow, other people too offered insights into Fr. Gleb's activities, the political and social context in which he operated, the Orthodox Church, and the former Soviet state. Thanks to:

- Viktor Popkov and Tat'iana Lebedeva, who operate an impressive bookstore and coffee shop in central Moscow and who, in the 1970s, were active members of the Christian Seminar in Moscow;
- Pavel Men, the brother of Fr. Aleksandr Men, who has a vast store of knowledge about his brother, Fr. Gleb, and their associates;
- Sergei Filatov, a distinguished sociologist of religion, whose studies of politics, religion, and society are invaluable sources of information about post-Soviet Russia; and
- Grigorii Kliucharev of the Russian Academy of Sciences, Institute of Sociology, who specializes in the study of Russian youth, education, values, and literacy, and with whom I have had many discussions about recent trends in Russian society.

Despite various newspapers and articles and a large book of reminiscences, a biography of Henry S. Dakin, the American entrepreneur and publisher, does not exist. I am grateful to Dakin's wife and daughter, Vergilia and Adriana Dakin, for their help in reconstructing his life and accomplishments, and to his associates, Jim Hickman and Anya Kucherev, for a series of interviews that elaborated on Dakin's interest in Russia. Hickman and Kucherev are key sources on Henry Dakin's efforts to forge connections between the American and Russian people outside the official channels of their governments. Although essentially a nonpolitical person, Dakin's publications of Russian samizdat materials led him eventually to Gleb Yakunin and the documents of the Christian Committee for the Defense of Believers' Rights in the USSR.

I thank Christine Worobec, Distinguished Research Professor Emerita and director of the NIU Series on Slavic, East European, and Eurasian Studies at Northern Illinois University, for her interest in and encouragement of this book on Yakunin, which came at an important time in my research. She read every page of my monograph and offered extremely helpful suggestions that greatly improved the analysis. Similarly, Dominic Erdozain of King's College London also read every page, and his recommendations proved invaluable for the focus and organization of the book. Amy Farranto, the senior acquisitions editor at Northern Illinois University Press, is a superb editor and consultant, whose professional and personal gifts go far beyond the merely academic. An expert stylist, she is a strong advocate for clear, concrete writing. Her editorial skills are impressive, and the interest she has demonstrated in my subject has been a constant source of inspiration.

Librarians at Mercer University, Duke University, and the University of North Carolina have made research for this book a pleasurable experience. I thank especially Cecilia Williams, the interlibrary loan supervisor, and Adam Griggs, the research services librarian, at Mercer; my sister Linda Daniel, Duke Libraries' teaching and learning Strategist; and Abbey Allred, library staff at the University of North Carolina at Chapel Hill, for their selfless service and expertise in locating sometimes obscure titles. These people have significantly enhanced the quality of the research for this book. In addition, research assistants, particularly Olivia Joyce Pakele, at the Hoover Library and Archives at Stanford University so willingly gave me the benefit of their knowledge and experience. My thanks to Karen M. Laun, Kristen Gregg, Cheryl Hirsch, and copyeditor Therese Malhame for their expertise and dedication to this book.

I want to express my gratitude to William D. Underwood, the president of Mercer University, for his emphasis on the relationship between teaching and research and for his personal interest in my work. I thank my colleagues in the history department at Mercer, as well as Deneen Senasi, the director of the Faculty Research and Writing Colloquium, and faculty colleagues in the colloquium whose suggestions and criticisms have strengthened my work. I thank Mary Pearson and Joseph Payne for their close reading of the manuscript and their extremely helpful critiques, Jerome Gratigny, the director of Academic Technology Services and Matt Adams at Information Technology Services at Mercer for providing the technological assistance that I needed at several important junctures of this work.

I owe a debt of gratitude to Clifford Foust, a professor of history at the University of North Carolina at Chapel Hill, who introduced me to Russian history and remained a mentor throughout my graduate school study and afterward. At his insistence, I applied to the IREX exchange program with the Soviet Union, and the year of living in Moscow and the enriching experience of working in the archives have had a major impact on my teaching and scholarship throughout my academic career.

I owe my largest debt to my wife Karol for her interest in my manuscript. She read each page numerous times and her comments strengthened the clarity and straightforwardness of my writing. Most of all, I am thankful for her creative and sustaining presence in my life.

Notes

Introduction

1. Senior Investigator for the Department of Internal Affairs of the Investigative Department of the KGB of the USSR, Leningrad Region (Starshii sledovatel' po OVD Sledstvennogo otdela UKGB SSSR po Leningradskoi oblasti), "Postanovlenie o proizvodstve obyska," September 27, 1979, reproduced in Elena Ivanovna Volkova, *Glyba Gleba: Zapreshchenneishii ierei Iakunin*, appendix: "Materialy 'Ugolovnogo dela No. 515 po obvineniiu Iakunina Gleba Pavlovicha' iz Tsentral'nogo arkhiva FSB Rossii"(St. Petersburg: Renome, 2021), 484.

2. Officers of the KGB Directorate in the city of Moscow and the Moscow region, "Protokol obyska," September 28, 1979, reproduced in Volkova, *Glyba Gleba*, 486.

3. Volkova, 292.

4. Officers of the KGB Directorate, "Protokol obyska," 487–95.

5. Officers of the KGB Directorate, 489.

6. Officers of the KGB Directorate, 495; and Volkova, *Glyba Gleba*, 293.

7. *Bulletin of the Swedish Mission* 3 (1979), Keston Archive, SU Ort 8/2, Yakunin file: 2.

8. Jane Ellis, "The Christian Committee for the Defence of Believers' Rights in the USSR," *Religion in Communist Lands* 8, no. 4 (1980): 289.

9. Anatolii Levitin-Krasnov, "KGB Search Linked to Poresh Investigation," October 4, 1979, Keston Archive, SU Ort 8/2 Yakunin file.

10. Viktor Popkov and Tat'iana Lebedeva, interview by author, Moscow, May 17, 2018.

11. Yuri Andropov, quoted in Joshua Rubenstein, "Introduction: Andrei Sakharov, the KGB, and the Legacy of Soviet Dissent," in *The KGB File of Andrei Sakharov*, ed. Joshua Rubenstein and Alexander Gribanov, trans. Ella Shmulevich, Efrem Yankelevich, and Alla Zeide (New Haven, CT: Yale University Press, 2005), 24.

12. In 1976, Aleksandr Il'ich Ginzburg (1936–2002), a journalist and poet, and Yuri Fedorovich Orlov (1924–2020), a nuclear physicist, were founding members of the Moscow Helsinki Group established to monitor violations of the human rights agreements that the Soviet government had signed. Anatolii Borisovich Shcharansky (1948–), a mathematician and computer programmer, served as spokesperson for some of the most influential human rights groups in the Soviet Union.

13. Joining Tat'iana Velikanova on the editorial staff were Tat'iana Khodorovich and Sergei Kovalev. Velikanova is discussed in more detail in chapter 6.

14. Anatolii Levitin-Krasnov, "Father Gleb Yakunin and Lev Regel'son," in *Letters from Moscow: Religion and Human Rights in the USSR*, ed. Jane Ellis (San Franscisco: H. S. Dakin, 1978), 1–9.

15. Levitin-Krasnov, 1.
16. Levitin-Krasnov, 6.
17. Feliks Svetlov and Zoia Krakhmal'nikova, "Tat'iana Velikanova i o. Gleb Iakunin arestovany," Moscow (November 1979), Keston Archive, *Arkhiv samizdata*, no. 3779.
18. Svetlov and Krakhmal'nikova.
19. Svetlov and Krakhmal'nikova. The authors' quotation from the Gospels comes from Matthew 25:35–36, 40.
20. Svetlov and Krakhmal'nikova, "Tat'iana Velikanova i o. Gleb Iakunin."
21. The Council for Religious Affairs, created by Stalin in May 1944 to supervise religious activity in the USSR, operated under the Council of Ministers.
22. Vladimir Alekseevich Kuroedov, *Religiia i tserkov' v Sovetskom gosudarstve* (Moscow: Izdatel'stvo politicheskoi literatury, 1981). Kuroedov's appointment and his elevation as chairperson of the Council for Religious Affairs in February 6, 1960, replacing his predecessor G. G. Karpov, signaled a renewed attack on the Orthodox clergy. For a history of Soviet religious policy of this period, see Tat'iana A. Chumachenko, *Church and State in Soviet Russia: Russian Orthodoxy from World War II to the Khrushchev Years*, ed. and trans. Edward E. Roslof (Armonk, NY: M. E. Sharpe, 2002).
23. See Vladimir Alekseevich Kuroedov, *Religiia i tserkov' v sovetskom obshchestve*, 2nd ed. (Moscow: Izdatel'stvo politicheskoi literatury, 1984), 3–4, 17.
24. Kuroedov, 192.
25. Kuroedov, 188–97.
26. Volkova, *Glyba Gleba*.
27. Georgii Vasil'evich Rovenskii, *Gleb Iakunin (1934–2014): Pravoslavnyi pravozashchitnik, sviashchennik, deputat, poet* (Shchyolkovo: Shchyolkovskii kraevedcheskii klub, 2021).
28. Sergei Sergeevich Bychkov, *Sviashchennik Gleb Iakunin. Nelegkii put' pravdoiskatelia* (Moscow: Eksmo, 2021).
29. Mark Philip Bradley, *The World Reimagined: Americans and Human Rights in the Twentieth Century* (New York: Cambridge University Press, 2016), 158–60.

1. Beginnings

1. Obshchestvo remeslennogo i zemledel'cheskogo trud sredi evreev (Soviet Union), *Materialy i issledovaniia*, no. 4: *Evrei v SSSR* (Tel Aviv: Aticot, 1929), 50.
2. "Ananyev," in *Encyclopedia Judaica*, ed. Cecil Roth (Jerusalem: Macmillan, 1971), vol. 2: 924; I. Michael Aronson, *Troubled Waters: The Origins of the 1881 Anti-Jewish Pogroms in Russia* (Pittsburgh, PA: University of Pittsburgh Press, 1990) 59, 110; "Ananyev, Ukraine," in *Jewish Virtual Library*, https:www.jewishvirtuallibrary.org/ananyev; and *Die Judenpogrome in Russland hrsg. im aufrage des Zionistischen hilfsfonds in London; von der zur erforschung der pogrome eingesetzten kommission*, ed. A. Linden, vol. 2 (Cologne: Jüdishcher verlag g.m.b.h., 1910), 134–37.
3. Anatolii Emmanuilovich Levitin-Krasnov, "Father Gleb Yakunin and Lev Regel'son," in *Letters from Moscow: Religion and Human Rights in the USSR*, ed. Jane Ellis (San Francisco: H. S. Dakin, 1978), 1.
4. Anatolii Emmanuilovich Levitin-Krasnov, *V poiskakh novogo grada: Vospominaniia*, pt. 3 (Tel Aviv: Izdatel'stvo Krug, 1980), 222.

5. Elena Volkova, *Glyba Gleba: Zapreshchenneishii ierei Iakunin* (St. Petersburg: Renome, 2021), 42.

6. Volkova, 225.

7. Valerii Arkad'evich Alekseev, *Illiuzii i dogmy* (Moscow: Polizdat, 1991) 359–61; and Ol'ga Iur'evna Vasil'eva, *Russkaia Pravoslavnaia Tserkov' v politike sovetskogo gosudarstva v 1943–1948* (Moscow: Institut rossiiskoi istorii RAN, 1999), 121, 207.

8. Fr. Gleb Yakunin, interview by author, Moscow, May 10, 2007.

9. Levitin-Krasnov, *V poiskakh novogo grada*, 225–26. Knut Hamsun (Knud Pedersen, 1859–1952), a Norwegian novelist and poet, whose works had a profound influence on many twentieth-century authors, received the Nobel Prize for Literature in 1920. One of his most widely read novels, *Pan*, written in 1894, features Lieutenant Thomas Glahn, an ex-military man and hunter, who lives alone with his dog Aesop in the forest, apart from the social world.

10. Volkova, *Glyba Gleba*, 48.

11. Zoia Afanas'evna Maslenikova, *Zhizn' ottsa Aleksandra Menia* (Moscow: Pristsel's, 1995), 117–18.

12. Yakunin, interview by author.

13. Yakunin, interview by author.

14. Sergei Borisovich Filatov, ed., *Religiozno-obshchestvenaia zhizn' rossiiskikh regionov*, vol. 2 (Moscow-St. Petersburg: Letnii sad, 2016), 3–4, 16–17, 23–24.

15. Zoia Afanasev'na Maslenikova, quoted in Wallace L. Daniel, *Russia's Uncommon Prophet: Father Aleksandr Men and His Times* (DeKalb: Northern Illinois University Press, 2016), 71.

16. The priests, Fr. Serafim (Batiukov) and Fr. Pyotr Shipkov, and the nun, Mother Mariia, are intimately portrayed in *Women of the Catacombs: The Underground Church in Stalin's Russia*, ed. and trans. Wallace L. Daniel, preface Archpriest Aleksandr Men, foreword Roy R. Robson (Ithaca, NY: Northern Illinois University Press / Cornell University Press, 2021), and in Aleksandr Men', *O sebe . . . Vospominaniia, interv'iu, besedy, pis'ma* (Moscow: Zhizn's Bogom, 2007), 27–60.

17. Yakunin, interview by author.

18. Aleksandr Men, *Istoriia religii v semi tomakh: V poiskakh puti, istiny, i zhizni* (Moscow: Slovo, 1991).

19. On this point, see Protoierei Aleksandr Borisov, "Dukhovnyi realizm ottsa Aleksandra Menia," in *Tserkovnaia zhizn' XX veka: Protoierei Aleksandr Men' i ego dukhovnye nastavniki; Sbornik materialov Pervoi nauchnoi konferentsii "Menevskie chteniia" (9-11 Sentiabria 2006 g.)*, ed. M. V. Grigorenko (Sergiev Posad: Izdanie prikhoda Sergievskoi tserkvi v Semkhoze, g. Sergiev Posad, 2007), 161.

20. Elena Volkova, "Poeticheskii manifest Pravoslavnoi reformatsii," foreword to Gleb Pavlovich Yakunin, *Khvalebnyi primitiv iurodivyi, v chest' Boga, mirozdan'ia, rodiny: Poema* (Moscow: Biblioteka PravLit, 2008), 5.

21. Yakunin, *Khvalebnyi primitiv*, 16.

22. Andrei Alekseevich Eremin, *Otets Aleksandr Men': Pastyr' na rubezhe vekov*, 2nd ed. (Moscow: Carte Blanche, 2001), 453.

23. Men', *Magizm i Edinobozhie*, vol. 2 of *Istoriia religii v semi tomakh*, 57.

24. Men', 58.

25. Lucien Lévy Bruhl, *La mentalité primitive*, 14th ed. (1923; repr., Paris: Presses Universitaires de France, 1947), 12–16.

26. Lucien Lévy Bruhl, quoted by Men', *Magizm i Edinobozhie*, 58.
27. Men', *Magizm i Edinobozhie*, 405.
28. Wallace L. Daniel, "Father Aleksandr Men's *Son of Man*," in *Voices of the Voiceless: Religion, Communism, and the Keston Archive*, ed. Julie deGraffenried and Zoe Knox (Waco, TX: Baylor University Press, 2019), 30–31.
29. Eremin, *Otets Aleksandr Men'*, 454. These pagan secular rituals, which emphasized folk magic, witchcraft, and fertility, were the opposite of the veneration of relics in Orthodox Christianity, which, as Robert Greene has pointed out, accentuated love and respect for the holy deceased (Robert H. Greene, *Bodies Like Bright Stars: Saints and Relics in Orthodox Russia* [DeKalb: Northern Illinois University Press, 2010], 160–71).
30. Men and Yakunin shared similar ideas about open and closed societies. According to both of them, Christianity teaches that one must always remain open to discovery and change.
31. Men', *O sebe*, 87.
32. Men', 88; and Yakunin, interview by author.
33. Aleksandr Men', "Vospominaniia o studencheskikh godakh," in *Khronika neraskrytogo ubiistva*, ed. Sergei Bychkov (Moscow: Russkoe reklamnoe izdatel'stvo, 1996), 146.
34. Men', *O sebe*, 88.
35. Yakunin, interview by author.
36. Valentine Bibikova, quoted in Volkova, *Glyba Gleba*, 48.
37. Maslenikova, *Zhizn' ottsa Aleksandra Menia*, 142.
38. Yakunin, interview by author.
39. The Russian historian Irina Ivanovna Osipova has identified large numbers of the catacomb churches in her *"O, Premiloserdyi . . . Budi s nami neotstupno. . . .": Vospominaniia veruiushchikh Istinno-Pravoslavnoi (Katakombnoi) Tserkvi: Konets 1920-kh–nachalo 1970-kh godov* (St. Petersburg: Kifa, 2011); and Irina Ivanovna Osipova, "Dokumenty po regionam i godam: Iz istorii gonenii Istinno-Pravoslavnnoi (Katakombnoi) Tserkvi: Konets 1920-kh–nachalo 1970-kh godov," *Mezhdunarodnoe istoriko-prosvetitel'skoe pravozashchitnoe i blagotvoritel'noe obshchestvo MEMORIAL* http://www.histor-ipt-kt.org/doc.html.
40. As late as the end of the twentieth century, catacomb churches received scant attention in history texts on the Orthodox Church. See Men, "Preface," in *Women of the Catacombs*, xxxiii.
41. Aleksandr Men', "Pis'mo k E. N.," in *"AEQUINOX": Sbornik pamiati o. Aleksandra Menia*, eds. I. G. Vishnevetskii and E. G. Rabinovich (Moscow: Carte Blanche, 1991), 182–202. See Elena Semenovna Men's description of the catacomb community in her "My Journey," in *Women of the Catacombs*, 101–35.
42. Yakunin, interview by author.
43. Yakunin, interview by author.
44. Yakunin, interview by author.
45. Aleksandr Men had long seen this ignorance, and in his teenage years had begun writing the story of the New Testament. It was published in 1968 in Brussels under the pen name of Immanuel Svetlov, with the title *Syn chelovecheskii* (*Son of Man*). See Immanuel Svetlov, *Syn chelovecheskii* (Brussels: Zhizn' s Bogom, 1968). The Moscow Patriarchate's recent publication of Fr. Aleksandr's collected writings included *Syn che-*

lovecheskii as the first volume in the series (Protoierei Aleksandr Men, *Sobranie sochinenii* [Moscow: Izdatel'stvo Moskovskoi Patriarkhii Russkoi Pravoslavnoi Tserkvi, 2015]).

46. Years later, when writing about the church's role in society, Yakunin wrote, "The Orthodox Church, founded in Rus' in 988, after 1927 existed only in the catacombs and in exile abroad." Gleb Yakunin, *Istoricheskii put' pravoslavnogo talibanstva* (Moscow: Profizdat, 2002), 12.

47. Yakunin, interview by author.

48. Maslenikova, *Zhizn' ottsa Aleksandra Menia*, 133–35.

49. Maslenikova, 154; Yakunin told Elena Volkova, his close friend and helpmate, that Men introduced Berdiaev to him in Irkutsk, and, emphasizing Berdiaev's importance, recommended that Yakunin should read him. Volkova, interview by author, September 12, 2015.

50. Nicolas Berdyaev, *Dream and Reality: An Essay in Autobiography*, trans. Katherine Lampert (1950; repr., New York: Collier Books, 1962).

51. Andrew Louth, *Modern Orthodox Thinkers: From the Philokalia to the Present* (Downer's Grove, IL: IVP Academic, 2015), 63.

52. Georgii Petrovich Fedotov, "Berdiaev the Thinker," http://cheboto.ns.ca/Philosophy/Sui-Generis/Berdyaev/essays/fedotov.htm.

53. Volkova, interview by author, September 11, 2015.

54. Nikolai Aleksandrovich Berdiaev, *Filosofiia svobody: Smysl tvorchestva; Opyt opravdaniia cheloveka* (1911; repr., Moscow: Izdatel'stvo "Pravda," 1989), 37, 95–96, 194–95, 255–57, 428.

55. Berdiaev, *Filosofiia svobody*, iv, 17, 28, 61.

56. Berdyaev, *Dream and Reality*, quoted in Louth, *Modern Orthodox Thinkers*, 67.

57. Fyodor Dostoevsky, *The Brothers Karamazov*, trans. and annotated Richard Pevear and Larissa Volokhonsky (New York: Farrar, Straus and Giroux, 1990), 255.

58. Berdiaev, *Filosofiia svobody*, 213–14.

59. Berdiaev, 223; and Nikolai Aleksandrovich Berdiaev, *The Destiny of Man*, trans. Natalie Duddington (New York: Harper's, 1960), 134.

60. For the context of and reasons for Men's expulsion from the institute, see Daniel, *Russia's Uncommon Prophet*, 86–88; and Men', *Khronika neraskrytogo ubiistva*, 133–34n5.

61. Iraida Yakunina, "Znakomstvo s Glebom," Arkhiv Yakunin, Moscow.

62. Iraida Yakunina, "Znakomstvo s Glebom."

63. Iraida Yakunina, "Znakomstvo s Glebom."

64. Iraida Yakunina, interview by author, October 28, 2016.

65. Yakunina, interview by author.

66. For a firsthand account of the beginning of Khrushchev's antireligion campaign, see Michael Bourdeaux, *One Word of Truth: The Cold War Memoir of Michael Bourdeaux and Keston College* (London: Darton, Longman and Todd, 2019), 54–92.

67. Nathaniel Davis, *A Long Walk to Church: A Contemporary History of Russian Orthodoxy*, 2nd ed. (Boulder, CO: Westview Press, 2003), 39–40.

68. In addition, as Davis reports, the restrictions on Orthodox religious institutions undermined the strength of the church at all levels. The number of theological seminaries declined from 8 to 3; more than two-thirds of the convents closed; in 1960 alone, 1,400 churches lost their registration in the Soviet Union. By 1961, according to official figures, the number of registered Orthodox communities declined from 13,415 to

approximately 11,500. Between 1961 and 1966, 4,219 Orthodox societies suffered the loss of their registration. Parents were forbidden by law to bring up their children as religious believers (Davis, *Long Walk to Church*, 32, 38, 41–42).

69. Volkova, *Glyba Gleba*, 74.
70. Iraida Yakunina, "Znakomstvo s Glebom."
71. Levitin-Krasnov, "Father Gleb Yakunin and Lev Regel'son," 3.
72. Iraida Yakunina, "Znakomstvo s Glebom."
73. Levitin-Krasnov, "Father Gleb Yakunin and Lev Regel'son," 4.
74. Levitin-Krasnov, 4.

2. The Letters

1. The letter addressed to Patriarch Aleksii I had an appendix offering some of the rationale for the submission of their letter, which was dated December 13, 1965. Eshliman and Yakunin sent copies of the letter to all active bishops in the Orthodox Church in the Soviet Union. The two priests sent copies of their letter to Chairman Podgorny, Prime Minister Aleksey Kosygin, and the Soviet prosecutor-general Roman Rudenko.

2. The articles from the international press cited in this paragraph are from the National Council of Churches, Department of Information, "News Release," July 2, 1966, 1–3; Victor S. Frank, "Church and State in the USSR," parts 1 and 2, *Tablet*, May 21 and 28, 1966, 580–81, 611–12; Editorial, "Russian Priests Condemn Soviet Council," *Christian Century*, June 15, 1966, 767, 820; Edmund Stevens, "Priests Protest at Russian Church's Ties with State," (London) *Times*, May 9, 1969; "Some Questions about Religion and the Church," an interview with Vladimir Kuroedov, published originally in *Izvestiia*, August 29, 1966, and reprinted in English in *Religion in Communist Dominated Areas* 5, no. 22 (November 30, 1966): 173–77.

3. The Soviet government closed more than ten thousand Orthodox Churches and scores of monasteries and convents from 1959 to 1964. Dimitry Pospielovsky, "Anti-Church Pressure in the Soviet Union," European Service General News Talk, April 26, 1966, 1, in Keston Archive, USSR Ort C/32. According to Russian government sources, between 1958 and 1966, the number of registered Orthodox communities declined by 5,949, a loss of 44 percent (Nathaniel Davis, *A Long Walk to Church: A Contemporary History of Russian Orthodoxy*, 2nd ed. [Boulder, CO: Westview Press, 2003], 43).

4. National Council of Churches, Department of Information, "News Release," July 2, 1966, pp. 1–3; Frank, "Church and State in the USSR," 580–81, 611–12; "Russian Priests Condemn Soviet Council," 767, 820; Stevens, "Priests Protest at Russian Church's Ties with State"; and "Some Questions about Religion and the Church."

5. The English historian Jane Ellis provides an extensive analysis of the Parish Reform and its effects, in *The Russian Orthodox Church: A Contemporary History* (London: Routledge, 1986), 53–77. An excerpt from the reform document was published in *Religion in Communist Lands* 9, no. 1 (1981): 24–27.

6. Pospielovsky, "Anti-Church Pressure," 2.

7. Wallace L. Daniel, *Russia's Uncommon Prophet: The Life and Times of Father Aleksandr Men* (DeKalb: Northern Illinois University Press, 2016); Pavel Volf'ovich Men, interview by author, Moscow, July 3, 2013; Zoia Afanas'evna Maslenikova, *Zhizn' ottsa Aleksandra Menia* (Moscow: Pristsel's, 1995), 204.

NOTES TO PAGES 35-39   253

8. Aleksandr Vladimirovich Men', *O sebe . . . Vospominaniia, interv'iu, besedy, pis'ma* (Moscow: Zhizn' s bogom, 2007), 112.

9. Men, 115.

10. Anatolii Emmanuilovich Levitin-Krasnov, "Otets Dmitrii Dudko," *Posev* 31, no. 1 (1975), 27.

11. Levitin-Krasnov, 27.

12. Levitin-Krasnov, 27.

13. A year later, in 1963, Dudko became a priest in the Moscow Church of St. Nicholas in the Preobrazhensky Cemetery, where a decade later he was well known for his sermons and his open-ended question-and-answer sessions that attracted large numbers of Russian youth.

14. Fr. Dmitrii Dudko's early life, career, and personality are portrayed in his *Podarok ot Boga: Kniga v piati chastiakh* (Moscow: Izdatel'stvo Sretenskogo monastyria, 2002); Anatolii Emmanuilovich Levitin-Krasnov, "O tekh, kogo nedavno-sudili," *Posev* 36, no. 11 (1980): 47–49; Sviashchenniki Gleb Yakunin and Iurii Ryzhkov, *Tri razgovora o proshlom, nastoiashchem, i budushchem Pravoslaviia, s prilozheniem kratkoi povesti o Moskovskoi Patriarkhii* (Moscow, 2006), http:/ / krotov.info / library / 28_ya / ku / nin_apz.htm; and Oliver Bullough, *The Last Man in Russia: The Struggle to Save a Dying Nation* (New York: Basic Books, 2013).

15. Sergei Sergeevich Bychkov, *Osvobozhdenie ot illiuzii* (Moscow: Tetis Pablishn, 2010), 34. Bychkov's biography of Yermogen is a detailed account of the archbishop's life, accomplishments, and struggles with the political and religious authorities.

16. "Archbishop Yermogen: A Great Russian Pastor," June 28, 1968, in Keston Archive, SU Ort 8/2, box 24, Individual Clergy, folder 2: Yermogen file.

17. "Archbishop Yermogen"; Archimandrite Afanasii (Kudiuk), "Vysokopreosviashchennyi arkhiepiskop Ermogen (Golubev)," *Zhurnal Moskovskoi Patriarkhii* (November 1978), 21.

18. "Archbishop Yermogen."

19. Anatolii Levitin-Krasnov, "Novosti iz Moskvy: Smert' Arkhiepiskopa Ermogena Golubeva," *Russkaia mysl'*, no. 3204 (May 18, 1978), 21.

20. Levitin-Krasnov, 21.

21. This account of Patriarch Aleksii's response to Archbishop Yermogen is taken from Yakunin and Eshliman's signed letter, which will be discussed later in this chapter.

22. Archpriest Afanasii (Kudiuk), "Vysokopreosviashchennyi arkhiepiskop Ermogen (Golubev)," 21.

23. Sesil' Vess'e, *Za vashu i nashu svobodu: Dissidentskoe dvizhenie v Rossii* (Moscow: Novoe literaturnoe obozrenie, 2015) 242–43; Mikhail Vital'evich Shkarovskii, *Russkaia Pravoslavnaia Tserkov' v XX veke* (Moscow: Veche, Lepta, 2010), 273–74; and Ludmilla Alexeyeva, *Soviet Dissent: Contemporary Movements for National, Religious, and Human Rights*, trans. Carol Pearce and John Glad (Middletown, CT: Wesleyan University Press, 1985), 249.

24. Michael Bourdeaux, "The Brave Stand of Archbishop Yermogen," *Liberty*, September–October 1968, 23. See also Keston College, "Archbishop Yermogen (Golubev)," May 25, 1978, in Keston Archive, SU Ort 8/2, box 24, Individual Clergy, folder 2: Yermogen file.

25. Men', *O sebe*, 27; and Fr. Gleb Yakunin, interview by author, Moscow, May 10, 2007.

26. "Editorial," *Pravda*, October 17, 1964, quoted in William Taubman, *Khrushchev: The Man and His Era* (New York: W. W. Norton, 2003), 620.

27. Shkarovskii, *Russkaia Pravoslavnaia Tserkov'*, 274; and Mikhail Borisovich Danilushkin et al., *Istoriia Russkoi Pravoslavnoi Tserkvi, 1917-1970: Ot vosstanovleniia Patriarshestva do nashikh dnei*, vol. 1 of *Trudy Russkoi pravoslavnoi akademii bogoslovskikh nauk i nauchno bogoslovskikh issledovanii, 1917–1970* (St. Petersburg: Voskresenie), 944.

28. Danilushkin et al., *Istoriia Russkoi Pravoslavnoi Tserkvi*, 944; Shkarovskii, *Russkaia Pravoslavnaia Tserkov'*, 274; and Men', *O sebe*, 145–46.

29. Men', *O sebe*, 143.

30. Yakunin, interview by author.

31. Yakunin, interview by author.

32. According to Yakunin, "Fr. Aleksandr Men', without reservation, shared our position, but we did not want to entangle him in this affair. I was a good priest; my parishioners liked me, but I never had the gift that Fr. Aleksandr had. I wasn't a brilliant preacher, as he was" (Yakunin, interview by author).

33. Yakunin, interview by author.

34. Fr. Gleb Yakunin and Fr. Nikolai Eshliman, "Otkrytoe pis'mo Ego Sviateishestvu, Sviateishemu Patriarkhu Moskovskomu i vseia Rusi, Aleksiiu," in Keston Archive, SU Ort 8/2, Yakunin file.

35. Yakunin and Eshliman, 34. See also Christian Föller, "Andersdenken (de) und Orthodoxie: Der Fall der Priester Nikolaj Ešliman und Gleb Jakunin: Inakomyliashchie and Orthodoxy: The Case of the Priests Nikolai Eshliman and Gleb Iakunin," *Jahrbücher Für Geschichte Osteuropas* 66, no. 3 (2018): 418–42.

36. Jubilee Bishops' Council of the Russian Orthodox Church, August 13–16, 2000, Moscow, "On the Fundamentals of the Social Conception of the Russian Orthodox Church," section III, 4, Church and State, https://incommunion.org/fundamentals-of-the-social-conception-of-the-russian-orthodox-church/.

37. Yakunin and Eshliman, "Otkrytoe pis'mo," 36.

38. Yakunin and Eshliman, 37.

39. Yakunin and Eshliman, 37.

40. Yakunin and Eshliman, 37–38.

41. Aleksandr Men', "Khristianstvo i tvorchestvo," in *Radostnaia vest' (lektsy)*, ed. M. V. Sergeeva (Moscow: Vita-Tsentr, 1992), 256, and, in the same volume, "Khristianskaia kultura na Rusi," 249–50; Wallace L. Daniel, "Father Aleksandr Men and the Struggle to Recover Russia's Heritage," *Demokratizatsiya* 17, no. 1 (Winter 2009), 85; and Daniel, *Russia's Uncommon Prophet*, 267.

42. Men', "Khristianstvo i tvorchestvo," 256.

43. Fr. Aleksandr castigated the church's intolerance toward independent thought among its adherents, which, he argued, sharply limited the creativity it needed to thrive. Fr. Aleksandr Men', "Mozhno li reformirovat' pravoslavnuiu tserkov': Neizvestnoe interv'iu Aleksandra Menia," *Nezavisimaia gazeta*, January 2, 1992, also published as "Problemy tserkvi iznutri," in *Kul'tura i dukhovnnoe voskhozhdenie*, ed. R. I. Al'betkova and M. T. Rabotiaga (Moscow: Iskusstvo, 1992), 440–45.

44. Yakunin and Eshliman, "Otkrytoe pis'mo," 38–41.

45. Gregory R. Freeze, "Handmaiden of the State? The Church in Imperial Russia Reconsidered," *Journal of Ecclesiastical History* 36, no. 1 (January 1985): 82–102.

46. See Gregory R. Freeze, "'Churching' 1917: The Church Crisis and the Parish Revolution," *Gosudarstvo, religiia, tserkov' v Rossii i za rubezhom* 37, nos. 1–2 (2019): 30–52.

47. Yakunin and Eshliman, "Otkrytoe pis'mo," 39–40.

48. Yakunin and Eshliman, 13.

49. Yakunin and Eshliman, 30.

50. Yakunin and Eshliman, 9.

51. Yakunin and Eshliman.

52. Sergei Bulgakov, *The Orthodox Church*, foreword by Thomas Hopko, revised translation by Lydia Kesich (1935; repr., Crestwood, NY: St. Vladimir's Seminary Press, 1988), 129.

53. Yakunin and Eshliman, "Otkrytoe pis'mo," 32.

54. Yakunin and Eshliman, 7, 12–14, 18.

55. Yakunin and Eshliman, 23–24.

56. Yakunin and Eshliman, 11.

57. Chief among these obstacles to the priest's duties were the policies and actions of the Council for Religious Affairs, which reported to the Council of Ministers of the USSR. Established in 1965, the Council for Religious Affairs (Sovet po delam religii) was created to oversee all religious activities in the Soviet Union. The council lasted until the dissolution of the USSR.

58. Yakunin and Eshliman, "Otkrytoe pis'mo," 18, 46–47.

59. Yakunin and Eshliman, iii, 11, 61–62.

60. Yakunin and Eshliman, 223. See also Nikolai Aleksandrovich Berdiaev's *The Destiny of Man*, trans. Natalie Duddington (New York: Harper's, 1960), 134.

61. Nikolai Nikolaevich Eshliman and Gleb Pavlovich Yakunin, "To the Chairman of the Presidium of the Supreme Soviet of the Union of Socialist Republics," in Michael Bourdeaux, *Patriarch and Prophets: Persecution of the Russian Orthodox Church Today* (New York: Praeger, 1970), 189–90.

62. Eshliman and Yakunin, "To the Chairman of the Presidium," 189.

63. Eshliman and Yakunin, 192.

64. Eshliman and Yakunin, 193–94.

65. Eshliman and Yakunin, 193.

66. Eshliman and Yakunin, 193. The letter to Chairman Podgorny referenced Articles 142 and 143 of the Penal Code of the USSR.

67. Eshliman and Yakunin, 191.

68. Yakunin, interview by author.

69. Men', *O sebe*, 135.

70. Men', 142.

71. Men', 143.

72. By wanting to wait until a "more propitious time," Men and others had in mind the political turmoil following the ouster of Premier Nikita Khrushchev in October 1964. Believing that the political uncertainties of the present time were not to their advantage, they thought the letters would be better received after the new government had taken shape and greater stability had returned.

73. Men', *O sebe*, 143.

74. Men', 145.

75. Men', 146.

76. Lev Regel'son, "Dnevnik: Lev Regel'son otvechaet ottsu Aleksandru Meniu: O bogoslovskoi shkole Feliksa Karelina," https://skurlatov.livejournal.com

77. Regel'son, "Dnevnik."

78. Danilushkin et al., *Istoriia Russkoi Pravoslavnoi Tserkvi*, 944–45; and Regel'son, "Dnevnik."

79. Danilushkin et al., *Istoriia Russkoi Pravoslavnoi Tserkvi*, 944; and Regel'son, "Dnevnik."

80. Men', *O sebe*, 148–49.

81. Men', 144–45.

82. Men', 149.

83. See their defense of the action, in Frs. Gleb Yakunin and Nikolai Eshliman, "Appeal to the Patriarch, the Holy Synod, and the Diocesan Bishops," May 12, 1966, in Bourdeaux, *Patriarch and Prophets*, 224.

3. The Awakening

1. Fr. Gleb Yakunin, interview by author, Moscow, May 10, 2007.

2. Jane Ellis, *The Russian Orthodox Church: A Contemporary History* (London: Routledge, 1988), 197.

3. "The Resolution of His Holiness Patriarch Aleksii I," May 23, 1966, communicated through the office of the Metropolitan of Krutitsy and Kolomna, diocesan bishop of Moscow, in Michael Bourdeaux, *Patriarch and Prophets: Persecution of the Russian Orthodox Church Today* (New York: Praeger, 1970), 226–27.

4. Bourdeaux, 226–27.

5. Frs. N. Eshliman and G. Yakunin, "Appeal to the Patriarch, Holy Synod and the Diocesan Bishops," May 12, 1966, in Bourdeaux, *Patriarch and Prophets*, 225. Eshliman and Yakunin wrote this appeal in response to an earlier accusation from Patriarch Aleksii I that by distributing their letter to Russian Orthodox bishops, they had violated canon law.

6. Yakunin, interview by author.

7. "Nikolai Eshliman, Russian Priest Dies at 57," Special to the *New York Times*, June 14, 1985, in Keston Archive, SU Ort, Yakunin file.

8. Yakunin, interview by author.

9. Vladimir Il'ich Lenin, "O znachenii voinstvuiushchego materializma," in *Polnoe sobranie sochineniia* (Moscow: Izdatel'stvo politicheskoi literatury, 1964), 45:28.

10. "Soviet Official Lectures on Religion," *Religion in Communist Lands* 6, no. 1 (Spring 1978), 32.

11. "Soviet Official Lectures," 33.

12. Igor Shafarevich, *Zakonodatel'stvo o religii v SSSR* (Paris: YMCA-Press, 1973); "Soviet Official Lectures," 33.

13. Tat'iana Goricheva, quoted by Ellis, *Russian Orthodox Church: A Contemporary History*, 392.

14. "Fr. Sergi Zheludkov Writes to Pavel Litvinov," March 30, 1968, in Bourdeaux, *Patriarch and Prophets*, 341.

15. Sviashchennik Sergei Zheludkov, "K razmyshleniam ob intellektual'noi svobode (Otvet Akademiku A. D. Sakharovu)," Keston Archive, SU Ort 8/ 2, Fr. S. Zheludkov, box 27, folder 3. Zheludkov wrote his letter after reading Sakharov's *Reflections on Progress, Peaceful Coexistence, and Intellectual Freedom*, in which the nuclear physicist discussed the nuclear age and called for freedom of thought and world government as the best means of preventing the nuclear destruction of the planet.

16. Zheludkov.

17. Zheludkov.

18. Zheludkov.

19. Details about Boris Talantov's life are found at the end of his letter, "Zhaloba, General'nomu prokuroru SSSR ot gr. Talantova Borisa Vladimirovicha (g. Kirov)," *Vestnik Russkogo studencheskogo khristianskogo dvizheniia*, no. 3 (89–90) (1968): 49–68; Xenia Dennen, "A Forgotten Christian Martyr: Boris Talantov," *Keston Newsletter*, no. 36 (2022): 28–34; and John B. Dunlop, "Dissent within the Orthodox Church: Boris Vladimirovich Talantov (1903–1971)," *Russian Review* 31 no. 3 (July 1972): 248–59.

20. Talantov wrote the first of the letters after he read the two open letters sent by Frs. Gleb Yakunin and Nikolai Eshliman to Patriarch Aleksii I and Chairman N. V. Podgorny in late 1965. "Bedstvennoe polozhenie Pravoslavnoi Tserkvi v Kirovskoi oblasti i rol' Moskovskoi Patriarkhii (Iz otkrytogo pis'ma Borisa Talantova ot 19 noiabria 1966 g.)," *Vestnik Russkogo studencheskogo khristianskogo dvizheniia*, no. 1 (3) (1967): 29–64. Eleven other Orthodox believers signed the letter.

21. Gleb Yakunin, "Menia otluchili ot tserkvi, kak L'va Toltstogo," interviewed by Andrei Morozov, September 3, 2004, in Keston Archive, SU Ort: Yakunin, Fr. Gleb.

22. On this problem, Talantov wrote a two-part essay, to which he gave the general title "The Moscow Patriarchate and Sergianism." Part 1 is titled "Sergianism, or Adaptation to Atheism (The Leaven of Herod)." Part 2 is titled "The Secret Participation of the Moscow Patriarchate in the Battle of the CPSU against the Orthodox Christian Church (The Crisis of the Church Administration)." Both parts, in English translation, can be found at http:www.orthodoxinfo.com>cat_tal. In 1968, Talantov wrote another theoretical essay titled "Sovetskoe obshchestvo, 1965–68," *Posev* 25, no. 9 (1969): 35–41.

23. Talantov, "Sergianism, or Adaptation to Atheism."

24. Talantov (emphasis in the original).

25. Talantov.

26. Fr. Michael Aksenov-Meerson, "The Russian Orthodox Church, 1965–1980," *Religion in Communist Lands* 9, nos. 3–4 (1981), 105.

27. Aksenov-Meerson, 106.

28. Yevgeni Pazukhin, "Charting the Russian Religious Renaissance," *Religion, State and Society* 23, no. 1 (1995), 61.

29. Victoria Smolkin, *A Sacred Space Is Never Empty: A History of Soviet Atheism* (Princeton, NJ: Princeton University Press, 2018), 155.

30. Fr. Michael Aksenov-Meerson, interview by author, Bethesda, Maryland, May 27, 2019. Fr. Meerson emigrated from the Soviet Union in 1972 and is presently head priest of Christ the Savior Orthodox Church in the Diocese of New York and New Jersey. See also the Russian writer Ludmilla Evgen'evna Ulitskaia's personal account of Fr. Aleksandr and his large influence on her in *Sviashchennyi musor: Rasskazy, esse* (Moscow: Astrel', 2012), 94–100.

31. Aksenov-Meerson, interview by author.

32. Protoierei Aleksandr Borisov, "Dukhovnyi realism ottsa Aleksandra Menia," in *Tserkovnaia zhizn' XX veka: Protoierei Aleksandr Men' i ego dukhovnye nastavniki; Sbornik materialov Pervoi nauchnoi konferenstsii "Menevskie chteniia" (Sentiabria 2006 g.)*, ed. M. V. Grigorenko (Sergiev Posad: Izdanie prikhoda Sergievskoi tserkvi v Semkhoze, g. Sergiev Posad, 2007), 163–65, 170–71.

33. Iurii Mikhailovich Tabak, interview by author, Moscow, October 19, 2008. Tabak, a writer and member of the Moscow intelligentsia, often went to see Fr. Aleksandr at Novaia Derevnia; Andrei Cherniak, interview by author, Moscow, May 24, 2007. Cherniak, a physicist and former atheist, spoke glowingly about his discussions with Fr. Aleksandr.

34. Anatolii Emmanuilovich Levitin-Krasnov was the first Orthodox Christian in the Soviet Union to join the movement for human rights. For the background and personality of Levitin-Krasnov, see Aleksandr Men', *O sebe . . . Vospominaniia, interv'iu, besedy, pis'ma* (Moscow: Izdatel'stvo Zhizn' s Bogom, 2007), 120–27; Anatolii Levitin-Krasnov, *Likhie gody: 1924–1942* (Paris: YMCA Press, 1977); A. I. (Mikhail Meerson-Aksenov), "Arest Krasnova-Levitina," *Vestnik Russkogo studencheskogo khristianskogo dvizheniia*, nos. 1–2 (95–96), 1970: 69–74; and Philip Walters, "Anatolii Levitin-Krasnov (1915–1991)," *Religion in Communist Lands* 19, vol. 3–4 (1991): 264–70. DOI: 10.1080/09637499108431520.

35. Anatolii Levitin-Krasnov, "Religion and Soviet Youth," *Religion in Communist Lands* 7, no. 4 (Winter 1979), 232–33.

36. Levitin-Krasnov, 237.

37. See the details on the people who flocked to his community in Anatolii Levitin-Krasnov, "Otets Dimitrii Dudko," *Posev* 31, 1 (1975), 26–36.

38. Fr. John Meyendorff, Foreword to Fr. Dmitrii Dudko, *Our Hope*, trans. Paul D. Garrett (Crestwood, NY: St. Vladimir's Seminary Press, 1977), 9.

39. Sviashchennik Dmitrii Dudko, *O nashem upovanii: Besedy* (Paris: YMCA-Press, 1976), 235–36. Fr. Dmitrii's ten conversational sermons with his parishioners are included in this volume in addition to a later eleventh session, which he conducted in his home. At the tenth session, two plainclothes police officers escorted Fr. Dmitrii out of the church. He was soon transferred to a rural church outside Moscow. For the threat that Fr. Dmitrii's growing reputation posed to Soviet authorities both in the Soviet Union and abroad, see Nadieszda Kizenko, "Father Dmitri Dudko and the Intersection of Late Cold War Underground, Official, and Diaspora Russian Orthodox Church Opinion," *Review of Ecumenical Studies* 14, no. 2 (2022): 289–309. DOI: 10.2478/ress-2022-0106. A collection of Fr. Dmitrii's sermons over a twenty-five-year period, 1960 to 1985, is included in Sviashchennik Dmitrii Sergeevich Dudko, *V ternine i pri doroge: Sbornik propovedei za 25 let* (Moscow: D. S. Dudko, 1993).

40. Marco Sabbatini, "The Pathos of Holy Foolishness in the Leningrad Underground," in *Holy Foolishness in Russia: New Perspectives*, ed. Priscilla Hunt and Svitlana Kobets (Bloomington, IN: Slavica, 2011), 337–52. See also Olga Tchepournaya, "The Hidden Sphere of Religious Searches in the Soviet Union: Independent Religious Communities in Leningrad from the 1960s to the 1970s," *Sociology of Religion* 64, no. 3 (2003): 377–88.

41. J. H. Hexter, *Reappraisals in History: New Views on History and Society in Early Modern Europe*, 2nd ed. (1961; repr., Chicago: University of Chicago Press, 1979), 38.

42. Anatolii Levitin-Krasnov, "Sol' zemli (Molodaia Rossiia)," *Russkaia mysl'*, no. 3282, pt. 1 (November 15, 1979), 14; Koenraad de Wolf, *Dissident for Life: Alexander Ogorodnikov and the Struggle for Religious Freedom in Russia* (Grand Rapids, MI: William B. Eerdmans, 2010), 55; and Jane Ellis, "USSR: The Christian Seminar," *Religion in Communist Lands* 8, no. 2 (Summer 1980), 94–95.

43. De Wolf, *Dissident for Life*, 64–65.

44. Alexander Ogorodnikov and Boris Razveev, "Letter to Dr. Philip Potter, General-Secretary of the WCC," August 5, 1976, *Religion in Communist Lands* 7, no. 1 (1979), 50.

45. The two individuals were Aleksandr Shchipkov, Tat'iana Shchipkova's son and a student at the institute where she taught, and Viktor Popkov, a staff member of the Smolensk Exhibition Hall. Participants from Smolensk included Elena Kashtanova, also a student at the Pedagogical Institute.

46. Tat'iana Nikolaevna Shchipkova, "Imeet li pravo sovetskii prepodavatel' na svobody sovesti," July–September 1978, in Khristianskii komitet zashchity prav veruiushchikh v SSSR, *Dokumenty khristianskogo komiteta zaschchity prav veruiushchikh v SSSR* (San Francisco: Washington Street Research Center, 1978), 4:497. An excerpt from this document is published in *Religion in Communist Lands* 8, no. 2 (Summer 1980): 106–9.

47. Shchipkova, "Imeet li pravo," 497–98.

48. Shchipkova, 498.

49. Tat'iana Shchipkova, "Spiritual Pilgrimage of Vladimir Poresh," appendix in Ellis, "USSR," 101–2.

50. Shchipkova, 101.

51. Shchipkova, 102.

52. Shchipkova, 102.

53. In October 1975, members of the "creative intelligentsia" in Leningrad formed a religious-philosophical seminar, which they called the "37," named after the apartment in which it first met. The Leningrad seminar differed in size and focus from its fellow organization in Moscow. Preeminent among its leaders was a young, talented Orthodox woman named Tat'iana Goricheva. Born in Leningrad, twenty-eight years old in 1975, Goricheva spent her childhood years immersed in books, because, she said, "only in books did people not live constantly with lies" (Tat'iana Goricheva, *Talking about God Is Dangerous: The Diary of a Russian Dissident* [New York: Crossroad, 1987], 12). For Goricheva and the underground culture in Leningrad in the late 1970s and 1980s, see Elizabeth Skomp, "The Marian Ideal in the Works of Tat'iana Goricheva and the Mariia Journals," in *Framing Mary: The Mother of God in Modern, Revolutionary, and Post-Soviet Culture*, ed. Amy Singleton Adams and Vera Shevzov (DeKalb: Northern Illinois University Press, 2018), 227–45.

54. Regel'son has a Facebook page that contains a wealth of information about him, Russian culture, and various other subjects, htpps//:www.facebook.com./lregelson.

55. Anatolii Levitin-Krasnov, "Father Gleb Yakunin and Lev Regel'son," in *Letters from Moscow: Religion and Human Rights in the USSR*, ed. Jane Ellis (San Francisco, CA: H. S. Dakin, 1978), 8.

56. Levitin-Krasnov, 8–9.

57. Lev Regel'son, *Tragediia russkoi tserkvi, 1917–1945*, afterword by Archpriest John Meyendorff (Paris: YMCA Press, 1977).

58. Alexander Ogorodnikov, "Pis'mo General'nomu Sekretariu Vsemirnogo Soveta Tserkvei D-ru Filippu Potteru," July 27, 1976, *Vestnik Russkogo khristianskogo dvizheniia*, nos. 3–4 (119) (1976), 305. In English: Ogorodnikov and Razveev, "Letter to Dr. Philip Potter," July 27, 1976, *Religion in Communist Lands* 4, no. 4 (1976), 46.

59. Tat'iana Lebedeva, interview by author, Moscow, May 17, 2018. Lebedeva grew up in Smolensk and attended the seminar under Shchipkova's direction, before moving to Moscow and joining the seminar there.

60. Ogorodnikov and Razveev, "Letter to Dr. Philip Potter," 49.

61. Mark Popovskii, "Khristianstvo molodeet," *Vol'noe slovo*, no. 29 (1978), 53.

62. Popovskii, 54.

63. Popovskii, 54. Ogorodnikov wrote an essay on this topic in which he lauded the Christian commitment, which he observed in the catacomb churches; see his "Kul'tura katakom, k opytu istorii pokoleniia," in *Obschchina: Zhurnal Khristianskogo Seminara po problemam religioznogo vozrozhdeniia*, ed. Aleksandr Ogorodnikov, no. 2 (1978): 28–31.

64. Ogorodnikov and Razveev, "Letter to Dr. Philip Potter," 49; on Ogorodnikov's journey, see also Philip Walters, "From Community to Isolation: Aleksandr Ogorodnikov," *Frontier*, January–February 1987, 2–5.

65. Alexander Ogorodnikov, "Khristianskii kruzhok v Moskve," *Vestnik Russkogo khristianskogo dvizheniia*, nos. 3–4 (119), 297.

66. Ogorodnikov, "Khristianskii kruzhok." In addition to these writers and philosophers, Ogorodnikov cited Pavel Florenskii, Nikita Struve, and Semen Frank.

67. Fr. Gleb Yakunin et al., "Appeal for the Glorification of Russian Martyrs in the USSR," May 25, 1975, in Yakunin and Regel'son, *Letters from Moscow*, 35. Yakunin, Regel'son, and Kapitanchuk asked Patriarch Pimen to take the lead in glorifying Russian martyrs, who, they said, served as lodestars for the kind of courageous, self-sacrificial models needed during difficult times.

68. Yakunin et al., 35.

69. Alexander Ogorodnikov, "Informatsionnoe soobshchenie ("Informational Message"), no. 5," May 22, 1978, in *Dokumenty khristianskogo komiteta*, 4:487. In English: *Dokumenty khristianskogo komiteta (Documents of the Christian Committee)*, 3:303–11.

70. Ogorodnikov, "Informatsionnoe soobshchenie," 488.

71. Ogorodnikov, 490.

72. Ogorodnikov, 490.

73. Vladimir Sergeevich Solov'ev, *Sobranie sochineniia*, 2nd ed. (St. Petersburg: Obshchestvennaia pol'za, 1911), 7:12.

74. Vladimir Sergeevich Solov'ev, *God, Man, and the Church: The Spiritual Foundations of Life*, trans. Donald Attwater (1937; repr., London: James Clarke, 2016), 102–5, 113–15, 118–20. God had endowed his creation with love and had given human beings the gift of freedom. When hate and revenge dominated human affairs, he emphasized, "they acted in opposition to the will of the Holy God."

75. Aleksandr Men', "Vladimir Solov'ev," in *Russkaia religioznaia filosofii: Lektsii* (Moscow: Khram sviatykh bessrebrenikov Kosmu i Damiana v Shubine, 2003), 31.

76. Vladimir Poresh, "Dai krovi—priimi Dukh," April 1977, *Obshchina*, no. 2: 21–23. *Arkhiv samizdata*, no. 3452, 123, in Keston Archive, SU Ort 11/10, box 28, Christian Seminar, folder 12.

77. Poresh, 22.

78. Ogorodnikov and Razveev, "Letter to Dr. Philip Potter," 50.

79. Nicholas Zernov, *Three Russian Prophets: Khomiakov, Dostoevsky, and Soloviev*, 3rd ed. (1911; repr., Gulf Breeze, FL: Academic International Press, 1944), 60. Khomiakov, like several of his major predecessors, based his theological writings on the need for human transformation. Although set in distant, bygone days, his portrayals were timeless, particularly as they related to the spiritual confrontation with violence and power. See Aleksei Stepanovich Khomiakov, "Neskol'ko slov pravoslavnogo khristianina o zapadnykh veroispovedaniiakh," in *Izbrannye sochineniia*, ed. N. S. Arsen'ev (New York: Izdatel'stvo imeni Chekhova, 1955), 252. When segregated, driven apart by violence and power, the organic community was shattered, misdirected, and profaned. Khomiakov viewed the isolated, self-directed individual as sick and fundamentally impotent (Khomiakov, 242–43).

80. Protoeirei Aleksandr Men', *Bibliia i literatura: Lektsii* (Moscow: Khram sviatykh bessrebrenikov Kosmu i Damiana v Shubine, 2002), 141, also quoted in Wallace L. Daniel, *Russia's Uncommon Prophet: Father Aleksandr Men and His Times* (Dekalb: Northern Illinois University Press, 2016), 275.

81. Aleksei Stapanovich Khomiakov, *Tserkov' Odna* (Moscow: Gosudarstvennaia publichnaia biblioteka, 1991), 22–23. *Tserkov' Odna* was published in Berlin in 1867, and in Russia not until 1879, nineteen years after Khomiakov's death.

82. Khomiakov, "Neskol'ko slov" 252. In *Tserkov' Odna*, Khomiakov made clear the distinction between the individual as an isolated being and the person as a member of the corporate body of the church. "The wisdom that lives within the human being," he wrote, "is not given to him individually, but as a member of the church, and it is given to him in part, without nullifying entirely his individual error, but to the church wisdom is given in the fullness of truth and without any mixture of error" (Khomiakov, *Tserkov' Odna*, 11).

83. Henri Bergson, *The Two Sources of Morality and Religion*, trans. R. Ashley Audra and Cloudesley Brereton, with the assistance of W. Horsfall Carter (Garden City, NY: Doubleday, Anchor Books, 1935).

84. Bergson, 266.

85. The closed society set narrow boundaries around morality and religion, excluded its members from interaction with outsiders, and exhibited little care regarding those outside the clan. These beliefs evolved from earlier pagan societies to which the closed society retained a close connection.

86. "The open society is one which is deemed in principle to embrace all humanity," Bergson maintained (Bergson, *Two Sources*, 267).

87. Czesław Miłosz, *The Captive Mind*, trans. Jane Zielonko (1951; repr., New York: Vintage International, Random House, 1990), 27–28.

88. Viktor Popkov and Tat'iana Lebedeva, interviews by author, Moscow, May 17, 2018.

4. Western Perceptions and Soviet Realities

1. Willem Adolph Visser 't Hooft, "Message of the Assembly," opening session, *Report of the First Assembly of the World Council of Churches Held at Amsterdam, August 2 to September 4, 1948*, ed. W. A. Visser 't Hooft (London: SCM Press, 1949), 10.

2. David Kelly, "Nairobi: A Door Opened," *Religion in Communist Lands* 4, no. 1 (Spring 1976), 4.

3. World Council of Churches, Central Committee, "Violence, Nonviolence, and the Struggle for Social Justice," August 28, 1973, *Ecumenical Review* 25, no. 4 (1973), 430.

4. World Council of Churches, Central Committee, "Violence," 430–46.

5. See also the helpful comments of Xenia Howard-Johnston [Dennen], "Editorial," *Religion in Communist Dominated Lands* 4, no. 1 (Spring 1976): 2–3.

6. Michael Bourdeaux, "The Pushkino-Nairobi Connection," in Keston Archive, SU Ort 8/2, Individual Clergy: Yakunin, Fr. Gleb (1974–1976), box 26, folder 4 (1 of 2); Michael Bourdeaux, *One Word of Truth: The Cold War Memoir of Michael Bourdeaux and Keston College* (London: Darton, Longman and Todd, 2019), 173.

7. In the 1970s, as Mark Philip Bradley has written, the emergence of the human rights movement signaled the growing belief in a "universal moral language." Portrayed as the "idea of our times," human rights had wide application; however, it also had a limited scope. Government leaders rarely related it to abuses in their own country but employed human rights almost exclusively to violations "outside the domestic sphere of the nation" (Mark Philip Bradley, *The World Reimagined: Americans and Human Rights in the Twentieth Century* [New York: Cambridge University Press, 2016], 200–201).

8. Fr. Gleb Yakunin and Lev Regel'son, "Obrashchenie k delegatam V Assembleia Vsemirnogo Soveta Tserkvei," October 16, 1975, *Arkhiv Samizdata*, No. 2380, in Keston Archive, SU Ort 8/2, Yakunin file. An English-language translation is included in Fr. Gleb Yakunin and Lev Regel'son, *Letters from Moscow: Religion and Human Rights in the USSR*, ed. Jane Ellis (San Francisco, CA: H. S. Dakin Co., 1978), 41–50, and *Religion in Communist Lands* 4, no. 1 (1976): 9–14. (For accounts of the assembly's reception of the "Appeal," see Kelly, "Nairobi," 4–8, and Elena Pozdreva, "The Report Card of the Moscow Patriarchate's Delegation in Nairobi," *Radio Liberty Research*, February 23, 1976, RL 104/76.)

9. Patriarch Tikhon, quoted in Yakunin and Regel'son, "Obrashchenie," 3.

10. Bourdeaux, "Pushkino-Nairobi Connection."

11. Yakunin and Regel'son, "Obrashchenie," 4.

12. Yakunin and Regel'son, 4.

13. Yakunin and Regel'son, 7.

14. Yakunin and Regel'son, 10.

15. Yakunin and Regel'son, 10.

16. Yakunin and Regel'son, 8.

17. Yakunin and Regel'son, 9.

18. Yakunin and Regel'son, 9.

19. Yakunin and Regel'son, 9–11.

20. Yakunin and Regel'son, 9.

21. Fr. Gleb Yakunin and Lev Regel'son, "Obrashchenie k khristianam Portugalii," April 3, 1975, in Keston Archive, SU Ort 8/2, Yakunin, Fr. Gleb file. An English translation of the letter is included in Yakunin and Regel'son, *Letters from Moscow*, 29–31.

22. Yakunin wrote several other letters between his and Regel'son's appeal to the church in Portugal and their next letter, which is discussed later in the text. They include Yakunin's "Politburo TsK. KPSS—Oktrytoe pis'mo," April 19, 1975, in Keston

Archive, SU Ort 8/2, Yakunin file, and in Yakunin and Regel'son, *Letters from Moscow*, 32–33. Yakunin protested the Soviet practice of the *subbotnik*, or "Red Saturday," a day of voluntary labor required of citizens on Lenin's birthday, April 22. In 1975, when it happened to fall on Easter Sunday, he requested that the *subbotnik* be moved to either May 1 or November 7. He, Lev Regel'son, and Viktor Kapitanchuk, wrote an additional letter, "Appeal for the Glorification of Russian Martyrs in the USSR," May 25, 1975, in Yakunin and Regel'son, *Letters from Moscow*, 34–40. In the letter, they encouraged the patriarch and church leaders to begin preparations for the glorification of martyrs who had perished in the early years of the Soviet period.

23. Yakunin and Regel'son, "Obrashchenie," 9.

24. Yakunin and Regel'son, 10.

25. "Iuvenalii, mitropolit eparkhii (Poiarkov, Vladimir Kirillovich)," www.patriarchia.ru/db/text/31765.html.

26. "Iuvenalii, mitropolit eparkhii."

27. Metropolitan Yuvenalii, "Russian Orthodox Response," *Religion in Communist Lands* 4, no. 1 (1976), 15. Metropolitan's Yuvenalii's letter is addressed to the editor of *Target*, the daily bulletin published by the Kenyan organizing committee of the WCC.

28. Yuvenalii, "Russian Orthodox Response," 15.

29. Yuvenalii, 15.

30. See, for example, the "Documentary Record Compiled by Alan Nichols of the Australian Delegation's Visit to the Soviet Union, Poland, and Yugoslavia," June 14, 1976–July 4, 1976, in Keston Archive, SU Ort 9/9: Visits from Foreign Delegations, 1967–1977, box 27, folder 12 (1 of 2).

31. Yuvenalii, "Russian Orthodox Response," 15.

32. Yuvenalii, 15–16.

33. "Russian Baptist Response," *Religion in Communist Lands* 4, no. 1 (Spring 1976), 16.

34. For a detailed discussion of the formation, organization, and persecution of Baptist and other Protestant communities, see Michael Bourdeaux, *Religious Ferment in Russia: Protestant Opposition to Soviet Religious Policy* (London: Macmillan, 1968).

35. World Council of Churches, *Breaking Barriers: The Official Report of the Fifth Assembly of the World Council of Churches, Nairobi, 23 November–10 December 1975*, ed. David M. Paton (London: SPCK, 1976), 168. For summaries of the proceedings, see also Kelly, "Nairobi," 4–8, and Bourdeaux, *One Word*, 172–76.

36. Bourdeaux, *One Word*, 172–76. Metropolitans Yuvenalii and Nikodim spoke in opposition to the amendment.

37. Mr. V. H. Davados (Church of North India) recommended closure. A vote then followed, but many of the delegates were unsure about what their vote actually entailed (Bourdeaux, *One Word*, 172–76).

38. They included Dr. T. B. Simatupang (Protestant, Indonesia), Mr. A. Buevskii (Russian Orthodox Church), and Dr. W. P. Thompson (Presbyterian Church, USA).

39. World Council of Churches, *Breaking Barriers*, 168.

40. Vitalii Borovoi, quoted in World Council of Churches, *Breaking Barriers*, 171.

41. World Council of Churches, 171.

42. Pimen, Patriarkh Moskovskii i vseia Rus, i chleny Sviashchennogo Sinoda, "Poslanie Sviashchennogo Sinoda o V Assemblee Vsemirnogo Soveta Tserkvei i ee rezul'tatakh," March 3, 1976, *Zhurnal Moskovskoi patriarkhii*, no. 4 (1976): 11.

43. Helene Posdeeff, "Geneva: The Defense of Believers' Rights," *Religion in Communist Lands* 4, no. 4 (Winter 1976), 5.

44. World Council of Churches, Central Committee, "Helsinki Colloquium: Memorandum on the Church's Role," July 24–28, 1976, *Ecumenical Review* 28, no. 4 (1976): 450–56.

45. Philip A. Potter, "The Churches and Religious Liberty in the Helsinki Signatory States," August 12, 1976, *Ecumenical Review* 28, no. 4 (1976), 450.

46. Jane Ellis, "The Background to Yakunin's and Regel'son's Activity," in Yakunin and Regel'son, *Letters from Moscow*, 134–35.

47. "Interview with Metropolitan Nikodim," *Moscow News*, February 7–14, 1976; extracts also published in Yakunin and Regel'son, *Letters from Moscow*, 136–38.

48. Yakunin and Regel'son, *Letters from Moscow*, 136.

49. Yakunin and Regel'son, 137. (In the interest of greater clarity, I have rearranged parts of this sentence.)

50. For a much different view, see the report of the Archbishop of Canterbury, Donald Coggan, who visited the Soviet Union in September 1977. He left a detailed account of his experiences in his "Communiqué on the Visit to the Russian Orthodox Church of His Grace Dr. Frederick Donald Coggan, the Archpriest of Canterbury, Primate of All England and Metropolitan," September 26, 1977, Moscow, marked "Confidential," in Keston Archive, SU Ort 9/9: Visits from Foreign Delegations, folder 13 (1977–1990) (2 of 2).

51. Ellis, "Background," 138.

52. Bourdeaux, *One Word*, 183.

53. Bourdeaux, 183.

54. Erich Weingartner, *Human Rights on the Ecumenical Agenda: Report and Assessment (Background Information of Commission of the Churches on International Affairs)* (Geneva: Commission of the Churches on International Affairs, 1983); Bourdeaux, *One Word*, 176–77; and Michael Bourdeaux, "The Russian Church, Religious Liberty and the World Council of Churches," *Religion in Communist Lands* 13, no. 1 (1985): 4–27.

55. Quoted in Bourdeaux, *One Word*, 177. On both theological and moral grounds, Canon Bourdeaux is especially critical of Weingartner's approach. He argued that Weingartner totally misunderstood the motives of those who defended religious liberty in the Soviet Union (Bourdeaux, "Russian Church," 21–24).

56. Bourdeaux, *One Word*, 188–89.

57. Rev. B. O. Fielding Clarke, "Letter," *Church Times*, October 17, 1980, 12 (emphasis in the original). Rev. Fielding Clarke served the Anglican Church in the town of Wirksworth, in the Derbyshire district, and noted that he had visited the USSR twelve times, often as a guest of the Russian Church. See also the testimonies of David Y. K. Wong, a Hong Kong architect and engineer and president of the Baptist World Alliance, Bishop Ian Sheville of Newcastle, Australia, and Bishop Robert Runcie of St. Albans Cathedral in Great Britain and the future Archbishop of Canterbury (1980–1991). The interview with David Wong was published in *Baptist Times*, August 26, 1976. Summary accounts of the latter three visits to the USSR were published in Keston College, "Western Church Leaders Report on Religion in the Soviet Union," *Religion in Communist Lands* 5, no. 1 (Spring 1977): 52–53.

58. See the collection of essays, *Voices of the Voiceless: Religion, Communism, and the Keston Archive*, eds. Julie deGraffenried and Zoe Knox (Waco, TX: Baylor University Press, 2019).

59. The journal *Religion in Communist Lands* began publication in 1973. It published a large number of extremely valuable primary and secondary source materials on religion, politics, and society in countries formerly under Communist rule.

60. "The world is now dominated by a new spirit," President Jimmy Carter emphasized in his inauguration speech on January 20, 1977. "Peoples more numerous and more politically aware are craving, and now demanding, their place in the sun—not just for the benefit of their own physical condition, but for basic human rights" (quoted in Bradley, *World Reimagined*, 123). Although the United States trailed Western European countries in defining human rights as a primary concern, the president's commitment likely strengthened the resolve of Yakunin and Regel'son to move more deliberately to seek support from sympathetic people in the United States. Henry Dakin would be one of those people (see chapter 5).

61. Others who called to testify in the hearings included David D. Klassen, a former prisoner in the Soviet Union, Lev E. Dobriansky, a professor in the Department of Economics at Georgetown University, and George Dobczansky, research director of Human Rights Research, Inc.

62. Felix Corley, "Obituary: Pastor Georgi Vins," *Independent*, January 17, 1998, https://www.independent.co.uk/news/obituaries-pastor-georgi-vins-1139170.html; Georgi Vins, *Testament from Prison*, trans. Jane Ellis (Weston, Ontario: David C. Cook, 1975); "Georgi Vins (Wiens) (1928–1998)," https://cmbs.mennonitebrethren.ca/personal_papers/vins-wiensgeorgi-1928-1998/; and Albert W. Wardin Jr., "Jacob J. Wiens: Mission Champion in Freedom and Repression," *Journal of Church and State* 28, no. 3 (Autumn 1986): 495–514.

63. Yakunin and Regel'son, "Obrashchenie," 11. Yakunin and Regel'son also mentioned the Latvian Baptist elder Yanis Smits and his family who, like members of other congregations, had applied for permission to emigrate.

64. Representative Buchanan noted that human rights advocates in thirteen countries, including the United States, had petitioned for Vins's release. Keston College in England, too, had taken a substantial interest in the case and petitioned for his release.

65. "Statement of Hon. John H. Buchanan, Jr., a Representative in Congress from the State of Alabama," June 24, 1976, in US Congress, House Committee on International Relations, *Religious Persecution in the Soviet Union*. Hearings before the Subcommittees on International Political and Military Affairs and on International Organizations. Committee on International Relations, 94th Cong., 2nd. sess., June 24 and 30, 1976, 2.

66. Bohdan R. Bociurkiw, "Statement to the House of Representatives," US Congress, *Religious Persecution in the Soviet Union*, 3.

67. Bociurkiw's "Statement" and "Prepared Statement" were included in US Congress, *Religious Persecution in the Soviet Union*, 2–27.

68. Anatolii Levitin-Krasnov, quoted in Bociurkiw, "Statement," 4.

69. Bociurkiw, "Statement" and "Prepared Statement," 4, 9–10. Bociurkiw's comments refer to the ferment among the intelligentsia that developed after Stalin's death

in March 1953, the loosening of censorship controls, and the publication of novels, poems, and other materials that represented a new wave of creative thought.

70. Bociurkiw, "Statement" and "Prepared Statement," 4–5.

71. "Statement of Prof. John Dunlop, German-Russian Department, Oberlin College," in US Congress, *Religious Persecution in the Soviet Union*, 53.

72. Dunlop, "Statement," 52.

73. Dunlop, 52–54.

74. According to Fr. Dmitrii Dudko, "a believing child is subjected to badgering, mockery and there have been cases when teachers have ripped the crosses off children" (quoted in Dunlop, "Statement," 55.

75. "Statement of Yanis Smits, Chairman, Council of Churches of Evangelical Christians and Baptists; Former Prisoner of the Soviet Union," June 24, 1976, in US Congress, *Religious Persecution in the Soviet Union*, 28. Klassen spoke of the insecurities his fellow believers had to endure, and he gave concrete descriptions of the physical and psychological abuses they had suffered.

76. In the hearings, Professor Lev E. Dobriansky emphasized the discrepancy between external and internal behavior (US Congress, *Religious Persecution in the Soviet Union*, 80).

77. Professor Bohdan Bociurkiw, in the discussion following the testimonies of Bociurkiw, Yanis Smits) and David Klassen, in US Congress, *Religious Persecution in the Soviet Union*, 37.

78. Bociurkiw, "Statement" and "Prepared Statement," 37–38.

79. In his criticism of church leaders, Fr. Gleb Yakunin had repeatedly claimed that they had lost the trust of the Russian people. See Yakunin and Regel'son, "Obrashchenie," 11, and earlier, Yakunin and Fr. Nikolai Eshliman's 1965 letter to Patriarch Aleksii, "Otkrytoe pis'mo Ego Sviateishestvu, Sviateishemu Patriarkhu Moskovskomu i Vseia Rusi, Aleksiiu," 3, in Keston Archive, SU Ort 8/2, Yakunin file.

80. Fr. Gleb Yakunin and Lev Regel'son, "To the General Secretary of the WCC, Philip Potter," March 6, 1976, in Helene Posdeeff, "Geneva," Appendix: "Russian Believers Write to WCC's General Secretary," *Religion in Communist Lands* 4, no. 4 (Winter 1976): 9–15.

81. US Congress, *Religious Persecution in the Soviet Union*, 88.

82. US Congress, 88.

83. In late April 1979, under President Jimmy Carter, an exchange of prisoners from the Soviet Union and the United States resulted in the release of Georgi Vins.

5. Gleb Yakunin, Henry Dakin, and the Defense of Religious Liberty

1. Khristianskii komitet zashchity prav veruiushchikh v SSSR, "Deklaratsiia," in *Dokumenty khristianskogo komiteta zashchity prav veruiushchikh v SSSR* (San Francisco: Washington Street Research Center, 1977), 1:1.

2. "Deklaratsiia," in *Dokumenty*, 1:1.

3. Mikhail Vital'evich Shkarovskii, *Russkaia Pravoslavnaia Tserkov' v XX veke* (Moscow: Veche, Lepta, 2010) 280–81.

4. Dimitry V. Pospielovsky, *Russkaia Pravoslavnaia Tserkov' v XX veke* (Moscow: Izdatel'stvo "Respublika," 1995), 359–60; and Dimitry V. Pospielovskii, *The Orthodox*

Church in the History of Russia (Crestwood, NY: St. Vladimir's Seminary Press, 1998), 343.

5. Jane Ellis, "The Christian Committee for the Defence of Believers' Rights in the USSR," *Religion in Communist Lands* 4, no. 4 (1980): 279; and Jane Ellis, *The Russian Orthodox Church: A Contemporary History* (London: Routledge, 1988), 291, 374.

6. Ellis, *Russian Orthodox Church: A Contemporary History*, 374.

7. At Tarasovka, and later at Novaia Derevnia, Kapitanchuk regularly participated in the discussion sessions Fr. Aleksandr Men led about church reform. There, too, he developed a close relationship with Yakunin (Aleksandr Men', *O sebe . . . Vospominaniia, interv'iu, besedy, pis'ma* [Moscow: Zhizn' s Bogom) 2007], 170, 173).

8. Tat'iana Lebedeva, interview by author, Moscow, May 17, 2018.

9. Ellis, "Christian Committee," 19.

10. The Moscow Group's formal name was "Public Group to Promote Fulfillment of the Helsinki Accords in the USSR" (Obshchestvennaia gruppa sodeistviia vypolneniiu Khel'sinskikh soglashenii v SSSR). Its membership included, in addition to Orlov, Sakharov's wife Elena Bonner, Liudmilla Alekseyeva, Aleksandr Ginzburg, Anatoly Marchenko, Anatoly Sharanskii, Petro Grigorenko, and others (Moscow Helsinki Group, "Ob obrazovanii obshchestvennoi gruppy sodeistviia vypolneniiu Khel'sinkskikh soglashenii v SSSR," in *Dokumenty Moskovskoi Khel'sinkskoi gruppy, 1976–1982*, ed. G. V. Kuzovkin and I. Zubarev (Moscow: Zatsepa, 2006).

11. University of Minnesota, Human Rights Library, "The Final Act of the Conference on Security and Cooperation in Europe," August 1, 1975, 14 I.L.M. 1292 (Helsinki Accords), http://www1.umn.edu/humanrts/osce/basics/finact75.htm.; Peter Slezkine, "From Helsinki to Human Rights Watch: How an American Cold War Monitoring Group Became an International Human Rights Institution," *Humanity* 5, no. 3 (Winter 2014), 348. See the interpretations by political leaders in the United States and the Soviet Union, in Patrick G. Vaughan, "Zbigniew Brzezinski and the Helsinki Final Act," in *The Crisis of Détente in Europe: From Helsinki to Gorbachev, 1975–1985*, ed. Leopoldo Nuti (London: Routledge, 2009), 11–25, and, in the same volume, Svetlana Savranskaya, "Human Rights Movement in the USSR after the Signing of the Helsinki Final Act, and the Reaction of Soviet Authorities," 26–40.

12. Fr. Gleb Yakunin, interview by author, Moscow, May 10, 2007.

13. A letter addressed to Pope John Paul II, sent on November 22, 1978, signed by Fr. Gleb Yakunin, Viktor Kapitanchuk, Vadim Shcheglov, and five members of the Catholic Committee for the Defense of Believers' Rights, explained this contention by saying that the "highest sphere of the human being is that of spiritual life." When spiritual freedom is violated, the core of human identity and purpose is also violated ("To Pope John Paul II, The Heads of the Autocephalous Orthodox Churches; Primate of the Anglican Church, Archbishop D. Coggan; The World Council of Churches; Community Christian Committees Which Defend Believers' Rights; and President of the United States, J. Carter)," November 22, 1978, in Alan Scarfe, ed., *Christian Committee for the Defense of Believers' Rights in the USSR: A Selection of Documents in Translation*, trans. Maria Belaeffa [Glendale, CA: Door of Hope Press, 1982], 112).

14. Nikolai Aleksandrovich Berdiaev, *Filosofiia svobody* (Moscow: A. I. Mamontova, 1911).

15. Yakunin, interview by author.

16. *Dokumenty*, 1:vii.

17. See, for example, "Zhaloby ot veruiushchikh prikhozhan sv. Nikol'skogo khrama g. Nikolaeva," December 25, 1975, in *Dokumenty khristianskogo komiteta*, 1:83–85; Prikhozhan sviato-nikol'skogo sobora, "Sviateishestvo Pimen, Patriarkh Moskvy i vseia Rossii: Zapros-Zhaloba," in *Dokumenty khristianskogo komiteta*, 1:94.

18. According to his wife, Vergilia, Henry Dakin had also learned basic Russian and could read simple Russian texts. Vergilia Passache Dakin, interview by author, Ukiah, CA, Zoom, July 9, 2020.

19. In the 1960s, while working at the Lawrence Berkeley National Laboratory, Dakin created a pocket-size radiation detector that remained in use for the next fifty years. He was well on his way to a successful career in the sciences.

20. As the newsletter of the Bancroft Library at the University of California, Berkeley, mourned, "The annals of California history scarcely record a comparable family tragedy." Dale L. Morgan, "Susanna Bryant Dakin," *Bancroftiana*, no. 40 (May 1967), 1.

21. Susanna Dakin, speaking at Henry S. Dakin Memorial 2d, https://www.youtube.com/watch?v=5ffyJRc1n9M.

22. Willis Harman, quoted in Kathleen Teltsch, "Fortune in Toys Helps to Put Americans and Russians in Touch," *New York Times*, November 16, 1988. See also the testimony of Ed Ellsworth, a technician who worked with Henry Dakin on various projects, in Ed Ellsworth, "Ed Ellsworth Biography," https://sunrisecenter.org/classes-events/core-teachers/ed-ellsworth/.

23. Adriana Dakin, interview by author, Ukiah, CA, Zoom, July 9, 2020.

24. Jim Hickman, interview by author, Cochabamba, Bolivia, Zoom, July 11, 2020.

25. Hickman, interview by author.

26. Henry Dakin's father, Richard, the originator of the world-famous Dakin Stuffed Animals toys, had built these human relationships with Russians through his commercial ventures. The Dakin brown bear toys became the official symbol of the Olympic Games, held in Moscow in 1980 (Teltsch, "Fortune in Toys").

27. Dakin believed in universal human rights, and he had a large interest in enhancing human relationships that strengthened those rights. In the mid-1970s, new forms of technology, such as desktop publishing, were only in their infancy, but Dakin used them to establish connections with the Soviet people.

28. See Nadezhda Beliakova, "Samizdat dlia tamizdata, ili Kak Kholodnaia voina povliiala na razvitie novogo zhanra pravoslavnogo samizdata," in *Acta samizdatika: Zapiski o samizdate: Al'manakh*, no. 5, ed. M. Ia. Sheinker (Moscow: Gosudarstvennaia publichnaia istoricheskaia biblioteka Rossii, 2020), 77–91.

29. See *A Chronicle of Current Events: Journal of the Human Rights Movement in the USSR* 58 (1981), 24.

30. "Deklaratsiia," in *Dokumenty*, 1:1.

31. "Zhaloby ot veruiushchikh prikhozhan sv. Nikol'skogo khrama g. Nikolaeva," December 25, 1975, in *Dokumenty*, 1:83–85.

32. "Zhaloby," 1:83.

33. "Zhaloby," 1:83.

34. "Zhaloby," 1:84. Chunikhin served as the local representative of the Council for Religious Affairs.

35. Archbishop Bogolep of Kirov and Nikolaev Diocese, "Ukaz," November 5, 1976, in *Dokumenty*, 1:99. Issuing the order, Archbishop Bogolep wrote, "The Church is the Lord's house, a temple of prayer and an assembly of peace creating people, where there must reign peace, love, unity of souls, and agreement, and not a place of brigandage, where rules evil, enmity, and contempt for one another."

36. A. Goritsvet, "Pod sen'iu sobora," *Iuzhnaia Pravda*, February 5, 1977.

37. "See "Zaiavlenie predsedatel'iu Tsentral'nogo raionogo suda g. Nikolaeva E. V. Pisaruk ot L. A. Mirchenko i drugikh prikhozhan," February 10, 1977; "Zapros-Zhaloba; V Narodnyi sud Tsentral'nogo raiona goroda Nikolaeva ot prikhozhan sviato-nikol'skogo sobora, N. K. Martinova, Z. K. Kliukina, i L. V. Seredavina," February 9, 1977; and Prikhozhan sviato-nikol'skogo sobora, "Sviateishchemu Patriarkhu Moskovskogo i vseia Rossii, Pimen, Zapros-Zhaloba," May 28, 1977, in *Dokumenty*, 1:86–89, 94–96.

38. "Sviateishchemu Patriarkhu Moskovskogo i vseia Rossii," May 28, 1977, in *Dokumenty*, 1:88–89. The May 28, 1977, letter represented the second of the two letters the Nikolaev parishioners sent to the patriarch.

39. "To Most Holy Patriarch of Moscow and All Russia, Pimen," December 16, 1978, in Scarfe, *Christian Committee*, 74–79.

40. "To Most Holy Patriarch," 76.

41. "To Most Holy Patriarch," 75.

42. "To Most Holy Patriarch," 75.

43. "To Most Holy Patriarch," 79.

44. See the pathbreaking book, Stephen Kotkin, *Magnetic Mountain: Stalinism As a Civilization* (Berkeley: University of Californian Press 1997), 218–21, 237.

45. For similar examples of "Bolshevik speak" and its purposes, see Andrew B. Stone, "'Overcoming Peasant Backwardness': The Khruschchev Antireligous Campaign and the Rural Soviet Union," *Russian Review* 67 (April 2008): 296–320.

46. Anastasia Kleimionova and other parishioners of the Holy Convent of Pechersk, "To the Most Holy Patriarch of Moscow and All Russia, Pimen," October 27, 1978, in Scarfe, *Christian Committee Documents*, 74.

47. Vladimir Zelinskii, "Pastva i pastyri," *Russkaia mysl'*, no. 3786 (July 28, 1979): 8–9.

48. Zelinskii, "Pastva i pastyri," 8. See, for example, the difficulties Fr. Aleksandr Men had with older women when he first arrived at his Akulino parish in 1958 in Wallace L. Daniel, *Russia's Uncommon Prophet: Father Aleksandr Men and His Times* (DeKalb: Northern Illinois University Press, 2016), 100–1.

49. Daniel, *Russia's Uncommon Prophet*, 74. Additional examples of the Church's appointed leaders reveal the harsh, inhumane qualities of priests' leadership roles. See, for example, Kleimionova et al., "To the Most Holy Patriarch," 74.

50. Evgeny Barabanov, "The Schism between the Church and the World," in *From under the Rubble*, ed. Alexander Solzhenitsyn, trans. A. M. Brock et al., under the direction of Michael Scammell, intro. Max Hayward (Boston: Little, Brown, 1974), 177.

51. Fr. Gleb Yakunin, "Doklad Sviashchennika Gleba Iakunina Khristianskomu komitetu zashchitu prav veruiushchikh v SSSR o sovremennom polozhenii Russkoi Pravoslavnoi Tserkvi i o perspektivakh religioznogo vozrozhdeniia Rossii," in *Dokumenty khristianskogo komiteta* (San Francisco: Washington Street Research Center, 1979),

11: 1128; English language copy (abridged): "The Russian Orthodox Church Today: Religious Revival in the USSR," in Scarfe, *Christian Committee Documents*, 23–40.

52. See Barabanov's comments in "Schism," 178–79, 187.

53. Fr. Lev Konin, "Prekratit' Psikhiatricheskie Repressii v SSSR," May 6, 1977, in *Dokumenty khristianskogo komiteta*, 1:113. Fr. Lev's biographical account is taken from a paper attached to the Christian Committee's documents.

54. Konin, 113.

55. Konin, 113.

56. Konin, 114.

57. Konin, 115.

58. Fr. Lev Konin, "Zaiavelenie," October 16, 1977, in *Dokumenty khristianskogo komiteta*, 1:111. Father Lev sent his "Appeal" for assistance to the Christian Committee for the Defense of Believers' Rights.

59. See also the case of Aleksandr Argentev, a member of the Moscow intelligentsia and a student in the process of finding his way, searching for his own identity, and expressing dissatisfaction with the Marxist-Leninist teachings of his schooling. He participated in the Christian Seminar, before the police sent him to a psychiatric clinic in the city in the summer of 1976. See his "Letter to Pimen, Most Holy Patriarch of Moscow and All Russia," written from Psychiatric Clinic no. 14, Moscow, July 21, 1976, in Keston Archive, SU 12/11. I, Individual Clergy: Fr. Gleb Yakunin, Fr. Nikolai Eshliman, Fr. Nikolai Gainov.

60. Konin, "Prekratit' Psikhiatricheskie Repressii," 115–16.

61. Katolicheskii komitet zashchity prav veruiushchikh, "XXXIV Sessii General'noi Assemblei OON, Pravitel'stvam k Parlamentam vsekh Stran," September 29, 1979, in *Dokumenty khristianskogo komiteta*, 12:1267. Conference participants recognized the Convention on the Rights of the Child, composed by the United Nations in 1959, as a foundational agreement.

62. Katolicheskii komitet zashchity prav veruiushchikh, "XXXIV Sessii General'noi Assemblei OON," 1267–68.

63. Katolicheskii komitet, 1268.

64. Katolicheskii komitet, 1268.

65. Katolicheskii komitet, 1268.

66. Tat'iana Ivanovna Sorokina, "Zaiavlenie," in Scarfe, *Christian Committee Documents*, 140.

67. After opening Sorokina's case, the district court turned the proceedings over to the regional court for further adjudication.

68. Oktiabrskii District People's Court, city of Taganrog, "Decision in the Name of the RSFSR," October 12, 1978, in Scarfe, *Christian Committee Documents*, 143.

69. Sorokina, "Zaiavlenie," 141.

70. Valeriia Petrovna Bondareko, "Letter to Christian Committee for the Defense of Believers' Rights in the USSR," 1977, in Hoover Archive, Stanford University, Papers of Henry S. Dakin, box 1, folder 1.

71. "Zaiavlenie ot veruiushchikh Riazanskoi obshchiny EkhB," August 19, 1979, in Hoover Archive, Stanford University, Papers of Henry S. Dakin, box 9, folder 3.

72. "Khristianam vsego mira, Komitetu zashchita prav cheloveka pri OON, Sovetu rodstvennikov uznikov," August 1978, in Hoover Archive, Stanford University, Papers of Henry S. Dakin, box 4, folder 5.

73. Yakunin, "Doklad," 1132.
74. Ellis, "Christian Committee," 282.
75. Yakunin, "Doklad," 1129, 1137.
76. Yakunin, 1128.
77. The great majority of Orthodox priests, Yakunin wrote, did little more than offer praises to God, paeans he considered useless (Yakunin, "Doklad," 1160).
78. Yakunin, 1160.
79. Such a purpose did not fit into what Yakunin described as the "cult-pious pharisaical mentality" of the church's present leadership. Yakunin, 1160; Father Gleb Yakunin, "The Present State of the Russian Orthodox Church and the Prospects for Religious Revival in Russia," in Sergei Pushkarov, Vladimir Rusak, and Gleb Yakunin, *Christianity and Government in Russia and the Soviet Union: Reflections on the Millennium* (Boulder, CO: Westview Press, 1989), 110–13.
80. Czesław Miłosz, *The Captive Mind*, trans. Jane Zielonko (1951; repr., New York: Vintage International, Random House, 1990), 201.
81. Yakunin, "Doklad," 1142–43.
82. Yakunin, 1167.
83. Yakunin, 1139.
84. Yakunin, 1167.
85. Yakunin, 1163–64.
86. Yakunin, 1166.
87. Yakunin, 1165. The biblical quotation is from Mark 2:21.
88. Yakunin, "Doklad," 1166.
89. The numbers of individuals and groups represented included Reformed Baptists—100; Catholics—49; True and Free Adventists—37; Reformed Baptists and Pentecostals—17, signing jointly; Georgian Orthodox—5; Jewish—2; various other groups—16. Letters, reports, and legal materials made up the remainder of the documents (Ellis, "Christian Committee," 290–91n10).
90. Metropolitan Nikodim, "The Russian Orthodox Church and the Ecumenical Movement," *Ecumenical Review* 21, no. 2 (1969): 116–29.
91. "Deklaratsiia," in *Dokumenty*, 1:1.
92. Fr. Gleb Yakunin et al. "Pravoslavnomu Vselenskomu Patriarkhu Dmitriiu," April 11, 1978, in *Dokumenty*, 1:159–63. An abridged copy of the letter was also published in *Religion in Communist Lands* 7, no. 3 (1979): 191–94.
93. Sviashchennik Gleb Yakunin, Viktor Kapitanchuk, and Vadim Shcheglov, "Ego Sviateishestu Pape Rimskomu, nasledniki Sviateishego Prestola Papy Ioanna-Pavla I," October 1, 1978, in *Dokumenty*, 5, pt. 2: 700–721. The second, "Letter to Pope John Paul II," November 22, 1978, in Scarfe, *Christian Committee Documents*, 111–15, proposed the creation of an international agreement on religious rights, corresponding to the 1975 Helsinki Accords on human rights. The third letter, "Pis'mo Pape Ioannu Pavlu II," April 2, 1979, decried the false claims of the Orthodox hierarchy and state representatives about religious freedom in the Soviet Union (Ellis, *Russian Orthodox Church: A Contemporary History*, 376–77).
94. Yakunin, "Doklad," 1134.
95. Yakunin, 1167.
96. Yakunin et al., "Pravoslavnomu Vselenskomu Patriarkhu Dmitriiu," 160.

97. "Deklaratsiia," in *Dokumenty*, 1:1.

98. Yakunin et al., "Pravoslavnomu Vselenskomu Patriarkhu Dmitriiu," 161.

99. James L. Rathenau, *Turbulence in World Politics: A Theory of Change and Continuity* (Princeton, NJ: Princeton University Press, 1990), 454.

100. When attached to the internet, which soon became a reality, telecommunications possessed, on many different levels, the capacity to bring people much closer together. For the political, economic, and social implications of this innovation, see Klaus Schwab, *Shaping the Future of the Fourth Industrial Revolution* (Redfern, New South Wales: Currency Press, 2018).

101. Anya Kucharev, a Russian émigré who began working for Dakin in 1980 as a translator and assistant, is a goldmine of information on the Esalen Institute in California, which hosted many Russian political leaders, cosmonauts, business executives, scientists, and others, bringing them together with Americans for relaxation and conversation (Anya Kucharev, interview by author, San Rafael, CA, email, July 24, 2020). Many details about Henry Dakin's initiatives in person-to-person diplomacy are included in the book of reminiscences *Henry S. Dakin: From Physics to Metaphysics and Guns to Toys*, ed. Laura Gail Drewes, foreword Vergilia Paasche Dakin (Petaluma, CA: Happy Medium Productions, 2020).

102. See Birgit Menzel, "New Age Diplomacy: The Diplomatic Role of the Esalen Institute in Ending the Cold War," in *New Age in Russia*, https://newageru.hypotheses.org/1903.

103. Vergilia Paasche Dakin, interview by author.

6. "I Thank God for the Fate He Has Given Me"

1. Norman Cohn, *The Pursuit of the Millennium: Revolutionary Messianism in Medieval and Reformation Europe and Its Bearing on Modern Totalitarian Movements* (New York: Harper, 1961), 314–15.

2. This anxiety was expressed in a variety of ways, including concerns about the Vatican's efforts to appeal to Soviet youth and the increased sale of books and other printed materials that were available in secondhand bookstores. See Yuri Andropov, chair of the Committee for State Security, "To the CC CPSU," Document 161. KGB, 25 March 1974; No. 788–A, Moscow; and "Decree of the Chairman of the State Commission of the USSR Council of Ministers for Publishing, Printing Presses and the Book Trade," Document 162, I, No. 346/DSP," Moscow, June 6, 1975, in *Religion in the Soviet Union: An Archival Reader*, ed. and trans. Felix Corley (New York: New York University Press, 1996), 267–69, 270–73.

3. Boris Roshchin, "Svobody religii i klepki," *Literaturnaia gazeta*, April 13 and 20, 1977. English translation in Fr. Gleb Yakunin and Lev Regel'son, *Letters from Moscow: Religion and Human Rights in the USSR*, ed. Jane Ellis (San Francisco: H. S. Dakin, 1978), 78–83.

4. Roshchin, "Svobody religii," 3, 11.

5. Roshchin, 8.

6. Roshchin, 7.

7. "Excerpts from the Transcript of a Press Conference at the House of Fr. Dmitrii Dudko, April 27, 1977, Referring to articles in *Literaturnaia gazeta*, April 13 and 20, 1977," in Keston Archive Ort 8/2: Yakunin, 1.

8. "Excerpts," 2.
9. "Excerpts," 1–2.
10. "Excerpts," 4.
11. "Excerpts," 3–4.
12. Yakunin estimated attendance at church services at Easter, as well as at Prayers of the Departed, had grown by 25 percent from the previous year ("Excerpts," 4).
13. See the letter written by two sympathizers who wrote in support of Fr. Gleb and other defenders of religious liberty and human rights: Alexei Zalesskii and Irina Zalesskaia, "Appeal to the Christians of Our Country," *Religion in Communist Lands* 4, no. 4 (1980): 292–93; Jane Ellis, "The Christian Committee for the Defense of Believers' Rights in the USSR," *Religion in Communist Lands* 8, no. 4 (1980), 287.
14. Fr. Gleb Yakunin, Hierodeacon Varsonofi Khaibulin, and Viktor Kapitanchuk, "Zaiavlenie Khristianskogo komiteta zashchity prav veruiushchikh v SSSR," December 29, 1977, in *Dokumenty khristianskogo komiteta zashchity prav veruiushchikh v SSSR* (San Francisco: Washington Street Research Center, 1977), 1:3. English translation in *Dokumenty khristianskogo komiteta zashchity prav veruiushchikh v SSSR*, vol. 3: *Izbrannye perevody dokumentov iz tomov 1, 2, 4* (San Francisco: Washington Street Research Center, 1977, 1978), 285.
15. For both Fonchenkov and Gainov, see "Avtobiografiia ottsa Vasiliia Fonchenkova," in *Dokumenty*,10:1077, and "Biograficheskaia spravka sviashchennika o. Nikolaia Gainova," *Russkaia mysl'*, no. 3292 (January 24, 1980), 5.
16. Ellis, "Christian Committee," 288.
17. "Excerpts," 2.
18. This fundamental point was emphasized in the founding of the Committee for the Defense of Believers' Rights in the USSR, specifically "to assist in putting Soviet legislation into practice." "Deklaratsiia," December 30, 1976, in *Dokumenty*, 1:1.
19. *Constitution (Fundamental Law) of the Union of Soviet Socialist Republics, Adopted at the Seventh (Special) Session of the Supreme Soviet of the USSR, Ninth Convocation, on October 7, 1977*, chap. 1, art. 6 (Moscow: Politizdat, 1977), https://constitution.org/cons/ussr77.txt.
20. Gleb Yakunin, Varsonofii Khaibulin, and Viktor Kapitanchuk, "Uvazhaemomu predsedateliu Konstitutsionnoi komissii Brezhnevy Leonidu Il'ichu" June 8, 1977, Moscow, in *Dokumenty*, 1:26–27. English translation in *Dokumenty*, 3:340–41.
21. Jane Ellis, *The Russian Orthodox Church: A Contemporary History* (London: Routledge, 1988), 255.
22. Fr. Gleb Yakunin, Varsonofii Khaibulin, and Viktor Kapitanchuk, "Otkrytoe pis'mo rukovodstvy radioveshchatel'nykh stantsii Golos Ameriki, Bi–Bi–Si, Nemetskaia Volna," November 11, 1977, in *Dokumenty*, 1:37–38; Ellis, *Russian Orthodox Church: A Contemporary History*, 256.
23. Leonard Ternovskii, "Podvig protivostoianiia,"*Posev* 36, no. 1 (1980): 2.
24. Andrei Sakharov, *Memoirs*, trans. Richard Lourie (New York: Alfred A. Knopf, 1990), 499. On the moral challenges the Soviet Union faced, see Philip Boobbyer, *Conscience, Dissent and Reform in Soviet Russia* (London: Routledge, 2005), 222.
25. *Constitution (Fundamental Law) of the Union of Soviet Socialist Republics, 1977*, chap. 1, art. 6.
26. As noted earlier, the KGB had Sakharov under observation for many years. The specific incident that resulted in his arrest was his leadership of a public demonstration protesting the Soviet Union's invasion of Afghanistan.

27. Ellis, *Russian Orthodox Church: A Contemporary History*, 422.

28. Ellis, 422. As Ellis notes, the charge of "forgery" derived from a summer work project in which Popkov and Burtsov supposedly inaccurately filed a worksheet with the foreman; the charge covered up the foreman's illegal assignment of long overtime hours that he had required the two young men to work.

29. "Appeal for the Release of Father Gleb Yakunin," in *Arkhiv Samizdata*, 3853, November 4, 1979, in Keston Archive, SU Ort 8/2: Individual Clergy, box 26, folder 6, Yakunin, Fr. Gleb (1978–1979).

30. Stanislav Zherdev, Anatolii Vlasov, and Nikolai Romanyuk, "'Declaration' (in Support of Fr. Gleb Yakunin)," November 4(?), 1979, in Keston Archive, SU Ort 8/2: Individual Clergy, box 26, folder 6, Yakunin, Fr. Gleb (1978–1979).

31. The announcement of the service appeared in the *Church of England Newspaper*, February 29, 1980, and "Special Service of Prayer for Jailed Russian Christians," *Catholic Herald*, February 29, 1980.

32. "Prayers of Protest in Montreal," *Orthodox Church*, March 1980, 2.

33. A photograph and brief story of this event appeared in the Russian émigré newspaper *Novoye Russkoe Slovo*, February 26, 1980, in Keston Archive, SU Ort 9/4: Western Reactions (1980–2000), box 27, folder 8 (2 of 2).

34. "Einheitlicher christlicher Appell für sowjetischen Priester, Gleb Yakunin," *Neue Zürcher Zeitung*, February 26, 1980.

35. (Anonymous), "Snova o 'dobrykh liudiakh novoi Rusi,'" *Russkaia mysl'* (March 13, 1980), 4.

36. See Oliver Bullough, *The Last Man in Russia: The Struggle to Save a Dying Nation* (New York: Basic Books, 2013), 193–201; Sesil' Vess'e, *Za vashu i nashu svobodu: Dissidentskoe dvizhenie v Rossii* (Moscow: Novoe literaturnoe obozrenie, 2015), 393–95.

37. Fr. Gleb Yakunin, "Doklad Khristianskomu komitetu zashchity prav veruiushchikh v SSSR o sovremennom polozhenii Russkoi Pravoslavnoi Tserkvi i o perspektivakh religioznogo vozrozhdeniia Rossii," August 15, 1979, in *Dokumenty Khristianskogo komiteta zashchity prav veruiushchikh v SSSR* (San Francisco: Washington Street Research Center, 1979), 11:1155–56. English translation (abridged) in Alan Scarfe, ed., *Christian Committee for the Defense of Believers' Rights in the USSR: A Selection of Documents in Translation*, trans. Maria Belaeffa (Glendale, CA: Door of Hope Press, 1982), 23–39.

38. Nicholas Ganson, "Orthodox Dissidence as De-Atomization: Father Dmitrii Dudko and His Battle with *Razobshchennost'*," *Soviet and Post-Soviet Review* 40 (2013): 100–103, 106–7.

Ganson further develops the theme of his earlier piece in his article on Fr. Vsevelod Shpiller, in which the well-known Orthodox priest contended that the inner spiritual life wrongly becomes objectified when it is mixed with political activism (Nicholas Ganson, "Truth Reveals Itself Through Love: Fr. Vsevelod Shpiller's Critique of Aleksandr Solzhenitsyn as a Pastoral Admonition," *Soviet and Post-Soviet Review* [2022]: 1–29, https://doi.org/:10.30965/18763324-BJA10075). See also Seraphim Rose (Father), "In Defense of Father Dimitry Dudko," *Orthodox Word* 92, no. 16 (1980): 115–22, 127–28.

39. Iraida Yakunina, interview by author, Moscow, email, October 28, 2016.

40. Mark Popovskii, *Zhizn' i zhitie Voina-Iasentskogo arkhiepiskopa i khiruga*, 2nd ed. (Tenafly, NJ: Hermitage, 1996). Yakunina, interview by author. Mark Popovskii, born in 1922 in Odesa, fought in World War II. After the war, he began working as a

freelance writer. In 1977, Popovskii emigrated from the Soviet Union, eventually settling in New York (http://www.columbia.edu/cu/web/eresources/archives/rbm/BAR_Popovskii/main.html).

41. Yakunina, interview by author.

42. Yakunina, interview by author.

43. The details of this meeting were recounted by Elena Volkova, a close friend and confidant of Fr. Gleb, interview by author, Moscow, September 11, 2015.

44. Volkova, interview by author, Moscow, September 17, 2016. Whether or not Iraida Georgievna made this decision, as Yakunin claimed, is a matter of dispute. Under the complex circumstances in which he found himself, Yakunin may have decided against confessing his alleged wrongdoing, but attributed this courageous decision to his wife Iraida (Elena Volkova, *Glyba Gleba: Zapreshchenneishii ierei Iakunin* [St. Petersburg: Renome, 2021], 328–29).

45. See Rodric Braithwaite, *Afgantsy: The Russians in Afghanistan, 1979–89* (New York: Oxford University Press, 2011).

46. Radio Free Europe/Radio Liberty, "Poland: Solidarity—The Trade Union That Changed the World," August 24, 2005, https://www.rferl.org/a/1060898.html.

47. CPSU CC Politburo, Protocol No. 210, "Decision Setting Up the Suslov Commission," August 25, 1980, and "Special Dossier on the Polish Crisis of 1980," August 28, 1980, Wilson Center Digital Archive, Library of Congress, Manuscript Division, Dmitriĭ Antonovich Volkogonov papers, 1887–1995, mm97083838, Reel 18, Container 27. Translated by Malcolm Byrne. https://digitalarchive.wilsoncenter.org/document/111230.

Newspapers in the Soviet Union carried no information about the size of the workers' strikes, noting only that the Polish Party and government were actively in combat against certain "negative phenomena" taking place in Poland (David Willis, "Moscow Stays Cool While Polish Order Yields; So Far, Kremlin Keeps Reign on Itself—and Hopes It Can Ride Out Crisis," *Christian Science Monitor*, August 25, 1980, 1).

48. "The Trial of Gleb Yakunin, 25–28 August 1980," *Chronicle of Current Events*, no. 58 (November 1980), https://chronicle-of-current-events.com/2016/01/12/58-3-the-trial-of-gleb-yakunin/.

49. Kevin Klose, "Orlov Trial Opens," *Washington Post*, May 16, 1978.

50. *Criminal Code of the RSFSR* (Washington, DC and Russian SFSR: United States Joint Publication Service, 1961).

51. "Trial of Gleb Yakunin."

52. Lev Regel'son, quoted in "Protsess nad sviashchennikom G. Iakuninym: Po vospominaniia rodnyk i znakomykh," in Keston Archive, SU Ort 8/2: Yakunin Trial (1980), box 50, folder 2 (2 of 2).

53. "Protsess nad sviashchennikom G. Iakuninym."

54. Viktor Popkov, in "Protsess nad sviashchennikom G. Iakuninym," and "Trial of Gleb Yakunin." David Atkinson (1940–2012) served as a conservative member of the UK Parliament and was elected seven times from 1977 to 2005. He often voiced strong criticism of the Soviet Union, in particular on human rights issues, and he played an active role in several international forums that highlighted human rights abuses.

55. When I interviewed him near his office in Sergiev Posad in the summer of 1994, Andrei Il'ich Osipov was serving as head of the Department of Graduate Studies at

the Theological Academy of the Moscow Patriarchy and chief editor of the Orthodox journal *Bogoslovskii Vestnik*. He changed his views to fit the times. He had become a strong nationalist who viewed the church as the central institution in Russia's national identity (Andrei Il'ich Osipov, interview with author, Sergiev Posad, June 11, 1994).

56. A. I. Osipov, in "Protsess nad sviashchennikom G. Iakuninym," and "Trial of Gleb Yakunin," August 25–28, 1980.

57. "Interview with Archimandrite Iosif: Reply to 'Western Propaganda,'" TASS, in Russian for Abroad, September 19, 1980, in Keston Archive, SU Ort 8/2: Yakunin; "Trial of Gleb Yakunin." Shortly after the trial, Archimandrite Iosif gave this interview in order to elaborate on what he had said at the trial and how, he maintained, Western accounts distorted his testimony.

58. "Interview with Archimandrite Iosif."

59. Feliks Karelin in "Protsess nad sviashchennikom G. Iakuninym," and "Trial of Gleb Yakunin." Karelin, the reader will recall, came to Fr. Aleksandr Men's church in the early 1960s, brought there by Yakunin, and was the chief writer of the letters Yakunin and Nikolai Eshliman sent to Patriarch Aleksii I and chair of the Presidium Nikolai Podgorny in 1965.

60. "Trial of Gleb Yakunin." Fr. Krivoi also testified that Fr. Gleb had once sold him an icon.

61. "Trial of Gleb Yakunin." According to the account in *A Chronicle of Current Events*, Yakunin and his associates knew Shushpanov to be a member of the KGB and had written to Patriarch Pimen about his danger to the church.

62. "Trial of Gleb Yakunin."

63. "Trial of Gleb Yakunin."

64. "Trial of Gleb Yakunin."

65. All quotes in this paragraph are from "Protsess nad sviashchennikom G. Iakuninym," and "Trial of Gleb Yakunin."

66. See Nigel Wade's excellent article "Dissident Priest Jailed," *Daily Telegraph*, August 29, 1980, in Keston Archive, SU Ort 8/2: Yakunin.

67. Wallace L. Daniel, "'I Am a Fighter by Nature': Fr. Gleb Yakunin and the Defense of Religious Liberty," in *The Dangerous God: Christianity and the Soviet Experiment*, ed. Dominic Erdozain (DeKalb: Northern Illinois University Press, 2017), 77.

68. Leonid Kolosov, "Komu sluzhil 'otets' Gleb," *Trud*, September 2, 1980.

69. Gregory of Nazianzus, *Select Orations*, trans. Martha Vinson (Washington, DC: Catholic University of America Press, 2003; John A. McGuckin, *St. Gregory of Nazianzus: An Intellectual Biography* (Crestwood NY: St. Vladimir's Seminary Press, 2001.

70. Aleksandr Men', "Poeziia sv. Grigoriia Bogoslova," in *Navstrechu khristu: Sbornik statei*, eds. Nataliia Grigorenko and Pavel Men (Moscow: Zhizn's Bogom, 2009), 7–30, originally published in *Zhurnal Moskovskoi Patriarkhii* 3 (1959): 62–67.

7. The Outcast

1. Nigel Wade, "Dissident Priest Jailed," *Daily Telegraph*, August 29, 1980, in Keston Archive, SU Ort 8/2: Yakunin. The journalist's reporting of Yakunin's case includes information on Velikanova's trial.

2. Andrei Sakharov et al., "Kto osuzhden?" August 29, 1980, *Arkhiv samizdata*, no. 4076, in Keston Archive, SU Ort 8/2: Yakunin.
3. Sakharov et al., "Kto osuzhden?"
4. Igumen Innokentii, "Rasprava," September 1980, p. 1, in *Arkhiv samizdata*, no. 1–6, in Keston Archive, SU Ort 8/2: Yakunin.
5. Igumen Innokentii, 3.
6. Igumen Innokentii, 4–5.
7. Igumen Innokentii, 6.
8. Igumen Innokentii, 6.
9. Sakharov et al., "Kto osuzhden?"
10. Mikhail Evgen'ev, "Prigovor Glebu Iakuninu," TASS, no. 50–54, August 28, 1980, in Keston Archive, SU Ort 8/2: Individual Clergy: Yakunin, box 24, folder 8, 1980.
11. Evgen'ev.
12. Evgen'ev.
13. Both Yakunin's associates, Regel'son and Kapitanchuk, admitted to being willing participants in writing a large number of letters and other documents sent to the West. But neither confessed to any illegal acts or to implicating Fr. Gleb in them.
14. Leonid Kolosov, "Komu sluzhil 'otets' Gleb?" *Trud*, September 2, 1980.
15. Kolosov.
16. Anya Kucherov, interview by author, San Rafael, CA, telephone, July 24, 2020 ; Adriana Dakin, interview by author, Ukiah, CA, Zoom, July 9, 2020.
17. Regel'son actively participated in the student seminars. He attended many of their meetings, and his views on Orthodox Christianity and the importance of the church's social role were shaped by the seminar sessions (Tat'iana Lebedeva, interview by author, Moscow, May 17, 2018). After the arrest of Alexander Ogorodnikov, Regel'son, older in age than most of the other participants, assumed the leadership position in the Christian Seminar. See Jane Ellis, "USSR: The Christian Seminar," *Religion in Communist Lands* 8, no. 2 (Summer 1980), 95–96.
18. Brothers in Christ, "Molodaia Rossiia–K Molodoi Amerike," dated late November to early December 1979, *Arkhiv Samizdata*, no. 4021, in Keston Archive, SU 12/11: Christian Seminar.
19. Vladimir Sergeevich Solov'ev, *God, Man, and the Church: The Spiritual Foundations of Life*, trans. Donald Attwater (1937, repr., London: James Clarke, 2016), xii–xv, 97–103.
20. Fr. Gleb Yakunin and Lev Regel'son, "Appeal to the Delegates of the 5th Assembly of the World Council of Churches," *Religion in Communist Lands* 4, no.1 (Spring 1976), 13.
21. "3,500 Clergy Petition Soviets," *Universe*, October 3, 1980.
22. Michael Bourdeaux, *One Word of Truth: The Cold War Memoir of Michael Bourdeaux and Keston College* (London: Darton, Longman and Todd, 2019), 238–39.
23. Anatolii Levitin-Krasnov, "O tekh, kogo nedavno sudili," *Posev* 36, no. 11 (November 1980), 47. In addition to Yakunin, Levitin-Krasnov included in his article sketches of Fr. Dmitrii Dudko, Lev Regel'son, Aleksandr Ogorodnikov, Tat'iana Velikanova, Tat'iana Shchipkova, and Vladimir Poresh.
24. Orthodox Church of Australia, "In Defense of Fr. Gleb Yakunin," October 7, 1980, in Keston Archive, SU Ort 8/2; Individual Clergy, box 26, folder 7: Yakunin, Fr. Gleb.

25. "Yakunin Appeal," *Keston News Service*, no. 119, March 12, 1981, and "Yakunin Appeal Reportedly Rejected," *Keston News Service*, no. 120, March 26, 1981.

26. Masha Gessen, "Inside the Gulags of the Soviet Union," *Literary Hub*, March 26, 2018, https:lithub.com/masha-gessen-inside-the-gulags-of-the-soviet-union/; and Masha Gessen and Misha Friedman, *Never Remember: Searching for Stalin's Gulags in Putin's Russia* (New York: Columbia Global Reports, 2018), 94.

27. Anne Applebaum, "Tales from the Gulag," World Monuments Fund (Fall 2003), 26.

28. Gessen and Friedman, *Never Remember*, 96.

29. See Colin McMahon, "Grim Prison Restored as a Reminder of Soviet-Era Cruelty," *Chicago Tribune*, July 26, 2000, https:www.chicagotribune.com/news/ct-xpm-2000-07-0007260337-story.html. Yuri Orlov had arrived at Perm no. 37 a year before Yakunin. He penned a graphic description of the physical setting of the camp in *Dangerous Thoughts: Memoirs of a Russian Life*, trans. Thomas P. Whitney [New York: William Morrow, 1991] 236, 238). Yakunin as well as Orlov spent many days in the isolation house and in similar conditions.

30. Orlov, *Dangerous Thoughts*.

31. "Fr. Gleb Yakunin Joins Protest Fast," *Keston News Service*, no. 124, May 21, 1981.

32. Fr. Gleb Yakunin Joins Protest Fast."

33. Anne Applebaum, *Gulag: A History* (New York: Doubleday, 2003), 542–43.

34. This fragment of life and labor in Perm-37 was written by Vardan Arutiunian, an Armenian, who served in the camp during the same period as Yakunin (Elena Ivanovna Volkova, *Glyba Gleba: Zapreshchenneishii ierei Iakunin* [St. Petersburg: Renome, 2021], 353).

35. Volkova, 353.

36. Volkova, 353.

37. The capacity to uphold one's personal dignity and resolve is emphasized in Alexander I. Solzhenitsyn's *One Day in the Life of Ivan Denisovich*, trans. Thomas P. Whitney (New York: Crest, Fawcett, 1963), and *The Gulag Archipelago, 1918–1956: An Experiment in Literary Investigation*, vol. 2, trans. Thomas P. Whitney (New York: Harper and Row, 1974), 656–64; Varlam Shalamov's *Kolyma Tales*, trans. John Glad (London: Penguin, 1994), 210–16; and Orlov, *Dangerous Thoughts*, 253.

38. Response of A. N. Bolshakov, junior counsel, head of the Perm Regional Procuracy, May 28, 1981, quoted by Fr. Gleb Yakunin, "Appeal to Western Christians," *Keston News Service*, no. 135, October 22, 1981.

39. Fr. Gleb Iakunin, "'Zaiavlenie' L. I. Brezhnevu o namerenii nachat' golodovku protesta protiv iz'iatiia i nego i drugikh veriushchikh religioznoi literatury," September 16, 1981, *Samizdat*, no. 4480, in Keston Archive, SU Ort 8/2: Yakunin, Fr. Gleb: Letters of Support (1979–1982), box 50, folder 1.

40. Yakunin, "Appeal."

41. Yakunin.

42. Yakunin.

43. Yakunin.

44. Mahatma Gandhi, *My Soul's Agony* (1933), in Mahatma Gandhi, *The Essential Writings*, ed. and intro. Judith M. Brown, Oxford World Classics, New Edition (Oxford: Oxford University Press, 2008), 224–25.

45. Yakunin, "Appeal."
46. "Priest Is Force-fed," *Church Times*, November 4, 1981.
47. "Fr. Gleb Yakunin Moved to Hospital," *Keston News Service*, no. 136, November 16, 1981; and "News of Fr. Gleb Yakunin's Health," *Keston News Service*, no. 137, November 19, 1981.
48. "Bible Is Returned," *Universe*, February 4, 1983, in Keston Archive, SU Ort 8/2: Yakunin, Fr. Gleb.
49. "Solitary Confinement for Fr. Gleb," *Keston News Service*, no. 166, January 27, 1983.
50. "Solitary Confinement for Fr. Gleb"; "Bible Is Returned"; "Izdevatel'stvo nad pravoslavnym sviashchennikom ottsom Glebom Iakuninym," dictated in the office of Keston College by Anatolii Levitin-Krasnov, August 2, 1982, in Keston Archive, SU Ort 8/2: Yakunin, Fr. Gleb.
51. In February 1973, Baptists in the United States awarded the Religious Freedom Award to the Christian Committee for the Defense of Believers' Rights, with Natal'ia Solzhenitsyn receiving the award on behalf of Fr. Gleb in a ceremony in New York. Later, Yakunin learned that the Church of England's Ross McWhirter Award for civic bravery would be given to him in a ceremony in London. Michael Bourdeaux accepted the award on Fr. Gleb's behalf and 250 British pounds were to be held in trust for Yakunin. *Baptist Times*, February 17, 1983, and *Church of England Newspaper*, April 12, 1985, in Keston Archive, SU Ort 8/2: Yakunin, Fr. Gleb.
52. Bella Bychkova Jordan and Terry G. Jordan-Bychkov, *Siberian Village: Land and Life in the Sakha Republic* (Minneapolis: University of Minnesota Press, 2001), 3–9; and James Forsyth, *A History of the Peoples of Siberia: Russia's North Asian Colony, 1581–1990* (New York: Cambridge University Press, 2008), 167, 194–95, 317–18.
53. "Fr. Gleb in Exile," *Keston News Service*, no. 214, December 6, 1984.
54. "Correction to Fr. Gleb's Exile Address," *Keston News Service*, no. 217, January 24, 1985.
55. Iraida Yakunina, interview with author, Moscow, email, October 28, 2016.
56. Levitin-Krasnov, "Izdevatel'stvo."
57. Elena Volkova, "To vasha Mama," Pamiati ottsa Gleba Yakunina, March 5, 2019, https://www.facebook.com/elenavolkova/posts.
58. Elena Volkova, interview by author, Moscow, September 17, 2016.
59. Volkova, "To vasha Mama." Volkova mentions a nun, Sister Agaf'eia, who also provided the children with significant assistance.
60. Volkova, interview by author, September 17, 2016.
61. Nadezhda Mandelstam, *Hope against Hope: A Memoir*, trans. Max Hayward, with an introduction by Clarence Brown (New York: Atheneum, 1970), 33.
62. Volkova, interview by author, September 12, 2015.
63. Gleb Pavlovich Yakunin, *Khvalebnyi primitiv iurodivyi, v chest' Boga, mirozdan'ia, rodiny: Poema*, with an introductory article by Elena Volkova (Moscow: Biblioteka Prav-Lit, 2008).
64. Yakunin, *Khvalebnyi primitiv*, 11.
65. Mariia Glebovna Yakunina, interview by author, May 23, 2018, Moscow.
66. Elena Volkova, "Poeticheskii manifest Pravoslavnoi reformatsii," in Yakunin, *Khvalebnyi primitivi*, 6.

67. Volkova, "Poeticheskii manifest," 6.
68. Volkova, 34–36.
69. Volkova, 40.
70. Yakunin, *Khvalebnyi primitiv*, 34–35.
71. Protoierei Aleksandr Borisov, "Dukhovnyi realizm ottsa Aleksandra Menia," in *Tserkovnaia zhizn' XX veka: Protoierei Aleksandr Men' i ego dukhovnie nastavniki: Sbornik materialov Pervoi nauchnoi konferentsii. "Menevskie chteniia (9–11 Sentiabria 2006 g.),"* ed. M. V. Grigorenko (Sergiev Posad: Izdanie prikhoda Sergievskoi tserkvi v Semkhoze, g. Sergiev Posad, 2007), 167.
72. Yakunin, *Khvalebnyi primitiv*, 35.
73. Yakunin, 35.
74. Yakunin, 22.
75. Yakunin, 109.
76. Yakunin, 114.
77. Yakunin, 97.
78. Yakunin, 88, 90–91. Yakunin quoted Iudushka Golovyov in Saltykov-Shchedrin's novel *The Golovyov Family*, who remarked that the Russian clergyman is "very devout, but in his affairs, he is ungodly, and in the lives of our native clergy, the spiritual is not primary" (Yakunin, *Khvalebnyi primitiv*, 90; and Volkova, "Poeticheskii manifest," 8).
79. Yakunin, *Khvalebnyi primitiv*, 88.
80. Yakunin, 42, 44, 52, 115.

8. Return

1. The rapidly shifting political landscape in the late 1980s and afterward is documented and analyzed in Geoffrey Hosking, *The Awakening of the Soviet Union* (Cambridge, MA: Harvard University Press, 1990); William Taubman, *Gorbachev: His Life and Times* (New York: W. W. Norton, 2017); Stephen F. Cohen, *The Victims Return: Survivors of the Gulag After Stalin* (Bloomsbury: I. B. Tauris, 2011); Geraldine Fagan, *Believing in Russia: Religious Policy after Communism* (London: Routledge, 2013); Irina Papkova, *The Russian Orthodox Church and Russian Politics* (New York: Oxford University Press, 2011); John Matlock, *Autopsy of an Empire: The American Ambassador's Account of the Collapse of an Empire* (New York: Random House, 1995); and Archie Brown, *Seven Years That Changed the World: Perestroika in Perspective* (Oxford: Oxford University Press, 2007).

2. Gleb Pavlovich Yakunin, *Khvalebnyi primitiv iurodivyi, v chest' Boga, mirozdan'ia, rodiny: Poema*, with an introductory article by Elena Volkova (Moscow: Biblioteka Prav-Lit, 2008), 17.

3. Richard Sakwa, *Russian Politics and Society*, 3rd ed. (London: Routledge, 2002), 9–13.

4. Taubman, *Gorbachev*, 353.

5. Mikhail Gorbachev, *Perestroika: New Thinking for Our Country and the World* (New York: Harper and Row, 1987), 91.

6. Sergii Chetverikov, *Optina Pustyn'*, 2nd ed. (Paris: YMCA Press, 1988), 81–82,84–85, 89, 101 ; Leonard J. Stanton, *The Optina Pustyn Monastery in the Russian Literary Imagination: Iconic Vision in the Works by Dostoevsky, Gogol, Tolstoy, and Others* (New York: Peter Lang, 1955), 81–82, 89, 101, 251.

7. Quoted in Michael Bourdeaux, *Gorbachev, Glasnost, and the Gospel* (London: Hodder and Stoughton, 1990), 44; see also Wallace L. Daniel, *The Orthodox Church and Civil Society in Russia* (College Station: Texas A&M University Press, 2006), 36.

8. Mikhail Vital'evich Shkarovskii, *Russkaia Pravoslavnaia Tserkov' v XX veka* (Moscow: Veche, Lepta, 2010), 404.

9. Shkarovskii, 406.

10. Yakunin, *Khvalebnyi primitiv*, 93, 111, 117. Wallace L. Daniel, "'I Am a Fighter by Nature': Fr. Gleb Iakunin and the Defense of Religious Liberty," in *The Dangerous God: Christianity and the Soviet Experiment*, ed. Dominic Erdozain (DeKalb: Northern Illinois University Press, 2017), 95.

11. A. Iu. Poslykhalin, *Istoriia gorodakh Shchyolkovo: Almanakh internet-zhurnala "Podmoskovnyi kraeved"* (Moscow: Akademizdat'sentr "Nauka," RAN, 2015), 5–6.

12. Georgii Rovenskii, *Gleb Iakunin (1934–2014): Pravoslavnyi pravozashchitnik, sviashchennik, deputat, poet* (Shchyolkovo: Shchyolkovskii kraevedcheskii klub, 2021), 8, 92–93.

13. Rovenskii, *Gleb Iakunin*, 8; and Poslykhalin, *Isoriia gorodakh*, 15–16. Shchyolkovo developed from the merger of four settlements and villages, including the village of Zhegalovo, where St. Nicholas Cathedral was located.

14. Natal'ia Pavlova, "Dolgaia doroga v mart," *Moskovskie novosti*, March 4, 1990.

15. Pavlova.

16. Evgeny Barabanov, "The Schism between the Church and the World," in *From Under the Rubble*, ed. Alexander Solzhenitsyn, trans. A. M. Brock et al., under the direction of Michael Scammell, intro. Max Hayward (Boston: Little, Brown, 1974), 176.

17. Pavlova, "Dolgaia doroga."

18. V. Kuzmenkii, "V poiskakh putevodnoi zvezdy: Inter'viu s Glebom Iakuninym," *Vechernii Novosibirsk*, August 14, 1990. A prominent human rights defender, author, and dissident, Anatoly Tikhonovich Marchenko (1938–1986) died during a hunger strike while in prison in Chistopol, Tatarstan. See Marchenko's autobiography, *My Testimony*, trans. Michael Scammell (New York: E. P. Dutton, 1969).

19. Sakwa, *Russian Politics and Society*, 141.

20. Sakwa, 141.

21. Oxana Antic, "The Russian Orthodox Church Moves towards Coming to Terms with Its Past," *RFE/RL, Report on the USSR* (March 8, 1991): 4.

22. Antic, "Russian Orthodox Church." One of these voices, the outspoken critic of the church's past complicity, Zoia Krakhmal'nikova, forcefully argued that church leaders had to admit their complicity with the police authorities. The regeneration of the church, she said, would only take place "when believers learn the whole truth about their pastors, who at the present are trying are trying to conceal this truth" (Zoia Krakhmal'nikova, "Skandal v blagorodnom semeistve: Prodolzhenie sleduet," *Stolitsa*, no. 14 (1992), 10.

23. Pavlova, "Dolgaia doroga."

24. Pavlova.

25. James J. Sheehan, "How History Can Be a Moral Science," in *Perspectives on History*, October 2005, https://www.historians.org/publications-and-directories/perspectives-on-history/october-2005/how-history-can-be-a-moral-science. In 2005, Sheehan served as president of the American Historical Association. His remarks followed those of his former teacher and colleague Gordon Wright, whose presidential address to the

American Historical Association in 1975, "History as a Moral Science," had stimulated a great deal of discussion about the moral lessons of history and whether historians should render moral judgments.

26. Petr L. Vail and Aleksandr A. Genis, *60-x: Mir sovetskogo cheloveka* (Ann Arbor, MI: Ardis, 1988), 180. Philip Boobbyer similarly emphasized this point in his *Conscience, Dissent and Reform in Soviet Russia* (London: Routledge, 2005), 223.

27. See Vladimir Nabokov, *Nikolai Gogol* (New York: New Directions, 1961); and Dian Laily Rachmawati, "Leo Tolstoy's Idea of Morality in His Short Stories' Characters," *Litera kultura* 2, no. 2 (2014): 1–18, https://cupdf.com>Documents.

28. Aleksandr Men', "Poeziia Sv. Grigoriia Bogoslova," in Men', *Navstrechu khristu: Sbornik statei*, ed. Nataliia Grigorenko and Pavel Men (Moscow: Zhizn's Bogom, 2009), 7–30, originally published in *Zhurnal Moskovskoi Patriarkhii* 3 (1959): 62–67; Aleksei Vasil'evich Govorov, *Sv. Grigorii Bogoslov, kak khristianskii poet 1886* (1886; repr., New York: Generic, 2019).

29. Kuzmenkii, "V poiskakh putevodnoi zvezdy."

30. R. Safarov, "Looking Around at the Pass," in *Perils of Perestroika: Viewpoints from the Soviet Press, 1989–1991*, ed. Isaac J. Tarasulo (Wilmington, DE: Scholarly Resources, 1992), 77. Safarov's article appeared in *Pravda* on July 28, 1990.

31. Patriarch Aleksi II, quoted by Serge Schmemann, "An Awakened Church Finds Russia Searching for Its Soul," *New York Times*, April 26, 1992, section 4.

32. Yevgenia Albats, *The State within a State: The KGB and Its Hold on Russia—Past, Present, and Future*, trans. Catherine A. Fitzpatrick (New York: Farrar, Straus and Giroux, 1994), 314. The church's connections to the KGB will be examined in chapter 9.

33. The symposium on "The Individual and Mass Consciousness" represented the third of a series of international conferences, cosponsored by the Catholic Academy of the episcopate of Rottenburg-Stuttgart and the Russian journal *Inostrannaia literatura* and held in the German town of Weingarten in May 1989. The materials of the three symposia can be found in *Inostrannaia literatura*, no. 5 (1989): 203–24; no. 5 (1990): 177–201; and no. 11 (1990): 203–22.

34. "Individual'noe i massovoe soznanie," *Inostrannaia litertura*, no. 11 (1990): 205.

35. "Individual'noe i massovoe soznanie," 213.

36. "Individual'noe i massovoe soznanie," 213.

37. See Jane Ellis's analysis of the 1929 law on religious associations and its social effects in *The Russian Orthodox Church: A Contemporary History* (1986; repr., London and New York: Routledge, 1988), 42–48.

38. According to Konstantin Kharchev, chair of the Council for Religious Affairs, six offices participated in the preparation and review of the new Soviet law: the Council for Religious Affairs, the Ministry of Justice, the Ministry of Foreign Affairs, the Committee for State Security (KGB), the Ministry of the Interior, and the state's prosecutor's office. Aleksandr Nezhnyi, "Treti razgovor s Kharchevem," *Ogonek* no. 44, October 1989, 11; and Nathaniel Davis, *A Long Walk to Church: A Contemporary History of Russian Orthodoxy*, 2nd ed. (Boulder, CO: Westview Press, 2003), 284n78.

39. See Giovanni Codevilla, "Commentary on the New Soviet Law on Freedom of Conscience and Religious Organizations," *Religion in Communist Lands* 19, nos. 1–2 (Summer 1991), 119. Codevilla provides the text of the Soviet law, published in *Pravda* on October 9, 1990.

40. Jane Ellis, *The Russian Orthodox Church: Triumphalism and Defensiveness* (New York: St. Martin's Press, 1996), 159–60.

41. Richard Sakwa, "Christian Democracy in Russia," *Religion, State and Society* 20, no. 2 (1992), 138–40. See Sakwa's informative history of Christian Democracy in Russia, its hope to develop civil society, and its desire to rebuild the political and economic structures in Russia. Richard Sakwa, "Christian Democracy and Civil Society in Russia," *Religion, State and Society* 22, no. 3 (1994): 273–303.

42. Yakunin served on the Committee on Freedom of Conscience, Denominations, Welfare, and Charity (Komitet po svobode sovesti, veroispovedaniyam, miloserdiiu i blagotvoritel'nosti). Fr. Polosin served as official chair.

43. The concurrent existence of the Russian and Soviet laws led to what Jane Ellis referred to as a "war of laws," in which Russian citizens remained uncertain over which to follow (Ellis, *Russian Orthodox Church: Triumphalism*, 163).

44. Harold J. Berman, *Justice in the USSR: An Interpretation of Soviet Law*, rev. ed. (New York: Vintage, 1963), 284.

45. See Jane Ellis's discussion of Konstantin Kharchev: "Some Reflections about Religious Policy under Kharchev," in *Religious Policy in the Soviet Union*, ed. Sabrina Petra Ramet (New York: Cambridge University Press, 1993), 90. Kharchev served as chair of the Council for Religious Affairs until June 1989.

46. Codevilla, "Commentary," 119.

47. On this question of independence, the Russian and Soviet laws affirmed the right of individuals to make their own judgment about religious belief without state interference. See Codevilla, "Commentary," 130. See also Anatolii Levitin-Krasnov's optimistic perspectives on religious life in the Soviet Union following his return in April 1990, after twenty-four years in forced emigration. While positive about the Soviet Union's casting aside the Stalinist framework, he nevertheless viewed his former country as standing on the edge of a precipice (Nadezhda Beliakova, "'I sviashchennik stanovitsia dobrym gostem v sovetskom obshchestve . . .': Religioznaia zhizn' Moskvy i Podmoskov'ia vesnoi 1990 goda v opisanii A. E. Levitina-Krasnova," *Istoricheskii kur'er* 2 [10], 2020]: 215–25, https://doi.org/10.31518/2618-9100-2020-2-17).

48. Codevilla, "Commentary," 130.

49. Codevilla, 130; Zakon Rossiiskoi Sovetskoi Federativnoi Sotsialiticheskoi Respubliki, "O svobode veroispovedanii," part 1, article 5, in *Sovetskaia Rossiia*, November 10, 1990.

50. See Codevilla, "Commentary," 131.

51. The 1990 Soviet law set forth a similar statement, although it did not underscore the right to atheistic teaching in the home, as proclaimed in the 1990 Russian law (Codevilla, "Commentary," 121, 134).

52. Zakon Rossiiskoi Sovetskoi Federativnoi, "O svobode veroispovedanii," part 1, article 21, *Sovetskaia Rossiia*, part 1, article 6.

53. Zakon Rossiiskoi Sovetskoi Federativnoi, "O svobode veroispovedanii"; and Codevilla, "Commentary," 121, 138–39.

54. Ellis, *Russian Orthodox Church: Triumphalism*, 160.

55. Liudmila Mikhailovna Vorontsova, "Razrushat' li muzei radi tserkovnogo vozrozhdeniia?" in *Religiia i demokratiia: Na puti k svobode sovesti*, vol. 2, ed. S. B. Filatov and D. E. Furman (Moscow: "Progress—Kul'tura,"1993), 69–82; Sergei Borisovich Filatov,

"Russkaia Pravoslovnaia Tserkov' i politicheskaia elita," in *Religiia i politika v postkommunisticheskoi Rossii*, ed. L. N. Mitrokhin (Moscow: Institut filosofii RAN, 1994), 108–9. Both Vorontsova and Filatov vividly portrayed the dilemmas involved in the process, particularly those related to the return of valuables.

56. Daniel, *Orthodox Church and Civil Society*, 56–59.

57. Filatov, "Russkaia Pravoslovnaia Tserkov'," 108–9.

58. Polosin's opening speech was published in *Sovetskaia Rossiia*, September 30, 1990.

59. For the vote and an account of the parliament chair Ruslan Khasbulatov's belief that the law needed to move forward quickly and with the support of a large majority of the deputies, see Ellis, *Russian Orthodox Church: Triumphalism*, 162.

60. Yakunin's comments were published in the stenographic account of the draft law's first reading, in *Sovetskaia Rossiia*, September 30, 1990.

61. Mariia Glebovna Yakunina, interview by author, Moscow, May 23, 2018.

62. See the comments by Deputy A. P. Surkov, from the Panfilovskii district of Moscow, during the first reading of the proposed new law, in *Sovetskaia Rossiia*, September 30, 1990. See also the comments of M. L. Malei, from the Pervomaiskii district of Moscow in the first session (*Sovetskaia Rossiia*, September 30, 1990).

63. Czesław Miłosz, *The Captive Mind*, trans. Jane Zielonko (1951; repr., New York: Vintage International, Random House, 1990), 175, 199.

64. Fr. Gleb Yakunin, "V sluzhenii kul'tu (Moskovskaia Patriarkhiia i kult' lichnosti Stalina)" in *Na puti k svobode sovesti*, ed. D. E. Furman and Fr. Mark (Smirnov) (Moscow: Progress, 1989), 172–206.

65. Yakunin, "V sluzhenii kul'tu," 173.

66. Yakunin, 174.

67. For more recent research on the complexities of the challenges facing Patriarch Tikhon and his attempted resolutions of them, see the observations of Scott M. Kenworthy, "Rethinking the Russian Orthodox Church and the Bolshevik Revolution," *Revolutionary Russia*, https://doi.org/10.1080/09546545.2018.1480893.

68. Yakunin, "V sluzhenii kul'tu," 184.

69. Yakunin, 193; citing Sviashchennik M. Zernov, "Moskva," *Zhurnal Moskovskoi Patriarkhii*, no. 10 (1947): 11–12.

70. Yakunin, "V sluzhenii kul'tu," 193.

71. Yakunin, 201. The church's seeming indifference to these holy martyrs offered clear proof, Yakunin said, of its spiritual apathy about one of the richest sources of moral regeneration in the church's treasury. Instead of spiritual connections to the martyrs, in its recent history, the church exhibited spiritual solidarity with their persecutors.

72. Fr. Gleb Yakunin, Viktor Kapitanchuk, and Lev Regel'son, "Appeal for the Glorification of Russian Martyrs in the USSR," May 25, 1975, in Fr. Gleb Yakunin and Lev Regel'son, *Letters from Moscow: Religion and Human Rights in the Soviet Union*, ed. Jane Ellis (San Francisco: H. S. Dakin, 1978), 34–40.

73. Yakunin, Kapitanchuk, and Regel'son, "Appeal for the Glorification," 35.

74. Yakunin, Kapitanchuk, and Regel'son, 35.

75. Yakunin, "V sluzhenii kul'tu," 203.

76. Yakunin, 203.

9. Lifting the Cover

1. "Zoia Krakhmal'nikova," in Xenia Dennen papers, Keston Archive, Soviet Union, Orthodox Subject Files; and Michael Bourdeaux, "Zoia Krakhmal'nikova," *Guardian*, May 12, 2008.

2. The authorities offered Krakhmal'nikova clemency if she agreed to sign papers stating she would no longer violate official policies, an agreement she refused to sign. After some delay, she was allowed to return to Moscow. Her husband, who had joined her in exile, was similarly released. "Zoia Krakhmal'nikova," in Xenia Dennen papers, Keston Archive.

3. Zoia Aleksandrovna Krakhmal'nikova, *Gor'kie plody sladkogo plena* (Montreal: Monastery Press, 1989), 10. As a spiritual daughter of Fr. Dmitrii Dudko, Krakhmal'nikova, whether in prison, the labor camp, or everyday life, maintained a constant "struggle for freedom," which she believed was a central theme of Orthodox Christianity. See Iakov Krotov, "S khristianskoi tochki zreniia," interview with Krakhmal'nikov's daughter Zoia Feliksovna Svetova and the writer and poet Vladimir Il'ich Iliushenko, http://krotov.info.library/17_r/radio_svoboda/20090117.htm; and Vladimir Iliushenko, "Geroi dukhovnogo soprotivleniia," https://old.prison.org/personal/krakmalnikova.shtml.

4. Krakhmal'nikova, *Gor'kie plody*, 10.

5. Iurii Sergeevich Sidorenko, *Tri dnia, kotorye oprokinuli bol'shevism: Ispoved' svidetelia, pokazaniia ochevidtsa* (Rostov-na-Donu: Izdatel'stvo Periodika Dona, 1991), 31; and James H. Billington, *Russia Transformed: Breakthrough to Hope, Moscow, August 1991* (New York: Free Press, 1992), 127–28. For a concise analysis of religion and the end of the Soviet government, see Michael Bourdeaux, "The Role of Religion in the Collapse of Communism," *Archiva Moldoviae* 5 (2013): 335–42.

6. "After the Coup," *Frontier*, September–October 1991, 15.

7. Vera Tolz, "Access to KGB and CPSU Archives in Russia," *RFE/RL Research Report* 1, no. 16 (April 17, 1992), 1.

8. Tolz, 1.

9. "Lev Ponomarov, "Za prava cheloveka," https://lenta.ru/lib/14163044. Ponomarov was also a member of the Helsinki Human Rights Watch and a founder of Memorial, the human rights organization created to honor the persecuted in the Soviet Union.

10. For biographical information on Fr. Viacheslav, see https:discoveringislam.org/dr_polosin.htm. See also Ali Viacheslav Polosin, "My Journey to Islam," https://www.islam.ru/en/content/story/polosin-ali-vyacheslav-my-journey-islam.

11. Iakov Krotov, "Religion and the Russian Press Since 1990: Journalists Most Actively Writing on Church Subjects," *East-West Church and Ministry Report* 10, no. 3 (Summer 2002): 10–13.

12. Aleksandr Nezhnyi, "Tret'e imia," *Ogonek* 4, January 25–February 1, 1992, 2–3.

13. Sergei Sergeevich Bychkov, *Sviashchennik Gleb Iakunin. Nelegkii put' pravdoiskatelia* (Moscow: Eksmo, 2021), 325.

14. Konstantin Mikhailovich Kharchev (b. 1934, in Gorky [Nizhnii Novgorod]), served as Soviet ambassador to Guyana and awaited an ambassadorship to the United Arab Emirates before he was appointed, in December 1984, to the chairmanship of the Council for Religious Affairs.

See Aleksandr Nezhnyi, "Tretii razgovor s Kharchevem," *Ogonek*, no. 44, October 1989, 9–11; John B. Dunlop, "KGB Subversion of the Russian Orthodox Church," *RFE/RL Research Report* 1, no. 12 (March 20, 1992), 51; Jane Ellis, "Some Reflections about Religious Policy under Kharchev," in *Religious Policy in the Soviet Union*, ed. Sabrina Petra Ramet (Cambridge: Cambridge University Press, 1993), 84–104.

15. "Govorit' vsiu pravdu—edinstvennyi put' Tserkovi," po materialam presskonferentsii v redaktsii zhurnal *Stolitsa*, posviashchennoi polozheniiu RPTs," *Stolitsa* 19, no. 2 (1992), quoted in Bychkov, *Sviashchennik Gleb Iakunin,*, 396.

16. Lev Ponomarev believed that this meeting resulted in Khasbulatov's decision to abort the commission's access to KGB archives (Aleksandr Nezhnyi, "Kamo griadeshi, sviataia tserkov'," *Ogonek*, nos. 18–19, May 1992, 12; and Yevgenia Albats, *The State within a State: The KBG and Its Hold on Russia: Past, Present, and Future*, trans. Catherine A. Fitzpatrick [New York: Farrar, Straus and Giroux, 1994], 314).

17. V. I. Lenin, quoted by Fr. Viacheslav Polosin, "Vechnyi rab ChK," *Izvestiia*, January 22, 1992.

18. Tsentral'nyi Arkhiv KGB, f. 6, op. 6/16, d. T-175, t. 1, l. 291, March 1983, in Keston Archive, SU Ort: Yakunin, Fr. Gleb (1991–1996), folder 4. Printed copies of Fr. Gleb's notes on his research in KGB archives may also be found on Iakov Krotov's website, http://krotov.info/4/texts/03_v/Vypiski_1992.htm.

19. Polosin, "Vechnyi rab." Polosin's citation of the fourth dream of Vera Pavlova referred to the most radical part of Nikolai Chernyshevsky's novel *What Is to Be Done?* (1863).

Her fourth dream is a modification of the European utopian ideal of the Crystal Palace and a society in which phalansteries, grand hotels that housed workers, and equality of the sexes predominated.

20. Polosin, "Vechnyi rab."

21. Mariia Glebovna Yakunina, interview by author, Moscow, May 23, 2018. Yakunin's attitude is confirmed by an example discussed later in this chapter.

22. Gleb Yakunin, "Abbat' vykhodit na sviaz '," interview by P. Vasil'ev, *Argumenty i fakty*, no. 1, January 8, 1992.

23. Nezhnyi, "Tret'e imia," 3.

24. Nezhnyi, 3.

25. Yakunin did not disclose "Drozdov" in his public revelation of the code names of agents. According to the English journalist Bruce Clark, Yakunin may have thought the patriarch a more enlightened leader and proponent of reform than the others whose names he revealed (Bruce Clark, *An Empire's New Clothes: The End of Russia's Liberal Dream* [London: Viking, 1995], 112). Moreover, as the newly elected patriarch, Aleksii II, represented to Yakunin a promising break from his predecessor Patriarch Pimen.

26. Nathaniel Davis, *A Long Walk to Church: A Contemporary History of Russian Orthodoxy*, 2nd ed. (Boulder, CO: Westview Press, 2003), 86.

27. Tsentral'nyi Arkhiv KGB, f. 1, op. 1, d. 360, l. 6, in Keston Archive, SU Ort: Yakunin, Fr. Gleb (1991–1996), folder 4.

28. A copy of the official document honoring Aleksii II by the KGB is published in Nezhnyi, "Kamo griadeshi," 13.

29. Albats, *State within a State*, 46.

30. "Dokumenty KGB," Tsentral'nyi Arkhiv KGB, February1984, f. 6, op. 7/16, U–175, t. 2, l. 163, in Keston Arhive, SU Ort: Yakunin, Fr. Gleb (1989–1993), folder 4.

31. "Dokumenty KGB," Tsentral'nyi Arkhiv KGB, February1984.

32. "Dokumenty KGB," Tsentral'nyi Arkhiv KGB, August 1988, f. 6, op.11, d. U–175, t. 3, l. 75, in Keston Archive, SU Ort: Yakunin, Fr. Gleb (1989–1993), box 50, folder 4; and Koenraad de Wolf, *Dissident for Life: Alexander Ogorodnikov and the Struggle for Religious Freedom in Russia*, trans. Nancy Forest-Flier, foreword David Alton (Grand Rapids, MI, 2010: Eerdmans), 199.

33. "Report on the Results of the Organisational and Agent-Operational Activity of the 4th Department of the 5th Directorate of the KGB," January 1986, in *Religion in the USSR: An Archival Reader*, ed. and trans. Felix Corley (New York: New York University Press, 1996), 375.

34. *Religion in the USSR: An Archival Reader*, 375.

35. Wallace L. Daniel, *Russia's Uncommon Prophet: Father Aleksandr Men and His Times* (DeKalb: Northern Illinois University Press, 2016), 232–33.

36. "Report on the Work of the 4th Department," January 1977, in *Religion in the USSR*, 365.

37. "Dokumenty KGB," Tsentral'nyi Arkhiv KGB, June 1988, f. 6, op. 10, d. Ts–175, t. 2, l. 111, in Keston Archive, SU Ort: Yakunin, Fr. Gleb (1989–1993), box 50, folder 4.

38. The KGB's report referred to the case of Fr. Georgii Edel'stein, "Dokumenty KGB," Tsentral'nyi Arkhiv KGB, June 1988, f. 6, op. 11, d. Z–175, t. 1, l. 239, in Keston Archive, SU Ort: Yakunin, Fr. Gleb (1989–1993), box 50, folder 4.

39. "Dokumenty KGB," Tsentral'nyi Arkhiv KGB, June 1988.

40. Tsentral'nyi Arkhiv KGB, f. 1, op. 5, d. 360, l. 32, January 1973, in Keston Archive, SU Ort: Fr. Gleb Yakunin (1989–1993), box 50, folder 4.

41. Tsentral'nyi Arkhiv KGB, f. 6, op. 6/16, d. T–175, t. 4, l. 256, October 1983; f. 6, op. 7/16, d. Y–175, t. 2, l. 32, January 1984; and f. 6, op. 12, d. Sh–175, t. 2, l. 233, July 1989, l. 32, in Keston Archive, SU Ort: Fr. Gleb Yakunin (1989–1993), box 50, folder 4.

42. Tsentral'nyi Arkhiv KGB, f. 6, op. 12, d. Sh–175, t. 2, l. 233, July 1989. Lieutenant-Colonel Evgenii Dmitrievich Kubyshkin, head of the 4th Department of the 5th Directorate of the KGB of the KGB, submitted the report to the Soviet Council of Ministers.

43. See Zoe Krakhmal'nikova, "Bliud uma: Revoliutsiia vsegda sut' iazycheskii bunt protiv Khrista," *Nezavisimaia gazeta*, January 10, 1992; Aleksandr Men', *Russkaia religioznaia filosofiia: Lektsii*, ed. Marina Nasonova (Moscow: Khram sviatykh bessrebrenikov Kosmy i Damiana v Shubine, 2003); Boris Viktorovich Raushenbakh, "Religiia i nravstvennost'," *Znamia*, no. 1 (January 1991): 204–16; and Dmitrii Sergeevich Likhachev, "Russkaia kul'tura: nasledie proshloe i real'naia sila segodnia," no. 24, *Sem'ia* 24 (June 15, 1988): 14–15.

44. Nezhnyi, "Tret'e imia," 2.

45. Nezhnyi, 3. For the security police's infiltration of the church in Ukraine and the delegation the police sent to the Church Council held soon after World War II, see Mark Krutov, "Episkopy na sluzhbe Lubianki: Istorii ierarkhoi ukrainskoi tserkvi, zaverbovannykh NKGB SSSR," January 23, 2018, https://www.svoboda.org/a/28989881.html.

46. Aleksandr Nezhnyi, "Ego blazhenstvo bez mitry i zhezla," *Ogonek* no. 48, November 1991, 8–10 and no. 49, December 1991, 21–22.

47. Nezhnyi, "Ego blazhenstvo," no. 48, 8–9 and no. 49, 20.

48. Nezhnyi, no. 49, 21.

49. Nezhnyi, no. 49, 21.

50. Nezhnyi, no. 49, 21.

51. Nezhnyi, "Tret'e imia," 2.

52. Nezhnyi, 2.

53. Nezhnyi, 3.

54. Bychkov, *Sviashchennik Gleb Iakunin*, 327.

55. Khrizostom (Martishkin), Archbishop of Vilnius and Lithuania, "Ia sotrudnichal s KGB . . . no ne byl stukachem," interview by Mikhail Pozdniaev, *Russkaia mysl'*, no. 3926 (April 24, 1992): 8–9.

56. Khrizostom (Martishkin), "Ia sotrudnichal," 8.

57. Khrizostom (Martishkin), "Ia sotrudnichal," 8.

58. Khrizostom (Martishkin), 8.

59. The biographical information on Archbishop Khrizostom is drawn from his later interview "Ia dobrovol'no sotrudnichal s KGB," *Moskovskii komsomolets*, November 30, 1993, parts of which are published in Bychkov, *Sviashchennik Gleb Iakunin*, 396–97.

60. Khrizostom (Martishkin), "Ia sotrudnichal," 8–9.

61. Khrizostom (Martishkin), 8–9.

62. Fr. Georgii Edel'stein, "Chekisty . . . v riasakh," interview by P. Lik'ianchenko," *Argumenty i fakty*, no. 36, September 12, 1991.

63. Yakunin, "Abbat' vykhodit na sviaz'."

64. John P. Burgess, *Holy Rus': The Rebirth of Orthodoxy in the New Russia* (New Haven, CT: Yale University Press, 2017), 8–23.

65. Khrizostom (Martishkin), "Ia sotrudnichal," 8–9.

66. In his later study of Orthodox priests, Ralph Della Cava drew important distinctions among members of the Russian Orthodox clergy, "Reviving Orthodoxy in Russia: An Overview of the Factions in the Russian Orthodox Church in the Spring of 1996," *Cahiers du Monde russe* 38, no. 3 (1997): 387–414.

67. A. Shushpanov, "Ispoved' byvshego agenta," interview by P. Luk'ianchenko, *Argumenty i fakty*, no. 8, February 26, 1992.

68. All the translators submitted five copies of each report. The first, Shushpanov said, "we left on the desk of the chairperson of the Department for External Relations of the Moscow Patriarchate (formerly Metropolitan Nikodim, later Metropolitan Yuvenalii), a second we sent to the Council for Religious Affairs, which was affiliated with the secret police, and the three remaining copies we provided for the KGB" (Shushpanov, "Ispoved' byvshego agenta").

69. Asked about his coworkers in the department, Shushpanov said that the majority of them either worked for the KGB or were allies of the agency. The Department for External Church Relations had a resident official of the KGB named "Colonel Vladimirov," whose real name was Aleksei Alekseevich Pogodin. "Colonel Vladimirov" arranged the special assignments for employees in the department (Shushpanov, "Ispoved' byvshego agenta").

70. Shushpanov.

71. Shushpanov.

72. "Vyvody Komissii: Ispol'zovanie TsK KPSS i KGB SSSR religioznykh organizatsii v antikonstitutsionnykh tseliakh" and "Chastnoe opredelenie Komissii Prezidenta Verkhovnogo Soveta Rossiisskoi Federatsii po rassledovaniiu prichin i obstoiatel'stv GKChP," March 6, 1992.

Typewritten copies in Keston Archive, SU Ort: Yakunin, Fr. Gleb (1989–1993), box 50, folder 4.

73. "Vyvody Komissii."

74. "Vyvody Komissii."

75. "Vyvody Komissii," 2.

76. "Vyvody Komissii," 2.

77. "Vyvody Komissii," 3.

78. "Vyvody Komissii," 5–6.

79. Jane Ellis, *Russian Orthodox Church: Triumphalism and Defensiveness* (New York: St. Martin's Press, 1996), 150–51.

80. Ellis, 150.

81. Ellis, 150–51. The pragmatic benefits of this church-state partnership could already be seen. In June 1991, during the inauguration ceremony in the Moscow Kremlin, President Yeltsin invited Patriarch Aleksii II to sit on the dais beside him as he took the presidential oath, and he had sought the patriarch's traditional blessing on the eve of his first presidential visit to the United States (Sergei Borisovich Filatov, "Russkaia Pravoslavnaia Tserkov' i politicheskaia elita," in *Religiia i politika v postkommunisticheskoi Rossii*, ed. L. N. Mitrokhin [Moscow: Institut filosofii RAN, 1994], 103); and "Yeltsin Attends Sunday Church Services," *Summary of World Broadcasts* 1408 B/1 (June 16, 1992).

82. Krakhmal'nikova, *Gor'kie plody*, 23.

83. Khrizostom (Martishkin), "Ia sotrudnichal," 8–9.

84. Michael Dobbs, "In Hard Times, No Time to Hunt Down KGB Agents," *International Herald Tribune*, February 12, 1992.

85. Clark, *Empire's New Clothes*, 112.

86. Sergei Borisovich Filatov, interview by author, Moscow, June 15, 1994.

87. Sergei Borisovich Filatov, "Pravoslavie v kontekste postkommunizma: 'Gosudarstvennaia tserkov" i svoboda sovesti," *Vek XX i mir* 1 (1992), 39. See also Filatov's "Russkaia Pravoslavnaia Tserkov ' i politicheskaia elita," in *Religiia i politika v postkommunicheskoi Rossii*, ed. L. N. Mitrokhin (Moscow: Institut filosofii RAN, 1994), 98–118.

88. Keith Armes, "Chekists in Cassocks: The Orthodox Church and the KGB," *Demokratizatsiya* 1, no. 4 (1993): 72–78; and Dunlop, "KGB Subversion," 52–53.

10. Priest and Politician

1. Ivan Levada, quoted in Joshua Yaffe, *Between Two Fires: Truth, Ambition, and Compromise in Putin's Russia* (New York: Tim Duggan Books, Random House, 2020), 11. In addition to Yaffe's work, illuminating studies of the years under review here include Masha Gessen, *The Future Is History: How Totalitarianism Reclaimed Russia* (New York: Riverhead Books, 2017); Catherine Belton, *Putin's People: How the KGB Took Back Russia and Then Took on the West* (New York: Farrar, Straus and Giroux, 2020); Stephen Kotkin, *Armageddon Averted: The Soviet Collapse, 1970–2000* (New York: Oxford University Press,

2008); *Aleksandr Nikolaevich Yakovlev: Izbrannye interviu: 1992–2005*, ed. A. A. Yakovlev (Moscow: Mezhdunarodnyi fond Demokratiia, 2009); and Lev Gudkov, Boris Dubin, and Yuri Levada, *Problema "elita" v segodniashnei Rossii: Razmyshleniia nad rezul'tatami sotsialogicheskogo issledovaniia* (Moscow: Fond Liberal'naia missiia, 2007).

2. For the ideological dissatisfaction and search for new ways of seeing the world from the Khrushchev to the Gorbachev periods, see Barbara Martin and Nadezhda Beliakova, eds., *Religious Life in the Late Soviet Union: From Survival to Revival (1960s–1980s)* (London: Routledge, 2023).

3. Sergei Borisovich Filatov, "Poslesovie: Religiia v postsovetskoi Rossii," in *Religiia i obshchestvo: Ocherki religioznoi zhizni sovremennoi Rossii*, ed. and comp. S. B. Filatov (Moscow: Letnii sad, 2002,) 471.

4. Patriarch Aleksi II, quoted by President Boris Yeltsin, "Yeltsin Comments on Cooperation with the Orthodox Church," *Interfax*, August 6, 1997.

5. Aleksandr Kyrlezhev and Konstantin Troitskii, "Sovremennoe rossiiskoe pravoslavie," pt. 1: "Tipologiia religioznogo soznaniia," *Kontinent*, no. 75 (January–March 1993), 242.

6. Maksim Shevchenko and Oleg Mramornov, "Prokliatye voprosy i sluzhenie religioznogo prostranstva," *Nezavisimaia gazeta-Religiia*, May 29, 1997. See also Aleksei Salmin, "Natsional'nyi vopros i religiia v kontekste gosudarstvennogo stroitel'sva v postkommunisticheskom mire," in *Liberalizm v Rossii: Sbornik statei*, ed. Iurii V. Krasheninnikov (Moscow: Znak, 1993), 21–45; John B. Dunlop, "The Russian Orthodox Church and Nationalism after 1988," *Religion in Communist Lands* 18, no. 4 (1990): 292–306; and Dmitrii Shusharin, "Porfirii Golovlev o svobode i vere," *Znamia* 3, no. 1 (March 1994): 191–200.

7. Viktor Aksiuchits, interview by author, Moscow, May 29, 1991; and Richard Sakwa, "Christian Democracy in Russia," *Religion, State and Society* 20, no. 2 (1992): 139–40.

8. Sakwa, "Christian Democracy in Russia," 141.

9. "Deklaratsiia Uchreditel'nogo Sobraniia Rossiiskogo Khristianskogo Demokraticheskogo Dvizheniia (RKhDD)," in *Khristianskie partii i samodeiatel'nye ob"edineniia: Sbornik materialov i dokumentov* (Moscow: Akademiia obshchestvennykh nauk pri TSK KPSS. Ideologicheskii otdel TsK KPSS, 1990), 119.

10. "Deklaratsiia," 118.

11. "Deklaratsiia," 116.

12. This is one of the main points Fr. Aleksandr Men stressed in his lecture on Solov'ev, as he emphasized that the Russian Church must follow the pathway connecting the church to the world (Protoierei Aleksandr Men', "Vladimir Solov'ev," in *Russkaia religioznaia filosofiia: Lektsii*, ed. Marina Nasonova [Moscow: Khram bessrebrennikov Kosmy i Damiana v Shubine, 2003], 36–47).

13. "Deklaratsiia," 120.

14. "Deklaratsiia," 121.

15. "Deklaratsiia," 121.

16. "Deklaratsiia," 121.

17. "Deklaratsiia," 122.

18. Both writers were discussed among members of the Russian intelligentsia, including the circles around Fr. Aleksandr Men, in which Yakunin participated (Wallace L. Daniel, *Russia's Uncommon Prophet: Father Aleksandr Men and His Times* [DeKalb: North-

ern Illinois University Press, 2016], 102–4, 180–82; and Aleksandr Men', *O sebe . . . Vospominaniia, interv'iu, besedy, pis'ma* [Moscow: Izdatel'stvo Zhizn' s Bogom, 2007], 111). See also Fr. Aleksandr's inclusion of Jacques Maritain and Nikolai Berdiaev among those he considered the most important thinkers of the twentieth century, in his *The Wellsprings of Religion*, vol. 1 of *Istoriia religii: V poiskakh puti, istiny, i zhizni*, trans. Alasdair MacNaughton, forewords by Wallace L. Daniel, Alasdair MacNaughton, and William Clegg (Yonkers, NY: St. Vladimir's Seminary Press, 2017), 38.

19. Sakwa, "Christian Democracy in Russia," 136.
20. "Deklaratsiia," 115.
21. "Deklaratsiia," 115.
22. "Osnovnye polozheniia politicheskoi programmy rossiisskogo khristianskogo demokraticheskogo dvizheniia," in *Khristianskie partii*, 102–4, 106–7; and "Deklaratsiia," 123.
23. Ernest Gellner, *Nationalism* (New York: New York University Press, 1997), 3–4, 102–3.
24. "Deklaratsiia," 124.
25. "Deklaratsiia," 124.
26. Aleksandr Sergeevich Pushkin, "Poltava," First Canto, quoted in "Deklaratsiia," https://go.gale.com/ps/i.do?p=LitRC&u=googlescholar&id=GALE|A259467586&v=2.1&it=r&sid=LitRC&asid=ab9c8124.
27. Mariia Glebovna Yakunina, interview by author, Moscow, email, February 5, 2021.
28. Mariia Glebovna Yakunina, interview by author, February 5, 2021.
29. Mariia Glebovna Yakunina, interview by author, February 5, 2021.
30. See Chernogolovka at http://chernogolovka.ru/about/index.ru.html?kk=bd15a3aad6.
31. According to Yakunin's daughter, despite Fr. Gleb's earlier inclination to remain a priest in Shchyolkovo, the urging of the scientists from Chernogolovka had a decisive influence (Mariia Glebovna Yakunina, interview by author, February 5, 2021).
32. "Deklaratsiia," 114.
33. "Osnovnye, polozheniia politicheskoi programmy," 113; and "Deklaratsiia," 116.
34. "Deklaratsiia," 116.
35. Mikhail Vital'evich, Shkarovskii, *Russkaia Pravoslavnaia Tserkov'* (Moscow: Veche, Lepta, 2010), 417–18; and T. Jeremy Gunn, "The Law of the Russian Federation on the Freedom of Conscience and Religious Associations from a Human Rights Perspective," in *Proselytism and Orthodoxy in Russia: The New War for Souls*, ed. John Witte Jr. and Michael Bourdeaux (Ossining, NY: Orbis), 260–61.
36. Fr. Gleb Yakunin, "Arkhiereiskomu Soboru Russkoi Pravoslavnoi Tserkvi, Obrashchenie," October 20, 1994, in Keston Archive, SU Ort 8/2: Individual Clergy: Yakunin, Fr. Gleb, box 50, folder 7 (18 of 19).
37. Fr. Gleb Yakunin, "Otkrytoe obrashchenie Prezidentu Rossiiskoi Federatsii El'tsinu B. N." March 21, 1995, 4, in Keston Archive, SU Ort 8/2: Individual Clergy, Yakunin, Fr. Gleb, box 26, folder 15.
38. Yakunin, "Otkrytoe obrashchenie."
39. Matthew Wyman and Stephen White, "Public Opinion, Parties, and Voters in the December 1993 Russian Elections," *Europe-Asian Studies* 47, no. 4 (June 1995), 598–600, 606.

40. Anthony Lewis, "Abroad at Home: When You Appease Fascism," *New York Times*, December 17, 1993; Joseph Albright and Marcia Kunstel, "Zhirinovsky—Russia's 'Frightening Fascist,'" *Atlanta Journal and Constitution*, February 6, 1994; and "Zhirinovsky A-Z," *Economist* 329, no. 7842, December 18, 1993, 38.

41. Mark Elliott and Anita Deyneka, "Protestant Missionaries in the Former Soviet Union," in *Proselytism and Orthodoxy*, 203, 209–10.

42. See *New Religions: A Guide; New Religious Movements, Sects, and Alternative Spiritualities*, ed. Christopher Partridge (New York: Oxford University Press, 2004); Eugene Clay, "The Church of the Transfiguring Mother of God and Its Role in Russian Nationalist Discourse, 1984–1999)," *Nova Religio: The Journal of Alternative and Emergent Religions* 3, no. 2 (April 2000): 320–49; and *Revisionism and Diversification in New Religious Movements*, ed. Eileen Barker (Farnham: Ashgate, 2013.) See the sociologist of religion Sergei Filatov's analysis of these religious groups and others, including several sects that practiced totalitarian methods, in Sergei Borisovich Filatov, "Posleslovie. Religiia v postsovetskoi Rossii, in *Religiia i obshchestvo: Ocherki religioznoi zhizhni sovremennoi Rossii*, ed. S. B. Filatov (Moscow: Letnii sad, 2002), 470–84. Despite the fears these nontraditional religions caused among the general public, most of these, he pointed out, failed to expand beyond their original numbers and were of short-run duration.

43. Aleksii II, Patriarch of Moscow and All Russia, "Iz vystupleniia na vstreche s administratsiei oblasti, Tambovskaia eparkhiia," August 10, 1993, in *Tserkov' i dukhovnoe vozrozhdenie Rossii: Slova, rechi, poslaniia, obrashcheniia, 1990–1998*, ed. Tikhon, Episkop Bronitskogo (Moscow: Izdatel'stvo Moskovskoi Patriarkhii, 1999), 302.

44. On the growth of church institutions, see Dimitry V. Pospielovskii, *The Orthodox Church in the History of Russia* (Crestwood, NY: St. Vladimir's Seminary Press, 1998), 368.

45. Daniel, *Russia's Uncommon Prophet*, 100–101.

46. Aleksii II, Patriarch of Moscow and All Russia, "Iz slova v Nikol'skom kafedral'nom sobore Iakutska," September 15, 1993, in *Tserkov' i dukhovnoe vozrozhdenie*, 308.

47. Aleksii II, Patriarch of Moscow and All Russia, "Iz slova v Nikol'skom kafedral'nom sobore Iakutska," 308.

48. Aleksii II, Patriarch of Moscow and All Russia, "Otvety na voprosy universiteta shtata Severnaia Karolina," 1991, in *Tserkov' i dukhovnoe vozrozhdenie*, 596.

49. Aleksii II, Patriarch of Moscow and All Russia, "Otvety na voprosy," 596.

50. Aleksii II, Patriarch of Moscow and All Russia, "Iz slova u chasovni v pamiat' moriakov, pogibshikh pri oborone Petropavlovska-Kamchatskogo v 1854 godu," September 16, 1993, in *Tserkov' i dukhovnoe vozrozhdenie*, 311.

51. Aleksii II, Patriarch of Moscow and All Russia, "Iz slova u chasovni v pamiat' moriakov," 311.

52. Aleksii II, Patriarch of Moscow and All Russia, "Iz slova u chasovni v pamiat' moriakov," 311; and Aleksii II, Patriarch of Moscow and All Russia, "Iz vystupleniia na vstreche s obshchestvennost'iu Volgograda," June 18, 1993, in *Tserkov' i dukhovnoe vozrozhdenie*, 291–92.

53. Aleksii II, Patriarch of Moscow and All Russia, "Iz vystupleniia na vstreche s administratsiei oblasti, Tambovskia eparkhiia," 302.

54. Aleksii II, Patriarch of Moscow and All Russia, "Iz vystupleniia na vstreche s administratsiei oblasti, Tambovskaia eparkhiia," 302.

55. Gleb Yakunin, "Letter to President Boris Yel'tsin," July 5, 1993, cited by Jane Ellis, *The Russian Orthodox Church: Triumphalism and Defensiveness* (New York: St. Martin's Press, 1996), 184.

56. Fr. Gleb Yakunin, statement at press conference in Moscow, July 21, 1993, quoted in Ellis, *Russian Orthodox Church: Triumphalism*, 185.

57. Aleksii II, Patriarch of Moscow and All Russia, "Iz vystupleniia na vstreche s administratsiei oblasti, Tambovskaia eparkhiia," 302.

58. Aleksii II, Patriarch of Moscow and All Russia, 302.

59. Aleksii II, Patriarch of Moscow and All Russia, "Dai Bog Rossii naiti dorogu k svetu," 1990, in *Tserkov' i dukhovnoe vozrozhdenie*, 828.

60. Aleksii II, Patriarch of Moscow and All Russia, "Iz slova na vstreche s tvorcheskoi i nauchnoi intelligentsiei Chuvashii," June 25, 1996, in *Tserkov' i dukhovnoe vozrozhdenie*, 318.

61. Aleksii II, Patriarch of Moscow and All Russia, 318.

62. Filatov, "Posleslovie, Religiia," 472–73.

63. "Iakunin, Gleb Pavlovich," in *Beloe dukhovenstov*, September 29, 2007, https://web.archive.org/web/2007092911643//http:www.ortho-rus.ru/cgi-bin/ps_file.cgi?4_3590.

64. "Iakunin, Gleb Pavlovich," 4.

65. "Iakunin, Gleb Pavlovich," 4.

66. "Iakunin, Gleb Pavlovich," 4.

67. The "Deklaratsiia" (114–15) of the Russian Christian Democratic Movement maintained that the church's withdrawal from politics had resulted in tragic circumstances in the past and would do so again. The church had to be involved in the real secular world or else it would suffer the consequences.

68. "Iakunin, Gleb Pavlovich."

69. Gleb Yakunin, "First Open Letter to Patriarch Aleksii II," January 19, 1994, *Religion, State and Society* 22, no. 3 (1994), 311–12. Yakunin correctly noted that Orthodox bishops and priests had served in the Fourth Duma in the years preceding the 1917 Revolution.

70. Yakunin, 311–12.

71. Yakunin, 312.

72. Yakunin, 316.

73. Gleb Yakunin, "Second Open Letter to Patriarch Aleksii II," February 11, 1994, *Religion, State and Society* 22, no. 3 (1994): 320–21.

74. Yakunin, 320–21.

75. Yakunin, "First Open Letter," 314.

76. Yakunin, 314.

77. Yakunin, 315. The file of the Memorial Society contains thirty Russian newspaper articles that detailed various aspects of Yakunin's political career in the 1990s, including work in the State Duma and his excommunication. See "Istoriia soprotivleniia rezhemu delo Iakunin Gleb," https://arch2.iofe.center/case/6864.

78. Ultraconservatives became especially incensed soon after Patriarch Aleksii II wrote to the chair of the Federal Assembly and expressed his displeasure at Fr. Gleb's defiance of the order of the Holy Synod. See Patriarch Aleksii II, "Letter to the Chairman of the State Duma of the Federal Assembly of the Russian Federation, Ivan Rybkin," *Religion, State and Society* 22, no. 3 (1994): 317–18.

79. Yakunin, "First Open Letter," 311.
80. Nikolai Vasil'ev, "Nas ne tronesh—my ne tronem, a zatronesh—spusku ne dadim," Portal Credo.ru, February 21, 2007, http://www.portal-credo.ru/site/?act=fresh&id=565.
81. Maksim Sokolov, "Chto bylo na nedele," *Kommersant*, September 16, 1995, 5.
82. Vasil'ev, "Nas ne tronesh."
83. Metropolitan Kirill of Smolensk and Kaliningrad, "Called to One Hope—The Gospel in Diverse Cultures," presented at the World Conference of Churches on World Mission and Evangelism, November 1996, Salvador, Bahai, and Brazil, in *Proselytism and Orthodoxy*, 73.
84. Filatov, *Religiia i obshchestvo*, 447–49; and Sergei Borisovich Filatov, "Sovremennaia Rossiia i sekty," *Inostrannaia literatura*, no. 8 (1996): 201–19.
85. See Yakunin's statement in Ellis, *Russian Orthodox Church: Triumphalism*, 185. Protestant communities of all kinds greatly expanded in the 1990s, from 900 in 1990 to 4,509 in 2001. Filatov, who is Russian Orthodox, considered such growth to be a positive movement because these groups reached people whom the Orthodox Church had not attracted (Sergei Borisovich Filatov, interview by author, Moscow, June 4, 2001; and Sergei Borisovich Filatov, "Protestantism in Postsoviet Russia: An Unacknowledged Triumph," *Religion, State and Society* 28, no. 1 [March 2000]: 93–104).
86. "Patriarch Rejects North American Standards of Freedom of Conscience," August 27, 1997, *Pravoslavie v Rossii*, http://www.stetson.edu/~psteeves/relnews/; Zoe Knox, *Russian Society and the Orthodox Church: Religion in Russia after Communism* (London: Routledge Curzon, 2005), 116–17.
87. Viktor Onuchko, "Pravoslavie, kul'tura, zemstvo: Otets Ioann; Razmyshleniia vslukh," *Nezavisimaia gazeta*, October 13, 1994; and Aleksandr Verkhovskii, "Tserkov' v politike i politika v tserkvi," in *Politicheskaia ksenofobiia: Radikal'nye gruppu, predstavleniia liderov, rol' tserkvi*, ed. Aleksandr Verkhovskii, Ekaterina Mikhailovskaia, and Vladimir Pribylovskii (Moscow: Izdatel'stvo OOO Panorama, 1999), 101–7.
88. Keith Armes, "Chekists in Cassocks: The Orthodox Church and the KGB," *Demokratizatsiya* 1, no. 4, 77.
89. "Ukrainian Patriarch and Yakunin Excommunicated by Russian Orthodox Church," *Eurasian Daily Monitor* 3, no. 37 (February 21, 1997): 1–2 (from Interfax-Ukraine, NTV, February 20, 1997), https://www.jamestown.org/org/program/ukrainian-patriarch-and-yakunin-excommunicated-by-russian-orthodox-church/.
90. "Iakunin, Gleb Pavlovich."
91. "Iakunin, Gleb Pavlovich."

11. Hope and the Twisted Road

1. Fr. Michael Meerson, interview by author, Bethesda, MD, May 29, 2019.
2. Dimitry V. Pospielovsky, *The Orthodox Church in Russia* (Crestwood, NY: St. Vladimir's Press, 1998), 357–58.
3. Gleb Yakunin, "Second Open Letter to Patriarch Aleksi II," *Religion, State and Society* 22, no. 3 (1994): 320–21; and Lev Ponomarev, quoted in "Iakunin, Gleb Pavlovich," July 21, 2022, https://oktmo.ru/stati/39373-yakunin-gleb-pavlovich.html.

4. Aleksandr Leonidovich Dvorkin, ed., *Sekty protiv tserkvi (Protsess Dvorkina)* (Moscow: Russkaia Pravoslavnaia Tserkov' Izdatel'stvo Moskovskoi Patriarkhii, 2000), 6–7.

5. Dvorkin's brochure, *Desiat' voprosov naviazchivomu neznakomtsu, ili Posobie dlia tekh, kto ne khochet byt' zaverbovannym*, is republished in Dvorkin, *Sekty protiv tserkvi*, 17–35.

6. Dvorkin, *Desiat' voprosov*, 20.

7. Marat Shterin and James T. Richardson, "The Yakunin vs. Dvorkin Trial and the Emerging Religious Pluralism in Russia," *Occasional Papers on Religion in Eastern Europe* 22, no. 1 (2002), https://digitalcommons.georgefox.edu/ree/vol22/iss1/1; and James Richardson and Marat Shterin, "Minority Religions and Social Justice in Russian Courts," *Social Justice Research* 12, no. 4 (1999), 402–4.

8. Dvorkin, "Ob"iasnenie po isku A. L. Dvorkina," in *Sekty protiv tserkvi*, 104.

9. "Rech' Gleba Iakunina," in *Sekty protiv tserkvi*, 160.

10. Perhaps, as Shterin and Richardson surmised, the court also found that Yakunin's recent excommunication from the church made him less than a credible plaintiff. See Shterin and Richardson, "Yakunin vs. Dvorkin Trial."

11. Emily B. Baran, "Negotiating the Limits of Religious Pluralism in Post-Soviet Russia: The Anticult Movement in the Russian Orthodox Church, 1990–2004), *Russian Review* 65, no. 4 (October 2006), 655–56.

12. The 1997 Law on Freedom of Conscience and Religious Associations has been widely discussed and analyzed. See W. Cole Durham Jr. and Lauren B. Homer, "Russia's 1997 Law on Freedom of Conscience and Religious Associations: An Analytical Appraisal," *Emory International Law Review* 12, no. 1 (Winter 1998): 101–246; Anatolii Viktorovich Pchelintsev, "Religiia i prava cheloveka," in *Religiia i prava cheloveka*, vol. 3 of *Na puti k svobode sovesti*, ed. L. M. Vorontsova, A. V. Pchelintsev, and S. B. Filatov (Moscow: Nauka, 1996), 7–11; John Witte Jr., Introduction to *Proselytism and Orthodoxy in Russia: The New War for Souls*, ed. John Witte Jr. and Michael Bourdeaux (Ossining, NY: Orbis, 1999), 1–27; and, in the same volume, Harold J. Berman, "Freedom of Religion in Russia: An Amicus for the Defendant," 265–83; and Lee Trepanier, "Nationalism and Religion in Russian Civil Society: An Inquiry into the 1997 Law 'On Freedom of Conscience,'" in *Civil Society and the Search for Justice in Russia*, ed. Christopher Marsh and Nikolas K. Gvosdev (Lanham, MD: Lexington Books, 2002), 57–73.

13. Russian Federal Law, "On Freedom of Conscience and on Religious Associations," trans. Lawrence A. Uzzell, *Emory International Law Review* 12, no. 1 (Winter 1998), 657.

14. Russian Federal Law, "On Freedom of Conscience," 664–65.

15. Zoia Krakhmal'nikova, quoted in Zoe Knox, *Russian Society and the Orthodox Church: Religion in Russia after Communism* (London: Routledge, 2005), 97.

16. Fr. Veniamin (Novik), *Pravoslavie. Khristianstvo. Demokratiia: Sbornik statei* (St. Petersburg: Aleteiia, 1999), 361. Embracing the principle of freedom of conscience, Fr. Veniamin noted, the Second Vatican Council had renounced the Syllabus.

17. Sergei Borisovich Filatov, "Posleslovie, Religiiia v postsovetskoi Rossii," in *Religiia i obshchestvo: Ocherki religioznoi zhizhni sovremennoi Rossii*, ed. and comp. S. B. Filatov (Moscow: Letnii sad, 2002), 472–73. The relationship between the Orthodox Church and the Russian government was fraught with tensions and sometimes outright distrust, as

Geraldine Fagan has convincingly demonstrated (Geraldine Fagan, *Believing in Russia: Religious Policy after Communism* [London: Routledge, 2013], 42–46).

18. Sviashchennik Gleb Yakunin, *Istoricheskii put' pravoslavnogo talibanstva* (Moscow: Profizdat, 2002), 30–32, 40. Despite Yakunin's contentions, a large gap existed between what the 1997 law proclaimed and its actual results. As Fagan has shown, at the grassroots level, practice varied and depended a great deal on the personal proclivities of local authorities (Fagan, *Believing in Russia*, 77–78).

19. Gleb Yakunin, "Menia otluchili ot tserkvi, kak L'va Tolstogo," interviewed by Andrei Morozov, September 3, 2004, in Keston Archive, SU Ort: Yakunin, Fr. Gleb.

20. Yakunin, "Menia otluchili."

21. Yakunin, "Menia otluchili."

22. Yakunin, *Istoricheskii put'*, 47.

23. Yakunin, *Istoricheskii put'*, 47.

24. Yakunin, *Istoricheskii put'*, 47–48. Yakunin cited Archimandrite Tikhon's interview with the Athenian newspaper *Khora*, which *Izvestiia* reprinted in Russia.

25. Yakunin, *Istoricheskii put'*, 48–49.

26. John P. Burgess, "The Theological Politics of the Icon of the New Martyrs and Confessors of Russia," *Journal of Church and State* 58, no. 3 (2015), 485–86.

27. Elena Volkova, email correspondence with author, May 31, 2023.

28. Volkova, email correspondence with author.

29. See Scott M. Kenworthy and Alexander S. Agadjanian, *Understanding World Christianity: Russia* (Minneapolis: Fortress Press, 2021), 263–68, 291–93, for an informative and engaging study of the Orthodox Church and the dilemmas it confronted in postcommunist Russia. As the authors point out, Orthodoxy represented a monolithic worldview but it encompassed a multiplicity of theological and social perspectives on how to relate to secular culture.

30. Sviashchennik Pavel Vladimirovich Bochkov and Protoierei Dionisii Martyshin, *"Dukh revoliutsii" v tserkvi* (St. Petersburg: Aleteiia, 2010), 8–9.

31. Sviashchennik Pavel Vladimirovich Bochkov, *Iurisdiktsionno-politicheskie tserkovnye raskoly postsovetskogo perioda* (Moscow: Editorial servis, 2010), 225.

32. "Spiski apostol'skoi preemstvennosti osnovannykh apostolami Pomestnykh Tserkvei," https://mir-angelica.ru/uchenie-o-vere/apostolskaya-pravoslavnaya-cerkov.html

33. "Spiski."

34. Bochkov, *Iurisdiktsionno-politicheskie tserkovnye raskoly*, 28.

35. Bochkov, 28–29.

36. Mother Mariia, quoted in Bochkov, *Iurisdiktsionno-politicheskie tserkovnye raskoly*, 29.

37. Sviashchenniki Gleb Yakunin and Iurii Ryzhkov, *Tri razgovora o proshlom, nastoiashchem, i budushchem Pravoslaviia, s prilozheniem kratkoi povesti o Moskovskoi Patriarkhii* (Moscow, 2006), http://krotov.info/library/28_ya/ku/nin_apz.htm.

38. Bochkov, *Iurisdiktsionno-politicheskie tserkovnye raskoly*, 225.

39. "Apostol'skaia Pravoslanaia Tserkov'," https://raskolniki.livejournal.com/2921.html.

40. Bochkov, *Iurisdiktsionno-politicheskie tserkovnye raskoly*, 230.

41. Bochkov, 226.

42. Bochkov, 225–26.
43. Mikhail Men, quoted in Judith D. Kornblatt, "Is Father Alexander Men' a Saint? The Jews, the Intelligentsia, and the Russian Orthodox Church," *Toronto Slavic Quarterly*, no. 70 (2003), http://sites.utoronto.ca/tsq/12/kornblatt12.shtmil.
44. Yakunin, "Menia otluchili."
45. Bochkov, *Iurisdiktsionno-politicheskie tserkovnye raskoly*, 55.
46. Sergei Sergeevich Bychkov, *Sviashchennik Gleb Iakunin. Nelekgii put' pravdoiskatelia* (Moscow: Eksmo, 2021), 5.
47. Yakunin and Ryzhkov, *Tri razgovora*.
48. Yakunin and Ryzhkov.
49. Yakunin and Ryzhkov.
50. Yakunin and Ryzhkov.
51. Yakunin and Ryzhkov. In Yakunin's view of *sobornost'*, the church community selected the priest, and priests, in turn, chose the bishop, a process that, he believed, served as a means of counteracting authoritarianism.
52. Yakunin, *Istoricheskii put'*, 52.
53. Mariia Glebovna Yakunina, interview by author, Moscow, February 5, 2021. The total number of Apostolic Orthodox Churches is unknown, although it likely remained much lower than that of other schismatic church organizations in Russia and Ukraine. Bochkov, "*Dukh revoliutsii*," 26.
54. "Spiski."
55. Vsemirnyi Russkii Narodnyi Sobor X, "Deklaratsiia o pravakh i dostoinstve cheloveka," April 6, 2006, www.patriarchia.ru/db/print/103235.html.
56. Sviashchennik Gleb Yakunin, "K vypusku alternativnoi deklaratsii mitropolita Kirilla 'o pravakh i dostoinstve cheloveka.'" I am grateful to Elena Volkova for providing this document from her personal archive.
57. Vsemirnyi Russkii Narodnyi Sobor X, "Deklaratsiia o pravakh."
58. Vsemirnyi Russkii Narodnyi Sobor X.
59. Yakunin, "K vypusku alternativnoi deklaratsii."
60. Vladimir Putin, "O provedenii spetsial'noi voennoi operatsii," February 24, 2023, https://en.kremlin.ru/events/president/news/67843.
61. Mariia Glebovna Yakunina, interview by author, email, February 5, 2021.
62. Only two of the three women actually performed the "Punk Prayer." The third was denied admittance to the Cathedral of Christ the Savior because she wanted to bring in her guitar. The three young women—Nadezhda Tolokonnikova, Mariia Alekhina, and Ekaterina Samutsevicha—and the significance of Pussy Riot's performance have been the subjects of many scholarly studies. See especially Mischa Gabowitsch, *Protest in Putin's Russia*, revised and updated (Cambridge: Polity Press, 2017), 161–94; Vera Shevzov, "Women on the Fault Lines of Faith: Pussy Riot and the Insider/Outsider Challenge to Post-Soviet Orthodoxy," *Religion and Gender* 4, no. 2 (2014): 121–44; and Dmitry Uzlaner, "The Pussy Riot Case and the Peculiarities of Russian Post-Secularism," trans. April French, *State, Religion and Church* 1, no. 1 (2014): 23–58.
63. "Russian Patriarch Says Punk Band 'Desecrated' Church," March 25, 2012, https://www.rferl.org/russia_church_punk_band_pussy_riot_/24526352.html.
64. Cathy Young, "Remembering the Russian Priest Who Fought the Orthodox Church," *Daily Beast*, December 28, 2014, updated April 14, 2017, https://www

.thedailybeast.com / remembering-the-russian-priest-who-fought-the-orthodox -church.

65. Sviashchennik Gleb Yakunin, "Khot' Lenin umer, no eshche ne vymer," *Bogu sluzhenie—stikhoslozhenie* (Moscow: privately printed book, n.d.), 85. The poem was written on December 12, 2012.

66. In October 2012, one of the group's members, Ekaterina Samutsevicha, appealed her sentence, and it was suspended. The other two members served until December 23, 2013, when they were released from prison after the State Duma granted them amnesty.

67. Bychkov, *Sviashchennik Gleb Yakunin. Nelegkii put' pravdoiskatelia* (Moscow: Eksmo, 2021). 347.

68. Mariia Glebovna Yakunina, interview by author, Moscow, email, February 5, 2021.

69. Yakunina, interview, February 5, 2021.

70. "Iakunin, Gleb Pavlovich," https://oktmo.ru/stat/39373-yakunin-gleb-pavlovich.html.

71. Boris Vladimirovich Talantov, "The Secret Participation of the Moscow Patriarchate in the Battle of the CPSU against the Orthodox Christian Church (The Crisis of the Church Administration)," part 2 of "The Moscow Patriarchate and Sergianism," http:www.orthodoxinfo.com/ecumenism/cat_tal. aspx; and Boris Vladimirovich Talantov, "Sovetskoe obshchestvo, 1965–68," *Posev* 25, no. 9 (1969), 41.

72. Fr. Gleb Yakunin, "Litsom k sobytiiu," conversation on Radio Liberty, April 20, 2003, quoted in Bychkov, *Sviashchennik Gleb Yakunin*, 358.

73. Viktor Popkov and Tat'iana Lebedeva, interview by author, Moscow, May 17, 2018. Popkov and Lebedeva, prominent members of the intelligentsia and former friends of Yakunin, manage a major bookstore in central Moscow.

74. Yakunin's belief in the coming transformation of Russia, on a practical level, shared several similarities with the "theology of hope" in the writings of the German theologian Jürgen Moltmann. "Hope," Moltmann wrote, "is nothing else than the expectation of those things which faith has believed to have been truly promised by God. Thus, faith believes God to be true; hope awaits the time when this truth shall be manifested." Jürgen Moltmann, *Theology of Hope: On the Ground and the Implications of a Christian Eschatology*, trans. James W. Leitch (New York: Harper and Row, 1967), 20. See also Jürgen Moltmann, *Religion, Revolution, and the Future*, trans. M. Douglas Meeks (New York: Charles Scribner's, 1969), 4–5, 203.

75. Irina Vladimirovna Karatsuba, quoted in Yakunin, *Bogu sluzhenie*, 3.

76. Nadezhda Mandelstam, *Hope against Hope: A Memoir*, trans. Max Hayward (New York: Atheneum, 1976), 96.

77. Lev Ponomarov, quoted in Elena Ivanovna Volkova, *Glyba Gleba: Zapreshchenneishii ierei Iakunin* (St. Petersburg: Renome, 2021), 17.

78. Valerii Borshchev, quoted in Yakunin, *Bogu sluzhenie*, 4.

79. Mariia Riabikova, quoted in Yakunin, *Bogu sluzhenie*, 5.

80. Heleen Zorgdrager, quoted in Yakunin, *Bogu sluzhenie*, 6.

BIBLIOGRAPHY

Essay on Archival Sources

The most significant sources for my study are in the Keston Archive. Formerly located in Oxford, England, and presently housed at Baylor University in Waco, Texas, the archive holds a vast array of primary documents on Fr. Gleb Yakunin and his activities in support of freedom of conscience. Beginning in the late 1950s, while he studied on the British exchange program with the Soviet Union, Michael Bourdeaux became aware of a second wave of the state's attempted extirpation of religious belief. He began to collect documents relating to this campaign, as well as the responses of individuals and groups who were determined to preserve their heritage and their religious and intellectual freedom. The Keston Archive had its origins in those efforts, and in subsequent years, it evolved into a major depository for documents and other materials concerning religion, politics, and the efforts of notable figures to protect a main source of Russia's cultural endowment from destruction.

Beginning in the mid-1960s, Bourdeaux and his associates became aware of Gleb Yakunin's significance in the defense of persecuted people. Keston served as a central depository of documents, letters, petitions, press clippings, and personal accounts of struggles to preserve religious rights in the Soviet Union and present-day Russia. More than twenty-five boxes of these materials relate to the topic of this book. The records of Yakunin's early life as an Orthodox priest are contained in his personal files (SU Ort 8/2, Yakunin; SU Ort 8/2, box 26: Individual Clergy: Yakunin, Fr. Gleb, box 26) and include an original copy of the famous letters that he and Fr. Nikolai Eshliman sent in 1965 to Patriarch Aleksii I and to Nikolai Podgorny, chair of the Soviet Presidium. A copy of the sensational letter written by Yakunin and Lev Regel'son to the delegates of the World Council of Churches, meeting in Nairobi, Kenya, is also found in the Yakunin files, as well as the responses from Metropolitans Nikodim and Yuvenalii, both of whom claimed that the charges of religious persecution represented falsifications. Yakunin, Regel'son and their colleagues faced severe criticisms from Soviet authorities in the late 1960s and 1970s. Reports from the press conferences in which they attempted to defend themselves and argued for a reality different from that presented by church and state authorities are included in Yakunin's personal files.

Despite his suspension from the Orthodox priesthood, the twenty years following the letters he and Eshliman sent to the patriarch proved significant in Yakunin's life. Although he enjoyed only limited participation in the Christian Seminar in Moscow, he witnessed evidence of a religious awakening among certain segments of the young intelligentsia. Primary materials from the seminar (SU 11/10, box 28: Christian Seminar) include an original copy of the samizdat journal *Obshchina*, lists of books discussed by seminar members, and the names of leading participants. Concurrently, in late December 1976, Yakunin and several of his colleagues created the Christian Committee for the Defense of Believers' Rights in the USSR. Keston Archive has nine of the original twelve volumes of the committee's documents, published by Henry S. Dakin's Research Center in San Francisco. The Christian Committee's ecumenical approach and its support for diverse religious communities in the Soviet Union are evidenced in the stories, grievances, and appeals incorporated in these documents. Although such records do not provide a complete picture of religious life, they offer a valuable, close-up view of many communities and their lived religious experiences. Adding to them is Yakunin's detailed "Report on the Orthodox Church Today and the Prospects for a Religious Revival in Russia," published in volume 11 of the Christian Committee's materials.

Yakunin's "Report" and the committee's published documents told a different story from the accounts of most foreign delegations that returned from visits singing the praises of religious freedom in the Soviet Union (SU Ort 9/9, box 27: Visits from Foreign Delegations, 1967–1977). Yakunin's work on the Christian Committee, his refusal to desist his activities, and his outspoken criticism of the Moscow Patriarchate's relationship to the government led to his arrest in 1979 and his trial in 1980. Keston Archive contains significant materials on these events, as well as on his subsequent imprisonment and exile to Yakutia province (SU Ort 8/2, box 50: Yakunin Trial). Supportive letters for him came from inside and outside the Soviet Union (SU Ort 8/2, boxes 26 and 27: Letters of Support, 1979–1982).

Release from exile in 1987 and reinstatement as a priest led to a new stage in Yakunin's life (SU Ort 8/2: Yakunin, Fr. Gleb [1989–1993]). Keston's holdings are particularly strong on the last years of the Soviet Union and the early part of the Russian government. These years resulted in Yakunin's entrance into politics, his election to the Russian Parliament, and his later selection to the parliamentary commission that investigated the relationship between the KGB and the Orthodox Church. The latter event produced a wealth of revelations from the previously closed KGB archives (Tsentral'nyi Arkhiv of the KGB, fonds 1, 5, and 6, in SU Ort 8/2, box 50: Yakunin, Fr. Gleb [1991–1996]). The final report, written by the chair Lev Ponomarev, summarized the commission's findings and also recommended safeguards to prevent the KGB's infiltration of the church (SU Ort 8/2: Yakunin, Fr. Gleb (1989–1993). Sadly, these recommendations, which might have divorced the church from the KGB, were not followed.

Thankfully, published sources are available on Yakunin's excommunication and the twilight years of his life. The papers of Xenia Dennen on Zoia Krakhmal'nikova and the files on Boris Talantov and Fr. Sergii Zheludkov in the Keston archive relate to similar purposes to which Yakunin devoted his life and service. They await further exploration by historians for the light they shine on efforts to free the mind from captivity.

In addition, the Hoover Archive at Stanford University in Palo Alto, California, proved invaluable to this book. The Henry S. Dakin papers in the archive contain the original materials for all twelve volumes of the Christian Committee for the Defense of Believers' Rights in the USSR.

Interviews by Author

Aksenov-Meerson, Fr. Michael, Bethesda, MD, May 27, 2019.
Aksiuchits, Viktor, Moscow, May 29, 1991.
Dakin, Adriana, Ukiah, CA, Zoom, July 9, 2020.
Dakin, Virgilia Pasche, Ukiah, CA, Zoom, July 9, 2020.
Filatov, Sergei Borisovich, Moscow, June 15, 1994, and June 4, 2001.
Hickman, Jim, Cochabamba, Bolivia, Zoom, July 11, 2020.
Kucharev, Anya, San Rafael, CA, July 24, 2020.
Lebedeva, Tat′iana, Moscow, May 17, 2018.
Men, Pavel Vol′fi ovich, Moscow, July 3, 2013.
Osipov, Andrei Il′ich, Sergiev Posad, June 11, 1994.
Popkov, Viktor, Moscow, May 17, 2018.
Tabak, Iurii Mikhailovich, Moscow, October 19, 2008.
Volkova, Elena Ivanovna, Moscow, September 11, 2015, and September 17, 2016.
Yakunin, Fr. Gleb Pavlovich, Moscow, May 10, 2007.
Yakunina, Iraida Georgievna, Moscow, email, October 28, 2016.
Yakunina, Mariia Glebovna, Moscow, May 23, 2018, and email, February 5, 2021.

Published Writings, Letters, and Appeals by Father Gleb Yakunin

Single author

"Abbat′ vykhodit na sviaz ′." *Argumenty i fakty*, no. 1, January 8, 1992.
"Appeal to Western Christians." *Keston News Service*, no. 135, October 22, 1981.
Bogu sluzhenie—stikhoslozhenie. Moscow: privately printed, n.d.
"Doklad Sviashchennika Gleba Iakunina Khristianskomu komitetu zashchitu prav veruiushchikh v SSSR o sovremennom polozhenii Russkoi Pravoslavnoi Tserkvi i o perspektivakh religioznogo vozrozhdeniia Rossii," August 15, 1979. In *Dokumenty khristianskogo komiteta*, 11:1128–68.
"First Open Letter to Patriarch Aleksii II," January 19, 1994. *Religion, State and Society* 22, no. 3 (1994): 311–16.
Istoricheskii put′ pravoslavnogo talibanstva. Moscow: Profizdat, 2002.
Khvalebnyi primitiv iurodivyi, v chest′ Boga, mirozdan′ia, rodiny: Poema. Introductory essay by Elena Volkova. Moscow: Biblioteka PravLit, 2008.
"Second Open Letter to Patriarch Aleksii II," February 11, 1994. *Religion, State and Society* 22, no. 3 (1994): 320–21.
"V sluzhenii kul′tu (Moskovskaia Patriarkhiia i kylt′ lichnosti Stalina)." In *Na puti k svobode sovesti*, edited by D. E. Furman and Fr. Mark (Smirnov), 172–206. Moscow: Progress, 1989.

Coauthored with

Eshliman, Fr. Nikolai. "Appeal to the Patriarch, the Holy Synod, and the Diocesan Bishops," May 12, 1966. In Bourdeaux, *Patriarch and Prophets*, 223–26.
Eshliman, Fr. Nikolai. "To the Chairman of the Presidium of the Supreme Soviet of the Union of Socialist Republics." In Bourdeaux, *Patriarch and Prophets*, 189–94.

Kapitanchuk, Viktor and Vadim Shcheglov. "Ego Sviateishestu Pape Rimskomu, nasledniki Sviateishego Prestola Papy Ioanna-Pavla I," October 1, 1978. In *Dokumenty khristianskogo komiteta*, vol. 5, pt. 2: 700–716.

Kapitanchuk, Viktor, Vadim Shcheglov, and Members of the Catholic Committee for the Defense of Believers' Rights. "Letter to Pope John Paul II, The Heads of Autocephalous Orthodox Churches, Primate of the Anglican Church, Archbishop D. Coggan, The World Council of Churches, Community Christian Committees, Which Defend Believers' Rights, and President of the United States, J. Carter," November 22, 1978. In Scarfe, *Christian Committee Documents*, 111–15.

Khaibulin, Hierodeacon Varsenofi, and Viktor Kapitanchuk. "Deklaratsiia." In *Dokumenty khristianskogo komiteta*, 1:1.

Khaibulin, Hierodeacon Varsonifi, and Viktor Kapitnachuk. "Otkrytoe pis'mo rukovodstvy radioveshchatel'nykh stantsii Golos Ameriki, Bi-Bi-Si, Nemetskaia Volna," November 11, 1977. In *Dokumenty Khristianskogo komiteta*, 1:37–38.

Khaibulin, Hierodeaon Varsonofi, and Viktor Kapitnachuk. "Zaiavlenie Khristianskogo komiteta zashchity prav veruiushchikh v SSSR," December 29, 1977. In *Dokumenty khristianskogo komiteta*, 1:3–4. English translation: *Dokumenty khristianskogo komiteta zashchity prav veruiushchikh v SSSR*, vol. 3: *Izbrannye perevody dokumentov iz tomov 1, 2*, 4:285–86.

Khailbulin, Hierodeacon Varsonifi, Viktor Kapitanchuk, and Vadim Sheglov. "Pravoslanomu Vselenskomu Patriarkhu Dmitriiu," April 11, 1978. In *Dokumenty kristianskogo komiteta*, vol. 1: 159–63.

Regel'son, Lev. *Letters from Moscow: Religion and Human Rights in the USSR*, edited by Jane Ellis. Keston, San Francisco: H. S. Dakin, 1978.

Regel'son, Lev. "To the General Secretary of the WCC, Philip Potter," March 6, 1976. In Helene Posdeeff, "Appendix: Russian Believers Write to WCC's General Secretary." *Religion in Communist Lands* 4, no. 4 (Winter 1976): 9–15.

Regel'son, Lev, and Viktor Kapitanchuk. "Appeal for the Glorification of Russian Martyrs in the USSR," May 25, 1975. In Yakunin and Regel'son, *Letters from Moscow*, 34–40.

Ryzhkov, Boris. *Tri razgovora o proshlom, nastoiashchem, i budushchem Pravoslaviia, s prilozheniem kratkoi povesti o Moskovskoi Patriarkhii*. Moscow, 2006. http://krotov.info/library/28_ya/ku/nin_apz.htm.

"Uvazhaemomu predsedateliu Konstitutsionnoi komissii Brezhnevy Leonidu Il'ichu," June 8, 1977. In *Dokumenty khristianskogo komiteta*, 1:26–27, and vol. 3: *Izbrannye perevody dokumentov iz tomov 1, 2*, 4:340–41.

Primary and Secondary Works

Note: Chapters included in edited volumes are not listed individually by author or by chapter title, but rather by the title of the entire work.

"AEQUINOX": *Sbornik pamiati o. Aleksandra Menia*, edited by I. G. Vishnevetskii and E. G. Rabinovich. Moscow: Carte Blanche, 1991.

Afanasii (Kuduik), Archimandrite. "Vysokopreosviashchennyi arkhiepiskop Ermogen (Golubev)." *Zhurnal Moskovskoi Patriarkhii*, no. 11 (November 1978): 21.

"After the Coup," *Frontier*, September–October 1991, 14–15.
A. I. (Mikhail Meerson-Aksenov). "Arest Krasnova-Levitina." *Vestnik Russkogo studencheskogo khristianskogo dvizheniia*, no. 1 (1970): 95–96, and no. 2 (1970): 69–74.
Aksenov-Meerson, Michael. "The Russian Orthodox Church, 1965–1980." *Religion in Communist Lands* 9, nos. 3–4 (1981): 101–10.
Albats, Yevgenia. *The State within a State: The KGB and Its Hold on Russia—Past, Present, and Future*. Translated by Catherine A. Fitzpatrick. New York: Farrar, Straus and Giroux, 1994.
Alekseev, Valerii Arkad'evich. *Illiuzii i dogmy*. Moscow: Polizdat, 1991.
Aleksii II, Patriarch. "Education and the Christian View of Man." *Russian Social Science Review* 35, no. 6 (November–December 1994): 45–48.
Aleksii II, Patriarch. "Letter to the Chairman of the State Duma of the Federal Assembly of the Russian Federation, Ivan Rybkin." *Religion, State and Society* 22, no. 3 (1994): 317–18.
Alexeyeva, Ludmilla. *Soviet Dissent: Contemporary Movements for National, Religious, and Human Rights*. Translated by Carol Pearce and John Glad. Middletown, CT: Wesleyan University Press, 1985.
"Ananyev." In *Encyclopedia Judaica*. Edited by Cecil Roth. Jerusalem: Macmillan, 1971. Vol. 2: 924.
"Ananyev, Ukraine." In *Jewish Virtual Library*. https:www.jewishvirtuallibrary.org/ananyev.
Antic, Oxana. "The Russian Orthodox Church Moves towards Coming to Terms with Its Past." *RFE/RL, Report on the USSR* (March 8, 1991): 4.
"Apostol'skaia Pravoslavnaia Tserkov'." https://raskolniki.livejournal.com/2921.html.
Applebaum, Anne. *Gulag: A History*. New York: Doubleday, 2003.
Applebaum, Anne. "Tales from the Gulag." World Monuments Fund (Fall 2003): 26–33.
Armes, Keith. "Chekists in Cassocks: The Orthodox Church and the KGB." *Demokratizatsiya* 1, no. 44 (1993): 72–78.
Aronson, I. Michael. *Troubled Waters: The Origins of the 1881 Anti-Jewish Pogroms in Russia*. Pittsburgh, PA: University of Pittsburgh Press, 1990.
Barabanov, Evgeny. "The Schism Between the Church and the World." In *From under the Rubble*, edited by Alexander Solzhenitsyn and translated by A. M. Brock, Milada Haigh, Marita Sapiets, Hilary Sternberg, and Harry Willets under the direction of Michael Scammell. Introduction by Max Hayward, 172–93. Boston: Little, Brown, 1974.
Baran, Emily B. "Negotiating the Limits of Religious Pluralism in Post-Soviet Russia: The Anticult Movement in the Russian Orthodox Church, 1990–2004. *Russian Review* 65, no. 4 (October 2006): 637–56.
Beliakova, Nadezhda. "'I sviashchennik stanovitsia dobrym gostem v sovetskom obshchestve.' . . . Religioznaia zhizn' Moskvy i Podmoskov'ia vesnoi 1990 goda v opisanii A. E. Levitina-Krasnova." *Istoricheskii kur'er* 2 [10], 2020]: 215–25. DOI: 10.31518/2618-9100-2020-2-17.
Beliakova, Nadezhda. "Samizdat dlia tamizdat, ili Kak Kholodnaia voina povliiala na razvitie novogo zhanra pravoslavnogo samizdata." In *Acta samizdatica / Zapiski o samizdate: Al'manakh*, no. 5, edited by M. Ia. Sheinker, 77–91. Moscow: Gosudarstvennaia publichnaia istoricheskaia biblioteka Rossii, 2020.

Belov, Anatolii Vasil'evich, and Andrei Dmitrievich Shilkin. *Diversiia bez dinamita*. 2nd ed. Moscow: Politizdat, 1976.
Belton, Catherine. *Putin's People: How the KGB Took Back Russia and Then Took on the West*. New York: Farrar, Straus and Giroux, 2020.
Berdiaev, Nikolai Aleksandrovich. *The Destiny of Man*. Translated by Natalie Duddington. New York: Harper's, 1960.
Berdiaev, Nikolai Aleksandrovich. *Filosofiia svobody: Smysl tvorchestvo*. Moscow: Pravda, 1989.
Berdyaev, Nicolas. *Dream and Reality: An Essay in Autobiography*. Translated by Katherine Lampert. 1950. Reprint, New York: Collier Books, 1962.
Bergson, Henri. *The Two Sources of Morality and Religion*. Translated by R. Ashley Audra and Cloudesley Brereton, with the assistance of W. Horsfall Carter. Garden City, NY: Doubleday, Anchor Books, 1935.
Berman, Harold J. *Justice in the USSR: An Interpretation of Soviet Law*. Rev. ed. New York: Vintage, 1963.
Billington, James H. *Russia Transformed: Breakthrough to Hope, Moscow, August 1991*. New York: Free Press, 1992.
"Biograficheskaia spravka sviashchennika o. Nikolaia Gainova." *Russkaia mysl'*, no. 3292, January 24, 1980, 5.
Bloch, Sidney, and Peter Reddaway. *Russia's Political Hospitals: The Abuse of Psychiatry in the Soviet Union*. London: Victor Gollancz, 1977.
Bochkov, Pavel Vladimirovich. *Iurisdiktsionno-politicheskie tserkovnye raskoly post-sovetskogo perioda*. Moscow: Editorial servis, 2010.
Bochkov, Pavel Vladimirovich, and Dionisii Martyshin. *"Dukh revoliutsii" v tserkvi*. St. Petersburg: Aleteiia, 2010.
Bogolep, Archbishop of Kirov and Nikolaev Diocese. "Ukaz," November 5, 1976. In *Dokumenty khristianskogo komiteta*, 1:99.
Boobyyer, Philip. *Conscience, Dissent and Reform in Soviet Russia*. London: Routledge, 2005.
Borisov, Protoierei Aleksandr. "Dukhovnyi realizm ottsa Aleksandra Menia." In *Tserkovnaia zhizn' XX veka: Protoierei Aleksandr Men' i ego dukhovnie nastavniki: Sbornik materialov Pervoi nauchnoi konferentsii.'Menevskie chteniia'" (9–11 Sentiabria 2006 g.)*,, edited by M. V. Grigorenko, 161–71. Sergiev Posad: Izdanie prikhoda Sergievskoi tserkvi v Semkhoze, g. Sergiev Posad, 2007.
Bourdeaux, Michael. "The Brave Stand of Archbishop Yermogen." *Liberty*, September–October 1968, 21–23.
Bourdeaux, Michael. *Gorbachev, Glasnost, and the Gospel*. London: Hodder and Stoughton, 1990.
Bourdeaux, Michael. *One Word of Truth: The Cold War Memoir of Michael Bourdeaux and Keston College*. London: Darton, Longman and Todd, 2019.
Bourdeaux, Michael. *Patriarch and Prophets: Persecution of the Russian Orthodox Church Today*. New York: Praeger, 1970.
Bourdeaux, Michael. *Religious Ferment in Russia: Protestant Opposition to Soviet Religious Policy*. London: Macmillan, 1968.
Bourdeaux, Michael. "The Role of Religion in the Collapse of Communism." *Archiva Moldoviae* 5 (2013): 335–42.

Bourdeaux, Michael. "The Russian Church, Religious Liberty and the World Council of Churches." *Religion in Communist Lands* 13, no. 1 (1985): 4–27.
Bradley, Mark Philip. *The World Reimagined: Americans and Human Rights in the Twentieth Century*. New York: Cambridge University Press, 2016.
Braithwaite, Rodric. *Afgantsy: The Russians in Afghanistan, 1979–89*. New York: Oxford University Press, 2011.
Brown, Archie. *Seven Years That Changed the World: Perestroika in Perspective*. Oxford: Oxford University Press, 2007.
Bruhl, Lucien Lévy. *La mentalité primitive*. 14th ed. 1923. Reprint, Paris: Presses Universitaires de France, 1947.
Bulgakov, Sergei. *The Orthodox Church*. Foreword by Thomas Hopko. Revised translation by Lydia Kesich. 1935. Reprint, Crestwood, NY: St Vladimir's Seminary Press, 1988.
Bullough, Oliver. *The Last Man in Russia: The Struggle to Save a Dying Nation*. New York: Basic Books, 2013.
Burgess, John P. *Holy Rus': The Rebirth of Orthodoxy in the New Russia*. New Haven, CT: Yale University Press, 2017.
Burgess, John P. "The Theological Politics of the Icon of the New Martyrs and Confessors of Russia." *Journal of Church and State* 58, no. 3 (2015): 483–507.
Bychkov, Sergei Sergeevich. *Sviashchennik Gleb Iakunin. Nelegkii put' pravdoiskatelia*. Moscow: Eksmo, 2021.
Bychkov, Sergei Sergeevich. *Osvobozhdenie ot illiuzii*. Moscow: Tetis Pablishn, 2010.
Bychkova Jordan, Bella, and Terry G. Jordan-Bychkov. *Siberian Village: Land and Life in the Sakha Republic*. Minneapolis: University of Minnesota Press, 2001.
"Chernogolovka." http://chernogolovka.ru/about/index.ru.html?kk=bd15a3aad6.
Chetverikov, Sergii. *Optina Pustyn'*. 2nd ed. Paris: YMCA-Press, 1988.
A Chronicle of Current Events: Journal of the Human Rights Movement in the USSR, 1972–80.
Chumachenko, Tat'iana A. *Church and State in Soviet Russia: Russian Orthodoxy from World War II to the Khrushchev Years*. Edited and translated by Edward E. Roslof. Armonk, NY: M. E. Sharpe, 2002.
Civil Society and the Search for Justice in Russia, edited by Christopher Marsh and Nikolas K. Gvosdev. Lanham, MD: Lexington Books, 2002.
Clark, Bruce. *An Empire's New Clothes: The End of Russia's Liberal Dream*. London: Viking, 1995.
Clay, Eugene. "The Church of the Transfiguring Mother of God and Its Role in Russian Nationalist Discourse, 1984–1999." *Nova Religio: The Journal of Alternative and Emergent Religions* 3, no. 2 (April 2000): 320–49.
Codevilla, Giovanni. "Commentary on the New Soviet Law on Freedom of Conscience and Religious Organizations." *Religion in Communist Lands* 19, nos. 1–2 (Summer 1991): 119–45.
Cohen, Stephen F. *The Victims Return: Survivors of the Gulag after Stalin*. Bloomsbury: I. B. Tauris, 2011.
Cohn, Norman. *The Pursuit of the Millennium: Revolutionary Messianism in Medieval and Reformation Europe and Its Bearing on Modern Totalitarian Movements*. New York: Harper, 1961.

BIBLIOGRAPHY

Constitution (Fundamental Law) of the Union of Soviet Socialist Republics: Adopted at the Extraordinary Seventh Session of the Supreme Soviet of the USSR of the Ninth Convocation on October 7, 1977. Moscow: Politizdat, 1977.
"Correction to Fr. Gleb's Exile Address." *Keston News Service*, no. 217, January 24, 1985.
CPSU CC Politburo, Protocol No. 210. "Decision Setting Up the Suslov Commission," August 25, 1980. Wilson Center Digital Archive, Library of Congress, Manuscript Division, Dmitriĭ Antonovich Volkogonov papers, 1887–1995, mm97083838, Reel 18, Container 27. Translated by Malcolm Byrne. https://digitalarchive.wilsoncenter.org/document/111230.
Criminal Code of the RSFSR. Washington, DC, and Russian SFSR: United States Joint Publication Service, 1961.
The Crisis of Détente in Europe: From Helsinki to Gorbachev, 1975–1985. Edited by Leopoldo Nuti. London: Routledge, 2009.
Dakin, H. S. "Statement on the Unauthorized Publication of Personal Correspondence in *Literaturnaia gazeta*." In Yakunin and Regel'son, *Letters from Moscow*, 120.
Dakin, Susanna. Speaking at Henry S. Dakin Memorial 2d. https://www.youtube.com/watch?v=5ffyJRc1n9M.
Dakin, Vergilia. "Henry Dakin: A Life Lived True, 1936–2010." *Mendocino Humanist*, December 14, 2010. https://ukiahcommunityblog.wordpress.com.
Daniel, Wallace L. "Father Aleksandr Men and the Struggle to Recover Russia's Heritage." *Demokratizatsiya* 17, no. 1 (Winter 2009): 73–91.
Daniel, Wallace L. "'I Am a Fighter by Nature': Fr. Gleb Yakunin and the Defense of Religious Liberty." In *Dangerous God: Christianity and the Soviet Experiment*, edited by Dominic Erdozain, 74–96. DeKalb: Northern Illinois University Press, 2017.
Daniel, Wallace L. *The Orthodox Church and Civil Society in Russia.* College Station: Texas A&M University Press, 2006.
Daniel, Wallace L. *Russia's Uncommon Prophet: Father Aleksandr Men and His Times.* DeKalb: Northern Illinois University Press, 2016.
Danilushkin, Mikhail Borislavich, gen.ed. *Istoriia Russkoi Pravoslavnoi Tserkvi, 1917–1970: Ot vosstanovleniia Patriarshestva do nashikh dnei.* Vol. 1 of *Trudy Russkoi pravoslavnoi akademii bogoslovskikh nauk i nauchno-bogoslovskikh issledovanii.* St. Petersburg: Voskresenie, 1997.
Davis, Nathaniel. *A Long Walk to Church: A Contemporary History of Russian Orthodoxy.* 2nd ed. Boulder, CO: Westview Press, 2003.
Della Cava, Ralph. "Reviving Orthodoxy in Russia: An Overview of the Factions in the Russian Orthodox Church in the Spring of 1996." *Cahiers du Monde russe* 38, no. 3 (1997): 387–414.
Dennen, Xenia. "A Forgotten Christian Martyr: Boris Talantov." *Keston Newsletter*, no. 36 (2022): 28–34.
De Wolf, Koenraad. *Dissident for Life: Alexander Ogorodnikov and the Struggle for Religious Freedom in Russia.* Translated by Nancy Forest-Flier. Foreword by David Alton. Grand Rapids, MI: Eerdmans, 2010.
Die Judenpogrome in Russland hrsg. im auftrage des Zionistischen hilfsfonds in London; von der zur erforschung der pogrome eingesetzten commission. Edited by A. Linden, 134–37. Vol. 2. Cologne: Jüdishcher verlag g.m.b.h., 1910.

Dostoevsky, Fyodor. *The Brothers Karamazov*. Translated and annotated by Richard Pevear and Larissa Volokhonsky. New York: Farrar, Straus and Giroux, 1990.
Dudko, Dmitrii Sergeevich. "KGB Subversion of the Russian Orthodox Church." *RFE/RL Research Report* 1, no. 12 (March 20, 1992): 51–53.
Dudko, Dmitrii Sergeevich. *O nashem upovanii: Besedy*. Paris: YMCA-Press, 1976.
Dudko, Dmitrii Sergeevich. *Our Hope*. Translated by Paul D. Garrett. Crestwood, NY: St. Vladimir's Seminary Press, 1977.
Dudko, Dmitrii Sergeevich. *Podarok ot Boga: Kniga v piati chastiakh*. Moscow: Izdatel'stvo Sretenskogo monastyria, 2002.
Dudko, Dmitrii Sergeevich. *V ternie i pri doroge: Sbornik propovedei za 25 let sluzheniia*. Moscow: D. S. Dudko, 1993.
Dunlop, John B. "Dissent within the Orthodox Church: Boris Vladimirovich Talantov (1903–1971)." *Russian Review* 31 no. 3 (July 1972): 248–59.
Dunlop, John B. "KGB Subversion of the Russian Orthodox Church." *RFE/RL Research Report* 1, no. 12 (March 20, 1992): 51–53.
Dunlop, John B. "The Russian Orthodox Church and Nationalism after 1988." *Religion in Communist Lands* 18, no. 4 (1990): 292–306.
Durham, W. Cole Jr., and Lauren B. Homer. "Russia's 1997 Law on Freedom of Conscience and Religious Associations: An Analytical Appraisal." *Emory International Law Review* 12, no. 1 (Winter 1998): 101–246.
Dvorkin, Aleksandr Leonidovich, ed. *Sekty protiv tserkvi (Protsess Dvorkina)*. Moscow: Russkaia Pravoslavnaia Tserkov', Izdatel'stvo Moskovskoi Patriarkhii, 2000.
Edel'stein, Fr. Georgii. "Chekisty . . . v riasakh." Interview by P. Lik'ianchenko." *Argumenty i fakty*, no. 36, September 12, 1991.
Ellis, Jane. "The Christian Committee for the Defence of Believers' Rights in the USSR." *Religion in Communist Lands* 4, no. 4 (1980): 279–98.
Ellis, Jane. *The Russian Orthodox Church: A Contemporary History*. London: Routledge, 1986.
Ellis, Jane. *The Russian Orthodox Church: Triumphalism and Defensiveness*. New York: St. Martin's Press, 1996.
Ellis, Jane. "USSR: The Christian Seminar." *Religion in Communist Lands* 8, no. 2 (1980): 92–112.
Ellsworth, Ed. "Ed Ellsworth Biography." https://sunrisecenter.org/classes-events/core-teachers/ed-ellsworth/.
Eremin, Andrei Alekseevich. *Otets Aleksandr Men': Pastyr' na rubezhe vekov*. 2nd ed. Moscow: Carte Blanche, 2001.
Fagan, Geraldine. *Believing in Russia: Religious Policy after Communism*. London: Routledge, 2013.
Fedotov, Georgii Petrovich. "Berdiaev the Thinker." http://cheboto.ns.ca/Philosophy/Sui-Generis/Berdyaev/essays/fedotov.htm.
Filatov, Sergei Borisovich. "Pravoslavie v kontekste postkommunizma: 'Gosudarstvennaia tserkov'' i svoboda sovesti." *Vek XX i mir* 1 (1992): 36–42.
Filatov, Sergei Borisovich. "Protestantism in Postsoviet Russia: An Unacknowledged Triumph." *Religion, State and Society* 28, no. 1 (2000): 93–104.
Filatov, Sergei Borisovich, ed. *Religiia i obshchestvo: Ocherki religioznoi zhizni sovremennoi Rossii*. Moscow: Letnii sad, 2002.

Filatov, Sergei Borisovich. *Religiozno-obshchestvenaia zhizn' rossiiskikh regionov.* Vol. 2. Moscow-St. Petersburg: Letnii sad, 2016.

Filatov, Sergei Borisovich. "Russkaia Pravoslavnaia Tserkov' i politicheskaia elita." In *Religiia i politika v postkommunicheskoi Rossii*, edited by L. N. Mitrokhin, 98–118. Moscow: Institut filosofii RAN, 1994.

Filatov, Sergei Borisovich. "Sovremennaia Rossiia i sekty." *Inostrannaia literatura*, no. 8 (1996): 201–19.

Föller, Christian. "Andersdenken (de) und Orthodoxie: Der Fall der Priester Nikolaj Ešliman und Gleb Jakunin = *Inakomysliashchie* and Orthodoxy: The Case of the Priests Nikolai Eshliman and Gleb Iakunin." *Jahrbücher Für Geshichte Osteuropas* 66, no. 3 (2018): 418–42.

Forsyth, James. *A History of the Peoples of Siberia: Russia's North Asian Colony, 1581–1990.* New York: Cambridge University Press, 2008.

"Fr. Gleb in Exile." *Keston News Service*, no. 214, December 6, 1984.

"Fr. Gleb Yakunin Joins Protest Fast." *Keston News Service*, no. 124, May 21, 1981.

"Fr. Gleb Yakunin Moved to Hospital." *Keston News Service*, no. 136, November 5, 1981.

Framing Mary: The Mother of God in Modern, Revolutionary, and Post-Soviet Culture. Edited by Amy Singleton Adams and Vera Shevzov. DeKalb: Northern Illinois University Press, 2018.

Freeze, Gregory R. "'Churching' 1917: The Church Crisis and the Parish Revolution." *Gosudarstvo, religiia, tserkov' v Rossii i za rubezhom* 37, nos. 1–2 (2019): 30–52.

Freeze, Gregory R. "Handmaiden of the State? The Church in Imperial Russia Reconsidered." *Journal of Ecclesiastical History* 36, no. 1 (January 1985): 82–102.

Gabowitsch, Mischa. *Protest in Putin's Russia.* Revised and updated. Cambridge: Polity Press, 2017.

Gandhi, Mahatma. *The Essential Writings.* Edited and introduction by Judith M. Brown. Oxford World's Classics. New Edition. Oxford: Oxford University Press, 2008.

Ganson, Nicholas. "Orthodox Dissidence as De-Atomization: Father Dmitrii Dudko and His Battle with *Razobshchennost'*." *Soviet and Post-Soviet Review* 40 (2013): 90–114.

Ganson, Nicholas. "Truth Reveals Itself Through Love: Fr. Vsevelod Shpiller's Critique of Aleksandr Solzhenitsyn as a Pastoral Admonition." *Soviet and Post-Soviet Review* (2022): 1–29. https://doi.org/10.30965/18763324-BJA10075.

"Georgi Vins (Wiens) (1928–1998)." https://cmbs.mennonitebrethren.ca/personal_papers/vins-wiensgeorgi-1928-1998/.

Gellner, Ernest. *Nationalism.* New York: New York University Press, 1997.

Gessen, Masha. *The Future Is History: How Totalitarianism Reclaimed Russia.* New York: Riverhead Books, 2017.

Gessen, Masha. "Inside the Gulags of the Soviet Union." *Literary Hub*, March 26, 2018. https:lithub.com/masha-gessen-inside-the-gulags-of-the-soviet-union/.

Gessen, Masha, and Misha Friedman. *Never Remember: Searching for Stalin's Gulags in Putin's Russia.* New York: Columbia Global Reports, 2018.

Gorbachev, Mikhail. *Perestroika: New Thinking for Our Country and the World.* New York: Harper and Row, 1987.

Goricheva, Tat′iana. *Talking about God Is Dangerous: The Diary of a Russian Dissident*. New York: Crossroad, 1987.
Govorov, Aleksei Vasil′evich. *Sv. Grigorii Bogoslov, kak khristianskii poet*. 1886. Reprint, New York: Generic, 2019.
The Great Purge Trials. Edited, with notes, by Robert C. Tucker and Stephen F. Cohen. Introduction by Robert C. Tucker. New York: Grosset and Dunlap, 1965.
Greene, Robert H. Greene, *Bodies Like Bright Stars: Saints and Relics in Orthodox Russia*. DeKalb: Northern Illinois University Press, 2010,
Gregory of Nazianzus. *Select Orations*. Translated by Martha Vinson. Washington, DC: Catholic University of America Press, 2003.
Gudkov, Lev Dmitrievich, Boris Dubin, and Yuri Levada. *Problema "elita" v segodniashnei Rossii: Razmyshleniia nad rezul′tatami sotsialogicheskogo issledovaniia*. Moscow: Fond Liberal′naia missiia, 2007.
Henry S. Dakin: From Physics to Metaphysics and Guns to Toys. Edited by Laura Gail Drewes. Foreword by Vergilia Paasche Dakin. Petaluma, CA: Happy Medium Productions, 2020.
Hexter, J. H. *Reappraisals in History: New Views on History and Society in Early Modern Europe*. 2nd ed. 1961. Reprint, Chicago: University of Chicago Press, 1979.
Holy Foolishness in Russia: New Perspectives. Edited by Priscilla Hunt and Svitlana Kobets. Bloomington, IN: Slavica, 2011.
Hosking, Geoffrey. *The Awakening of the Soviet Union*. Cambridge, MA: Harvard University Press, 1990.
Howard-Johnston [Dennen], Xenia. "Editorial." *Religion in Communist Dominated Areas* 4, no. 1 (Spring 1976): 2–3.
"Iakunin, Gleb Pavlovich." In *Beloe dukhovenstov*, September 29, 2007. https://web .archive.org/web/2007092911643/http:www.ortho-rus.ru/cgi-bin/ps_file.cgi ?4_3590.
Iliushenko, Vladimir Il′ich. "Geroi dukhovnogo soprotivleniia." https://old.prison .org/personal/krakmalnikova.shtml.
"Individual′noe i massovoe soznanie." *Inostrannaia literatura*, no. 11 (1990): 203–22.
"Istoriia soprotivleniia rezhemu delo Iakunin Gleb." https://arch2.iofe.center/case /6864.
"Iuvenalii, mitropolit eparkhii (Poiarkov, Vladimir Kirillovich)." www.patriarchia.ru /db/text/31765.html
Jubilee Bishops' Council of the Russian Orthodox Church, August 13–16, 2000, Moscow. "On the Fundamentals of the Social Conception of the Russian Orthodox Church." Section 3, Church and State. https://incommunion.org /fundamentals-of-the-social-conception-of-the-russian-orthodox-church/.
Kelly, David. "Nairobi: A Door Opened." *Religion in Communist Lands* 4, no. 1 (Spring 1976): 4–17.
Kenworthy, Scott M. "Rethinking the Russian Orthodox Church and the Bolshevik Revolution." In *Revolutionary Russia*. https://doi.org/10.1080/09546545.2018 .1480893.
Kenworthy, Scott M., and Alexander S. Agadjanian. *Understanding World Christianity: Russia*. Minneapolis, MN: Fortress Press, 2021.

Keston College. "Western Church Leaders Report on Religion in the Soviet Union." *Religion in Communist Lands* 5, no. 1 (Spring 1976): 52–53.
Khomiakov, Aleksei Stepanovich. *Izbrannye sochineniia*. Edited by N. S. Arsen'ev. New York: Izdatel'stvo imeni Chekhova, 1955.
Khomiakov, Aleksei Stepanovich. *Tserkov' odna*. Moscow: Gosudarstvennaia publichnaia istoricheskaia biblioteka, 1991.
Khristianskie partii i samodeiatel'nye ob"edineniia: Sbornik materialov i dokumentov. Moscow: Akademiia obshchestvennykh nauk pri TsK KPSS. Ideologicheskii otdel TsK KPSS, 1990.
Khristianskii komitet zashchity prav veruiushchikh v SSSR. *Dokumenty khristianskogo komiteta zashchity prav veruiushchikh v SSSR*. 12 vols. San Francisco: Washington Street Research Center, 1977–1979.
Khrizostom (Martishkin), Archbishop. "Ia sotrudnichal s KGB . . . no ne byl stukachem." Interview by Mikhail Pozdniaev. *Russkaia mysl'*, no. 3926 (April 24, 1992): 8–9.
Khronika neraskrytogo ubiistva, edited by Sergei Bychkov, 144–50. Moscow: Russkoe rekamnoe izdatel'stvo, 1996.
Kizenko, Nadieszda. "Father Dmitri Dudko and the Intersection of Late Cold War Underground, Official, and Diaspora Russian Orthodox Church Opinion." *Review of Ecumenical Studies* 14, no. 2 (2022): 289–309. DOI: 10.2478/ress-2022-0106.
Knox, Zoe. *Russian Society and the Orthodox Church: Religion in Russia after Communism*. London: Routledge Curzon, 2005.
Kornblatt, Judith D. "Is Father Alexander Men' a Saint? The Jews, the Intelligentsia, and the Russian Orthodox Church." *Toronto Slavic Quarterly*. http://sites.utoronto.ca/tsq/12/kornblatt12.shtmi.
Kotkin, Stephen. *Armageddon Averted: The Soviet Collapse, 1970–2000*. New York: Oxford University Press, 2008.
Kotkin, Stephen. *Magnetic Mountain: Stalinism as a Civilization*. Berkeley: University of California Press, 1997.
Krakhmal'nikova, Zoe. *Gor'kie plody sladkogo plena*. Montreal: Monastery Press, 1989.
Krakhmal'nikova, Zoe. "Skandal v blagorodnom semeistve: Prodolzhenie sleduet." *Stolitsa*, no. 14 (1992): 9–11.
Krotov, Iakov. "Religion and the Russian Press Since 1990: Journalists Most Actively Writing on Church Subjects." *East-West Church and Ministry Report* 10, no. 3 (Summer 2002): 10–13.
Krotov, Iakov. "S khristianskoi tochki zreniia." Interview with Krakhmal'nikov's daughter Zoia Feliksovna Svetova and the writer and poet Vladimir Il'ich Iliushenkov. http://krotov.info.library/17_r/radio_svoboda/20090117.htm.
Krutov, Mark. "Episkopy na sluzhbe Lubianki: Istorii ierarkhoi ukrainskoi tserkvi, zaverbovannykh NKGB SSSR, January 23, 2018. https://www.svoboda.org/a/28989881.html.
Kuroedov, Vladimir Alekseevich. *Religiia i tserkov' v sovetskom gosudarstve*. Moscow: Izdatel'stvo politicheskoi literatury, 1981.

Kuroedov, Vladimir Alekseevich. *Religiia i tserkov' v sovetskom obshchestve*. 2nd ed. Moscow: Izdatel'stvo politicheskoi literatury, 1984.
Kuroedov, Vladimir Alekseevich (interview). "Some Questions about Religion and the Church." *Religion in Communist Dominated Areas* 5, no. 22 (November 30, 1966): 173–77.
Kyrlezhev, Aleksandr, and Konstantin Troitskii. "Sovremennoe rossiiskoe pravoslavie." Part 1: "Tipologiia religioznogo soznaniia." *Kontinent*, no. 75 (January–March 1993): 241–62.
Lenin, Vladimir Il'ich. "O znachenii vointsvuiushchego materializma." In *Polnoe sobranie sochineniia*. 5th ed., 45:23–33. Moscow: Izdatel'stvo politicheskoi literatury, 1964.
Letters from Moscow. Edited by Jane Ellis. San Francisco: H. S. Dakin, 1978.
Levitin-Krasnov, Anatolii Emmanuilovich. "Father Gleb Yakunin and Lev Regelson." In *Letters from Moscow: Religion and Human Rights in the USSR*, 1–9.
Levitin-Krasnov, Anatolii Emmanuilovich. *Likhie gody: 1924–1942*. Paris: YMCA-Press, 1977.
Levitin-Krasnov, Anatolii Emmanuilovich. "Novosti iz Moskvy: Smert' Arkhiepiskopa Ermogena Golubeva." *Russkaia mysl'*, no. 3204 (May 18, 1978), 21.
Levitin-Krasnov, Anatolii Emmanuilovich. "O tekh, kogo nedavno sudili." *Posev* 36, no. 11 (November 1980): 47–49.
Levitin-Krasnov, Anatolii Emmanuilovich. "Otets Dmitrii Dudko." *Posev* 31, no. 1 (1975): 26–37.
Levitin-Krasnov, Anatolii Emmanuilovich. "Religion and Soviet Youth." *Religion in Communist Lands* 7, no. 4 (Winter 1979): 232–37.
Levitin-Krasnov, Anatolii Emmanuilovich. "Sol' zemli (Molodaia Rossiia)." *Russkaia mysl'*, no. 3282, part 1, November 15, 1979, p. 14.
Levitin-Krasnov, Anatolii Emmanuilovich. *V poiskakh novogo grada: Vospominaniia*, pt. 3. Tel-Aviv: Izdatel'stvo Krug, 1980.
Liberalizm v Rossii: Sbornik statei. Edited by Iurii V. Krasheninnikov. Moscow: Znak, 1993.
Likhachev, Dmitrii Sergeevich. "Russkaia kul'tura: nasledie proshloe i real'naia sila segodnia." *Sem'ia*, no. 24 (June 15, 1988): 14–15.
Louth, Andrew. *Modern Orthodox Thinkers: From the Philokalia to the Present*. Downer's Grove, IL: IVP Academic, 2015.
Mandelstam, Nadezhda. *Hope against Hope: A Memoir*. Translated by Max Hayward. Introduction by Clarence Brown. New York: Atheneum, 1970.
Marchenko, Anatoly. *My Testimony*. Translated by Michael Scammell. New York: E. P. Dutton, 1969.
Martin, Barbara and Nadezhda Beliakova, eds. *Religious Life in the Late Soviet Union: From Survival to Revival (1960s -1980s)*. London: Routledge, 2023.
Maslenikova, Zoia Afanas'evna. *Zhizn' ottsa Aleksandra Menia*. Moscow: Pristsel's, 1995.
Matlock, John. *Autopsy of an Empire: The American Ambassador's Account of the Collapse of an Empire*. New York: Random House, 1995.
McGuckin, John A. *St. Gregory of Nazianzus: An Intellectual Biography*. Crestwood, NY: St. Vladimir's Seminary Press, 2001.

Men', Aleksandr. *Bibliia i literatura*: Lektsii. Moscow: Khram sviatykh bessrebrenikov Kosmu i Damiana v Shubine, 2002.
Men', Aleksandr. *Istoriia religii v semi tomakh: V poiskakh puti, istiny, i zhizni*. Vol. 2: *Magizn i Edinobozhie: Religioznyi put' chelovechestva do epokhi velikikh Uchitelei*. Moscow: Slovo, 1991.
Men', Aleksandr. *Kul'tura i dukhovnnoe voskhozhdenie*. Edited by R. I. Al'betkova and M. T. Rabotiaga. Moscow: Iskusstvo, 1992.
Men', Aleksandr. *Navstrechu khristu: Sbornik statei*. Edited by Nataliia Grigorenko and Pavel Men. Moscow: Zhizn' s Bogom, 2009.
Men'. Aleksandr. "Poeziia sv. Grigoriia Bogoslova." In *Navstrechu khristu*, 7–30.
Men', Aleksandr. *O sebe . . . Vospominaniia, inter'viu, besedy, pis'ma*. Moscow: Izdatel'stvo Zhizn' s Bogom, 2007.
Men', Aleksandr. *Radostnaia vest' (lektsy)*. Edited by M. V. Sergeeva. Moscow: Vita-Tsentr, 1992.
Men', Aleksandr. *Russkaia religioznaia filosofiia: Lektsii*. Edited by Marina Nasonova. Moscow: Khram sviatykh bessrebrenikov Kosmy i Damiana v Shubine, 2003.
Men', Aleksandr. *Sobranie sochinenii*. Vol. 1: *Syn chelovecheskii*. Moscow: Izdatel'stvo Moskovskoi Patriarkhii Russkoi Pravoslavnoi Tserkvi, 2015.
Men', Aleksandr. *The Wellsprings of Religion*. Translated by Alasdair MacNaughton. Forewords by Wallace L. Daniel, Alasdair MacNaughton, and William Clegg. Yonkers, NY: St Vladimir's Seminary Press, 2017.
Menzel, Birgit. "New Age Diplomacy: The Diplomatic Role of the Esalen Institute in Ending the Cold War." In *New Age in Russia*. https://newageru.hypotheses.org/1903.
Miłosz, Czesław. *The Captive Mind*. Translated by Jane Zielonko. 1951. Reprint, New York: Vintage International, 1990.
Moltmann, Jürgen. *Religion, Revolution, and the Future*. Translated by M. Douglas Meeks. New York: Charles Scribner's, 1969.
Moltmann, Jürgen. *Theology of Hope: On the Ground and the Implications of a Christian Eschatology*. Translated by James W. Leitch. New York: Harper and Row, 1967.
Morgan, Dale L. "Susanna Bryant Dakin." *Bancroftiana*, no. 40 (May 1967): 1.
Moscow Helsinki Group. "Ob obrazovanii obshchestvennoi gruppy sodeistviia vypolneniiu Khel'sinkskikh soglashenii v SSSR." In *Dokumenty Moskovskoi Khel'sinkskoi gruppy, 1976-1982*, edited by G. V. Kuzovkin and D. I. Zubarev. Moscow: Zatsepa, 2006.
Nabokov, Vladimir. *Nikolai Gogol*. New York: New Directions, 1961.
New Religions: A Guide; New Religious Movements, Sects, and Alternative Spiritualities. Edited by Christopher Partridge. New York: Oxford University Press, 2004.
"News of Fr. Gleb Yakunin's Health." *Keston News Service*, no. 137, November 19, 1981.
Nezhnyi, Aleksandr. "Ego blazhenstvo bez mitry i zhezla." *Ogonek*, no. 48, November 1991, 8–10, and no. 49, December 1991, 21–22.
Nezhnyi, Aleksandr. "Kamo griadeshi, sviataia tserkov'?" *Ogonek*, nos. 18–19, May 1992, 12–13.
Nezhnyi, Aleksandr. "Tret'e imia." *Ogonek*, no. 4, January 25–February 1, 1992, 2–3.

Nezhnyi, Aleksandr. "Tretii razgovor s Kharchevem." *Ogonek*, no. 44, October 1989, 9–11.
Nezhnyi, Aleksandr. "Zakon i sovest '." *Ogenek-88: Luchshie publikatsii god*, compiled by L. Gushin, S. Kliamkin, and V. Iumashev, 318–23. Moscow: Ogonek, 1989
Nikodim (Rotov), Metropolitan. "The Russian Orthodox Church and the Ecumenical Movement." *Ecumenical Review* 21, no. 22 (1969): 116–29.
Obshchestvo remeslennogo i zemledel'cheskogo trud sredi evreev (Soviet Union). *Materialy i issledovaniia*, no. 4: *Evrei v SSSR*. Tel Aviv: Aticot, 1929.
Obshchina: Zhurnal Khristianskogo Seminara po problemam religioznogo vozrozhdeniia. Edited by Aleksandr Ogorodnikov, no. 2 (1978).
Ogorodnikov, Alexander. "Khristianskii kruzhok v Moskve." *Vestnik Russkogo studencheskogo dvizheniia*, nos. 3–4 (119) (1976): 296–301.
Ogorodnikov, Alexander. "Pis'mo General'nomu Sekretariu Vsemirnogo Soveta Tserkvei D-ru Filippu Potteru," July 27, 1976. *Vestnik Russkogo khristianskogo dvizheniia*, nos. 3–4 (119) (1976): 304–8.
Ogorodnikov, Alexander, and Boris Razveev. "Letter to Dr. Philip Potter, General Secretary of the WCC," August 5, 1976. *Religion in Communist Lands* 7, no. 1 (1979): 48–50.
Orlov, Yuri. *Dangerous Thoughts: Memoirs of a Russian Life*. Translated by Thomas P. Whitney. New York: William Morrow, 1991.
Osipova, Irina Ivanovna. "Dokumenty po regionam i godam: Iz istorii gonenii Istinno-Pravoslavnnoi (Katakombnoi) Tserkvi: Konets 1920-kh–nachalo 1970-kh godov." *Mezhdunarodnoe istoriko-prosvetitel'skoe pravozashchitnoe i blagotvoritel'noe obshchestvo MEMORIAL.* http://www.histor-ipt-kt.org/doc.html.
Osipova, Irina Ivanovna. *"O, Premiloserdyi . . . Budi s nami neotstupno. . . ."* Vospominaniia veruiushchikh Istinno-Pravoslavnoi (Katakombnoi) Tserkvi: Konets 1920-kh–nachalo 1970-kh godov. St. Petersburg: Kifa, 2011.
Papkova, Irina. *The Russian Orthodox Church and Russian Politics*. New York: Oxford University Press, 2011.
"Patriarch Rejects North American Standards of Freedom of Conscience," August 27, 1997. *Pravoslavie v Rossii*. http://www.stetson.edu/~psteeves/relnews.
Pazukhin, Yevgeni. "Charting the Russian Religious Renaissance." *Religion, State and Society* 23, no. 1 (1995): 57–94.
Perils of Perestroika: Viewpoints from the Soviet Press, 1989–1991. Edited by Isaac J. Tarasulo. Wilmington, DE: Scholarly Resources, 1992.
Pimen, Patriarch of Moscow and All Russia. "Speech at the Solemn Meeting of the Soviet Peace Committee." *Journal of the Moscow Patriarchate*, no. 11 (November 1977): 36.
Pimen, Patriarkh Moskovskii i vseia Rus, i chleny Sviashchennogo Sinoda. "Poslanie Sviashchennogo Sinoda o V Assemblee Vsemirnogo Soveta Tserkvei i ee rezul'tatakh," March 3, 1976. *Zhurnal Moskovskoi Patriarkhii*, no. 4 (1976): 7–13.
Politicheskaia ksenofobiia: Radikal'nye gruppu, predstavleniia liderov, rol' tserkvi. Edited by Aleksandr Verkhovskii, Ekaterina Mikhailovskaia, and Vladimir Pribylovskii. Moscow: Izdatel'stvo 000 Panorama, 1999.

Polosin, Ali Viacheslav. "My Journey to Islam." http:www.islam.ru/en/content/story/polosin-ali-vyacheslav-my-journey-islam.
Ponomarov, Lev. "Za prava cheloveka." https://lenta.ru/lib/14163044.\
Popovskii, Mark. "Khristianstvo molodeet." *Vol'noe slovo*, no. 29 (1978): 53–55.
Popovsky, Mark. *Zhizn' i zhitie Voina-Iasentskogo arkhiepiskopa i khiruga*, 2nd ed. Tenafly, N. J.: Hermitage, 1996.
Posdeeff, Helene. "Geneva: The Defense of Believers' Rights." *Religion in Communist Lands* 4, no. 4 (Winter 1976): 4–8.
Poslykhalin, A. Iu. *Istoriia gorodakh Shchyolkovo: Almanakh internet-zhurnala "Podmoskovnyi kraeved."* Moscow: Akademizdat'sentr "Nauka" RAN, 2015.
Pospielovsky, Dimitry V. *The Orthodox Church in the History of Russia*. Crestwood, NY: St Vladimir's Seminary Press, 1998.
Pospielovsky, Dimitry V. *Russkaia Pravoslavnaia Tserkov' v XX veke*. Moscow: Izdatel'stvo "Respublika," 1995.
Potter, Philip A. "The Churches and Religious Liberty in the Helsinki Signatory States," August 12, 1976. *Ecumenical Review* 28, no. 4 (October 1976): 448–49.
Pozdreva, Elena. "The Report Card of the Moscow Patriarchate's Delegation in Nairobi." *Radio Liberty Research*, February 23, 1976, RL 104/76.
Proselytism and Orthodoxy in Russia: The New War for Souls. Edited by John Witte Jr. and Michael Bourdeaux. Ossining, NY: Orbis, 1999.
Pushkarov, Sergei, Vladimir Rusak, and Gleb Yakunin. *Christianity and Government in Russia and the Soviet Union: Reflections on the Millennium*. Boulder, CO: Westview Press, 1989.
Putin, Vladimir. "O provedenii spetsial'noi voennoi operatsii," February 24, 2023. http://en.kremlin.ru/events/president/news/67843.
Rachmawati, Dian Laily. "Leo Tolstoy's Idea of Morality in His Short Stories Characters." *Litera kul'tura* 2, no. 2 (2014): 1–18.
Radio Free Europe/Radio Liberty. "Poland: Solidarity—The Trade Union That Changed the World," August 24, 2005. https://www.rferl.org/a/1060898.html.
Rathenau, James. L. *Turbulence in World Politics: A Theory of Change and Continuity*. Princeton, NJ: Princeton University Press, 1990.
Raushenbakh, Boris Viktorovich. "Religiia i nravstvennost'." *Znamia* 1, no. 1 (January 1991): 204–16.
Regel'son, Lev. "Dnevnik: Lev Regel'son otvechaet ottsu Aleksandry Meniu: O bogoslovskoi shkole Feliksa Karelina." https://skurlatov.com/327853.html.
Regel'son, Lev. htpps//:www.facebook.com./lregelson.
Regel'son, Lev. *Tragediia russkoi tserkvi, 1917–1945*. Afterword by Archpriest John Meyendorff. Paris: YMCA-Press, 1977.
Religiia i demokratiia: Na puti k svobode sovesti. Vol. 2, edited by S. B. Filatov and D. E. Furman. Moscow: "Progress—Kul'tura," 1993.
Religiia i politika v postkommunisticheskoi Rossii. Edited by L. N. Mitrokhin. Moscow: Institut filosofii RAN, 1994.
Religiia i prava cheloveka. Vol. 3 of *Na puti k svobode sovesti*. Edited by L. M. Vorontsova, A. V. Pchelintsev, and S. B. Filatov. Moscow: Nauka, 1996.
Religion in the Soviet Union: An Archival Reader. Edited and translated by Felix Corley. New York: New York University Press, 1996.

Religious Policy in the Soviet Union. Edited by Sabrina Petra Ramet. New York: Cambridge University Press, 1993.

Revisionism and Diversification in New Religious Movements. Edited by Eileen Barker. Farnham: Ashgate, 2013.

Richardson, James T., and Marat Shterin. "Minority Religions and Social Justice in Russian Courts: An Analysis of Recent Cases." *Social Justice Research* 12, no. 4 (1999): 393–408.

Rose, Seraphim (Father). "In Defense of Father Dimitry Dudko." *Orthodox Word* 92, no. 16 (1980): 115–22, 127–28.

Rovenskii, Georgii Vasil'evich. *Gleb Iakunin (1934–2014): Pravoslavnyi pravozashchitnik, sviashchennik, deputat, poet*. Shchyolkovo: Shchyolkovskii kraevedcheskii klub, 2021.

Rubenstein, Joshua. "Introduction: Andrei Sakarov, the KGB, and the Legacy of Soviet Dissent." In *The KGB File of Andrei Sakharov*, edited and annotated by Joshua Rubenstein and Alexander Gribanov. Translated by Ella Shmulevich, Efrem Yankelevich, and Alla Zeide, 1–85. New Haven, CT: Yale University Press, 2005.

Rudova, Larisa. "Bergsonism in Russia: The Case of Bakhtin." *Neophilogus* 80, no. 2 (April 1996): 175–88.

"Russian Baptist Response." *Religion in Communist Lands* 4, no. 1 (Spring 1976): 16–17.

"Russian Dissidents: Mopping Up." *Economist*, 273, no. 7108, November 24, 1979, 56.

Russian Federal Law. "On Freedom of Conscience and Religious Associations." Translated by Lawrence A. Uzzell. *Emory International Law Review* 12, no. 1 (Winter 1998): 657–80.

Russkaia Pravoslavnaia Tserkov', Otdel vneshnikh tserkovnykh sviazei. "Tserkov' i gosudarstvo." Section 5: "Osnovy sotsial'noi kontseptsii Russkoi Pravoslavnoi Tserkvi." https://mospat.ru/ru/documents/social-concepts/; English translation: https://mospat.ru/en/documents/social-concepts/.

Sakharov, Andrei Dmitrievich. *Memoirs*. Translated by Richard Lourie. New York: Alfred A. Knopf, 1990.

Sakharov, Andrei Dmitrievich. *Progress, Coexistence and Intellectual Freedom*. Introduction, Afterword, and Notes by Harrison E. Salisbury. New York: New York Times, 1968.

Sakwa, Richard. "Christian Democracy and Civil Society in Russia." *Religion, State and Society* 22, no. 3 (1994): 273–303.

Sakwa, Richard. "Christian Democracy in Russia." *Religion, State and Society* 20 no. 2 (1992): 135–68.

Sakwa, Richard. *Russian Politics and Society*. 3rd ed. London: Routledge, 2002.

Scarfe, Alan, ed. *Christian Committee for the Defense of Believers' Rights in the USSR: A Selection of Documents in Translation*. Translated by Maria Belaeffa. Glendale, CA: Door of Hope Press, 1982.

Schwab, Klaus. *Shaping the Future of the Fourth Industrial Revolution*. Redfern, New South Wales: Currency Press, 2018.

Shafarevich, Igor Rostislavovich. *Zakonodatel'stvo o religii v SSSR*. Paris: YMCA-Press, 1973.

Shalamov, Varlam. *Kolyma Tales*. Translated by John Glad. London: Penguin, 1994.
Shchipkova, Tat'iana Nikolaevna. "Imeet li pravo sovetskii prepodavatel' na svobody sovesti?" July–September 1978. In *Dokumenty khristianskogo komiteta*, 4:497–506.
Shchipkova, Tat'iana Nikolaevna. "Spiritual Pilgrimage of Vladimir Poresh." *Religion in Communist Lands* 8, no. 2 (Summer 1980): 101–3.
Sheehan, James J. "How History Can Be a Moral Science." *Perspectives on History*, October 2005. https://www.historians.org/publications-and-directories/perspectives-on-history/october-2005/how-history-can-be-a-moral-science–
Shevzov, Vera. "Women on the Fault Lines of Faith: Pussy Riot and the Insider/Outsider Challenge to Post-Soviet Orthodoxy." *Religion and Gender* 4, no. 2 (2014): 121–44.
Shilkin, Andrei Dmitrievich, and Anatolii Vasil'evich Belov. *Diversiia bez Dinamita*. 2nd ed. Moscow: Politizdat, 1976.
Shkarovskii, Mikhail Vital'evich. *Russkaia Pravoslavnaia Tserkov' v XX veke*. Moscow: Veche, Lepta, 2010.
Shterin, Marat, and James T. Richardson. "The Yakunin vs. Dvorkin Trial and the Emerging Religious Pluralism in Russia." *Occasional Papers on Religion in Eastern Europe* 22, no. 1 (2002). https://digitalcommons.georgefox.edu/ree/vol22/iss1/1.
Shusharin, Dmitrii. "Porfirii Golovlev o svobode i vere." *Znamia* 3, no. 1 (March 1994): 191–200.
Sidorenko, Iurii Sergeevich. *Tri dnia, kotorye oprokinuli bol'shevism: Ispoved' svidetelia, pokazaniia ochevidtsa*. Rostov-na-Donu: Izdatel'stvo Periodika Dona, 1991.
Slezkine, Peter. "From Helsinki to Human Rights Watch: How an American Cold War Monitoring Group Became an International Human Rights Institution." *Humanity* 5, no. 3 (Winter 2014): 345–70.
Smolkin, Victoria. *A Sacred Space is Never Empty: A History of Soviet Atheism*. Princeton, NJ: Princeton University Press, 2018.
"Solitary Confinement for Fr. Gleb." *Keston News Service*, no. 166, January 27, 1983.
Solov'ev, Vladimir Sergeevich. *God, Man, and the Church: The Spiritual Foundations of Life*. Translated by Donald Attwater. 1937. Reprint, London: James Clarke, 2016.
Solov'ev, Vladimir Sergeevich. *Sobranie sochinenii*. 2nd ed. 10 vols. St. Petersburg: Obshchestvennaia pol'za, 1901–1914.
Solzhenitsyn, Alexander I. *The Gulag Archipelago, 1918–1956: An Experiment in Literary Investigation*. Vol. 2. Translated by Thomas P. Whitney. New York: Harper and Row, 1974.
Solzhenitsyn, Alexander I. *One Day in the Life of Ivan Denisovich*. Translated by Thomas P. Whitney. New York: Crest, Fawcett, 1963.
"Soviet Official Lectures on Religion." *Religion in Communist Lands* 6, no. 1 (Spring 1978): 32–33.
"Special Dossier on the Polish Crisis of 1980," August 28, 1980. Wilson Center Digital Archive, Library of Congress, Manuscript Division, Dmitrii Antonovich Volkogonov papers, 1887–1995, mm97083838, Reel 18, Container 27. Translated by Malcolm Byrne. https://digitalarchive.wilsoncenter.org/document/111230.

"Spiski apostol'skoi preemstvennosti osnovannykh apostolami Pomestnykh Tserkvei." https://mir-angelica.ru/uchenie-o-vere/apostolskaya-pravoslavnaya-cerkov.html.
Stanton, Leonard J. *The Optina Pustyn Monastery in the Russian Literary Imagination: Iconic Vision in the Works by Dostoevsky, Gogol, Tolstoy, and Others.* New York: Peter Lang, 1995.
Stone, Andrew B. "'Overcoming Peasant Backwardness': The Khrushchev Antireligious Campaign and the Rural Soviet Union." *Russian Review* 67 (April 2008): 296–320.
Svetlov, Immanuel [Aleksandr Men']. *Syn chelovecheskii.* Brussels: Zhizn's Bogom, 1968.
Talantov, Boris Vladimirovich. "Bedstvennoe polozhenie Pravoslavnoi Tserkvi v Kirovskoi oblasti i rol' Moskovskoi Patriarkhii (Iz otkrytogo pis'ma Borisa Talantova ot 19 noiabria 1966 g.)." *Vestnik Russkogo studencheskogo khristianskogo dvizheniia,* no. 1 (83) (1967): 29–64.
Talantov, Boris Vladimirovich. "The Moscow Patriarchate and Sergianism." https://www.orthodoxinfo.com>cat_tal.
Talantov, Boris Vladimirovich. "Sovetskoe obschchestvo, 1965–68." *Posev* 25, no. 9 (1969): 35–41.
Talantov, Boris Vladimirovich. "Zhaloba, General'nomu prokuroru SSSR ot gr. Talantova Borisa Vladimirovicha (g. Kirov)." *Vestnik Russkogo studencheskogo khristianskogo dvizheniia,* nos. 3–4 (89–90) (1968): 49–68.
Taubman, William. *Gorbachev: His Life and Times.* New York: W. W. Norton, 2017.
Taubman, William. *Khrushchev: The Man and His Era.* New York: W. W. Norton, 2003.
Tchepournaya, Olga. "The Hidden Sphere of Religious Searches in the Soviet Union: Independent Religious Communities in Leningrad from the 1960s to the 1970s." *Sociology of Religion* 64, no. 3 (2003): 377–88.
Ternovskii, Leonard. "Podvig protivostoianiia." *Posev* 36, no. 1 (1980): 2.
Tolz, Vera. "Access to KGB and CPSU Archives in Russia." *RFE/RL Research Report* 1, no. 16 (April 17, 1992): 1.
"To vasha Mama." Pamiati ottsa Gleba Iakunina, blog entry by Elena Volkova, March 5, 2019.
"The Trial of Gleb Yakunin, 25–28 August 1980." *A Chronicle of Current Events,* no. 58 (November 1980). https://chronicle-of-current-events.com/2016/01/12/58-3-the-trial-of-gleb-yakunin/.
Tserkov' i dukhovnoe vozrozhdenie Rossii: Slova, rechi, poslaniia, obrashcheniia, 1990–1998. Edited by Tikhon, Episkop Bronitskogo. Moscow: Izdatel'stvo Moskovskoi Patriarkhii, 1999.
Tserkovnaia zhizn' XX veka: Protoierei Aleksandr Men' i ego dukhovnie nastavniki: Sbornik materialov Pervoi nauchnoi konferentsii "Menevskie chteniia (9–11 sentiabria 2006 g.). Edited by M. V. Grigorenko. Sergiev Posad: Izdanie prikhoda Sergievskoi tserkvi v Semkhoze, g. Sergiev Posad, 2007.
"Ukrainian Patriarch and Yakunin Excommunicated by Russian Orthodox Church." *Eurasian Daily Monitor* 3, no. 37 (February 21, 1997): 1–2 (from Interfax-Ukraine, NTV, February 20, 1997). https://www.jamestown.org/program/ukrainian-patriarch-and-yakunin-excommunicated-by-russian-orthodox-church/.

Ulitskaia, Ludmilla Evgen′evna. *Sviashchennyi musor: Rasskazy, esse*. Moscow: Astrel′, 2012.
University of Minnesota, Human Rights Library. "The Final Act of the Conference on Security and Cooperation in Europe," August 1, 1975, 14 I.L.M. 1292 (Helsinki Declaration). http://www1.umn.edu/humanrts/osce/basics/finact75.htm.
US Congress, House Committee on International Relations. *Religious Persecution in the Soviet Union*. Hearings before the Subcommittees on International Political and Military Affairs and on International Relations. Committee on International Relations, 94th Cong., 2nd sess., June 24 and 30, 1976.
Uzlaner, Dmitry. "The Pussy Riot Case and the Peculiarities of Russian Post-Secularism." Translated by April French. *State, Religion and Church* 1, no. 1 (2014): 23–58.
Vail, Peter L., and Aleksandr A. Genis. *60-x: Mir sovetskogo cheloveka*. Ann Arbor, MI: Ardis, 1988.
Vasil′ev, Nikolai. "Nas ne tronesh—my ne tronem, a zatronesh—spusku ne dadim." Portal Credo.ru, February 21, 2007. http://www.portal-credo.ru/site/?act=fresh&id=.
Vasil′eva, Ol′ga Iur′evna. *Russkaia Pravoslavnaia Tserkov′ v politike sovetskogo gosudarstva v 1943–1948*. Moscow: Institut rossisskoi istorii RAN, 1999.
Veniamin (Novik). *Pravoslavie. Khristianstvo. Demokratiia: Sbornik statei*. St. Petersburg: Aleteiia, 1999.
Vess′e, Sesil′. *Za vashu i nashu svobodu: Dissidentskoe dvizhenie v Rossii*. Moscow: Novoe literaturnoe obozrenie, 2015.
Vins, Georgi. *Testament from Prison*. Translated by Jane Ellis. Weston, Ontario: David C. Cook, 1975.
Visser 't Hooft, Willem Adolph. "Message of the Assembly." In *Report of the First Assembly of the World Council of Churches Held at Amsterdam, August 2 to September 4, 1948*, edited by W. A. Visser 't Hooft. London: SCM Press, 1949.
Voices of the Voiceless: Religion, Communism, and the Keston Archive. Edited by Julie deGraffenried and Zoe Knox. Waco, TX: Baylor University Press, 2019.
Volkova, Elena Ivanovna. *Glyba Gleba: Zapreshchenneishii ierei Iakunin*. St. Petersburg: Renome, 2021.
Vorontstova, Liudmila Mikhailovna. "Razrushat′ li muzei radi tserkovnogo vozrozhdeniia?" In *Religiia i demokratiia: Na puti k svobode sovesti*. Vol. 2, edited by S. B. Filatov and D. E. Furman, 69-82. Moscow: Progress—Kul′tura, 1993.
Vsemirnyi Russkii Narodnyi Sobor, X. "Deklaratsiia o pravakh i dostoinstve cheloveka," April 6, 2006. www.patriarchia.ru/db/print/103235.html.
"Vypiski sviashch: Gleba Iakunina iz otchetov KGB o rabote s agentami-sotrudnikami Moskovskoi patriarkhii." http://krotov.info.
Walters, Philip. "Anatolii Levitin-Krasnov, 1915–1991." *Religion in Communist Lands* 19, nos. 3–4 (1991): 264–70. DOI: 10.1080/09637499108431520.
Wardin, Albert W. Jr. "Jacob J. Wiens: Mission Champion in Freedom and Repression." *Journal of Church and State* 28, no. 3 (Autumn 1986): 495–514.

Weingartner, Erich. *Human Rights on the Ecumenical Agenda: Report and Assessment (Background Information of Commission of the Churches on International Affairs).* Geneva: Commission of the Churches on International Affairs, 1983.
Women of the Catacombs: Memoirs of the Underground Church in Stalin's Russia. Edited and translated by Wallace L. Daniel. Preface by Archpriest Aleksandr Men. Foreword by Roy R. Robson. Ithaca, NY: Northern Illinois University Press/ Cornell University Press, 2021.
World Council of Churches. *Breaking Barriers: The Official Report of the Fifth Assembly of the World Council of Churches, Nairobi, 23 November–10 December 1975.* Edited by David M. Paton. London: SPCK, 1976.
World Council of Churches, Central Committee. "Helsinki Colloquium: Memorandum on the Church's Role," July 24–28, 1976. *Ecumenical Review* 28, no. 4 (1976): 450–56.
World Council of Churches, Central Committee. "Violence, Nonviolence, and the Struggle for Social Justice," August 28, 1973. *Ecumenical Review* 25, no. 4 (1973): 430–46.
Wyman, Matthew, and Stephen White. "Public Opinion, Parties, and Voters in the December 1993 Russian Elections." *Europe-Asian Studies* 47, no. 4 (June 1995): 591–614.
Yaffe, Joshua. *Between Two Fires: Truth, Ambition, and Compromise in Putin's Russia.* New York: Tim Duggan Books, Random House, 2020.
Yakovlev, Aleksandr Nikolaevich. *Izbrannye intervi: 1992–2005.* Edited by A. A. Yakovlev. Moscow: Mezhdunarodnyi fond Demokratiia, 2009.
"Yakunin Appeal." *Keston News Service*, no. 119, March 12, 1981.
"Yakunin Appeal Reportedly Rejected." *Keston News Service*, no. 120, March 26, 1981.
"Yeltsin Attends Sunday Church Services." *Summary of World Broadcasts* 1408 B/1 (June 16, 1992).
Young, Cathy. "Remembering the Russian Priest Who Fought the Orthodox Church," December 28, 2014, updated April 14, 2017. https://www.thedailybeast.com/remembering-the-russian-priest-who-fought-the-orthodox-church.
Yuvenalii, Metropolitan. "Russian Orthodox Response." *Religion in Communist Lands* 4, no. 1, (Spring 1976): 15–16.
Zalesskii, Alexei, and Irina Zalesskaia. "Appeal to the Christians of Our Country." *Religion in Communist Lands* 4, no. 4 (1980): 292–93.
Zelinskii, Vladimir. "Pastva i pastyri." *Russkaia mysl'*, no. 3786 (July 28, 1979): 8–9.
Zernov, Sviashchennik M. "Moskva." *Zhurnal Moskovskoi Patriarkhii*, no. 10 (1947): 11–12.
Zernov, Nicholas. *The Russian Religious Renaissance of the Twentieth Century.* New York: Harper and Row, 1963.
Zernov, Nicholas. *Three Russian Prophets: Khomiakov, Dostoevsky, and Soloviev.* 3rd ed. 1911. Reprint, Gulf Breeze, FL: Academic International Press, 1944.

Index

Figures are indicated by "f" following page numbers.

Adventists, 114–16, 208, 271n89
Afghanistan, Soviet invasion of (1979), 3, 129, 131, 273n26
Aitmatov, Chinghiz, 163
Aksakov, Ivan Sergeevich, 45
Aksenov-Meerson, Michael, 59, 60, 257n30
Aksiuchits, Viktor, 164, 168, 200–204, 201f
Albats, Yevgenia, 184
Aleksenko, Leonid Demianovich, 105–6
Alekseyeva, Liudmilla, 267n10
Aleksii I (patriarch of Moscow): on church-state relations, 54; letter to (1965), 31–32, 39–54, 57, 85, 91, 113, 252n1, 257n20, 276n59; Stalin's cult of personality and, 169–70; suspension of Yakunin from priesthood, 1, 54, 101; Yermogen and, 38, 253n21
Aleksii II (patriarch of Moscow): challenges facing, 209–10, 213, 218; KGB and, 183–84, 187, 286n25, 286n28; on missionaries, 208, 211, 217; pressure from church factions, 197; on revitalization of Russian Orthodox Church, 162–63, 199; on Ukrainian independence, 219; Yakunin and, 204, 210–17, 293n78; at Yeltsin's inauguration, 289n81
All-Russian Church Council (1917–1918), 42–43, 45, 214–15, 221–22, 229, 232
American Historical Association, 281–82n25
American Orthodox Church (AOC), 115
Andropov, Yuri, 2, 143, 155
antireligion campaigns: Bolsheviks and, 45, 55, 106, 179, 181; ideological basis of, 63; of Khrushchev, 7, 28–29, 33, 38, 53, 89, 91, 167–68, 251n66; persecution and, 75–76; propaganda, 13, 28, 106, 121; of Stalin, 89, 167–68. *See also* atheism
antisemitism, 11, 27
Apostolic Orthodox Church (AOTs), 8, 228–33, 231f, 297n53

Applebaum, Anne, 144
Argentev, Aleksandr, 270n59
Arnold, John, 87
Arutiunian, Vardan, 278n34
atheism: Bolsheviks and, 43, 44, 58; in cultural history, 33; in educational settings, 13, 59, 92, 109; in literature, 108; resistance to, 22, 128; scientific, 92, 109; of Yakunin, 13, 15, 26, 35. *See also* antireligion campaigns
Atkinson, David, 134, 141, 275n54
authoritarianism: criticisms of, 8; mass systems of belief and, 163; Miłosz on, 9–10; reemergence of, 222–27; Russian Orthodox Church and, 113, 169–72, 197, 208, 215, 224
Autocephalous Orthodox Church, 90, 115, 197, 219

Baptists: Christian Committee and, 279n51; illegal operations, 114–15; Irkutsk community, 20; missionaries, 208, 211–12; persecution of, 78, 81, 263n34; Reformed, 89–90, 116, 271n89; Riazan', 112; Southern, 208
Barabanov, Evgenii, 106–7, 158
Baran, Emily, 224
Beak, David, 141
Belov, Aleksei, 238f
Berdiaev, Nikolai: Dudko and, 36; Marxism renounced by, 24–25; *The Meaning of Creativity*, 25; Men on, 24, 291n18; on personalism, 26, 203; *The Philosophy of Freedom*, 25–26, 29, 98; rediscovery of, 43, 50, 65, 67; Yakunin and, 24–27, 29, 153, 251n49
Bergson, Henri, 69, 71–72
Berman, Harold J., 165
Bibikova, Valentina, 20–21

321

Bloom, Anthony, 97, 128
Bochkov, Pavel, 228, 230
Bociurkiw, Bohdan R., 88, 90–93, 265–66n69
Bogdanova, Paulina, 184–85
Bogolep (archbishop of Kirov and Nikolaev), 269n35
Bolotov, Vasilii, 50
Bolsheviks: antireligion campaigns of, 45, 55, 106, 179, 181; atheism promoted by, 43, 44, 58; church-state relations and, 21, 22, 58, 167, 172–73; language of, 106, 269n45. *See also* Communist Party
Bondarenko, Valeriia Petrovna, 112
Bonner, Elena, 98, 138, 267n10
Borovoi, Vitalii, 82
Borshchev, Valerii, 242
Bourdeaux, Michael, 76, 87–88, 128, 142, 264n55, 279n51
Bradley, Mark Philip, 262n7
Brezhnev, Leonid, 3, 124, 128, 143, 145, 155, 170
Bruhl, Lucien Lévy, 18
Buchanan, John H., 90, 265n64
Buddhism, 212, 224
Bukovsky, Vladimir, 133, 192
Bulgakov, Sergei, 25, 43, 46, 50, 67, 153
Burgess, John, 191
Burtsev, Vladimir, 127, 274n28
Bychkov, Sergei Sergeevich, 8–9, 189, 230–31, 237, 253n15

canon law: on church-state relations, 195; on geographical dominion, 115; Nikodim on, 86; violations of, 33, 54, 188, 214, 222, 256n5; Yakunin-Eshliman letters on, 44
Carter, Jimmy, 265n60, 266n83
Catacomb Church, 16, 20–22, 229, 250nn39–41, 251n46, 260n63
Catherine the Great (Russian Empire), 11, 35
Catholic Church: Committee for the Defense of Believers' Rights, 109, 267n13; converts from Russian Orthodox Church, 12; corruption in, 226; decline of, 55; illegal operations, 114–15; Irkutsk community, 16, 19–20; missionaries and, 208; persecution of, 78; reconciliation with Russian Orthodox Church, 116; Syllabus, 225, 295n16
censorship, 57, 70, 130, 227, 266n69
Chebrikov, Viktor, 183
Chekhov, Anton, 110, 161
Chernenko, Konstantin, 155
Cherniak, Andrei, 258n33

Chernyshevsky, Nikolai, 286n19
Christian Committee for the Defense of Believers' Rights: archives, 2, 100, 103–13; Baptists and, 279n51; Dakin and, 7, 9, 102–3, 112, 115–16, 118; founding members, 7, 95–97, 111f; on freedom of conscience, 98, 100, 116–17; KGB and, 95, 119, 122–23; letters written by, 116–17, 124; purpose of, 95–99, 112, 116–18, 273n18; on religious persecution, 96, 98, 111–12, 117
Christianity: conversion to, 15, 17–19, 22, 24, 35, 62, 67, 123, 176; education on, 210; freedom and, 18, 25, 26; Lenin on, 55; open forms of, 19, 250n30; politics and, 196, 201–3; Shchipkova on, 63; Solov'ev on, 69, 142, 260n74. *See also specific denominations*
Christian Seminar: KGB and, 2, 68–69, 127; origins of, 62–63; participants, 63–68, 114, 134, 239, 259n45, 260n59, 270n59, 277n17; reading list for, 69–72, 260n66
Chunikhin (Council for Religious Affairs representative), 104, 268n34
Church of England, 128, 274n31, 279n51
church-state relations: Aleksii I on, 54; authoritarianism and, 169–72; Bolsheviks and, 21, 22, 58, 167, 172–73; canon law on, 195; Kuroedov on, 5; Levitin-Krasnov on, 91, 283n47; Nikodim on, 85, 86; normalization of, 55; parish reform and, 33–34, 38, 54; remodeling, 164–71; separation of, 48, 80, 92, 168, 172, 195–96, 212; Yakunin-Eshliman letters on, 32, 41–48
Clark, Bruce, 286n25
Clarke, B. O. Fielding, 87, 264n57
closed societies, 8, 71–72, 159, 250n30, 261n85
Codevilla, Giovanni, 165–66
Coggan, Donald, 264n50
Cohn, Norman, 120
Cold War, 9, 32, 76, 84, 87–88, 93, 118
Coles, Robert, 77
Committee for State Security. *See* KGB
Communist Party: archives, 178; criticisms of, 162, 200–202; ideology, 57–58, 90, 108, 117, 120, 124, 158, 200; religious persecution and, 73, 75, 88; Yakunin-Eshliman letters on, 43. *See also* Bolsheviks
Congress of People's Deputies, 7, 159, 164–65, 178–79, 200
conscience, freedom of: activism, 1, 3, 142, 179; for children, 109–10; Christian

Committee on, 98, 100, 116–17; Congress of People's Deputies on, 164; constitutional guarantee, 2, 5, 89, 166; democracy and, 163, 217, 218, 224; Helsinki Accords on, 98; as human right, 98, 163, 168; suppression of, 6, 77, 96, 146; Yakunin-Eshliman letters on, 47. *See also* Law on Freedom of Conscience and Religious Associations

Constitution of Soviet Union: on church-state relations, 48, 92; on Communist Party, 124; freedoms guaranteed by, 2, 5, 47, 89, 166; violations of, 2, 31, 33, 48, 103, 195, 218

Convention on the Rights of the Child (United Nations), 270n61

Corley, Felix, 89

Council for Religious Affairs: abuses of power within, 47–48, 104; beneficial work of, 80; establishment of, 248n21, 255n57; Furov and, 55; KGB and, 182, 186, 190; Kharchev and, 179, 283n45, 285n14; Kuroedov and, 5, 38, 248n22; RCDM's calls for abolition of, 203

Council of Ministers, 80, 248n21, 255n57

Czechoslovakia, Soviet invasion of (1968), 64

Dakin, Adriana, 101

Dakin, Henry S.: background of, 100–101, 268nn18–19; Christian Committee and, 7, 9, 102–3, 112, 115–16, 118; on human rights, 268n27; person-to-person diplomacy and, 118, 272n101; Regel'son and, 120–21, 141; Washington Street Research Center, 6, 101, 103, 118, 141

Dakin, Richard, 268n26

Dakin, Susanna, 101

Dakin, Vergilia, 118, 268n18

Dashkov, Georgii, 45

Davis, Nathaniel, 251–52n68

"Declaration of Human Rights and Dignity" (2006), 233–35

Della Cava, Ralph, 288n66

democracy: creative, 202–3; foundations of, 240; freedom of conscience and, 163, 217, 218, 224; Russian Orthodox Church and, 80–81, 197, 214–15; Soviet movement toward, 156, 159–61, 166, 168–69; threats to, 225, 234

Denisenko, Mikhail Antonovich. *See* Filaret, Metropolitan

Dimitrios I (patriarch of Constantinople), 116

Dobczansky, George, 265n61

Dobriansky, Lev E., 265n61, 266n76

Dostoevsky, Fyodor, 26, 43, 51, 156, 161

Dudko, Dmitrii: arrest of, 126–28; confession by, 129–30; Krakhmal'nikova as spiritual daughter of, 285n3; in labor camp, 36; Levitin-Krasnov on, 4, 36, 277n23; parish assignments, 37, 253n13; personality of, 36, 61, 114, 253n14; on religious persecution, 266n74; Roshchin's portrayal of, 121; sessions held by, 61–63, 258n39; Yakunin-Eshliman letters and, 49

Dunlop, John, 88, 91–92

Dvorkin, Aleksandr Leonidovich, 222–24

Edel'stein, Georgii, 177f, 190, 191, 200, 201f, 287n38

education: atheistic agenda, 13, 59, 92, 109; freedom of thought in, 207; political change and, 202–3; religious, 65, 161–62, 166–67, 209–10, 212; religious persecution in schools, 92, 266n74

Ellis, Jane, 85–86, 96, 113, 252n5, 274n28, 283n43

enlightened patriotism, 203–4

Esalen Institute (California), 118, 272n101

Eshliman, Nikolai: "Appeal to the Patriarch, Holy Synod and the Diocesan Bishops" (1966), 256n5; death of, 55; letter to Aleksii I (with Yakunin, 1965), 31–32, 39–54, 57, 85, 91, 113, 252n1, 257n20, 276n59; letter to Supreme Soviet Chairman (with Yakunin, 1965), 31, 39, 47–53, 91, 255n66, 257n20, 276n59; parish assignments, 36; personality of, 35, 54–55; photograph of, 42f; suspension from priesthood, 7, 54

Fagan, Geraldine, 296nn17–18

Filaret, Metropolitan, 183, 186–88, 197, 219–21

Filatov, Sergei Borisovich, 197, 213, 217, 284n55, 292n42, 294n85

Florenskii, Pavel, 43, 50, 260n66

Fonchenkov, Vasilii, 123

Frank, Semen, 32, 260n66

Frank, Victor, 32

Fraser, Donald M., 88

freedom: of assembly, 203; of belief, 1, 59, 98; Berdiaev on, 25–26, 29, 36; of choice, 25, 26, 60, 71; Christianity and, 18, 25, 26; of expression, 57, 59; of speech, 57, 59, 98, 153, 203. *See also* conscience, freedom of; religious freedom; thought, freedom of

Freeze, Gregory, 44
Furov, Vasilii Grigor'evich, 55–56

Gainov, Nikolai, 123, 237
Gandhi, Mahatma, 146
Ganson, Nicholas, 130, 274n38
Gavriil, Archimandrite, 106
Genis, Aleksandr, 160–61
Ginzburg, Aleksandr, 2, 247n12, 267n10
Gogol, Nikolai, 43, 67, 153, 154, 156, 161
Golubev, Aleksii Stepanovich. *See* Yermogen, Archbishop
Gorbachev, Mikhail, 7, 155–57, 159, 165–66, 176–77, 199
Goricheva, Tat'iana, 56–57, 259n53
Greene, Robert, 250n29
Gregory of Nazianzas, 137, 161
Grigorenko, Petro, 267n10
gulag. *See* labor camps

Hamsun, Knut, 14, 249n9
Harman, Willis, 101
Helsinki Accords (1975): Monitoring Group, 3, 98, 247n12, 267n10; Point 7 of Final Act, 81, 98; signatory states, 82, 85, 98; violations of, 81, 88, 98
Helsinki Human Rights Watch, 285n9
Hexter, J. H., 62
Hickman, Jim, 102
Holloway, Richard, 81, 82
Howard-Johnston, Xenia, 88
human rights: activism, 2–3, 57, 89, 98, 102, 109, 133, 143–44, 242; for children, 109–10, 270n61; Dakin on, 268n27; "Declaration of Human Rights and Dignity," 233–35; freedom of conscience, 98, 163, 168; legal processes and, 138–39; United States on, 265n60, 265n64; Universal Declaration of Human Rights, 233–35; violations of, 3, 93, 95, 103, 247n12, 262n7; WCC and, 74, 75, 77, 84, 87. *See also* Helsinki Accords
hunger strikes, 146–47, 281n18

"The Individual and Mass Consciousness" symposium (1989), 163, 282n33
Innokentii (Orthodox monk), 139–40, 213
Institute of Zoology (Irkutsk), 7, 14–24, 27, 28, 100–101, 251n60
Irkutsk (Siberia): Aleksii II in, 210; exile of Khrizostom to, 190; Institute of Zoology in, 7, 14–24, 27, 28, 100–101, 251n60; labor camps in, 22; religious communities in, 16, 19–24

Islam. *See* Muslims and Islam
Ivanov, Viacheslav, 43, 153
Ivashura, Galina Afanas'evna, 112

Jehovah's Witnesses, 78, 223
Jews and Judaism, 11, 27, 55, 78, 190, 224
John Chrysostom (saint), 206–7
John Paul I (pope), 117
John Paul II (pope), 114, 117, 267n13, 271n93

Kapitanchuk, Viktor: arrest of, 127, 130, 277n13; Christian Committee and, 96–97, 99, 111; letter to Pimen (1975), 67; on martyrs, 172–73, 260n67, 263n22; at Men's parish, 97, 267n7; photographs, 99f, 111f; as witness at Yakunin's trial, 132, 133, 140, 141; Yakunin-Eshliman letters and, 40, 50, 51
Karamzin, Nikolai, 45
Karatsuba, Irina, 240
Karelin, Feliks, 40, 42f, 50, 51, 132, 134–35, 276n59
Kashtanova, Elena, 259n45
Kazantsev, Nikodim, 45
Keston College (England): Cold War and, 9, 88; founding members, 87; petition for Vin's release, 265n64; *Religion in Communist Lands*, 88, 265n59, 271n92; on Yakunin, 128, 142, 146–47
KGB: Aleksii II and, 183–84, 187, 286n25, 286n28; archives, 7, 8, 178–89, 196, 286n16, 286n18; arrests, 1–3, 89, 108, 112, 122–30; Christian Committee and, 95, 119, 122–23; Christian Seminar and, 2, 68–69, 127; coup attempts and resurgence, 177–78, 195–96, 198; Russian Orthodox Church and, 178–97, 222, 229; searches of Yakunin's home, 1–2, 119, 130; WCC and, 79, 186–87
Khaibulin, Varsonofi, 56, 96–97, 111, 111f
Kharchev, Konstantin, 179, 282n38, 283n45, 285n14
Khar'iuzov, Bishop N. A., 172
Khasbulatov, Ruslan, 180, 284n59, 286n16
Khodorovicha, Natalia, 102
Khomiakov, Aleksei, 25, 43, 67, 69–71, 261n79, 261nn81–82
Khrizostom, Archbishop, 189–91, 196–97, 288n59
Khrushchev, Nikita: antireligion campaigns, 7, 28–29, 33, 38, 53, 89, 91, 167–68, 251n66; anti-Stalin speech (1956), 21, 56; church-state relations and, 34; criticisms

of, 40, 53, 107; dismissal of, 39, 44, 47–48, 54, 255n72; labor camps and, 143
Kireevskii, Ivan, 156
Kireevskii, Pyotr, 67
Kirill, Metropolitan, 173, 217, 233–36
Kiselev, Alexei A., 88
Klassen, David D., 92–93, 265n61, 266n75
Kleimionova, Anastasiia, 106
Kolosov, Leonid, 141
Konin, Lev, 107–8, 270n53, 270n58
Kosygin, Aleksey, 252n1
Kotkin, Stephen, 106
Krakhmal'nikova, Zoia, 4–5, 175–77, 177f, 196, 225, 281n22, 285nn2–3
Krotov, Iakov, 230
Kubyshkin, Evgenii Dmitrievich, 287n42
Kucharev, Anya, 272n101
Kuraev, Andrei, 196
Kuroedov, Vladimir Alekseevich, 5–6, 38, 248n22
Kyrlezhev, Aleksandr, 199

labor camps: Burtsev in, 127; conditions in, 22, 143–46, 151, 278n29, 278n34; Dudko in, 36; Orlov in, 144–46, 278n29; Popkov in, 127, 134; Shchipkova in, 127; Talantov in, 58; Yakunin in, 9, 143–47, 150–51, 154–55, 159, 242, 278n29
Law on Freedom of Conscience and Religious Associations (1990 & 1997), 164–68, 217–18, 222–25, 295n12
Law on Religious Associations (1929), 164, 282n37
Lebedeva, Tat'iana, 66, 97, 239, 240f, 260n59, 298n73
Lefortovo Prison (Moscow), 3, 125, 129–33, 139, 142–43, 176
Lenin, Vladimir, 55, 181, 263n22
Leningrad: Ecclesiastical Seminary, 108; ideological crisis in, 122; religious-philosophical seminars in, 51, 64, 66, 259n53; Theological Academy in, 183; underground literary movement in, 61–62, 259n53
Leontiev, Konstantin, 43
letters. See Yakunin, Gleb, letters by
Levada, Yuri, 198
Levitin-Krasnov, Anatolii: on church-state relations, 91, 283n47; on Dudko, 4, 36, 277n23; human rights activism, 258n34; marriage of, 149; on Regel'son, 4, 65, 277n23; Roshchin's portrayal of, 121; as teacher, 60–61; on Yakunin, 4, 13, 14, 30, 142; Yakunin-Eshliman letters and, 49

Lomonosov, Mikhail, 43
Lubentsova, Valentina G., 133, 135–36
Luther, Martin, 226
Lysenko, Nikolai, 216

Mandel'stam, Nadezhda, 150, 240–41
Mandel'stam, Osip, 150
Marchenko, Anatoly, 159, 267n10, 281n18
Maritain, Jacques, 203, 291n18
martyrs, 6, 46, 76, 172–73, 227, 235, 260n67, 263n22, 284n71
Marxism, 24–25, 65, 90
Marxism-Leninism, 5, 157, 230, 270n59
Maslenikova, Zoia, 16
Meerson, Mikhail, 221
Men, Aleksandr: Apostolic Orthodox Church and, 230, 231f; on Berdiaev, 24, 251n49; on creativity, 18, 44, 254n43; death of, 44, 163, 230; History of Religion, 17–19, 152; at Institute of Zoology, 7, 14–24, 27, 251n60; on Karelin, 50, 51; KGB surveillance of, 184, 185; on Khomiakov, 70–71; lecture on Solov'ev, 290n12; Magic and Monotheism, 17–18; parish assignments, 34–35, 60, 97, 210, 254n32, 269n48; personality of, 34, 35, 114; Son of Man, 250–51n45; The Wellsprings of Religion, 291n18; Yakunin-Eshliman letters and, 40, 43–44, 49–51; Yakunin's relationship with, 7, 14–24, 29, 35, 239
Men, Mikhail, 230
Miłosz, Czesław, 9–10, 72, 114, 169
missionaries, 208–9, 211–12, 217, 224, 292n42
Moltmann, Jürgen, 298n74
moral regeneration, 172, 187–91, 284n71
Moscow: Christian Seminar, 2, 62–72, 260n59; Helsinki Monitoring Group, 3, 98, 247n12, 267n10; ideological crisis in, 122; Lefortovo Prison, 3, 125, 129–33, 139, 142–43, 176; messianic vision of, 171–72; Olympic Games (1980), 3, 126, 129, 268n26; Theological Academy and Seminary, 28–29, 35, 36, 123, 132, 178, 187
Moscow Patriarchate: AOC and, 115; criticisms of, 8, 24, 114, 116, 207–8, 214–15, 222, 271n79; Department for External Church Relations, 123, 135, 182, 192–93, 233, 288n69; Department of Foreign Relations, 79; Holy Synod, 38, 45, 82–83, 156–57, 183, 196, 213–16, 232, 293n78; Journal of the Moscow Patriarchate, 4, 65, 106, 171, 182, 196; Men's collected writings published by, 250–51n45; restoration of, 53, 214, 215. See also specific patriarchs
Muslims and Islam, 20, 55, 78, 212, 224

nationalism: bourgeois, 91; in Russia, 198–200, 208, 214–18, 224–28; in Soviet era, 76, 171, 203, 207
New Faith, 10, 114
Nezhnyi, Aleksandr Iosifovich, 179–80, 182–83, 188, 194
Nikodim, Metropolitan, 79, 85–86, 116, 117, 186, 263n36

Ogorodnikov, Aleksandr, 3, 62–70, 121, 145–46, 184–85, 260n63, 260n66, 277n17, 277n23
Old Believers, 16
Olympic Games (1980), 3, 126, 129, 268n26
open societies, 71–72, 159, 197, 217, 222, 250n30, 261n86
Orlov, Yuri, 2, 98, 133, 144–46, 247n12, 267n10, 278n29
Osipov, Andrei Il'ich, 132, 134, 275–76n55
Osipova, Irina Ivanovna, 250n39

paganism, 18, 57, 137, 152, 201, 250n29, 261n85
Pasolini, Pier Paolo, 62
Paul, Anna, 112
Paul VI (pope), 87
Pavlova, Natal'ia, 159
Payne, Ernest, 81–82
Pentecostals, 78, 110, 114–16, 208, 271n89
perestroika, 156, 159–60, 164, 185, 199
Perm-37 labor camp, 143–47, 150–51, 154–55, 278n29, 278n34
persecution. *See* religious persecution
personalism, 26, 203
person-to-person diplomacy, 118, 272n101
Peter the Great (Russian Empire), 15, 41, 43–45
Pimen (patriarch of Moscow): criticisms of, 117; death of, 162, 187; Dudko sessions suspended by, 61, 62; letters to, 67, 100, 103–6, 276n61; martyrs and, 172, 260n67; meeting with Gorbachev, 156–57
Pitirim, Metropolitan, 182, 196
Pius IX (pope), 225
Podgorny, Nikolai, 31, 39, 48, 53, 91, 252n1, 255n66, 257n20, 276n59
poems. *See* Yakunin, Gleb, writings by
Pogodin, Aleksei Alekseevich, 288n69
Poiarkov, Vladimir Kirillovich. *See* Yuvenalii, Metropolitan
Poland: partition of, 11; Soviet interventions in, 9, 132; workers' strikes in, 131–32, 275n47

Polosin, Viacheslav, 164, 167–68, 178–82, 196, 200–204, 284n58, 286n19
Ponomarev, Lev Aleksandrovich, 178–79, 193–96, 242, 285n9, 286n16
Popkov, Viktor, 66, 68, 127, 132, 134, 239, 240f, 259n45, 274n28, 298n73
Popov, L. M., 132
Popovskii, Mark, 66–67, 130, 274–75n40
Poresh, Vladimir, 63–66, 69–70, 145–46, 277n23
Pospielovsky, Dimitry, 96, 221
Potter, Philip, 82, 84, 92, 93, 187
Primakov, Evgenii, 180
propaganda: Aleksii II on, 211; antireligious, 13, 28, 106, 121; anti-Soviet, 5–6, 87, 120, 138, 140, 176; religious, 64, 112, 114
Protestantism. *See specific denominations*
Pugo, Boris, 196
Pushkin, Alexander, 43, 160, 161, 204
Pussy Riot, 236–37, 297n62, 298n66
Pustoutov, Iosif, 132, 134, 276n57
Putin, Vladimir, 226–27, 233, 235–37

Razveev, Boris, 220
RCDM. *See* Russian Christian Democratic Movement
Reddaway, Peter, 87–88
Regel'son, Lev: "Appeal to Christians in Portugal" (1975), 78, 133; arrest of, 126, 128, 130, 277n13; Christian Seminar and, 63–66, 72, 277n17; Dakin and, 120–21, 141; Facebook page, 259n54; Furov on, 56; letter to Pimen (1975), 67; letter to WCC (1975), 9, 73, 75–81, 87, 91–92, 134, 142; Levitin-Krasnov on, 4, 65, 277n23; on martyrs, 172–73, 260n67, 263n22; photograph of, 99f; *The Tragedy of the Russian Orthodox Church, 1917–1945*, 65; as witness at Yakunin's trial, 132, 133, 140; Yakunin-Eshliman letters and, 40, 50, 51
religion: culture and, 43–44; education on, 65, 161–62, 166–67, 209–10, 212; in Irkutsk, 16, 19–24; politics and, 4, 91, 220–22, 241, 293n69; science and, 15, 43, 69. *See also* antireligion campaigns; church-state relations; Council for Religious Affairs; missionaries; World Council of Churches; *specific religions and denominations*
religious freedom: activism, 1, 3, 8, 72; constitutional guarantee, 47; Helsinki Accords on, 98; Marxism-Leninism on, 5; restrictions on, 218; WCC position on, 81–84; Western views of, 86–91, 93;

INDEX   327

Yakunin-Eshliman letters on, 47; Year of Religious Freedom, 116
religious persecution: Christian Committee on, 96, 98, 111–12, 117; Communist Party and, 73, 75, 88; data collection on, 9, 83, 92–93, 96, 263n34; at labor camps, 146; letter to Aleksii I on (1965), 31; letter to WCC on (1975), 7, 75–79, 92, 142; psychiatric hospitals and, 77, 92, 108, 117, 270n59; in schools, 92, 266n74; Soviet response to accusations of, 80–81, 85–86; Western reactions to, 87–88, 92, 94, 128–29
religious tolerance, 73, 181–82, 187
Riabikova, Mariia, 242
Richardson, James T., 295n10
Ridiger, Aleksii Mikhailovich. *See* Aleksii II
Ronionova, Evgeniia Petrovna, 188
Rosenau, James, 118
Roshchin, Boris, 120–21
Rossel, Jacques, 81, 82
Rovenskii, Georgii Vasil'evich, 8
Rudenko, Roman, 112, 252n1
Runcie, Robert, 264n57
Russia: authoritarianism in, 222–27; education system in, 207; missionaries in, 208–9, 211–12, 217, 224, 292n42; nationalism in, 198–200, 208, 214–18, 224–28; political framework for, 177, 178, 198, 202–3; religious diversity in, 199; Ukraine invasion (2022), 235. *See also* Soviet Union; *specific leaders*
Russian Christian Democratic Movement (RCDM), 164, 179, 200–205, 207, 283n41, 293n67
Russian Church Abroad, 197
Russian Orthodox Church: abuses of power within, 103–7, 193, 195, 207, 269n49; authoritarianism and, 113, 169–72, 197, 208, 215, 224; Catholic converts in, 12; criticisms of, 3, 24, 26–27, 37, 41, 125–26, 205; decline of, 7, 28–29, 33, 45, 55, 251–52n68, 252n3; democracy and, 80–81, 197, 214–15; excommunication of Yakunin, 7, 220–22, 293n77, 295n10; gathering of young priests, 32–37, 39, 49–51; KGB collusion with, 178–97, 222, 229; parish reform, 33–34, 38, 40, 49, 54, 252n5; perestroika and, 156, 159–60, 164; public loss of trust in, 93, 103, 107, 266n79; reconciliation with Catholic Church, 116; revival of, 39, 44, 49, 59, 91, 156–57, 162–68, 199–200, 209; ritualistic practices, 7, 13, 16, 250n29; WCC membership, 74, 76, 116; Yakunin's report on

(1979), 113–15, 117. *See also* canon law; church-state relations; martyrs; Moscow Patriarchate; *specific leaders and sects*
Russian Revolution (1917), 12, 44, 78, 103, 115, 121, 173, 214

St. Petersburg. *See* Leningrad
Sakharov, Andrei: arrest and exile, 127, 138, 155, 273n26; death of, 178; human rights activism, 2–3, 89; *Reflections on Progress, Peaceful Coexistence, and Intellectual Freedom*, 257n15; on Velikanova, 125, 138–40; on Yakunin, 138–40, 159
Sakwa, Richard, 156, 159, 283n41
Saltykov-Shchedrin, Mikhail, 153, 280n78
samizdat publications: Christian Committee and, 100, 102–3; *A Chronicle of Current Events*, 3, 125, 247n13, 276n61; on freedom of thought, 57; Keston College and, 88; *Nadezhda*, 176; by Regel'son, 65; on religious persecution, 96; on Yakunin, 5, 128, 139
Schapiro, Leonard, 87–88
schools. *See* education
Scott, Edward, 82
Semenova, Iraida Georgievna. *See* Yakunina, Iraida Georgievna
Seraphim of Sarov (saint), 173
Sergei, Metropolitan, 21, 58, 91, 170, 229
Sergius of Radonezh (saint), 173
Shafarevich, Igor, 56
Shcharansky, Anatolii, 2, 247n12, 267n10
Shcheglov, Vadim, 97–98, 123
Shchipkov, Aleksandr, 259n45
Shchipkova, Tat'iana, 63–66, 68–69, 127, 259n45, 277n23
Shchyolkovo, 8, 157–58, 204–6, 281n13, 291n31
Sheehan, James, 160, 281n25
Sheville, Ian, 264n57
Shkarovskii, Mikhail Vital'evich, 96
Shpiller, Vsevelod, 274n38
Shterin, Marat, 295n10
Shushpanov, Aleksandr, 135, 140, 192–93, 276n61, 288nn68–69
Siberia: exile of Yakunin to, 7, 9, 147–51, 149f, 154–55; labor camps in, 9, 22, 150–51, 155; missionaries in, 89. *See also* Irkutsk
Simanskii, Sergei Vladimirovich. *See* Aleksii I
Skaredov, G. I., 132–34
Smirnov, Aleksandr, 230
Smits, Yanis, 88, 92–93, 265n63

INDEX

sobornost' (conciliarity), 7–8, 36, 71, 203, 215, 226, 229, 232, 297n51
Solov'ev, Vladimir, 43, 45, 50, 67, 69, 142, 153, 156, 201, 260n74, 290n12
Solzhenitsyn, Aleksandr, 102, 129, 135, 278n37
Solzhenitsyn, Natalia, 102, 279n51
Sorokin, Sergei Ivanovich, 110–11
Sorokina, Tati'ana Ivanovna, 110–11, 270n67
Soviet Union: Afghanistan invasion (1979), 3, 129, 131, 273n26; conspiracy theories in, 119–22; Council of Ministers, 80, 248n21, 255n57; Czechoslovakia invasion (1968), 64; democratization in, 156, 159–61, 166, 168–69; dissolution of, 7, 156, 197, 216, 218; famine (1921–1922), 75–76, 172; moral challenges for, 94, 273n24; nationalism in, 76, 171, 203, 207; Poland, interventions in, 9, 132; religious awakening in, 56, 66–67, 96, 113, 119–20, 122, 273n12. *See also* authoritarianism; Bolsheviks; Cold War; Communist Party; Constitution of Soviet Union; KGB; religion; Russia; *specific leaders and locations*
Spengler, Michael, 193
Stalin, Joseph and Stalinism: antireligion campaigns, 89, 167–68; collectivization campaign, 36; Council for Religious Affairs and, 248n21; critiques of, 21, 56–58; cult of power and personality, 18, 169–71, 173; death of, 39, 143, 265–66n69; labor camps under, 143, 144; Moscow Patriarchate restored by, 53, 215; purges by, 6, 39
Struve, Nikita, 260n66
Stryzhik, Pyotr, 103–6, 114
subbotnik (Red Saturday), 263n22
Suslov, Mikhail, 132
Svetlov, Feliks, 4–5, 175–76
Sychev, Vladimir, 185

Tabak, Iurii Mikhailovich, 258n33
Talantov, Boris Vladimirovich, 58–59, 191, 239, 257nn19–20, 257n22
telecommunications, 118, 272n100
thought, freedom of: activism, 1, 10, 257n15; in education, 207; Helsinki Accords on, 98; in Russian literature, 153, 154; suppression of, 10, 57–59, 64, 77
Tikhon (patriarch of Moscow), 75–76, 91, 153, 170, 172, 284n67
Timoshevskii, V. N., 185–86
Tishkovskaia, Evgeniia, 216

Tolstoy, Leo, 43, 156, 161
Troitskii, Konstantin, 199
Trubetskoi, Nikolai and Evgenii, 50
True Orthodox Church, 58, 229
Turgenev, Ivan, 156
Tyutchev, Fyodor, 43

Ukraine: independence movement, 189, 219; Russian invasion (2022), 235; Jewish population, 11; Nikolaev Church, 103–5, 269n38; religious persecution, 111–12
Ukrainian Autocephalous Church, 90, 197, 219
Ukrainian Orthodox Church, 189, 197, 219, 222
Ulitskaia, Ludmilla Evgen'evna, 257n30
Union of Soviet Socialist Republics (USSR). *See* Soviet Union
Universal Declaration of Human Rights (United Nations), 233–35

Vail, Pyotr, 160–61
Velikanova, Tat'iana Mikhailovna, 3, 5, 125–26, 127f, 138–40, 239–40, 247n13, 276n1, 277n23
Veniamin, Metropolitan, 172, 225, 295n16
Vinikov, Viacheslav, 149, 181, 227
Vins, Georgi, 88–90, 94, 123, 265n64, 266n83
Vins, Peter, 88–89
Volkova, Elena, 1, 8–9, 14, 151, 227, 251n49, 275n43
Vorontsova, Liudmila Mikhailovna, 283n55

Walesa, Lech, 132
Weingartner, Erich, 87, 264n55
Wong, David Y. K., 264n57
World Council of Churches (WCC): Geneva meeting (1976), 84; Helsinki Colloquium (1976), 84; human rights and, 74, 75, 77, 84, 87; KGB and, 79, 186–87; Kirill's address to (1996), 217; letter to (1975), 7, 9, 73, 75–81, 87, 91–92, 134, 142; membership of Russian Orthodox Church, 74, 76, 116; Nairobi Assembly (1975), 75–86, 89–92, 96, 134; on religious freedom, 81–84
World War II, 27, 39, 53, 59, 91, 168, 171, 274n40
Wright, Gordon, 281–82n25

Yakunin, Aleksandr (son of Gleb), 96, 97f, 125, 126f
Yakunin, Gleb: Aleksii II and, 204, 210–17, 293n78; Apostolic Orthodox Church and,

8, 228–33; arrest of, 1, 3, 7, 96, 122–28; atheism of, 13, 15, 26, 35; birth (1934), 6, 12; Christian Seminar and, 66, 67, 72, 114; conversion to Christianity, 15, 17–19, 22, 24, 35; death (2014), 8, 221, 238; election to Congress of People's Deputies, 7, 159, 161, 161f, 164, 200; election to Federal Assembly of State Duma, 215–17, 293n77; excommunicated from Russian Orthodox Church, 7, 220–22, 293n77, 295n10; exile to Siberia, 7, 9, 147–51, 149f, 154–55; family background, 6–7, 12–13, 15; health challenges, 236–38; at Institute of Zoology, 7, 14–24, 27, 28, 100–101; KGB archive investigations and, 178–79, 182–87, 286n18; in labor camp, 9, 143–47, 150–51, 154–55, 159, 242, 278n29; in Lefortovo Prison, 3, 125, 129–31, 139, 142–43; libel case against Dvorkin, 222–24; marriage and children, 3, 7, 10, 27–30, 96, 97f, 125, 126f; on martyrs, 172–73, 260n67, 263n22, 284n71; ordination into priesthood, 7, 30; personality of, 10, 12–14, 24, 30, 35, 182; photographs of, 42f, 83f, 97f, 99f, 111f, 201f, 241f; portrayals of, 3–9, 120–21, 140–42, 159, 185, 220; press conferences, 95, 121–23; RCDM and, 164, 179, 200–205, 207; seminary education, 28–29; at Shchyolkovo parish, 157–58, 204–6, 291n31; suspension and defrocking from priesthood, 1, 7, 54, 78, 101, 213–22; trial and sentencing, 131–42, 192. *See also* Christian Committee for the Defense of Believers' Rights

Yakunin, Gleb, letters by: to Aleksii I (with Eshliman, 1965), 31–32, 39–54, 57, 85, 91, 113, 252n1, 257n20, 276n59; to Aleksii II (1993), 216; to Aleksii II (1994), 214–15; to Brezhnev (1981), 145; to Pimen (1975), 67; to Supreme Soviet Chairman (with Eshliman, 1965), 31, 39, 47–53, 91, 255n66, 257n20, 276n59; to WCC (1975), 7, 9, 73, 75–81, 87, 91–92, 134, 142; to Yeltsin (1995), 207–8

Yakunin, Gleb, writings by: "Appeal for the Glorification of Russian Martyrs in the USSR" (1975), 172–73, 260n67, 263n22; "Appeal to Christians in Portugal" (1975), 78, 133; "Appeal to the Patriarch, Holy Synod and the Diocesan Bishops" (1966), 256n5; "Appeal to Western Christians" (1981), 145–46; "Eulogy of a Simpleminded Fool of God" (1981), 151–53, 155; "In Service to the Cult" (The Moscow Patriarchate and Stalin's Cult of Personality) (repub. 1989), 169–73; poetry, 17, 35, 147, 150–53, 155, 157; report on Russian Orthodox Church (1979), 113–15, 117

Yakunin, Pavel Ivanovich (father of Gleb), 12–13

Yakunina, Anna (daughter of Gleb), 96, 125, 126f, 148

Yakunina, Iraida Georgievna (wife of Gleb): background, 27, 28; KGB and, 2, 130–31; marriage and children, 3, 7, 10, 27–30, 96, 97f, 125, 126f; opposed to Gleb confessing, 131, 275n44; visits to Gleb in prison and exile, 130–31, 144, 148

Yakunina, Klavdiia Iosifovna (mother of Gleb), 6–7, 12–15, 30

Yakunina, Mariia (daughter of Gleb): birth, 30; family environment, 96, 125; on Gleb's health challenges, 237; on Gleb's personality, 182; photographs, 97f, 126f, 238f; on Shchyolkovo's parish, 205–6, 291n31; visit to Gleb in exile, 148

Yeltsin, Boris, 177–79, 198, 206–8, 213, 217, 224–26, 289n81

Yermogen, Archbishop, 37–40, 48, 49, 253n15, 253n21

Yuvenalii, Metropolitan, 79–81, 85, 182, 186, 263n27, 263n36

Zagryazkina, E. B., 135

Zdanovskaia, Klavdiia Iosifovna. *See* Yakunina, Klavdiia Iosifovna

Zdanovskaia, Lidiia Iosifovna, 149–50, 227

Zernov, Mikhail, 171

Zernov, Nicholas, 70

Zheludkov, Sergei, 57–59, 257n15

Zhirinovsky, Vladimir, 208, 216

Zorgdrager, Heleen, 242

www.ingramcontent.com/pod-product-compliance
Lightning Source LLC
Chambersburg PA
CBHW030002240426
43672CB00007B/792